RHETORICAL CITIZENSHIP AND PUBLIC DELIBERATION

RHETORIC AND DEMOCRATIC DELIBERATION
VOLUME 3

EDITED BY CHERYL GLENN AND J. MICHAEL HOGAN
THE PENNSYLVANIA STATE UNIVERSITY

Editorial Board:

Robert Asen (University of Wisconsin–Madison)
Debra Hawhee (The Pennsylvania State University)
Peter Levine (Tufts University)
Steven J. Mailloux (University of California, Irvine)
Krista Ratcliffe (Marquette University)
Karen Tracy (University of Colorado, Boulder)
Kirt Wilson (The Pennsylvania State University)
David Zarefsky (Northwestern University)

Rhetoric and Democratic Deliberation is a series of groundbreaking monographs and edited volumes focusing on the character and quality of public discourse in politics and culture. It is sponsored by the Center for Democratic Deliberation, an interdisciplinary center for research, teaching, and outreach on issues of rhetoric, civic engagement, and public deliberation.

Other books in the series:

Karen Tracy, *Challenges of Ordinary Democracy:
A Case Study in Deliberation and Dissent*

Samuel McCormick, *Letters to Power:
Public Advocacy Without Public Intellectuals*

RHETORICAL CITIZENSHIP AND PUBLIC DELIBERATION

EDITED BY **CHRISTIAN KOCK** AND **LISA S. VILLADSEN**

The Pennsylvania State University Press | University Park, Pennsylvania

Library of Congress Cataloging-in-Publication Data

Rhetorical citizenship and public deliberation / edited by Christian Kock and Lisa S. Villadsen.
    p.   cm. — (Rhetoric and democratic deliberation)
Summary: "A collection of essays examining citizenship as a discursive phenomenon, in the sense that important civic functions take place in deliberation among citizens and that discourse is not prefatory to real action but in many ways constitutive of civic engagement"—Provided by publisher.
Includes bibliographical references and index.
ISBN 978-0-271-05387-5 (cloth : alk. paper)

1. Citizenship.
2. Deliberative democracy.
3. Political participation.

I. Kock, Christian.
II. Villadsen, Lisa S., 1968– .

JF801.R52 2012
323.601'4—dc23
            2012009583

Copyright © 2012 The Pennsylvania State University
All rights reserved
Printed in the United States of America
Published by The Pennsylvania State University Press,
University Park, PA 16802-1003

The Pennsylvania State University Press is a member of the Association of American University Presses.

It is the policy of The Pennsylvania State University Press to use acid-free paper. Publications on uncoated stock satisfy the minimum requirements of American National Standard for Information Sciences—Permanence of Paper for Printed Library Material, ANSI Z39.48–1992.

This book is printed on Nature's Natural, which contains 30% post-consumer waste.

CONTENTS

Introduction: Citizenship as a Rhetorical Practice /
Christian Kock and Lisa S. Villadsen   1

SECTION I: TRACING RHETORICAL CITIZENSHIP AS CONCEPT AND PRACTICE

1   Deliberative Democracy: Mapping Out the Deliberative Turn in Democratic Theory / *Kasper Møller Hansen*   13

2   The Making of Truth in Debate: The Case of (and a Case for) the Early Sophists / *Manfred Kraus*   28

3   The Search for "Real" Democracy: Rhetorical Citizenship and Public Deliberation in France and the United States, 1870–1940 / *William Keith and Paula Cossart*   46

SECTION II: PUBLIC DELIBERATION AS RHETORICAL PRACTICE

Part 1   Considering Norms of Communicative Behavior

4   The Respect Fallacy: Limits of Respect in Public Dialogue / *Italo Testa*   69

5   Dialectical Citizenship? Some Thoughts on the Role of Pragmatics in the Analysis of Public Debate / *Niels Møller Nielsen*   86

6   Provocative Style: The Gaarder Debate Example / *Marie Lund Klujeff*   101

7 Virtual Deliberations: Talking Politics Online in Hungary / *Ildikó Kaposi*   115

Part 2   Critiques of "Elite" Discourse

8 Dis-playing Democracy: The Rhetoric of Duplicity / *Kristian Wedberg*   137

9 Rhetoric of War, Rhetoric of Gender / *Berit von der Lippe*   153

10 Speaking of Terror: Norms of Rhetorical Citizenship in Danish Public Discourse / *Lisa S. Villadsen*   169

11 "This May Be the Law, but Should It Be?": Tony Blair's Rhetoric of Exception / *Bart van Klink and Oliver W. Lembcke*   181

Part 3   Rhetorical Citizenship Across Communicative Settings

12 I Agree, but . . . : Finding Alternatives to Controversial Projects Through Public Deliberation / *James McDonald*   199

13 Deliberation as Behavior in Public / *Tatiana Tatarchevskiy*   218

14 Homing in on the Arguments: The Rhetorical Construction of Subject Positions in Debates on the Danish Real Estate Market / *Sine Nørholm Just and Jonas Gabrielsen*   232

15 Danish Revue: Satire as Rhetorical Citizenship / *Jette Barnholdt Hansen*   249

SECTION III: TOWARD BETTER DELIBERATIVE PRACTICES

16 Presidential Primary Debate as a Genre of Journalistic Discourse: How Can We Put Debate into the Debates? / *John Adams and Stephen West*   267

17 A Tool for Rhetorical Citizenship: Generalizing the
    Status System / *Christian Kock*   279

18 Interpretive Debates Revisited / *Georgia Warnke*   296

    About the Contributors   315

    Index   321

INTRODUCTION:
CITIZENSHIP AS A RHETORICAL PRACTICE

Christian Kock and Lisa S. Villadsen

The assemblies . . . will deliberate better when all are deliberating jointly, the common people when with the notables and these when with the masses.
—Aristotle, *Politics*

There is a relationship between attentiveness and care, and to care about democracy is to care whether and how citizens speak.
—Robert Hariman, "Amateur Hour: Knowing What to Love in Ordinary Democracy"

Citizenship has long been a keyword among educators, philosophers, and political theorists. Using the phrase "rhetorical citizenship" as a unifying perspective, this book aims to develop an understanding of citizenship as a discursive phenomenon in the sense that important civic functions take place in deliberation among citizens, and that discourse is not prefatory to real action but is in many ways constitutive of civic engagement. The book pursues this aim by bringing together, in a cross-disciplinary effort, contributions by scholars in fields that rarely intersect.

Liberal vs. Republican Notions of Citizenship

For the most part, discussions as well as implementations of citizenship have focused on those aspects of it that are central to the "liberal" tradition of social thought—that is, questions of the freedoms and rights of citizens and groups.

The essays in this volume give voice to a "republican" conception in the thinking about citizenship. Seeing participation and debate as central to being a citizen, this tradition looks back to the Greek city-states and republican Rome.

Citizenship, in this sense of the word, is basically, we argue, *rhetorical* citizenship. Rhetoric, in this view, is at the core of being a citizen.

"Deliberative Democracy"

Our concern to see citizenship as rhetorical parallels the trend in modern political theory that sees the essence of democracy in the idea of *deliberation*. If we are to connect these two ideas, citizenship and deliberation, and reflect constructively on their meaning in present-day democracy, then we should talk not only about rights and freedoms but also about rhetoric.

Aristotle was the first major thinker to connect these notions; deliberation (*boulē, bouleusis*) is central to his political, ethical, and rhetorical thought. To deliberate, he says, is to reflect on the pros and cons of "things that are in our control and are attainable by action" (*Nicomachean Ethics*, 1112b). His ethics focuses on deliberation followed by choice (*proairesis*) in the individual. Rhetoric is deliberation in public about communal choice: its function "is to deal with things about which we deliberate, but for which we have no systematic rules" (*Rhetoric*, 1357a). This also makes clear why Aristotle saw rhetoric "as an offshoot of Dialectic and of the science of Ethics, which may be reasonably called Politics" (*Rhetoric*, 1356a). Politics is the highest art, since its goal is to strive for the good life for all citizens; but this can only be achieved by wise choices, and these depend on public deliberation, that is, on rhetoric.

A similar rationale informed the conference "Rhetorical Citizenship and Public Deliberation," held in Copenhagen in October 2008, where the chapters in this book were originally presented. Reflection on citizenship in a democracy must concern itself with public deliberation, and hence with rhetoric.

Is Deliberation Possible?

It is sometimes assumed that in modern states "direct" democracy, as known from ancient city-states, is unworkable, so citizens cannot really be deliberators. If citizenship, as in the liberal tradition, is understood mainly as the rights and freedoms accorded to citizens, then individuals tend to be seen as participants in the political process only insofar as they elect representatives who govern the land. Also, the "liberal" view of democracy tends to see citizens as constituencies (or "segments") with given and stable preferences. Democracy, in such a view, is like a marketplace, and citizens are like consumers whose needs, interests, and preferences follow from socioeconomic parameters. Elected representatives, in turn, are like channels relaying the preferences of their constituencies into legislation and governance, rather than deliberators arguing about what is best for the polity.

One corollary of this is that the assumed function of deliberation shrinks. A minor role is assigned to persuasion, which moves individuals from supporting a policy to opposing it, or vice versa. Citizens vote; representatives bargain and negotiate. A further, and stronger, corollary is that people are primarily concerned about maximal preference fulfillment. Widespread views posit that people's preferences may be exhaustively expressed in terms of their perceived personal (or even personal *economic*) utility, regardless of what might be best for the polity. Modern political communication, with its reliance on marketing techniques that target segments selectively, appealing to their assumed group preferences, bears witness to this.

The fragmentation of the citizenry implied by these views and trends points to an important reason to reinvigorate the republican-rhetorical aspect of citizenship. If politics is about the best interest of the polity rather than merely the aggregated interests of mutually insulated segments, then *public* deliberation is called for. That need is accentuated by another current megatrend: multiculturalism. As diverse cultures increasingly seek access and acceptance in modern democracies, it is natural that concerns over collective identity, social cohesion, and the difficulties of intersegmental communication (if any) come to the fore. Much thinking on citizenship in social philosophy and democratic theory has addressed issues connected with multiculturalism, and that goes for thinking within the liberal-democratic tradition, too, but it remains fair to say that this thinking, for all its differences, has dealt primarily with freedoms, rights, and duties (or negations of them)—not with the discursive aspects of democracy in multicultural societies.

Deliberation as Speaking and Listening

If citizenship is understood as essentially deliberative, it necessarily implies two complementary discursive manifestations: deliberating citizens, and their elected representatives, must not only speak but listen. Democracy becomes less like a marketplace and more like a forum. Deliberation means "weighing"; and that, when applied to public issues, implies holding together all reasons and considerations relevant to the issue—not only those of one's own that speak for a given policy but also others that may speak against it, and that one has not yet considered.

The need to listen as well as to speak is further accentuated in complex societies like our own, where new media (such as new digital services), new opportunities, and new threats seem to multiply exponentially. Globalization and digital media are two major factors creating increased attention to national and global citizenship, and to the opportunities and the need to communicate across space and other barriers. Much hope has been invested in the supposed empowering potential of the Internet as a means for anybody to have a say; as to whether and how that promise will be made good, assessments differ, and all the data are not yet in.

A primarily rights-based, liberal conception of citizenship becomes less adequate in postmodern societies characterized by self-reflexivity and globalization, just as the view of the individual as having a fixed identity with fixed preferences loses plausibility. As many social theorists in our time have made clear, the individual's identity has become a life-long project of learning, adaptation, and transformation. The idea, easily enhanced by classical conceptions of liberal democracy, that we are all more or less what we are, each of us with interests and preferences that primarily reflect our sociological habitus, becomes less credible. The more diverse a society becomes, the more pressing is the need for public reflection on what is best for the society as such and not just for its segments—in other words, the need for deliberation, for rhetoric.

An immediate implication is that elected representatives must be deliberators rather than just negotiators. But it also becomes increasingly urgent that citizens themselves take part in public exchange that invokes not only segment interests but also the common good. As a leading political theorist and proponent of deliberative democracy, John Dryzek, has recently argued, "A deliberative democracy cannot easily be sought in a single forum. Instead, it should be sought in the contributions of multiple sites—and representations across these sites. Rhetoric can enable effective communication between differently situated actors, and can both establish and maintain deliberative systems" (2010, 320).

But rhetorical citizenship has more to it than deliberative exchange among representatives and citizens across multiple sites. In a modern polity it is not only possible but also necessary that citizens deliberate even when they are not public agents in deliberation. They will need not only to attend to the deliberation of their elected or would-be representatives and other public debaters but also, on that basis, to deliberate tacitly, in their own minds, as well as among themselves, on who has made the best case for what the polity should do—and who accordingly deserves their support, at elections or in between.

So, for citizens in deliberative democracy, the relevance of rhetoric is at least twofold: to become an active agent in such a democracy, the citizen must be a deliberative rhetor; and even citizens at the receiving end of public deliberation (newspaper readers, TV viewers, audiences at public debates, etc.) must themselves engage in "inner" deliberation. Rhetorical citizenship is concerned with citizens' output as well as their critical engagement with public deliberation. Careful monitoring of the public deliberation they hear or see is an important part of their deliberative engagement. In Dryzek's words, "Representative democracy and the deliberative system make rhetoric necessary. But its well-known hazards remain. So we still need some way to sort defensible uses of rhetoric from undesirable uses" (2010, 327).

In this view, there is a need for rhetoric in a deliberative democracy as well as for critical observation, description, and evaluation of the rhetoric that does occur—not just discourse by public officials or candidates but also other forms of discursive participation in public debate, partly to get a broader view of what is out there, but also to understand more fully the empowering and emancipatory aspects of rhetoric in society.

Rhetoricians Meet Deliberative Democrats

As the rhetorical scholar Robert Hariman has noted, "understanding, appreciating, and improving democratic participation is impeded by both the rationality standards of deliberative democracy theorists and classical rhetoric's ideal of eloquence" (2007, 222). This is a call for scholarly approaches that better account, and can offer suggestions, for actual civic discourse. Discourse cannot be studied merely as a theoretical or idealized notion. Public discourse is concrete, manifest, omnipresent, visible, and accessible to all; anyone can relate to it, and it is the conduit of numerous societal functions and dynamisms. We offer the concept of rhetorical citizenship as a way of conceptualizing the discursive, processual, participatory aspects of civic life. As Hauser puts it, "A public's essential characteristic is its shared activity of exchanging opinion. Put differently, *publics do not exist as entities but as processes; their collective reasoning is not defined by abstract reflection but by practical judgment; their awareness of issues is not philosophical but eventful"* (1999, 64).

Several rhetoricians have engaged deliberative democracy with appreciation of its focus on the actual discursive aspects of democratic systems as well as its concern with strengthening public participation in civic life. Multiple varieties of public discourse may be seen as instantiations of citizenship. Hauser's seminal work (1999) on "vernacular rhetoric" helped reorient rhetorical scholars' concern with political rhetoric to include informal and everyday instances of civic interaction. Dan Brouwer and Robert Asen have suggested the metaphor of "modality" as a vehicle for studying and being public (2010). We share their affirmation of plurality in public activity and in scholarship. This volume thus brings together multiple disciplinary traditions of studying public discourse, as well as a variety of case studies; together they argue that our individual contributions to civic life can take many forms as we are called on in a range of different roles, for example, as voters, members of interest groups, employees or students with certain affiliations, even as family to individuals who rely on public care facilities. In his "discourse theory of citizenship," Asen similarly encourages us to view citizenship as a "mode of public engagement" and thereby recognize "fluid, multimodal, and quotidian enactments of citizenship in a multiple public sphere" (2004, 191), seeing democracy more as a "guiding spirit that informs human interaction" than as "a set of institutions or specific acts" (196). A rhetorically based understanding of public debate can risk engaging difference without that risk leading to reduced commitment; rather, "a commitment to engaging others privileges norms of inclusion and fairness" (201).

A rhetorical focus has a special regard for individual actors in the public arena, not just the eloquent politician or NGO representative but also the person watching an election debate on TV, chiming in with a point of view through a blog on civic issues, collecting signatures from passersby on a windy street to stop municipal budget cuts, or deciding to join a local interest group.

Focusing on how citizens actually deliberate allows us to consider both macro and micro practices, but always with an eye to the significance for the individuals involved. For example, what forms of participation does a particular discursive phenomenon encourage—and by whom? How are speaking positions allotted and organized? What discursive norms inform a particular public forum? What possibilities are there for "ordinary" citizens to engage in public discourse? How do some people come to see themselves as legitimate voices in public debate? How does one assess arguments on public issues?

While rhetorical citizenship as a concept has no ideological bent, it is clearly normative in its attention to notions of empowerment, inclusivity, and discourse ethics. Among several scholars who study norms of engagement and expectations in public deliberation is Robert Ivie, who identifies as a key challenge "how to communicate politically without an exclusionary aim for consensus and unity or a reduction of difference to total otherness" (2002, 278). In his call for "rowdy" deliberation, Ivie seeks a rhetorical conception of deliberation that promotes democratic practice in the here and now rather than postponing it to a hypothetical future, disciplined by the illusion of rational consensus (278). He applauds Iris Marion Young's argument that an adequate understanding of political deliberation must encompass rhetoric as a necessary and positive attribute, but he extends the thought and argues that democratic deliberation is best understood as primarily rhetorical. Such an understanding is tantamount to accepting political discussion as essentially agonistic and robust enough to accommodate a measure of disagreement as sound and genuinely democratic.

Citizenship and Rhetorical Agency

Many of these concerns are central to a second theoretical strand that informs our thinking on rhetorical citizenship: the concept of *rhetorical agency*, which has gained attention by highlighting issues of voice, power, and rights. In rhetorical studies it has shown a way across an unproductive chasm, with traditionalist, rhetor-centered, instrumental notions of rhetoric on the one side and poststructuralist, constructivist conceptions on the other. Cheryl Geisler observes that the concept spans instrumental aspects of rhetoric as well as social, institutional, political, and cultural factors that condition a speaker's access to speaking and being heard (2004, 12–13). Focusing on the complexity of rhetorical events, it invites us to consider contextual factors that influence the particular event, and to underscore the structural aspects and the fluid nature of rhetorical force: for example, a person who enjoys institutional authority in one setting may have difficulty gaining a hearing in another.

A Cross-Disciplinary Effort

For years, many scholarly disciplines have engaged the idea of citizenship, but too often their thinking has moved in relatively closed circuits. Scholars need to pool their insights and communicate, as well as learn, across disciplinary boundaries. This book aims to show that no one scholarly angle is sufficient, yet all are necessary. Its interdisciplinarity—to say nothing of the broad range of nationalities it represents—is one feature that sets this volume apart from most work on citizenship so far, including the rhetorical studies we have alluded to. The careful study of authentic public communication as it actually takes place is traditionally one of rhetoricians' strong suits; here they have something to offer to scholars from other disciplines who also study the workings of democracy. Political scientists and philosophers have not traditionally engaged in precisely this kind of study, but they have much to offer by way of both conceptual analysis and empirical research.

We believe that the concept of rhetorical citizenship embraces scholarship from a range of disciplines, including communication studies, discourse analysis, and political philosophy, as well as fields outside the humanities such as political science and sociology. The concept may serve as an umbrella term covering a range of scholarly approaches to communication in the public, and particularly the political, sphere. Finally, the concept is well suited to mediate between theory and critical inquiry.

The chapters in this volume address in one aspect or another a general concern with the makeup and enhancement of public deliberation. The book adopts a rhetorical lens, even as it brings together authors from multiple disciplines. This rhetorical perspective emphasizes a diversity of actual deliberative practices, holding its conceptualizations accountable to, as many authors put it, a vernacular practice that considers how everyday people participate in and practice citizenship, and how everyday practices might be enhanced. The volume presents work on the possibilities for, obstacles to, and potentialities in public deliberation, as well as critical case studies of such engagement, organized in three broadly defined sections.

Section I, "Tracing Rhetorical Citizenship as Concept and Practice," considers the historical roots of deliberation as a concept and a practice. Three chapters suggest that those who wish to give more attention to the discursive aspects of democracy might look back for insight and precedent—not just to the immediate past, where notions of deliberative democracy sprang up in many quarters, but all the way back to those original "rhetorical citizens," the Greek Sophists, as well as to practical attempts in the not so distant past to implement democracy as a discursive phenomenon.

Section II, "Public Deliberation as Rhetorical Practice," comprises twelve chapters that address criteria of various kinds that either do or arguably could influence in positive ways the manner in which public deliberation is currently practiced. The first two chapters in the section take a theoretical, even a philosophical approach; the other ten look at specific contemporary practices and instances of political and other public talk, representing several countries and addressing physical as well as mediated and virtual subsections of the public sphere.

Section III, "Toward Better Deliberative Practices," looks forward. Ranging from the specific genre of presidential primary debates to a general consideration of social and ethical controversies, it offers three chapters that consider how public deliberative debates might become more constructive without prescribing consensus.

This might be a fitting note on which to end this introduction. Unlike many earlier exponents of deliberative democracy, we believe that proponents of rhetorical citizenship do not hold up the achievement of full agreement or the elimination of conflict as guiding ends. Harmony is not unison. Nor are the chapters in this collection.

REFERENCES

Aristotle. 1926. *Rhetoric*. Translated by J. H. Freese. Vol. 22 of *Aristotle in Twenty-three Volumes*. Cambridge: Harvard University Press.
———. 1934. *Nicomachean Ethics*. Translated by H. Rackham. Vol. 19 of *Aristotle in Twenty-three Volumes*. Cambridge: Harvard University Press; London: William Heinemann.
———. 1944. *Politics*. Translated by H. Rackham. Vol. 21 of *Aristotle in Twenty-three Volumes*. Cambridge: Harvard University Press; London: William Heinemann.
Asen, Robert. 2004. "A Discourse Theory of Citizenship." *Quarterly Journal of Speech* 90:189–211.
Brouwer, Daniel C., and Robert Asen. 2010. "Introduction: Public Modalities, or the Metaphors We Theorize By." In *Public Modalities: Rhetoric, Culture, Media, and the Shape of Public Life*, ed. Daniel C. Brouwer and Robert Asen, 1–32. Tuscaloosa: University of Alabama Press.
Dryzek, John. 2010. "Rhetoric in Democracy: A Systemic Appreciation." *Political Theory* 38 (3): 319–39.
Geisler, Cheryl. 2004. "How Ought We to Understand the Concept of Rhetorical Agency? Report from the ARS." *Rhetoric Society Quarterly* 34:9–17.

Hariman, Robert. 2007. "Amateur Hour: Knowing What to Love in Ordinary Democracy." In *The Prettier Doll: Rhetoric, Discourse, and Ordinary Democracy*, ed. Karen Tracy, James P. McDaniel, and Bruce Gronbeck, 218–50. Tuscaloosa: University of Alabama Press.

Hauser, Gerard A. 1999. *Vernacular Voices: The Rhetoric of Publics and Public Spheres*. Columbia: University of South Carolina Press.

Ivie, Robert L. 2002. "Rhetorical Deliberation and Democratic Politics in the Here and Now." *Rhetoric and Public Affairs* 5:277–85.

SECTION I

TRACING RHETORICAL CITIZENSHIP AS CONCEPT AND PRACTICE

The chapters in this section are united by attempts to trace the ancestry, the emergence, and the growth of ideas of rhetorical citizenship and deliberative democracy, in theory and in practice.

Kasper Møller Hansen, a political scientist, views deliberative democracy as a model that values deliberation rather than participation as the key element in democracy; it seeks its justification in the quality of the deliberation, not the number of speakers involved. Hansen reminds us that academic interest in issues of deliberative democracy is not just a current fad but builds on a strong tradition. In fact, several political thinkers throughout history have addressed the concept of deliberation under a variety of names. Emphasizing its strong historical roots in the republican tradition, Hansen discusses its role in the work of Jean-Jacques Rousseau, Alexis de Tocqueville, John Stuart Mill, and John Dewey. In addition, Hansen introduces the thinking on democracy of the Danish theologian Hal Koch and goes on to trace the revitalization of the deliberative understanding of democracy in modern scholarship, emphasizing its wide distribution over many academic fields.

Manfred Kraus, a classical scholar, goes even further back and discusses the ancient Sophists' views about truth and human *logos* to make a case for their relevance to a concept of rhetorical citizenship. Their key contribution is the idea of establishing socially relevant truth in open public debate. Without their analysis of the functions of *logos*, rhetoric would not exist; and without rhetoric, the very idea of a responsible and self-determined citizen would not be possible. In Kraus's analysis, the sophistic treatment of operational truth regarding the contingencies of human life, and the Sophists' belief in the necessity of constant negotiation between contradictory points of view, as in the political assemblies and law courts of Athens, have laid the groundwork for the concept of citizenship. Our participatory democracy is in dire need of self-responsible, assertive, and independently thinking citizens—just the kind of citizens whom the Sophists' teachings aimed to educate.

William Keith and Paula Cossart, representing communication studies and sociology, respectively, also take a historical approach. Their aim is to understand the function and eventual lack of appeal of public forums where citizens might exercise their rhetorical citizenship. Their chapter thus presents the volume's first case study. Comparing France in the late nineteenth century and the United States in the early twentieth, they find that in both cases, as people attempted to enact their role as citizen deliberators, the norms and practices they developed embodied a vision of rational citizenship, showing surprising parallels, whether successes or failures. The authors see rhetorical citizenship as the set of deliberative practices through which citizens enact their citizenship. They argue that, historically, the emergence of public deliberative events (citizen juries, town halls, and the like) was driven by a "crisis of republicanism": a widespread doubt that democratic institutions and government policies reflect the will of the public. The chapter seeks to draw lessons for contemporary deliberative projects, in particular on inherent tensions in rhetorical citizenship.

The three chapters in this section work together to outline key conceptual precursors of rhetorical citizenship by tracing the emergence of the notion of deliberative democracy and showing how, in the rhetorical tradition, ideas about free and critical discursive interaction were central to the idea of a civic community. While the remainder of the volume deals primarily with contemporary examples and issues of rhetorical citizenship, Keith and Cossart's case study shows how—including at the level of practice—rhetorical citizenship has a rich history, important in itself and an important source for understanding current challenges that beset attempts to organize public discussion forums.

I

DELIBERATIVE DEMOCRACY:
MAPPING OUT THE DELIBERATIVE TURN IN
DEMOCRATIC THEORY

Kasper Møller Hansen

Deliberative democracy is the current buzzword in contemporary democratic thought, but the concept is deeply rooted in the republican democratic tradition. Researchers often forget these democratic roots in their hurry to "jump on the bandwagon." This chapter shows how deliberation appears in the writings of five important political thinkers within the republican tradition in order to identify the roots of deliberative democracy. It also investigates the contemporary rise of deliberative democracy and explains why the deliberative turn suddenly occurred. To begin, a brief general account of deliberative democracy will be helpful.

Deliberative Democracy

Political discussion and deliberation are important elements in democratic theory. Deliberation has always been central to democracy, though with varying degrees of intensity. In ancient Greece and the city-states of the Middle Ages and the Renaissance, citizens would gather in assemblies to debate issues before making decisions. The term *deliberation* comes from the Latin *libra*, a scale on which to weigh or balance. In this sense, deliberation is often simply translated as "careful consideration." More specifically, deliberation can be defined as "an unconstrained exchange of arguments that involves practical reasoning and potentially leads to a transformation of preferences" (Cooke 2000, 948; see also Hansen 2004, 98; Hansen and Andersen 2004).

Deliberative democracy is a model of democracy that emphasizes deliberation (as opposed to participation) as the focal point. Thus the quality of the deliberation, not the number of speakers, justifies deliberative democracy. Deliberative democracy is based on deliberation that is mutually justifiable and expressed with mutual respect for arguments offered by other citizens. Accountability is achieved through continuous deliberation between politicians and citizens, and political equality is constituted through active deliberation. Preferences are considered as endogenously given, that is, as created within the deliberative process. The decision-making process consists of deliberation supplemented by majority voting. It is the quality of the deliberation, not the number of speakers or the degree of descriptive representation among them, that constitutes democratic legitimacy (Dryzek and Niemeyer 2008; Hansen 2004; Hansen and Andersen 2004).

In a manner of speaking, deliberative democracy represents a view of democracy where every step in the decision-making process is infused with deliberation. While deliberative democracy has become the most popular concept in current discussions of democracy, political thinkers have actually addressed the concept of deliberation throughout history.

Deliberative Democracy—A Long Tradition

To illustrate how deliberation has been conceived, I will focus on four political thinkers: Jean-Jacques Rousseau, Alexis de Tocqueville, John Stuart Mill, and John Dewey. As a supplement to these four internationally renowned thinkers, I will introduce the Danish theologian Hal Koch (1945–1991) as the deliberative democrat he was, although he was never directly identified as such.

Rather than delve into the complex political works of these political theorists in detail, my focus is on how deliberation is considered in different parts of their work. These political theorists discussed deliberation in various aspects of public life, but always within the context of democracy. This chapter casts light on how key political theorists discussed related aspects of democracy, fully cognizant that their theories are of a much more complex and sophisticated nature. The aim is simply to show that deliberation is not a new phenomenon, first considered by political theorists and other thinkers in recent decades, but is in fact part of a long republican tradition. I hope that this discussion of earlier political theorists can inspire contemporary discussions on deliberative democracy, but I make no claim that interpretations of these earlier theorists constitute guidelines for such discussions.

Rousseau on Deliberation

Jean-Jacques Rousseau (1712–1778) was one of the first political thinkers from a plebeian background. In fact, he remained rather poor throughout his life. This might explain why he was so concerned about political equality in a time dominated by the rational outlook of the Enlightenment. Rousseau continued the social contract theories of Hobbes (1651) and Locke (1690), but because of his strong belief in liberty, he rejected Hobbes's position that the individual must be completely submissive to the sovereign. In Rousseau's social contract, everyone submits to everyone else, and thus to no one in particular. Accordingly, the individual remains just as free as he was before the contract, as each individual gains an equivalent share of the whole for any losses, as well as an increased capacity to preserve what he owns (Rousseau 1999, 455–56). Rousseau is one of the first political thinkers since the ancient Greeks explicitly to emphasize deliberation in the political process. His strong belief in the sovereignty of the people and their right to self-government led Rousseau to argue for "direct" or "city-state" democracy, whereby citizens could take part directly in the decision-making process. As such, governance by representatives should not be tolerated, as it would enslave the people and violate the right to self-government. As Rousseau emphasizes in his famous statement about the English, "The people of England regards itself as free; but it is grossly mistaken; it is free only during the election of the members of parliament. As soon as they are elected, slavery overtakes it, and it is nothing" (470). Deliberation is essential in the process of self-government, as it transforms self-interest into a common interest, or, in Rousseau's words, "particular wills are substituted for general will in public deliberation." Rousseau goes on to say that there "are two general rules that may serve to regulate this relation [between particular wills and the general will]. First, the more grave and important the questions discussed, the nearer should the opinion that is to prevail approach unanimity. Secondly, the more the matter in hand calls for speed, the smaller the prescribed difference in the number of votes may be allowed to become: where an instant decision has to be reached, a majority of one vote should be enough" (472).

While the first statement emphasizes deliberation as a means of transforming self-interest into common interest and asserts that if important questions are at stake, deliberation should approach unanimity, the second holds that when speed is of the essence, unanimity and consensus can be sacrificed, and a difference of one vote can decide the matter. This view of deliberation as a means of transforming differing opinions into common interest also prevails in contemporary approaches to deliberation (e.g., Habermas 1984. See Hansen 2010 for a critical discussion of consensus as a result of deliberation. The challenge is that a goal of consensus in deliberation tends to depress the plurality of the arguments).

Although this reading of Rousseau betokens his partiality for deliberation, he also warns that "long debates, dissensions and tumult proclaim the ascendancy of particular interests and the decline of the State" (471). Thus Freeman (2000, 377) and Elster (1998, 14) interpret Rousseau as being against deliberation. Nevertheless, it could be argued that Rousseau warns against distorted deliberation, that is, excessive deliberation marked by tumult. Either way, the examples above illustrate how the concept of deliberation has been relevant in theories of democracy for centuries.

Tocqueville on Deliberation

Another important political observer is Alexis de Tocqueville (1805–1859), who is often studied for his fascination with American society during his travels in the United States in the 1830s. In particular, Tocqueville's preoccupation with Americans' participation in local institutions, voluntary associations, and civil society in general has been the subject of much scholarly study (e.g., Barber 1984, 234–35; Mansbridge 1983, 41). Thus Tocqueville is interpreted as an advocate of what has come to be known as communitarianism (Putnam 2000, 24). Deliberation and discussion are also part of Tocqueville's fascination with American society, as described in *Democracy in America*. This emerges in his description of American debate culture, where he claims that Americans find such amusement in deliberation that some seek entertainment in debating clubs rather than the theater (1835, 289). He also describes how discussions continue as long as the majority is undecided, "but as soon as its decision is irrevocably pronounced, everyone is silent, and the friends as well as the opponents of the measure unite in assenting to its propriety" (304). This shows how important discussion was in decision-making procedures, but also that everyone, according to Tocqueville, supported the decision as soon as it was made. Tocqueville describes American jury deliberations in the 1830s as the "most efficacious means for the education of the people which society can employ" (330). But juries are important not only for their educational effect but also because they promote attention to the common good among the citizenry: "By obliging men to turn their attention to other affairs than their own, it rubs off that private selfishness which is the rust of society" (329). Like Rousseau, Tocqueville emphasizes how discussion can extend a narrow focus on self-interest and promote broader interest in societal affairs.

Mill on Deliberation

John Stuart Mill (1806–1873) similarly emphasized the educational effect of participation and deliberation, writing of "the practical part of the political education of a free people, taking them out of the narrow circle of personal and family selfishness, and accustoming them to the comprehension of joint interests, the management of joint concerns—habituating them to act from public or semipublic motives, and guide their conduct by aims which unite instead of isolating them from one another" (1962, 243–44). Mill's strong advocacy of liberty of speech also has relevance for why deliberation has been justified as central to the political process. Mill makes the argument for free speech on four grounds. First, if an opinion is not allowed to be expressed, then how will we know whether or not it is true? By denying expression to an opinion, we assume our own infallibility; that is, we assume that the current truth is unquestionable. Second, even if silenced opinions are untrue, they may be part of a new perception of the truth; it is only by the collision of different opinions that the entire truth will prevail. Third, even if the current perception of the truth is entirely correct, liberty of speech is necessary. The truth would otherwise turn into prejudice, and people would forget the rational grounds upon which it was based. Finally, the meaning of the truth will be endangered if freedom of expression is violated, as the truth becomes a "formal profession" and prevents the development of the current belief based on rational arguments or personal experiences (180–81). The fourth argument makes clear that Mill believes that free speech offers a means by which to arrive at a "truth"; however, these four grounds for liberty of speech also form a strong argument that deliberation should be part of the political process in order to secure a decision based on "rational grounds."

Dewey on Deliberation

The American philosopher and educational theorist John Dewey (1859–1952) has been called the first political thinker in the twentieth century to advocate the need to give deliberation a more central position in democratic theory (Eriksen and Weigård 1999, 152; Eriksen 1995). In his work on democracy, Dewey argues that voting procedures and expert decisions in government must be supplemented by popular participation; otherwise, democracy will turn into a technocracy in which a class of experts will rule, remote from every common interest. Public consultation is important even when decisions are carried out through majority rule, as it allows interest to be created, articulated, and communicated within the political system (1984, 364–65): "The essential need . . . is the improvement of the methods and conditions of debate, discussion and persuasions" (365).

Koch on Deliberation

As part of his advocacy of general education in the postwar period, the Danish theologian Hal Koch (1904–1963) wrote a book, published in 1945, titled *What Is Democracy?* This book and the lectures he gave on the influential Danish bishop N. F. S. Grundtvig (1783–1872) had a strong emphasis on general education. Koch considered this work to be his contribution to the Danish resistance against the German Nazi regime. The book is infused with the conviction that general education would lead to democracy and liberty. Koch emphasized deliberation as the essence of democracy. Democracy, he felt, could not be defined simply as a model or a system; instead, it represented a way of life and a frame of mind. Democracy was thus much more comprehensive and complex than the mere use of elections and voting to reach decisions on behalf of society. For Koch, democracy was the deliberative process among conflicting actors who carefully examined the issues at stake in a sincere attempt to reach a more truthful and justified understanding of conflicting interests through deliberation. As such, he wrote, "It is the deliberation (dialogue) and the mutual understanding and respect that are the nature of democracy" (1991, 16, my translation). This suggests that a decision based on a deliberative process serves not only a single person or class but the common good (20). In Koch's view, voting is a justified and legitimate democratic procedure only if it is undertaken after an issue has been carefully deliberated upon. The distribution of votes indicates how effective the deliberation has been in considering the common good. Thus any democratic decision is always relative and merely approximates the "right" decision. The deliberative process never stops; it is continuous (24–25). If the attempt to reach a mutual understanding in the case of conflicting opinions fails, Koch believes that society is bound to end in a situation reminiscent of Hobbes's state of nature, in which people's lives are considered "solitary, poor, nasty, brutish and short," and each individual merely attempts to maximize his own self-interest (Hobbes 1994, 76). Given this outcome, Koch saw no true alternative to deliberation.

The aim of this brief discussion of the five political thinkers has been to demonstrate that deliberation is not merely a contemporary phenomenon that developed in the twentieth century; instead, it has deep roots in the republican tradition of democratic theory.

This conclusion is also supported by the writings of the American founding fathers. James Madison (1987, 126) advocated the filter of deliberation through which public opinion must be matured in order to improve its quality and include the common interest. It is important to understand the two sides of Madison's argument. On the one hand, he argues that deliberation is required because the poor (pure) quality of the public's raw opinions and deliberation encourages the substitution of self-interest for common interest. On the other hand, deliberation is needed because it means stronger popular control of decision-making procedures. The two arguments are not contradictory or mutually exclusive but represent two very different assumptions about popular control and the quality of public opinion.

Although deliberative democracy can be traced back to the republican tradition of democratic theory, this is seldom recognized in contemporary work on deliberative democracy. Rather, researchers tend to refer only to contemporary writers, forgetting the roots of the tradition. To better understand the developing field of deliberative democracy, and why deliberation has reappeared as the focus of study among contemporary political thinkers, let us turn now to present-day discussions.

Mapping the Rise of Deliberative Democracy

Within the past few decades, the concept of deliberation has revitalized the theoretical debate on political and democratic theory in applied empirical research as well as in many new initiatives to involve citizens in public decision making. In political theory, Habermas, Rawls, and more recently Bohman, Gutmann and Thompson, and Dryzek have developed more or less all-embracing theories with strong deliberative elements. In applied empirical research, James S. Fishkin and Robert Luskin's "deliberative polls" and Ned Cosby's "citizens' juries" have been applied worldwide (Fung 2003; Hansen 2004).

Contemporary deliberative democracy has been heavily influenced by two thinkers: Rawls and Habermas. The legacy and inspiration of these two philosophers become apparent in many parts of the theory. Despite the work of Habermas and Rawls on deliberation, however, the concept of deliberation did not prosper until the late 1980s, as indicated in figure 1.1.

According to Bohman (1998) and later Dryzek (2000) and Chambers (2003), echoed by many others, democracy theory has taken a "deliberative turn." Of course, the true believers in deliberative democracy may not need much evidence; however, others might be more interested in empirical evidence with which to investigate this further. Such evidence also provides an opportunity to identify the root of this deliberative turn. One way of empirically investigating the focus on deliberative democracy is to evaluate the 517 academic articles published about deliberative democracy between 1989 and 2010, as this gives us an idea of the attention and popularity the concept has achieved.

As figure 1.1 indicates, academic debate on deliberative democracy increased dramatically in the 1990s. The social science and the arts and humanities citation indices of the Thomson Reuters Web of Knowledge (formerly the ISI Web of Knowledge), an academic citation indexing and

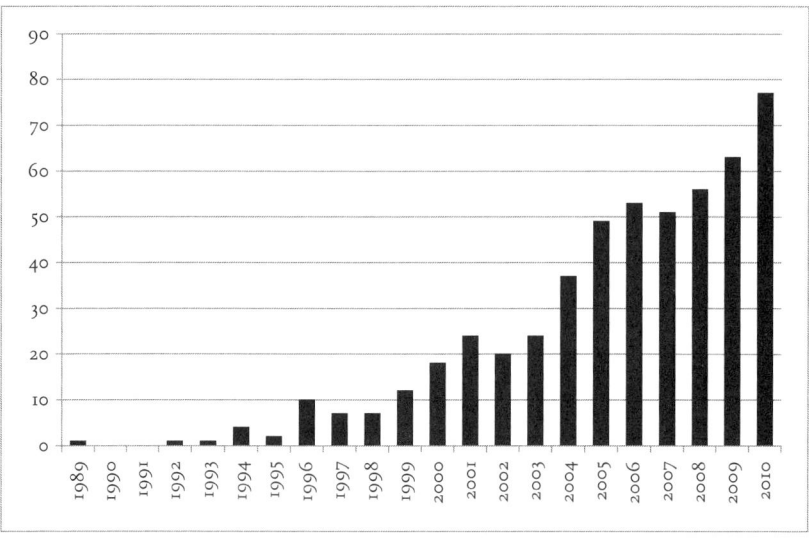

Fig. 1.1 Number of academic articles on deliberative democracy, 1989–2010

Note: These articles were found through a combined search of Thomson Reuters Web of Knowledge—the social science citation index and the arts and humanities citation index—by searching for the phrase "deliberative democracy" in title, summary, and keywords in the English language only. The search includes journals from 1956 onward, but no articles on deliberative democracy were found until 1989. Search conducted 2 May 2011.

search service, indicate that only nine academic articles on deliberative democracy were published in these fields in the period 1956–95, and none before 1989, against 508 in the period 1996–2010. If we divide the articles by subject area, we find that 22 percent of the articles on deliberative democracy have been published in the field of political science (fig. 1.2).

It is hardly surprising that the largest and broadest field, political science, has the greatest number of published articles on deliberative democracy. But the fact that 26 percent of the articles are spread over the "Others" category, which comprises sixty-four different fields, indicates that the concept has been applied in very different disciplines and has thus traveled far beyond the discipline within which it was first conceptualized. Figures 1.1 and 1.2 provide strong evidence of the deliberative turn, as the concept of deliberative democracy has received increased attention in the space of a few years.

Even though, as argued above, the term *deliberation* and its use in relation to the concept of democracy have long traditions, figure 1.1 shows that deliberative democracy was rediscovered in the late 1980s. The phrase was first coined by Bessette (1980) and was used again in his later book, *The Mild Voice of Reason* (1994), but attention to deliberative democracy really picked up in the early 1990s.

One might speculate as to why attention increased so dramatically at this time. As Carole Pateman (2000) said of the dramatic shift, "I get up one

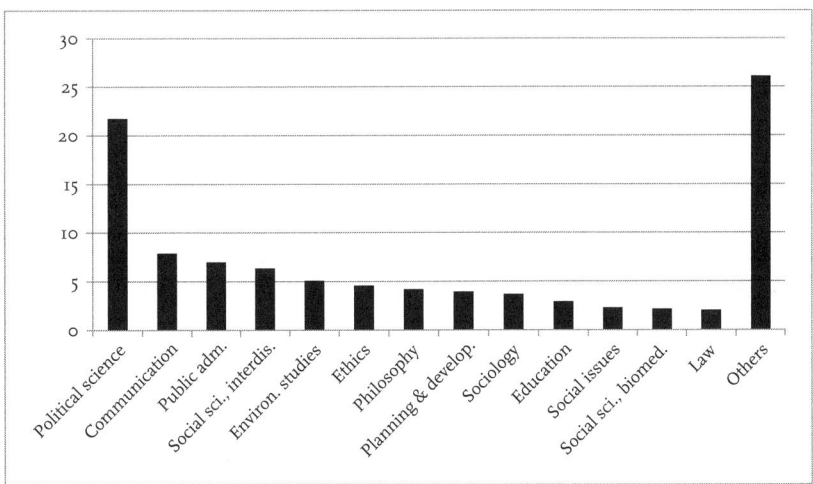

Fig. 1.2 The 517 articles on deliberative democracy divided by subject area (%)

Note: See note to fig. 1.1. Thomson Reuters Web of Knowledge—social science citation index and the arts and humanities citation index—groups some journals under more than one subject area; thus *N* in this analysis is 786.

day and everybody is talking about deliberative democracy." At first glance, it certainly seems as though this happened almost overnight. Upon further consideration, one finds several explanations of what contributed to this shift. First, several articles and books were published, independent of one another, within a few years on the subject of deliberation (e.g., Cohen 1989; Dryzek 1990; Fishkin 1991; Manin 1987). With the exception of Cohen, who cites Manin's article, none of the publications refers to any of the others. Second, the shift can be explained to some degree by the renewed interest in Habermas's work in the wake of the 1989 translation of his 1962 book *The Structural Transformation of the Public Sphere*. For example, Cohen, Manin, Dryzek, and Fishkin all refer to Habermas's works. Yet another explanation relates to a general trend among researchers to jump on the bandwagon (Peng 1994). Thus deliberative democracy has become a fashionable term, but this is not to say that the term is without content. It has been argued that deliberative democracy connects the liberal and republican traditions within democratic theory (Gutmann and Thompson 1996, 27; Habermas 1996). The concept of deliberative democracy has also moved the debate between liberal and republican approaches to democracy to a point that seems to allow many approaches to democracy to find common ground for their arguments, providing a broad synthesis between opposites (e.g., laypeople vs. elites, individuals vs. collectives, and local vs. global), thus appealing to a broad range of students of democracy. Furthermore, it appears that writers who previously applied the concepts of liberal or participatory democracy have now found a common concept for their work in the emerging field of deliberative democracy.

It is also possible to relate the focus on deliberative democracy to the general reaction to the individualization of society, the growing lack of trust in politicians, the gap between politicians and the public, and general tendencies relating to the impact of globalization on social norms and values. These features relate to the theoretical ideal that many deliberative democrats try to address with the theory of deliberative democracy and the alternative methods for involving citizens in decision making. Finally, the emphasis on deliberation and deliberative democracy is also part of a general trend within political theory and the normative debate on democracy, according to which normative theory must relate to the empirical reality of contemporary society (e.g., Smith 2004).

Figures 1.3 and 1.4 take the analysis a step further. They confirm the extent to which publications have spread out across fields. Figure 1.3 shows that although the journals *Political Theory* and *Political Studies* have published the most articles on deliberative democracy, these two journals only account for a limited share of the total of 517 articles. Once again, this illustrates the wide diffusion of the concept.

The diffuse study of deliberative democracy is also confirmed when we consider the number of citations of the 517 articles (fig. 1.4). Again, the "Others" category accounts for more than 60 percent of these citations. This indicates that references are not clustered around a few articles but are spread across many.

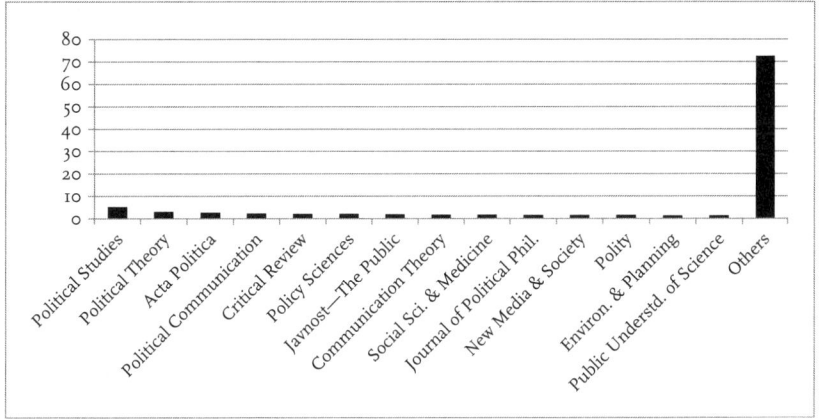

Fig. 1.3 *The 517 articles on deliberative democracy divided by journal (%)*

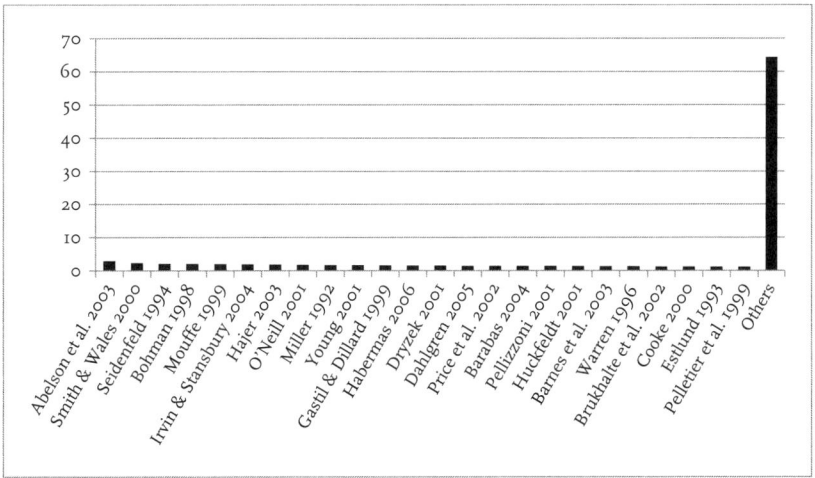

Fig. 1.4 *Number of citations as of 2010 (%)*
Note: The 517 articles were cited 3,588 times by 2010.

Conclusion

Contemporary studies of deliberative democracy often focus on how deliberation positively affects the decision-making process, forgetting that deliberative democracy has deep roots in classical political thinkers such as Rousseau, Tocqueville, Mill, Dewey, and Koch. Thus deliberative democracy is hardly a recent phenomenon among political thinkers, although scholars sometimes give that impression. Deliberative democracy builds upon the republican tradition of democratic thinking. A more careful look at the increased attention to deliberative democracy among researchers shows that although the legacy of the republican tradition is strong, there are few common reference points, and the concept is widely distributed across fields and journals. This might be so because the concept of deliberative democracy has spread rapidly across many fields in which various traditions have had different focus points. This shows the dynamics of a development concept, but also that researchers might have a tendency to invent the wheel over and over again.

REFERENCES

Abelson, J., P. G. Forest, J. Eyles, P. Smith, E. Martin, and F. P. Gauvin. 2003. "Deliberations About Deliberative Methods: Issues in the Design and Evaluation of Public Participation Processes." *Social Science and Medicine* 57 (2): 239–51.

Andersen, V. N., and K. M. Hansen. 2007. "How Deliberation Makes Better Citizens—The Deliberative Poll on the Euro." *European Journal of Political Research* 46 (4): 531–56.

Barabas, J. 2004. "How Deliberation Affects Policy Opinions." *American Political Science Review* 98 (4): 687–701.

Barber, B. R. 1984. *Strong Democracy: Participatory Politics for a New Age*. Berkeley and Los Angeles: University of California Press.

Barnes, M., J. Newman, A. Knops, and H. Sullivan. 2003. "Constituting 'the Public' in Public Participation." *Public Administration* 81 (2): 379–99.

Bessette, J. M. 1980. "Deliberative Democracy: The Majority Principle in Republican Government." In *How Democratic Is the Constitution?* ed. R. A. Goldwin and W. A. Schambra, 102–16. Washington, D.C.: American Enterprise Institute for Public Policy Research.

———. 1994. *The Mild Voice of Reason: Deliberative Democracy and American National Government*. Chicago: University of Chicago Press.

Bohman, J. 1996. *Public Deliberation: Pluralism, Complexity, and Democracy*. Cambridge: MIT Press.

———. 1998. "Survey Article: The Coming of Age of Deliberative Democracy." *Journal of Political Philosophy* 6 (4): 400–425.

Burkhalter, S., J. Gastil, and T. Kelshaw. 2002. "A Conceptual Definition and Theoretical Model of Public Deliberation in Small Face-to-Face Groups." *Communication Theory* 12 (4): 398–422.

Chambers, S. 2003. "Deliberative Democratic Theory." *Annual Review of Political Science* 6:307–26.

Cohen, J. 1989. "Deliberation and Democratic Legitimacy." In *The Good Polity: Normative Analysis of the State*, ed. A. Hamlin and P. Pettit, 17–34. Oxford: Basil Blackwell.

Cooke, M. 2000. "Five Arguments for Deliberative Democracy." *Political Studies* 48 (2): 947–69.

Dahlgren, P. 2005. "The Internet, Public Spheres, and Political Communication: Dispersion and Deliberation." *Political Communication* 22 (2): 147–62.

Dewey, J. 1984. *The Public and Its Problems*. In *John Dewey—The Later Works, 1925–1953*, vol. 2, *1925–1927*, ed. J. A. Boydston, 235–372. Carbondale: Southern Illinois University Press. (Orig. pub. 1927.)

Dryzek, J. S. 1990. *Discursive Democracy: Politics, Policy, and Political Science*. Cambridge: Cambridge University Press.

———. 2000. *Deliberative Democracy and Beyond: Liberals, Critics, Contestations*. Oxford: Oxford University Press.

———. 2001. "Legitimacy and Economy in Deliberative Democracy." *Political Theory* 29 (5): 651–69.

———. 2005. "Deliberative Democracy in Divided Societies—Alternatives to Agonism and Analgesia." *Political Theory* 33 (2): 218–42.

Dryzek, J. S., and S. J. Niemeyer. 2008. "Discursive Representation." *American Political Science Review* 102 (4): 481–93.

Elster, J. 1998. "Introduction." In *Deliberative Democracy*, ed. J. Elster, 1–18. Cambridge: Cambridge University Press.

Eriksen, E. O. 1995. "Introduksjon til en deliberativ politikkmodel." In *Deliberativ politikk: Demokrati i teori og praksis*, ed. E. O. Eriksen, 11–30. Bergen, Norway: TANO.

Eriksen, E. O., and J. Weigård. 1999. *Kommunikativ handling og deliberativt demokrati: Jürgen Habermas' teori om politikk og samfunn*. Bergen, Norway: Fakboklaget.

Estlund, D. M. 1993. "Who's Afraid of Deliberative Democracy—On the Strategic Deliberative Dichotomy in Recent Constitutional Jurisprudence." *Texas Law Review* 71 (7): 1437–77.

Fishkin, J. S. 1988. "The Case for a National Caucus—Taking Democracy Seriously." *Atlantic*, August, 16–18.

———. 1991. *Democracy and Deliberation: New Directions for Democratic Reform*. New Haven: Yale University Press.

———. 1997. *The Voice of the People: Public Opinion and Democracy*. 2nd ed. New Haven: Yale University Press.

Freeman, S. 2000. "Deliberative Democracy: A Sympathetic Comment." *Philosophy and Public Affairs* 29 (4): 371–418.

Fung, A. 2003. "Recipes for Public Spheres: Eight Institutional Design Choices and Their Consequences." *Journal of Political Philosophy* 11 (3): 338–67.

Gastil, J., and J. P. Dillard. 1999. "Increasing Political Sophistication Through Public Deliberation." *Political Communication* 16 (1): 3–23.

Gutmann, A., and D. Thompson. 1996. *Democracy and Disagreement*. Cambridge: Belknap Press of Harvard University Press.

Habermas, J. 1984. *The Theory of Communicative Action: Reason and the Rationalization of Society*. Cambridge: Polity Press.

———. 1989. *The Structural Transformation of the Public Sphere: An Inquiry into a Category of Bourgeois Society*. Cambridge: Polity Press.

———. 1996. *Between Facts and Norms: Contributions to a Discourse Theory of Law and Democracy*. Cambridge: MIT Press.

———. 2006. "Political Communication in Media Society: Does Democracy Still Enjoy an Epistemic Dimension? The Impact of Normative Theory on Empirical Research." *Communication Theory* 16 (4): 411–26.

Hajer, M. 2003. "Policy Without Polity? Policy Analysis and the Institutional Void." *Policy Sciences* 36 (2): 175–95.

Hansen, K. M. 2004. *Deliberative Democracy and Opinion Formation*. Odense: University Press of Southern Denmark.

———. 2010. "The Equality Paradox of Deliberative Democracy: Evidence from a National Deliberative Poll." In *Political Discussion in Modern Democracies*, ed. M. Wolf, L. Morales, and K. Ikeda, 26–43. London: Routledge.

Hansen, K. M., and V. N. Andersen. 2004. "Deliberative Democracy and the Deliberative Poll on the Euro." *Scandinavian Political Studies* 27 (3): 261–86.

Hobbes, T. 1994. *Leviathan*. Indianapolis: Hackett. (Orig. pub. 1651.)

Huckfeldt, R. 2001. "The Social Communication of Political Expertise." *American Journal of Political Science* 45 (2): 425–38.

Irvin, R. A., and J. Stansbury. 2004. "Citizen Participation in Decision Making: Is It Worth the Effort?" *Public Administration Review* 64 (1): 55–65.

Koch, H. 1991. *Hvad er demokrati?* 5th ed. Copenhagen: Gyldendal. (Orig. pub. 1945.)

Locke, J. 1980. *The Second Treatise of Government*. Indianapolis: Hackett. (Orig. pub. 1690.)

Luskin, R. C., J. S. Fishkin, and R. Jowell. 2002. "Considered Opinions: Deliberative Polling in Britain." *British Journal of Political Science* 32:455–87.

Madison, J., A. Hamilton, and J. Jay. 1987. *The Federalist Papers*, ed. I. Kramnick. New York: Penguin. (Orig. pub. 1788.)

Manin, B. 1987. "On Legitimacy and Political Deliberation." *Political Theory* 15 (3): 338–68.

Mansbridge, J. J. 1983. *Beyond Adversary Democracy*. 2nd ed. Chicago: University of Chicago Press.

Mill, J. S. 1962. *On Liberty*. New York: Meridian. (Orig. pub. 1859.)

Miller, D. 1992. "Deliberative Democracy and Social Choice." *Political Studies* 40:54–67.

Mouffe, C. 1999. "Deliberative Democracy or Agonistic Pluralism?" *Social Research* 66 (3): 745–58.

O'Neill, J. 2001. "Representing People, Representing Nature, Representing the World." *Environment and Planning C: Government and Policy* 19 (4): 483–500.

Pateman, Carol. 2000. Oral presentation at the conference "Deliberating About Deliberative Democracy," University of Texas at Austin, 4–6 February.

Pelletier, D., V. Kraak, C. McCullum, U. Uusitalo, and R. Rich. 1999. "The Shaping of Collective Values Through Deliberative Democracy: An Empirical Study from New York's North Country." *Policy Sciences* 32 (2): 103–31.

Pellizzoni, L. 2001. "The Myth of the Best Argument: Power, Deliberation, and Reason." *British Journal of Sociology* 52 (1): 59–86.

———. 2003. "Uncertainty and Participatory Democracy." *Environmental Values* 12 (2): 195–224.

Peng, Y. 1994. "Intellectual Fads in Political Science—The Cases of Political Socialization and Community Power Studies." *PS:Political Science and Politics* 27 (1): 100–108.

Price, V., J. N. Cappella, and L. Nir. 2002. "Does Disagreement Contribute to More Deliberative Opinion?" *Political Communication* 19 (1): 95–112.
Putnam, R. D. 2000. *Bowling Alone*. New York: Touchstone.
Rawls, J. 1971. *A Theory of Justice*. London: Oxford University Press.
———. 1996. *Political Liberalism: With a New Introduction and the "Reply to Habermas."* New York: Columbia University Press.
Rousseau, J.-J. 1999. "The Social Contract." In *Great Political Thinkers: From Plato to the Present*, 6th ed., ed. W. Ebenstein and A. Ebenstein, 452–72. Fort Worth: Harcourt College Publishers. (Orig. pub. 1762.)
Seidenfeld, M. A. 1994. "Syncopated Chevron: Emphasizing Reasoned Decisionmaking in Reviewing Agency Interpretations of Statutes." *Texas Law Review* 73:83–138.
Sigelman, L. 2006. "The *American Political Science Review* Citation Classics." *American Political Science Review* 100 (4): 667–69.
Smith, G., and C. Wales. 2000. "Citizens' Juries and Deliberative Democracy." *Political Studies* 48 (1): 51–65.
Smith, R. M. 2004. "Reconnecting Political Theory to Empirical Inquiry, or A Return to the Cave." In *Theory and Inquiry in American Politics*, ed. E. D. Mansfield and R. Sisson, 60–88. Columbus: Ohio University Press.
Tocqueville, A. de. 1835. *Democracy in America*. New York: Bantam.
Warren, M. E. 1996. "Deliberative Democracy and Authority." *American Political Science Review* 90 (1): 46–60.
Young, I. M. 2001. "Activist Challenges to Deliberative Democracy." *Political Theory* 29 (5): 670–90.

2

THE MAKING OF TRUTH IN DEBATE:
THE CASE OF (AND A CASE FOR) THE EARLY SOPHISTS

Manfred Kraus

When someone describes a debate as sophistic, there is little probability that he or she actually intends to praise it. Rather, the term indicates that the debate is regarded as employing unfair or at least questionable means, such as bluffs, captious or quibbling arguments, or even fallacies or spurious reasoning, also known as sophisms. It may further mean that a controversy has been initiated for controversy's sake, without any deeper interest in the subject matter at stake. The term "sophistic" has long suffered—and still does—from deprecatory and reprobative overtones. It instantly evokes the association of stupendous rhetorical brilliance, on the one hand, coupled with ethical meanness, ruthlessness, and a lack of moral responsibility, on the other. It is as if the ancient Greek thinkers we commonly call Sophists have acquired this bad reputation as retribution for their fine but brief hour of sweeping success in the fifth and fourth centuries BCE, as the Austrian historian of philosophy Theodor Gomperz once splendidly put it (1922, 351). The view we have of the individuals whom we categorize as Sophists is still heavily biased by the unfavorable picture that Plato and Aristotle, first and foremost, drew of them. Plato generally portrayed them as a kind of negative counterpart to his teacher Socrates, and the caricature of the sophistic practice of eristic debate sketched in dialogues such as the *Euthydemus* is a major trait in this unfavorable picture. Aristotle, for his part, was mainly interested in the Sophists as the champions of a special technique of fallacious reasoning and arguing that he called eristic—that is, polemical or contentious—reasoning, the fallacies of which he set about analyzing and stripping bare in his treatise *On Sophistical Refutations*.

Dedicated to the memory of Michael C. Leff, a wonderful rhetorician and a great citizen.

The ill repute of sophistic thinking in general was shared by the art of rhetoric, most prominently so in Plato, distinctly less so in Aristotle. Students of my generation were still brought up within a tradition in which Plato and the philosophers were the good guys, and the Sophists and rhetoricians were the bad guys. There was a clear-cut black-and-white picture: philosophers were interested in truth, Sophists and rhetoricians in mere appearances. Philosophers cared for justice and moral goodness, Sophists and rhetoricians for the quick success, no matter at what cost or by what means. Philosophers acted out of love of truth, Sophists and rhetoricians out of greed for profit. Yet, in the later decades of the last century, a fundamental change was brought about by what has been called the rhetorical turn or, more recently, the neosophistic turn.[1]

The Neosophistic Turn

The first impulse that triggered this change was started by discussions about totalitarianism and democracy that took place after World War II. Since Karl Popper first denounced Plato as a totalitarian in his 1945 book *The Open Society and Its Enemies*, and at the same time hailed the Sophists as the advocates and representatives of a more colorful democratic and pluralistic culture, the tables started turning piecemeal in favor of the Sophists. After some first inklings in the 1970s, when scholars such as W. K. C. Guthrie and G. B. Kerferd began to reassess the historical role of the early Sophists, the 1980s in particular saw a virtual explosion of scholarly interest in the Sophists and rhetoric and heard a many-voiced cry for a "new" age of sophistry and a "new" sophistic rhetoric in particular. One of the spearheads of this movement was John Poulakos, with his provocative essay "Toward a Sophistic Definition of Rhetoric" (1983b; see also 1984 and 1987). Others were to join him soon. Scholars such as Roger Moss (1982) and Jasper Neel (1988) aspired to make a "case for sophistry." The late Michael Leff (1987), based on Robert Scott (1967), investigated the epistemic function of rhetoric, followed later on by Daniel Royer (1991) and Bruce McComiskey (1994). Susan Jarratt (1987) stipulated a "sophistic historiography" that would introduce the idea of subversive change and disruption as opposed to continuity, and Sharon Crowley (1989) made "a plea for the revival of sophistry" as opposed to "technologized" rhetoric. From 1988 onward, Takis Poulakos joined his brother's approach in a number of essays, in the 1990s Bruce McComiskey called for a "postmodern sophistics" (1993) and a "neo-sophistic rhetorical theory" (1994), and Victor Vitanza (1991, 1997) advocated a "third sophistic." Both John Poulakos (1995) and Bruce McComiskey (2002) assembled their thoughts in major monographs. In 1988 Brian Vickers also ventured a "defence of rhetoric" against its Platonic denigration. Common to all of these works is the twofold demand not only that the rhetorical activities of the Sophists be reappraised and defended from a historical point of view against the philosophers' attacks, but that their basic theories and concepts also be appropriated for use in the pluralistic societies of the late twentieth and twenty-first centuries.

In this new interpretation, everything appears in a different light. Now the Sophists are looked upon favorably as partisans of democracy, pluralism, political freedom, and open debate, whereas Plato, as their chief opponent, appears as an intolerant aristocrat, totalitarian, and dogmatist who takes delight in suppressing dissenting opinions. This picture is still black and white, only the black has turned white, and vice versa (cf. Schiappa 1991c, 14–15). It is easy to see that there may be a similar overstatement here, as in the traditional view.

The core of Poulakos's interpretation is the notion of a "sophistic rhetoric" as an elaborate theory in its own right, with its own rules and standards, based on a concept of society not much unlike our own, which could thus smoothly be translated into contemporary implementation. Poulakos singles out the following five distinctive traits of ancient "sophistic rhetoric": (1) the conception of rhetoric as a *téchnē*, a practical art (vs. theoretical science, *epistḗmē*, in the Platonic sense); (2) a clear emphasis on style as personal expression; (3) the attention given to *kairós*, the opportune moment (vs. immutable, eternal truths; see Baumlin 1984; White 1987); (4) the importance attributed to *to prépon*, the appropriate (and thus to the individual situation and the individual audience); and (5) the interest in *to dunatón*, the possible or potential (vs. the factual, on which the dogmatists build their own truth-based systems) (Poulakos 1983b, 36).

In 1990, Poulakos's inspired but somewhat naïve approach was severely taken to task in a reply to his first essay by Edward Schiappa (1990c; see also 1991c), which triggered a seesaw of polemics, contained in the same issue of *Philosophy and Rhetoric* (Poulakos 1990; Schiappa 1990b; see also Schiappa 1991c and 1991b, 69–77). While in principle not questioning an adaptation of the concept at issue to contemporary practice, Schiappa points out that there must be a methodical difference between the rational construction of a contemporary neosophistic rhetorical theory (of which Leff 1987 and Jarratt 1987 would be outstanding examples) and the historical reconstruction of authentic sophistic doctrines (1990c, 193), on which latter task, in Schiappa's view, Poulakos's approach falls short in several respects; nor does he keep the two tasks properly apart. First, Schiappa argues, it is anachronistic to speak of a theory of "rhetoric" in the Sophists, since the term *rhētorikḗ* is not attested prior to Plato (e.g., *Gorgias* 449c), who may even have first coined the term in a polemical sense (see also Schiappa 1990a; 1991b, 39–63; 1991c, 8; 1999, 14–29; Cole 1991, 2). Second, the so-called Sophists were not a homogeneous group but a collection of individuals so diverse that it is difficult to generalize about "sophistic" views of rhetoric and persuasive discourse, and "individual studies of the Sophists are a logically prior task to that of constructing a general sophistic view" (Schiappa 1990c, 201). Moreover, according to Schiappa, there is but thin evidence for a technical use of *kairós* in the ancient Sophists (203), and even less for *to prépon* (203–4). As for the possible (which term Poulakos appears to employ in a more or less Aristotelian sense), Schiappa finds little reason to claim that the Sophists held anything remotely similar to a "doctrine" of *to dunatón* (204–7).

Bearing all this in mind—and even more recent contributions sympathetic to Poulakos's, such as McComiskey's (2002), mostly acknowledge these points—we will try to keep the historical reconstruction of sophistic doctrines apart from speculations about the usefulness of their contemporary appropriation. Our reflections will concentrate on the Sophists' opinions about truth and whether and how they thought it could be attained. We will try to identify the social and political conditions under which these views were developed, and the gnoseological, epistemological, and linguistic doctrines on which they were based. Yet we may nonetheless also dare to ask in what respect and under which circumstances the Sophists' views about truth and human *logos* may have ultimately contributed to the development of a concept of rhetorical citizenship, based on the fundamental idea of the negotiation and establishment of socially relevant truth in open public debate. Only in a final section will we dare to point out how and where these doctrines may still inform the basic charters of our own pluralistic and "neosophistic" societies.

Who Were the Sophists?

Let us begin by clarifying whom we are actually talking about. The obvious place to start is with the list of names included in the section dedicated to the "Older Sophists" in the second volume of Diels and Kranz's magisterial edition of the *Fragments of the Presocratics* (1952, 252–416), edited in English by Sprague (1972): these are Protagoras of Abdera, Gorgias of Leontini, Prodicus of Ceos, Thrasymachus of Chalcedon, Hippias of Elis, Antiphon of Rhamnus, and Critias of Athens, plus a couple of anonymous texts such as the *Dissoi Logoi* (*Twofold Arguments*) and the *Anonymus Jamblichi*. From this list most of the partisans of "neosophistic rhetoric" select their references (cf., e.g., Poulakos 1983b, 47). But the list creates a problem (Schiappa 1991c, 6–8). There are other names that are not on it, such as Callicles and Polus, Euthydemus and Dionysodorus, and even for those on it, boundaries are blurred: Protagoras, for instance, was at times also regarded as a philosopher (Diogenes Laertius 9.50); Critias was a politician and oligarch, and so was Antiphon, who was also a teacher and a practitioner of rhetoric (if the Sophist and the orator of the same name are in fact the same person). On the other hand, Aristophanes, in the *Clouds*, regarded even Socrates as a Sophist, and this may well be how most Athenians felt (for a description of the Sophist applicable to Socrates even in Plato's *Sophist*, see Quandahl 1989, 344–46). In the strict sense of the word, the majority of the "Older Sophists" were not even "Pre-Socratics." Except for Protagoras and Gorgias, most of them were younger than Socrates.

Literally, a *sophistés* is neither more nor less than a master and/or expert practitioner in a particular field of art. The term is used for Solon and Pythagoras (Herodotus 1.29.1, 4.95.2), as well as for poets in general (Pindar, e.g., *Isthmian* 5.28). *Sophía*, too, originally meant cleverness in practical things (see, e.g., Plato, *Protagoras* 321d). There is one distinctive trait that would seem to mark the Sophists: their habit of charging fees. Yet it has recently been argued that in doing so they only rendered explicit a practice that was already common in many areas of education yet was usually practiced on a basis of mutual bartering (Fredal 2008).

Geographically, the Old Sophistic was at the same time a global and a communal phenomenon. Most of the early Sophists originated in remote parts of the Greek *oecumene*. Yet their activities miraculously centered on the one and only polis of Athens, within a very limited period. In this respect, the Athens of the late fifth and the early fourth centuries BCE was a veritable global village that in a unique way provided the soil in which the Old Sophistic would grow and prosper.

By the same token, however, the great majority of the Older Sophists had no citizenship and hence no civic rights in Athens, which is to say that, except for the Athenians Antiphon and Critias, they were excluded from speaking publicly in political debate as well as in court proceedings. Consequently, their public activity had to concentrate on the education of young citizens and the coaching of Athenian politicians in the role of spin doctors. Pericles, for instance, is known to have been coached by Protagoras, to whom he offered patronage, and had his sons educated by him (Stadter 1991). Some Sophists, such as Gorgias and Hippias, acted as ambassadors of their native cities.

Thus, although the opinions and teachings of the Sophists may differ in various respects, there are still enough common traits and interests to entitle us to band them together; yet in doing so we should probably not regard them as anything like a philosophical school, but rather as an intellectual movement with many faces—one that nonetheless disturbed, shaped, and changed Athenian society. And their ideas were clearly hovering everywhere in the intellectual sphere of Athens in a particular period of its history.

The Historical *Kairós*

In that particular period, Athens was indeed the ideal setting for the emergence of such a movement. After the overthrow of the last of the tyrants at the end of the sixth century, Athens had developed a system of democratic governance unique among Greek cities (although it was also exported to some other cities). Political life was based on the principles of *isonomía* (equality before the law), *isēgoría* (equal right to speak), and *parrhēsía* (freedom of speech). Both political decisions and judicial verdicts, in which almost all male citizens were actively involved, were based on the practice of controversial free speech. Moreover, during most of the years 431 to 404 BCE, Athens was at war against Sparta, a situation that provided ample occasion for political debate and ambassadorial negotiations. During that period, the political system was far from stable. Twice, in 411 and in 404, Athens saw oligarchic revolutions, in which two of the major Sophists, Antiphon and Critias, were prominently involved and, as a consequence, lost their lives. This, by the way, demonstrates that it would be naïve to associate the Sophists generally with the aim "to disempower the powerful and empower the powerless" (Poulakos 1987, 99) or with ideas of liberalism and democracy, as some proponents of the "neosophistic" approach do (e.g., Poulakos 1987, 99–101; Poulakos 1989b, 13–14; Crowley 1989, 327, 329) (see Schiappa 1991c, 9–10; McComiskey 2002, 6, 19–20).

Besides these political developments, the period was also characterized by the transition of Athenian society from orality to literacy and to a culture of writing (cf. Poulakos 1989b, 11). This process has been brilliantly described by Havelock (1982; see also Connors 1986). In fact, this antithesis of orality and writing permeates nearly all essential cultural and political features of fifth- and fourth-century Athens, among them poetry, oratory, and philosophy, to name only the most prominent.

The Sophists and Debate

After Schiappa (1990a; 1991b, 39–63; 1999, 14–29) and Cole (1991, 2) pointed out that the word *rhētorikḗ* was still unknown to the fifth century, it is obvious that the early Sophists could not possibly have reflected on this term, let alone developed anything like a theory of "rhetoric" in a strict sense. The pivotal term that is truly at the center of their reflections is *lógos* ("one of the most equivocal terms in the Greek language," Schiappa 1991c, 8), that is, meaningful human speech. This term, however, comprises a lot more than just political and forensic oratory. It equally refers to the texts produced by scientists and natural philosophers, to all kinds of poetry and religious narratives, and to any meaningful linguistic utterance in general. As it appears, all the Sophists were deeply interested in the nature and functions of *lógos*, in its relation to reality, its influence on the human soul, and its internal structures, or, expressed in modern terms, in its semantics, pragmatics, and syntax, but particularly in its character as a specifically human phenomenon (cf. Gagarin 2002, 23; Hoffman 2002).

On the other hand, it also appears that the Sophists regarded the "art of *lógoi*" (their way of referring to what was later called "rhetoric") basically as an art of combat, a competition. Plato, in *Protagoras* (335a4–8), has the Abderite boast that he has won any competition of *logoi* in which he was himself master of the rules; in the *Gorgias* (456c7–457c2), he makes the Sophist from Leontini compare rhetoric with boxing, fencing, and wrestling. The pivotal term in all these passages is *agṓn*, "competition." In the *Sophist* (225a2–226a4), one of the subdivisions of the "competitive art" (*agōnistikḗ*) is the art of "contradictory arguing," or "speaking against" (*antilogikḗ*), which becomes Plato's standard term for what he thinks is the general sophistic practice of using *logos*. This description may not be inappropriate on this point, since references to *agṓn*, *antilogía*, and combative or competitive arts can be found all over the Sophists' original texts. For instance, the title of a work by Protagoras, *Antilogiai*, alludes exactly to the technique described by Plato, and the title of another of his works, *Kataballóntes* (namely, *lógoi*, i.e., *Overthrowing Arguments*), employs a metaphor clearly borrowed from wrestling.

This is significant, for sports imply rules and umpires, champions and prizes. The *agṓn* of *lógoi* that the Sophists have in mind is thus more than mere altercation; it is a well-regulated competition, supervised by impartial umpires—a formal debate in the full sense of the word. This obsession with the agonistic principle is not surprising, since the formal confrontation of two opposite speeches had been a standard feature of Greek poetry and prose from Homer to tragedy, comedy, and the historians (Froleyks 1973).

Moreover, the same principle was institutionalized by the mid-fifth century in the Athenian political and judicial systems. Because of the huge number of members of the political assembly (a minimum of six thousand citizens constituted a quorum), very strict rules had to be imposed. For instance, nobody was allowed to digress from the point at issue, or to speak twice on the same point.

Rules were even stricter for judicial debate in the popular courts, in which juries were also huge (MacDowell 1978, 36). There was a fixed sequence of speeches: for their pleading, both plaintiff and defendant had two speeches each, in alternating sequence (249). The time allotted to each speaker was strictly limited and meticulously monitored by the water clock (Aristotle, *Constitution of Athens* 67.2-3; MacDowell 1978, 249-50). Any digression from the issue was strictly prohibited (Aristotle, *Constitution of Athens* 67.1). The jury's final decision was irrevocable; appeals were not permitted.

Since the Sophists lived and practiced in Athens in the midst of that kind of cultural and institutional environment, they certainly had every opportunity to experience and imbibe the rules of formal debate.

The Sophists and Truth

It may seem ironic that probably in no other period was there more written about truth than in the age of the Sophists. Protagoras's work *Overthrowing Arguments* had *On Truth* as an alternate title; Antiphon, too, wrote a book *On Truth*, fragments of which have been discovered on papyrus (see

Gagarin 2002, 63–92). Gorgias opens his *Encomium of Helen* with the amazing statement that the best adornment of *lógos* is truth, and the word "truth" recurs later in that speech (*Helen* 2, 13; Poulakos 1983a, 8). Likewise, in his *Defence of Palamedes*, the speaker intends to flatter the judges by expressing his hope to persuade them by revealing the truth (*Palamedes* 33; see also 4, 24, 35).

The Greek word for "truth" in all these instances is *alḗtheia*, which literally translates as "unhiddenness" or else "unforgetfulness," depending on whether an objective or a subjective perspective is emphasized. But for "speaking truth" the Greeks had still another intriguing expression: *ta ónta légein*, which means "saying what is." This raises a fundamental problem: if truth is defined as the correlation of a linguistic expression to what is, then the truth of a statement (a *logos*) can only be assessed if we possess an independent way of knowing how things are in reality. But in this respect even earlier Greek thinkers were skeptical. Around 500 BCE, Xenophanes of Colophon expressed the view that precise knowledge was unattainable to mortals, and that everything our senses perceive is mere appearance (*dókos*, frg. 34). Parmenides of Elea also subscribed to the unreliability of the senses (fragment 7.3–5), which only yield appearances (*dóxai*, fragments 1.30; 8.51), but he also developed an ontology that postulates the absolute a priori truth (*alḗtheia*) of Being as established by mere thought. This "Eleatic" theory of ontological truth was later adopted by Plato, who, based on this view, developed his theory of the Forms.

This Eleatic view of truth as an eternal and monolithic entity, however, was strongly challenged by the Sophists. Protagoras, for instance, in *On Truth*, formulated the so-called *homo mensura* statement: man is the measure of all things, of things being that (or how) they are, and of things not-being that (or how) they are not (fragment 1), which is supposed to say that as things appear to any particular individual, so they are for this individual. This may be (and has been) called gnoseological relativism. But most probably this is a direct polemic against Parmenides. Protagoras also formulated the associated theory that, with respect to anything, two contradictory statements can validly be confronted with each other (fragment 6a; see Jarratt 1991, 49–53), which became the basic principle of the technique of *antilogía* or "antilogic" (cf. Schiappa 1991b, 89–102; Bialostosky 1995). In a similar way Gorgias attacked Eleatic ontology. In his *On What Is Not, or On Nature*, he defended the following statements, which clearly contradict the Eleatic axioms: there is nothing; and even if there is something, it is unknowable; and even if it both is and is knowable, it cannot be communicated to others (Sextus, *Against the*

Mathematicians 65; Pseudo-Aristotle, *On Melissus, Xenophanes, Gorgias* 979a, 12–13). With such views, Gorgias eliminates any reliable criterion of truth. There will be no way of distinguishing false statements from true ones. All statements will be gnoseologically equal.

This is further underpinned by the linguistic and semiotic views expressed in his argument against communicability. Being a sign, Gorgias argues, *logos* will always be fundamentally different and separated from its object. As a consequence, two individuals can never communicate with each other about reality, since what is being transported from one individual to the other is always *logos*, but never its object (Pseudo-Aristotle 980b, 3–8). At best, the external object itself, if it happens to be immediately present and can be viewed by both partners to the conversation, may provide a valid interpretation of the *logos* (Sextus 85). These and similar considerations are also supported by the extensive linguistic studies practiced by many Sophists (Havelock 1983; Kraus 2006a, 9–12).

For Gorgias, then, *logos* has neither a semantic nor a communicative function. It is completely severed from reality (Rosenmeyer 1955, 231–32). Yet it still does enter into the human mind (Segal 1962). Its functions are described at length in the *Encomium of Helen*. In that regard, Gorgias maintains, *logos* is a great master (*Helen* 8; "master" or "adept" is what the Greek word *dynástēs* here actually means). Its powers are compared to those of medical drugs, magical incantations, or physical force. It can create, eliminate, or modify at will all sorts of emotions in the human soul. But it can just as well affect and manipulate the various appearances and opinions (*dóxai*) treasured in the soul (*Helen* 11, 13). Since there is no criterion of truth, it may easily replace one *dóxa* by another that is more powerful. This is probably what Protagoras has in mind when he speaks of "making the weaker *logos* the stronger" (fragment 6b; Schiappa 1991b, 103–13). As typical examples of such processes of overpowering and replacing *logoi* with other *logoi*, Gorgias invokes the debates of scientists, pleadings in court, and the quarrels of philosophers (*Helen* 13).

At this point it becomes evident that pleadings in court can especially serve as a master model for this theory. As Antiphon's preserved speeches, and in particular the series of model speeches called the *Tetralogies*, unmistakably illustrate, in homicide trials, as a rule, the factual truth of the event lies completely in the dark, and there is little hope that it can ever be revealed. What are available are various and manifold *dóxai*, the diverse narratives offered by the opposing parties and the witnesses (see Gagarin 2002, 126). All the jury has to go on is the greater or lesser plausibility of these narratives

(*Tetralogy* 2.4.1–2). This is expressed by the Greek term *eikós*, which is usually translated as probability or verisimilitude but is better rendered as plausibility or appropriateness (Kraus 2006b; Hoffman 2008). Plausibility can in no way be measured against ontological truth, since, as Gorgias has argued, the latter is not attainable. Instead, it will have to be gauged by its greater or lesser coherence with the jury's general experience of life, with similar cases they have come to know earlier, or with the testimony of eyewitnesses (*hoi paragenómenoi*, e.g., Antiphon, *Tetralogy* 1.1.9). But once the jurors have reached a verdict, their irrevocable decision will create a new reality. If they declare a defendant guilty, legally he or she will *be* guilty, no matter whether he or she truly is so in a metaphysical sense. That will be simply irrelevant, since the verdict is irrevocable. Justice, in this case, may be said not to be *found* but *established* as the result of an open debate.

Likewise, in political matters, whenever a political assembly makes a decision following the guidance of *eikós* (for instance, if war be waged or peace be kept), this decision will immediately be put into effect and will presumably have a serious impact on the lives of individual citizens. *Eikós* is often associated with the concept of *dóxa* (appearance). In the *Phaedrus* (273a–b), Plato quotes a definition—allegedly by the Sicilian Tisias, one of the legendary inventors of rhetoric—that states that *eikós* is what appears (good) to the majority. It is significant that the phrase *édoxen têi boulêi kai tôi dêmôi* (literally, "it appeared to the council and the people") is the standard Greek expression for legally effective decisions made by a public assembly (Poulakos 2001, 66; cf. Lagogiannē-Geōrgakarakou and Mpourazelēs 2007).

The experience of the procedures actually practiced in law courts and public assemblies, coupled with elaborate theories on gnoseological skepticism and relativism, may in fact have brought about the radically new sophistic attitude toward truth that in certain circumstances regarded truth as basically negotiable, the result of intersubjective agreement attained by serious deliberation conducted in open and unrestricted public debate. On this account, truth is that which has some kind of significant impact on us, that which makes some noticeable difference to our lives. This obviously rejects any ontological foundation of truth; it may be called a functional or operational concept of truth.

This concept, however, was by no means applied universally or indiscriminately by the Sophists. Antiphon, in *On Truth*, makes an illuminating distinction. Truths, he says, may be of two kinds; they may be either by nature (*phúsei*) or by custom and convention (*nómōi*). It would be silly, for instance, to argue by means of *lógos* against the fact that it is with our eyes that we see and with our ears that we hear, since this is a fact by nature. But other "truths," for instance, the distinction between Greeks and barbarians, opinions no less commonly valid among the majority of Greeks, may be debated, contested, even revised (fragments 44A.2–3, 44B.2; cf. Gagarin 2002, 66–67). With this distinction, the operational concept of truth is restricted to the realm of human life and society but may not be extended to areas in which the laws of nature apply. The treatise *Dissoí lógoi, Twofold Statements*, may be an illuminative illustration of how the Sophists believed human knowledge could be essentially furthered by systematically juxtaposing contradictory statements and having them debated freely in order to find out which would be more powerful.

The Sophists, Rhetoric, and Citizenship

Even if the Sophists did not themselves establish a veritable theory of rhetoric, their general views on *logos* and its powers provided the basis for the development of a systematic theory in the course of the fourth century. The concepts of *eikós* and *dóxa*, for instance, play pivotal roles both in the anonymous *Rhetoric to Alexander* and in Aristotle's *Rhetoric*, the two theoretical treatises on rhetoric preserved from the mid-fourth century. As the fields widened in which open debate was practiced, the need for something like rhetoric became inevitable. The localization of the domain of rhetoric in the field of the contingencies that affect human life made it a powerful tool for resolving conflicts. And the antilogical principle that in open dissent both sides should be heard and have equal rights has become constitutive of any egalitarian and democratic society. Even the general consciousness of the relativity of human opinions and values as expressed by the early Sophists may turn into a strong intellectual weapon and an effective means of immunization against totalitarianism and doctrinairism of any kind.

At least in our time, the practice of rhetoric and debate has thus become basic to the concept of democracy, even if this link was not yet fully perceived—and clearly not always practiced—by all the early Sophists. Protagoras, if we believe Plato, seems to have been the one who meddled most directly in Athenian democratic politics. In Plato's dialogue he avows his commitment to the practice of "making men into good citizens" (*Protagoras* 319a), even if these are not his but Socrates' words. In his ensuing "Great Speech," a eulogy on the "art of citizenship" (*politikḗ tékhnē*), there is much talk about education (*paideía*), but the word "rhetoric" (or any related synonym) does not occur.

Gorgias always remained an alien and outsider, even if he once intervened with a mock funeral oration (see Poulakos 1989a). Antiphon and Critias, on the other hand, were Athenian citizens actively involved in politics, but their attitudes were anything but democratic. Hence there was—perhaps with the exception of Protagoras (see Farrar 1988, 71–98)—no firm link between the sophistic views on the "art of *lógoi*" and democratic citizenship.

But without the Sophists' analysis of the functions of *logos*, rhetoric would not be; and without rhetoric, the very idea of a responsible and self-determined citizen would not be. It is thus legitimate to say that the sophistic analysis of operational truth with respect to the contingencies of human life, and the Sophists' belief in the necessity of constant negotiation between contradictory points of view as observed in the Athenian practice of political assemblies and law courts, laid the ground for the concept of citizenship.

The Modern Neosophistic World

Does our own postmodern time qualify as a neosophistic age in this sense? Ours is an age of constant public deliberation conducted in speech, be it in politics, in courts, or elsewhere. Certainly, in law courts, the power of mere and sheer rhetoric has been somewhat domesticated. Jurisprudential and jurisdictional expertise is more important today than in the days of the Sophists. And we do have the right of appeal. But, as litigants or defendants, do we not still feel exposed to the judge's or jury's verdict, which we know will be based, at least partly, on an open debate of conflicting views?

Politics, in our Western representative parliamentary democracies, is a business of constant negotiation and coalition making, based on talk and debate. Maybe the real deliberative process of decision making nowadays occurs less in parliament, since parliamentary groups and their party whips exert a disciplining influence, but decisions are nonetheless usually premeditated in open debate within influential smaller circles and behind closed doors. Yet, on the other hand, in our age of mass media communication, the effect of broadcast public debate on the electorate and its parliamentary representatives can hardly be overrated, not to speak of the influence of advertising and sales promotion even on our very private decisions.

But ours is also an age of intensified relativism, even with respect to what traditionally were commonly accepted values. Nothing can be taken for granted any longer; everything must be negotiated and assert itself anew each time in open debate. The range of public deliberation has broadened. Even in domains traditionally associated with the exact sciences, subjective appearances suddenly seem to reemerge and sometimes even to prevail over "objective" measurement. In addition to measured air temperature, for example, there is also a "felt" or "apparent" air temperature (perceived by the individual body, and depending on wind chill and humidity factors); in addition to the calculated inflation rate there is now also an "apparent" or "perceived" inflation rate; and it is the latter terms that really seem to matter, if we believe meteorological and economic forecasters. This is a truly neo-Protagorean trait that openly challenges any Platonic, metaphysical idea of epistemic certainty. Furthermore, we have learned from scholars such as Thomas Kuhn that not even in the so-called hard sciences are paradigm shifts brought about by strictly scientific demonstration but by open debate and persuasion among leading scientists. One *dóxa* is ultimately replaced by another by means of debate. And this is of course even more true of the human sciences. Hence the notion that truth may be contingent and situational (depending on *kairós*) as well as community-related (observing *to prépon*), and can be generated by way of open debate on the basis of contradictory claims is also part of a current worldview that evokes whatever of Poulakos's features of ancient sophistic rhetoric survives Schiappa's criticism. This endows rhetoric with a clear epistemic function in singling out, testing, and establishing acceptable views by way of persuasion, exactly as postulated by some of the early Sophists such as Gorgias and Antiphon (and more recently by Robert Scott 1967 and Michael Leff 1987). Contemporary debates about a rhetoric of inquiry and the epistemic function of rhetoric in science (be it as a primary source of knowledge or only as part of scientific discourse) also attest to this. Thus, more so than ever, the method of constant open and public debate about unsettled problems, practiced by all groups within society, is one of the most powerful basic charters informing Western pluralistic and egalitarian societies. In politics, the fundamental notion of metaphysical uncertainty leads to a toleration of others' deviating opinions, but also to the responsible participation of citizens in decisions of the democratic state. But this system of participatory democracy is in desperate need of self-responsible, assertive, and independent-thinking citizens—exactly the kind of individual characters the Sophists once sought to bring about by their large-scale educational project.

REFERENCES

Baumlin, James S. 1984. "Decorum, Kairos, and the 'New' Rhetoric." *Pre/Text* 5:171–83.
Bialostosky, Don H. 1995. "Antilogics, Dialogics, and Sophistic Social Psychology: Michael Billig's Reinvention of Bakhtin from Protagorean Rhetoric." In *Rhetoric, Sophistry, Pragmatism*, ed. Steven Mailloux, 82–93. New York: Cambridge University Press.
Cole, Thomas. 1991. *The Origins of Rhetoric in Ancient Greece*. Baltimore: Johns Hopkins University Press.
Connors, Robert J. 1986. "Greek Rhetoric and the Transition from Orality." *Philosophy and Rhetoric* 19:38–65.
Consigny, Scott. 1991. "Gorgias and the Subversion of *Logos*." *Pre/Text* 12:225–35.
———. 1996. "Edward Schiappa's Reading of the Sophists." *Rhetoric Review* 14:253–69.
———. 2001. *Gorgias, Sophist and Artist*. Columbia: University of South Carolina Press.
Crowley, Sharon. 1989. "A Plea for the Revival of Sophistry." *Rhetoric Review* 7:318–34.
Diels, Hermann, and Walther Kranz, eds. 1952. *Die Fragmente der Vorsokratiker: Griechisch und Deutsch*. 6th ed. Vol. 2. Zurich: Weidmann.
Enos, Richard Leo. 1976. "The Epistemology of Gorgias' Rhetoric: A Re-examination." *Southern Speech Communication Journal* 42:35–51.
Farrar, Cynthia. 1988. *The Origins of Democratic Thinking: The Invention of Politics in Classical Athens*. Cambridge: Cambridge University Press.
Fredal, James. 2008. "Why Shouldn't the Sophists Charge Fees?" *Rhetoric Society Quarterly* 38:148–70.
Froleyks, Walter Johannes. 1973. "Der Agōn Logōn in der antiken Literatur." PhD diss., University of Bonn.
Gagarin, Michael. 1986. *Early Greek Law*. Berkeley and Los Angeles: University of California Press.
———. 2001. "Did the Sophists Aim to Persuade?" *Rhetorica* 19:275–91.
———. 2002. *Antiphon the Athenian*. Austin: University of Texas Press.
Garner, Richard. 1987. *Law and Society in Classical Athens*. New York: St. Martin's Press.
Gomperz, Theodor. 1922. *Griechische Denker: Eine Geschichte der griechischen Philosophie*. 4th ed. Edited by Heinrich Gomperz. Vol 1. Berlin: Vereinigung Wissenschaftlicher Verleger.
Guthrie, William K. C. 1971. *The Sophists*. Cambridge: Cambridge University Press.
Harrison, A. R. W. 1998. *The Law of Athens*. 2 vols. 2nd ed. London: Duckworth.
Havelock, Eric. 1982. *The Literate Revolution in Greece and Its Cultural Consequences*. Princeton: Princeton University Press.
———. 1983. "The Linguistic Task of the Presocratics." In *Language and Thought in Early Greek Philosophy*, ed. Kevin Robb, 7–82. La Salle, Ill.: Hegeler Institute.
Hays, Steve. 1990. "On the Skeptical Influence of Gorgias' *On Non-Being*." *Journal of the History of Philosophy* 28:327–37.
Hoffman, David C. 2002. "Logos and Pluralism: The Foundations of the Sophistic Movement." In *The Philosophy of Communication*, vol. 1, ed. Konstantine Boudouris and John Poulakos, 92–99. Athens: Ionian Publications.
———. 2008. "Concerning *Eikos*: Social Expectation and Verisimilitude in Early Attic Rhetoric." *Rhetorica* 26:1–29.
Jarratt, Susan. 1987. "Toward a Sophistic Historiography." *Pre/Text* 8:9–26.
———. 1991. *Rereading the Sophists: Classical Rhetoric Refigured*. Carbondale: Southern Illinois University Press.
Kennedy, George A. 1963. *The Art of Persuasion in Greece*. Princeton: Princeton University Press.
Kerferd, George B. 1981. *The Sophistic Movement*. Cambridge: Cambridge University Press.

Kraus, Manfred. 2006a. "Antilogia—Zu den Grundlagen sophistischer Debattierkunst." In *Rhetorik der Debatte*, ed. Olaf Kramer, 1–13. Tübingen: Niemeyer.
———. 2006b. "Nothing to Do with Truth? *Eikós* in Early Greek Rhetoric and Philosophy." In *Papers on Rhetoric VII*, ed. Lucia Calboli Montefusco, 129–50. Rome: Herder Editrice.
Kuhn, Thomas S. 1970. *The Structure of Scientific Revolutions*. 2nd ed. Chicago: University of Chicago Press.
Lagogiannē-Geōrgakarakou, Maria, and Kōstas Mpourazelēs, eds. 2007. *Édoxen tēi boulēi kai tōi dēmōi: Hē athēnaikḗ dēmokratía miláei me tis epigraphés tēs*. Athens: Ministry of Culture.
Leff, Michael C. 1978. "In Search of Ariadne's Thread: A Review of the Recent Literature on Rhetorical Theory." *Central States Speech Journal* 29:73–91.
———. 1987. "Modern Sophistic and the Unity of Rhetoric." In *The Rhetoric of the Human Sciences: Language and Argument in Scholarship and Public Affairs*, ed. John S. Nelson, Allan Megill, and Donald N. McCloskey, 19–37. Madison: University of Wisconsin Press.
MacDowell, Douglas M. 1978. *The Law in Classical Athens*. Ithaca: Cornell University Press.
McComiskey, Bruce. 1992. "Disassembling Plato's Critique of Rhetoric in the *Gorgias* (447a–466a)." *Rhetoric Review* 11:79–90.
———. 1993. "Postmodern Sophistics: Appearance and Deception in Rhetoric and Composition." In *Rhetoric in the Vortex of Cultural Studies*, ed. Arthur Walzer, 83–91. St. Paul: Rhetoric Society of America.
———. 1994. "Neo-Sophistic Rhetorical Theory: Sophistic Precedents for Contemporary Epistemic Rhetoric." *Rhetoric Society Quarterly* 24 (3–4): 16–24.
———. 2002. *Gorgias and the New Sophistic Rhetoric*. Carbondale: Southern Illinois University Press.
Moss, Roger. 1982. "The Case for Sophistry." In *Rhetoric Revalued*, ed. Brian Vickers, 207–24. Binghamton, N.Y.: Center for Medieval and Early Renaissance Studies.
Neel, Jasper. 1988. *Plato, Derrida, and Writing*. Carbondale: Southern Illinois University Press.
Popper, Karl. 1945. *The Open Society and Its Enemies*. 2 vols. London: Routledge and Kegan Paul.
Poulakos, John. 1983a. "Gorgias' *Encomium to Helen* and the Defense of Rhetoric." *Rhetorica* 1 (2): 1–16.
———. 1983b. "Toward a Sophistic Definition of Rhetoric." *Philosophy and Rhetoric* 16:35–48.
———. 1984. "Rhetoric, the Sophists, and the Possible." *Communication Monographs* 51:215–26.
———. 1987. "Sophistical Rhetoric as a Critique of Culture." In *Argument and Critical Practices: Proceedings of the Fifth SCA/AFA Conference on Argumentation*, ed. Joseph W. Wenzel, 97–101. Annandale, Va.: Speech Communication Association.
———. 1990. "Interpreting Sophistical Rhetoric: A Response to Schiappa." *Philosophy and Rhetoric* 23:218–28.
———. 1993. "Terms for Sophistical Rhetoric." In *Rethinking the History of Rhetoric: Multidisciplinary Essays on the Rhetorical Tradition*, ed. Takis Poulakos, 53–74. Boulder: Westview Press.
———. 1995. *Sophistical Rhetoric in Classical Greece*. Columbia: University of South Carolina Press.
Poulakos, Takis. 1988. "Towards a Cultural Understanding of Classical Epideictic Oratory." *Pre/Text* 9:147–68.

———. 1989a. "The Historical Intervention of Gorgias' Epitaphios: The Genre of Funeral Oration and the Athenian Institution of Public Burials." *Pre/Text* 10:90–99.

———. 1989b. "Intellectuals and the Public Sphere: The Case of the Older Sophists." In *Spheres of Argument: Proceedings of the Sixth SCA/AFA Conference on Argumentation*, ed. Bruce E. Gronbeck, 9–15. Annandale, Va.: Speech Communication Association.

———. 1994. "Human Agency in the History of Rhetoric: Gorgias's *Encomium of Helen*." In *Writing Histories of Rhetoric*, ed. Victor Vitanza, 59–80. Carbondale: Southern Illinois University Press.

———. 2001. "Isocrates' Use of *Doxa*." *Philosophy and Rhetoric* 34:61–78.

———. 2004. "Isocrates' Civic Education and the Question of Doxa." In *Isocrates and Civic Education*, ed. Takis Poulakos and David Depew, 44–65. Austin: University of Texas Press.

Quandahl, Ellen. 1989. "What Is Plato? Inference and Allusion in Plato's *Sophist*." *Rhetoric Review* 7:338–48.

Rosenmeyer, Thomas G. 1955. "Gorgias, Aeschylus, and *Apate*." *American Journal of Philology* 76:225–60.

Royer, Daniel J. 1991. "New Challenges to Epistemic Rhetoric." *Rhetoric Review* 9:282–97.

Schiappa, Edward. 1990a. "Did Plato Coin *Rhêtorikê*?" *American Journal of Philology* 111:460–73.

———. 1990b. "History and Neo-Sophistic Criticism: A Reply to Poulakos." *Philosophy and Rhetoric* 23:307–15.

———. 1990c. "Neo-Sophistic Rhetorical Criticism or the Historical Reconstruction of Sophistic Doctrines?" *Philosophy and Rhetoric* 23:192–217.

———. 1991a. "The Beginnings of Greek Rhetorical Theory." In *Rhetorical Movement: Essays in Honor of Leland M. Griffin*, ed. David Zarefsky, 5–33. Evanston: Northwestern University Press.

———. 1991b. *Protagoras and Logos: A Study in Greek Philosophy and Rhetoric*. Columbia: University of South Carolina Press.

———. 1991c. "Sophistic Rhetoric: Oasis or Mirage?" *Rhetoric Review* 10:5–18.

———. 1992. "*Rhêtorikê*: What's in a Name? Toward a Revised History of Early Greek Rhetorical Theory." *Quarterly Journal of Speech* 78:1–15.

———. 1995. "Isocrates' *Philosophia* and Contemporary Pragmatism." In *Rhetoric, Sophistry, Pragmatism*, ed. Steven Mailloux, 33–60. New York: Cambridge University Press.

———. 1999. *The Beginnings of Rhetorical Theory in Classical Greece*. New Haven: Yale University Press.

Scott, Robert L. 1967. "On Viewing Rhetoric as Epistemic." *Central States Speech Journal* 18:9–17.

Segal, Charles P. 1962. "Gorgias and the Psychology of the Logos." *Harvard Studies in Classical Philology* 66:99–155.

Sprague, Rosamond Kent, ed. 1972. *The Older Sophists: A Complete Translation by Several Hands of the Fragments in Die Fragmente der Vorsokratiker, ed. by Diels-Kranz, with a New Edition of Antiphon and of Euthydemus*. Columbia: University of South Carolina Press, 1990. Reprint, Indianapolis: Hackett, 2001.

Stadter, Philip A. 1991. "Pericles Among the Intellectuals." *Illinois Classical Studies* 16:111–24.

Vickers, Brian. 1988. *In Defence of Rhetoric*. Oxford: Clarendon Press.

Vitanza, Victor J. 1991. "'Some More' Notes: Toward a 'Third' Sophistic." *Argumentation* 5:117–39.

———. 1993. "Some Rudiments of Histories of Rhetorics and Rhetorics of Histories." In *Rethinking the History of Rhetoric*, ed. Takis Poulakos, 193–239. Boulder: Westview Press.

———. 1997. *Negation, Subjectivity, and the History of Rhetoric*. New York: State University of New York Press.

White, Eric Charles. 1987. *Kaironomia: On the Will-to-Invent*. Ithaca: Cornell University Press.

Yunis, Harvey. 1996. *Taming Democracy: Models of Political Rhetoric in Classical Athens*. Ithaca: Cornell University Press.

3

THE SEARCH FOR "REAL" DEMOCRACY:
RHETORICAL CITIZENSHIP AND PUBLIC DELIBERATION IN
FRANCE AND THE UNITED STATES, 1870–1940

William Keith and Paula Cossart

Rhetorical citizenship is that set of communicative and deliberative practices that in a particular culture and political system allow citizens to enact and embody their citizenship, in contrast to practices that are merely "talking about" politics. We argue that historically the turn to public deliberative techniques, such as forums, citizen juries, town halls, and public meetings, has been motivated by a "crisis of republicanism," a belief that instabilities in the voting process or government structures have created a mismatch between the will of the public and government policies; it includes both the case of a frail new republican regime and the case of an established regime in transition. We attempt a comparison of two cases: France in the late nineteenth century and the United States in the early twentieth. In both settings, as people attempted to enact their role as citizen deliberators, they developed norms and practices that embodied a vision of rational, discursive citizenship. Despite different cultures and histories, the cases contain surprising parallels, successes, and failures. We conclude by reflecting on lessons for contemporary deliberative projects, in particular reflecting on the fundamental tensions in rhetorical citizenship.

Contexts and Goals for Public Deliberation

In both our cases, public meetings became the site at which people became, in a sense, citizens—where they were constituted as citizens by speaking. In some cases, this might have meant just showing up, in others, more commonly, speaking in a particular way, with civility, reason, and decorum.

U.S. Forums

The forum movement in the United States began in the first decade of the twentieth century with the establishment of the Ford Hall Forum in Boston. The context, however, was an American tradition of adult education. While the system of public education for children had by 1920 made at least an eighth-grade education nearly universal, there was no adult system of continuing education, but there were successive projects, including the lyceums and the Chautauquas, distinguished less by common content or goals than by their character as public meetings. While sometimes "lyceum" and "Chautauqua" (and "forum") referred to a building or location, the terms more essentially meant a mode of interaction. In each case people got together, as citizens, to learn. In the case of lyceums, the subject was the latest literary and scientific knowledge. Lyceums were founded in towns large and small, starting in New England and spreading through the Midwest. They were essentially school buildings for adults, who might go there to look at permanent exhibits in natural history or technology, or take instruction in useful skills. But they also offered instruction in the liberal arts tradition, including speeches by famous orators of the day, and staged debates on political topics. They flourished from the 1820s to the 1860s (Ray 2005), when they began to decline, as public funding shifted to public schools.

The Chautauqua began as a site of Methodist religious instruction, though it quickly developed a more general educational mission, filling the gap left by the fading lyceums. A Sunday school teacher in Akron, Ohio, decided in 1874 that his congregation needed a permanent, rural site for religious retreat, education, and renewal. In a town in upstate New York on Lake Chautauqua, Methodists founded the "Mother Chautauqua," which consisted of a building and some land; once established, they soon moved beyond religious themes and invited the best speakers and intellectuals of the day. The original site was soon supplemented in two ways. First, towns throughout the Midwest founded "Chautauqua assemblies," usually in rural areas just outside town, and popular lecturers came there as well. Second, "Chautauqua Society Literary Circles" were held in people's homes all over the country; a group of neighbors (usually women) would order materials on a variety of topics from the Mother Chautauqua and study them. Chautauquas began to fade in the 1890s; a traveling version, more entertainment than substance, was popular from about 1906 to 1925 (Rieser 2003).

Yet the United States was changing rapidly during this period. From 1880 to 1920, the country went from being predominantly rural to primarily urban, from agricultural to industrial. Waves of immigration had rendered major cities polyglot mixtures of Old and New World cultures and traditions, so part of the challenge of adult education was imparting not only civic knowledge but civic traditions. The forums grafted the tradition of face-to-face discussion from lyceums and Chautauquas onto the goal of civic education; this vision of civic education took on a new dimension, since the forums educated citizens on two levels. First, like the television and radio news programs of today, they addressed the current policy and political topics that citizens needed to know about, and participants had a chance to learn from experts, just as they do now when seeing them interviewed. But organizers imagined a second, deeper level of learning. While these meetings always addressed civic topics, they were now imagined as enactments of town meetings, the ideal mode of democratic interaction. Forum advocates thought people in these meetings were learning to communicate like citizens, to make democracy visible as a form of life. By the 1920s, the common term for this type of communication was "discussion," as opposed to debate, as well as to platform speaking. These forums, by and large, had what Aristotle called "internal ends" ("an end desired for its own sake," *Ethica Nichomachea* 1.2.1) and embodied John Dewey's "consummatory moment" (Westbrook 1992, 377ff.); they simply *were* democracy, in themselves. But this immediately presents a crucial question: since democracy is also a form of governance, what is the connection between these meetings and governance? The struggle between wanting the forums to make a difference to policy and politics and believing that they didn't need to make a difference dogged forum supporters.

The French Réunion Politique

If one can say that political forums in late nineteenth-century France were motivated by the crisis of republican governance, it is because they sprang from a wish to consolidate the institutions of the new Third Republic. The republicans arrived in power mistrusting the people. Why? First, the French people had ceded power to Emperor Napoleon III by their overwhelming vote in the plebiscite of 1852. Second, the empire was followed by the insurrectional government of the Paris Commune, which seared in the republican memory the idea that urban mobs are naturally violent. When the Third Republic was installed in the years 1870–80, Republicans needed the people to support their institutions but at the same time feared that the mobs might seize power.

So they pursued two parallel and connected goals. First, they sought the formation of people as rational citizens—a vast enterprise of civic education (Rosanvallon [2001, 470] refers to it as "demopedic fervor"). It functioned on the one hand to make individuals forget their social differences while they were preoccupied with the public good, and on the other hand to inculcate decent and discreet modes of behavior, far from the passions of the *communards*. A second objective was to solidify the new republican institutions through popular support: to make participants the sort of people who express themselves through opinion, not action (Reynié 1998). The legitimate form of political participation avoided both the direct action of crowds and interest group pressure on the government, thus promoting calm public opinion, united around the common good. This public opinion could not be obtained merely by asking citizens what they thought on political questions but only after discussion between citizens; it was opinion born in the confrontation of ideas presented as arguments. The political technology considered most effective for making people into citizens with peaceful opinions was the political forum (*réunion politique*), defined as an organized assembly where speakers gave political talks. These speakers were sometimes just citizens desiring to speak. More often, they were people occupying public positions or candidates for them. (They were not experts, as in the U.S. forum movement.) In 1881 the republican government adopted a law instituting real freedom of assembly, although some rules remained that framed the exercise of it. Already in 1868, at the end of the empire, a law had been adopted loosening the prohibition on forums: several forums could be held, although often by dodging the law. But the republican legislation was incomparably more liberal: "Public forums are free," declared its first article.

If the political forum was thus celebrated as the participatory political mode authorizing the assembly of citizens in the public interest, it was because of the republican belief in face-to-face debate, where the better argument would win. Debate should allow people to overcome ideologies; ideology was perceived negatively by republicans in power, who saw it as without rational foundation. Fundamentally, this reflected a faith in individual reason, "the sole guide to social and political action" (Déloye 1997, 69), and the conviction that reason necessarily wins in an open debate. Consider the words of the republican deputy Jules Simon, talking in the legislative body under the empire on 13 March 1868: "Do you fear the popular forums to the point that you think that whenever they're assembled, error, and not truth, will prevail? I have confidence in truth . . . it will succeed in the long run; neither sophistries, nor passions, nor anger maintain strength before the cold and severe language of truth." Simon thus defended the freedom of assembly with the idea that the assembly of citizens is the best way to banish exaggerations, by confronting them with what he called "the greatest force in the world, reason." Political forums would be more effective in the exchange of ideas than newspapers, where the debate is indirect.

Besides, the expression of opinions in the press was reserved for a small, privileged group, while forums were a truly democratic form of expression, open to all. In the last third of the century, the debate forum—the *réunion contradictoire*—was the most widespread and legitimate form of public forum. It was where people of diverse opinions came to directly contrast their ideas; the republicans were always wary of the potential of private forums to include only like-minded people. These were rarer than debate forums owing to the deep mistrust of forums' gathering together people around one set of ideas. The memory of the "clubs" of 1789, 1848, and 1871 was always present (clubs were understood as associations organized as if they were forums, a hybrid form between the two modes of participation, association and forum), and the law of 1881 included a specific provision forbidding such clubs. It is also for this reason that publicity was essential to the forums that republicans valorized: private forums were more likely to divide people according to the similarity of their opinions.

Finally, it must be emphasized that the citizen assemblies were not truly part of decision making. Republicans never envisaged creating the means to revisit the outcomes of governmental deliberation. One often finds, especially in the republican press, criticism of the forums as parodies of the parliament or courts, the only legitimate sites of decision making. The products of these forums were nothing more than peaceful public opinion and a public of rational citizens (for more detail, see Cossart 2010).

Enacting Rhetorical Citizenship: Meetings and Forums

Both the problems and the effectiveness of forums in both contexts depended on the details of their organization. "Bringing people together" is a fine idea, but practical specifics make a substantial difference. If the forum is a means for enacting citizenship, different methods will yield different varieties of citizens. In each of our historical examples, the details of interaction reveal the cultural and political dimensions of citizenship.

The Federal Forum Project

While many different formats for forums were attempted, almost all their salient features are visible in those organized by John Studebaker, first in Des Moines, Iowa (1932–34, funded by the Carnegie Corporation of New York), and then across the United States, when Studebaker became commissioner of education (where he sponsored the Federal Forum Project, 1936–41). (For more detail on the forums, see Keith 2007, chapters 8 and 9.)

How did these forums differ from the old "town hall meetings" and Chautauqua assemblies? They differed, in part, owing to their physical arrangements; the spatial organization of the Des Moines forums was extremely clever. Previous forums had generally been established at one location, like Cooper Union or town hall in New York City; people were expected to come from across the city to attend, and the crowds were often very large. In Des Moines, Studebaker solved this problem by using public school buildings. Educators in the 1920s often expressed frustration because perfectly good school buildings were empty about two-thirds of each week (i.e., nights and weekends). Studebaker had long been interested in using them for adult education; he recognized that there were more elementary schools than middle schools, and more middle schools than high schools, in a medium-sized city like Des Moines, which had a population of 144,000 at that time (Studebaker 1935, 50). Elementary schools were neighborhood-based (so that small children could walk to school easily), whereas middle schools covered several neighborhoods and high schools a slightly larger territory. So elementary schools were the basic forum location for the "neighborhood forums"; there were eighteen of these. "Central forums" took place in the middle schools and "citywide forums" in the high schools; there were eight of these altogether. The city was divided into five roughly equal geographic sections to ensure that these forums were accessible to all. In fact, most participants lived pretty close to the forums they attended (51). In 1933–34, there were 556 neighborhood forums, compared to twenty-two larger ones, and in 1934–35, 538 to fifteen. The neighborhood forums were held twice a month; only forum leaders who could stay for the entire series were hired, so that there would be consistency of leadership. If residents missed their local neighborhood forum, they could attend one later the same week at a nearby school on the same topic. Local forums were held weekly, citywide forums each Monday of the season. Forums used their ninety minutes consistently. The first fifteen minutes were given to announcements and "spot news," breaking news that participants (voting through a show of hands) wanted to discuss briefly, especially if it was relevant to the evening's topic. After the spot news, the speaker for the evening spoke for about forty-five minutes, followed by thirty-plus minutes of discussion or questions and answers (Studebaker and Williams 1937, 27). Despite the preference for discussion, generally it accounted for less than half the program, usually about thirty minutes. Forums typically distinguished between the speaker, an expert or professional, and the leader, who conducted the meeting and led the discussion, although sometimes they were the same person. The leader had to frame the topic and manage the discussion, keeping it interesting and not too confrontational, while the speaker had to clarify issues and supply enough background information to make discussion possible; in small forums with lots of discussion, the quality of the leader was crucial, while in large city-county forums, which needed to attract and hold large audiences, the speaker was more important (41).

Ironically, discussion might be stifled by the public nature of forums; many participants wished to avoid publicity, indicating that freedom of discussion could be limited by the perceived opinion of one's neighbors, since participants admitted that they didn't want their names in the newspapers. Even in the best of circumstances, the spark of discussion did not always burst into flame, which is perhaps not surprising. Factors other than the leader or speaker might suppress discussion. Mary Ely mentioned "'forum cranks,' 'forum pests' or 'forum hounds' (as they are variously called), the inveterate, long-winded speech-makers who appear in almost every forum and may wreck the discussion if they are not held in check" (Ely 1937, 184). Some people just had a single issue, and no matter what the topic, they turned a question into a speech about that issue; audiences and chairpersons were always uncomfortable with this kind of inappropriate behavior. Yet sometimes forums did fulfill their promise. Ely, wife of Richard Ely (of the League for Political Education and the Town Hall in New York), worked for the American Association for Adult Education, and in 1937 she did a cross-country fact-finding tour to see how the forums worked in practice. Her account of the class diversity of the Portland, Oregon, forums is especially interesting, partly because it pointed out how well the forums could function and partly because it was more the exception than the rule. An economics professor from Reed College gave a talk that year titled "Should the Workers Have the Right to Strike?" Ely recounted that "the morning after the first meeting a longshoreman came into the forum office to express his disapproval of the manner in which the subject had been handled. It was suggested that he talk with the forum leader.

'I wouldn't know how to talk to a college professor,' he objected. But an interview was arranged, and the difficulty was talked out, not as between college professor and longshoreman but as between man and man. The lecture was revamped and greatly improved. It was given on the second night . . . and the question period was unusually animated" (155).

This comes close to the ideal of the forums: people from different parts of society sharing knowledge through discussion and advancing the common understanding of a social or political problem. Often, unfortunately, the result was more like standard educational experiences: an expert speaks, audience members ask some questions for clarification, and everyone goes home. Also, some methods of presentation stifled discussion; Ely noted that the practice of staging debates instead of speeches "must be regarded as a failure," since the focus on winning a case invariably overwhelmed the positive values of discussion (189).

La Réunion Contradictoire: *The Debate Forum*

What form did debate forums take? The first striking thing to notice is that forums became a massive phenomenon, with a sizeable portion of the population participating, especially in urban areas. In Paris, during the period preceding voting day, half the voters might attend a forum (Offerlé 1993, 90). The infatuation with political forums was such that, in large towns, it became a pleasant way to pass an evening, and not only during an election campaign. Forums were numerous and frequent—held many times per week in the large towns, and often several at the same time—and the size of the crowd was also impressive, often hundreds or even thousands. They were crucially important during campaigns and played a role in vetting candidates. As for their location, unlike American forums, in nineteenth-century France the forums could not be held in schools, no doubt because they were not explicitly considered adult "education" (similar to that given to children in schools). Educational objectives were nonetheless implicit, but it was more a question of the formation of rational citizens than of education per se. It was not a question of bringing in experts to enhance citizen knowledge of public affairs. In 1907 Prime Minister Clemenceau opposed the use of schoolyards for forums, citing the risks linked to "tubercular spittle." Sixty percent of the forums were held in ballrooms at the end of the Second Empire, others in concert halls, wine shops, theaters, or even circuses (Dalotel, Faure, and Freiermuth 1980, 47–48).

These rooms weren't free, and organizers frequently had to charge entrance fees, though these were often optional and modest. One can see the affront to the fully democratic character of the assembly, and the practice was sometimes criticized. Beyond financial barriers, there were other limitations on equal participation. The 1881 law said that only those enjoying "civil and political rights" could convene public forums. This excluded women, who could thus not organize public forums without male organizers. Women were nevertheless commonly present; while generally seen less often at the platform than in the audience, they distinguished themselves as speakers at specific forums, those centered on women's issues. Another type of discrimination in certain forums followed from their location. Some forums, because of the neighborhood in which they were located, drew a more working-class group, some a more middle-class group. Nevertheless, police informers often mentioned the social class of the participants in a forum, inferred from their manner of dress.

There was no set process for speaking times, choosing the order of speakers, or managing the question period (in election forums, one can nonetheless identify some unspoken rules, notably that candidates would make their case before the debate began). It must also be emphasized that the committee (*le bureau*) played an important role. The "formation of a committee and the designation of a president who were charged with maintaining calm and order according to the rules" revealed that forums were characteristically organized "in direct reference to the parliamentary model" (Roussellier 2001, 45). The committee ensured good progress in the debate and enabled different types of arguments to be heard. Frequently, at the opening of a session, the president said a few words noting that all points of view should be heard. The committee was composed of at least three people, a president and two assessors, either designated beforehand by the organizers or elected by the assembly (either by acclamation, by a show of hands, or by silent acquiescence—which sometimes resulted in brawls).

The forums ordinarily centered on an agenda drawn from public life: unemployment, public transportation, the rights of women, various elections, etc. But participants often led the debate in another direction, taking the theme as a point of departure. These presentations could take two forms: they might be made from the platform, which was obviously not always open to all, or from the room.

Speeches at the platform were sometimes very long; it was not unusual for a speaker to talk for more than an hour. Performance demanded great effort, as it was not always easy to be heard over the huge, boisterous assembly in rooms with terrible acoustics, not designed for such forums: loudspeakers were not available (they weren't in use until the second half of the 1920s, and weren't employed commonly in public forums until the 1930s). So a certain kind of eloquence existed, specific to public forums, harder for some to master than for others. Jean-Jacques Courtine describes this as "the rhetorical education of a powerful voice that assimilated the forum to a spoken opera" (1990, 158).

The room would not stay quiet without intervention; it was sometimes difficult to distinguish the time given to speeches from the platform and to the audience. The speakers were often interrupted by remarks or questions. This was particularly striking in the forums held near election time. We can see the public assuming an important role, notably because people in the room would ask many detailed questions of the candidates speaking before them; it was not only their competitors to which candidates had to respond. We may distinguish three principal types of questions posed to candidates. They often concerned the past of the candidate, his previous positions, and the ways in which he had or hadn't been useful to the community. Next, they might focus on the positions of the candidate in the present campaign: did he fully accept the platform established by the committee? Would he maintain his candidacy or throw his support to another if he lost on the first ballot? Finally, questions focused on what the candidate would do if elected. These questions characteristically aimed at very specific points, such as how the candidate would vote on this or that question. While the public sometimes allowed the candidate to respond at length, he was just as frequently interrupted in the middle of an explanation by a question or an argument. Unfortunately, press and police reports generally did not identify the persons posing these questions; they used vague expressions like "a participant demanded," "a voter posed a question addressed to," "many questions were asked about," "someone spoke up about."

Discussion

In both France and the United States, the popularity of the organized forum was relatively brief, around twenty to thirty years. What did it accomplish, and why did it fade? What can we learn from it? The answers to these questions are remarkably similar in both the U.S. and French cases. In the case of the U.S. forums, the federal program ended in 1941, although some local forums kept going, sometimes for a short while, sometimes for many years. In contrast, as we will see, to determined and organized interference with the function of the forums in France, in the United States, over the long run, they died peaceful deaths from lack of interest. Even as interest in them was growing, World War II loomed, and as the country began gearing up for war, people became less interested in talk than in the growing economy and foreign threats to world peace. The federal government began shedding Depression-era programs, and the Federal Forum Project was one of them.

Part of the problem was that many people were unemployed in the 1930s and thus had time to participate, and they increasingly went back to work as the economy improved. The economic insecurity that led many people to want to discuss alternatives to capitalism began to fade, and the lure of socialist and communist ideas weakened. To an extent, forums had been like social occasions: not quite entertainment but (at their best) exciting and informative. People typically dressed up for them, and there was a good number of repeat participants; samples of attendance showed that many people came nearly every week, no matter what the topic. In the postwar era, particularly with the arrival of television, the forum as entertainment decreased in popularity. Some of the forums attached to particular institutions survived, such as the City Club of Cleveland, Ohio (established in 1916), or the Milwaukee Turners (founded in 1853, meetings conducted in German until 1940), and continue to hold meetings to this day. *America's Town Meeting of the Air* continued on radio until 1956, but *American Mercury Presents: Meet the Press* debuted on radio in 1945 and in 1947 became the radio program that continues to this day on television.

The French forums had been encouraged by the republican reform legislation of 1881, which permitted an exchange of ideas between participants, but they did not last long. The republican project for the pacification of public opinion and the development of political civility by participation in debate forums confronted a double diversion from the end of the 1880s that spelled the end of forums as a site for debate.

The first diversion was the practice of resorting to noise or violence with the intention of suppressing discussion and stifling the expression of contrary opinions. A systematized and increasingly premeditated obstruction by noise tended to impede all discussion in public forums. The "interrupters" and "obstructionists," as they were called in newspaper and police reports, were for a time mostly outnumbered by the anarchists, to the point of being considered "forum spoilsports" by a journalist writing in the republican daily

Le Matin on 31 July 1887. The Boulangists (critics of the Republic assembled under General Boulanger in the late 1880s) were also accused of disrupting the tone of the forums with noise. They even recruited paid personnel, who were not necessarily their ideological allies, to create noise and distraction while opposition speakers were speaking (Mollier 2004). By the end of the century, obstruction constituted a fully established practice of those who attended the forums: it marked a major part of the forums held around the Dreyfus affair. At the same time, violence at forums increased, and generally the same groups were implicated. Not only the rhetorical violence of the speakers but also physical violence grew. Certainly, the altercations had been numerous in the past, but by the end of the decade the violence was more frequent and, above all, more organized, intentional, and planned. The republican press, as an observer of the disrupted forums, pointed out that the manners of the forums had evolved in an opposite sense to what they expected: the virtuous citizens, whom during the first years following the law of 1881 one hoped to see assembled for debate, seemed to abandon the forums, leaving room for individuals incapable of accepting different points of view, who sought to silence adversaries through noise or force.

The second diversion was connected to the first: from the end of the century onward, one can observe an increasing resort to meetings that could be classified as demonstration forums. There was a growing organization and participation in this type of forum—as with most contemporary political rallies—whose aim was not, in the end, to assemble people with diverse opinions so that they could deliberate public issues, but rather to show the force of preconstituted groups and assert previously formed opinions. The Boulangist period and then the Dreyfus affair had been particularly marked by this type of large assembly. It was thus during the belle époque that the word "meeting" (the same word is employed in French; occasionally during the nineteenth century it was transformed into *métingue*) began to replace "forum" (in the political sense of *réunion*) to designate such assemblies in press and police reports. Although that term was already in common use, at the turn of the century it became increasingly employed as a synonym for large forums of partisans of a common cause. The phenomenon was also promoted by the law of 1901, which authorized political associations, and by the resulting birth of the political parties. After World War I, these demonstration forums, in which the platform was of a single political color, surged at the expense of the debate forums. In the case of socialist and communist forums between the wars, we have been able to find evidence that a number of them were organized as demonstrations of force, and were described as such, particularly in the partisan press. The force was displayed by the sheer number of persons assembled and demonstrations of unity at the finale, a display of enthusiasm that might or might not be sincere. It appeared more important that the crowd should seem united in the same emotion, and commentators on forums systematically remarked on this shared emotion. The forum had been transformed into "a politics which poured out a liturgy and in which the masses, by their physical presence and their emotional participation, played an essential role" (Burrin 1986, 18). When the right was granted by law in 1881, the forum had been conceived as, and was in part, a place of debate, but it had diverged from that vision and was used as a mode of collective action.

How should we explain the failure of the forums as places of debate? One of the principal questions that emerge from our inquiry concerns the effects of the frequently large gap between citizen deliberation and effective public decision making. Was the failure of deliberative mechanisms not a foregone conclusion, given the chasm between fostering deliberation and influencing elected officials? That the participants themselves reported few results from their deliberations on public decisions was to have important effects. Many authors have emphasized it when observing the contemporary experiences with deliberation. "What purpose does deliberation serve if not from the perspective of action?" ask Loïc Blondiaux and Yves Sintomer (2002, 31). The debates' lack of influence on the choices made by representatives might cause the demobilization and withdrawal of citizens from places of deliberation. It might also drive the growth of disillusionment with the political system: if they are perceived as mere "democratic lures" (Blondiaux 2004, 19), these deliberative moments can again worsen the crises of representation that they are, in part, put in place to resolve. The great distance between deliberation and decision can finally bring about the temptation to transform deliberative assemblies into means of action, which is exactly what we see at the turn of the twentieth century.

In the case of the United States, understanding the forums as civic education was both a strength and a weakness. It allowed for a variety of formats, tailored to local interests and traditions, and fit in cleanly with other American traditions, such as the lyceum and the Chautauqua. It figured forums as mimicking deliberation without having to tie them directly to action. In this way, participation allowed people to speak *as citizens* to other citizens, and so constitute a civic identity. The setup of the forum and its rules for civility were all intended not just to inculcate civil discourse but to enact it, make it real, without having to be tied to specific legislative processes and institutions.

Yet in the end that was a great weakness; forums served the idealized standard of discursive citizenship at the expense of connecting to the levers of power. Ultimately, participants end up frustrated—if one can watch televised discussion on *Meet the Press*, why go to a forum, whose results get one no closer to influencing legislation? The satisfaction of enacting one's civic duty doesn't seem to be quite as motivating as actually influencing the course of events. Consider the civil rights movement in the United States. One could argue that after hundreds of "forums" conducted in churches across the South and the rest of the country, change was finally accomplished through protest and coordinated political action.

Despite a vigorous resurgence of interest in public deliberation in the United States, focused on face-to-face talk, the idea of a forum, especially involving political candidates, has clearly degenerated (Gastil and Keith 2005). The first two presidential election cycles of the twenty-first century have seen the emergence of "town hall meetings," which are little more than stage-managed public relations events, where no one unfriendly to the candidate is allowed in, and all questions are vetted by the organizers.

Conclusion

These points lead us to two fundamental lessons from the forum movements in both France and the United States, lessons that are relevant to contemporary efforts at public deliberation. The first involves the contradictory possibilities implied by government involvement. The government is well situated to organize forums, since it has the money and access to resources; private organizers are often partisan, and their programs are necessarily not comprehensive (the most comprehensive ones in the United States are run by the Kettering Foundation and America Speaks). Yet not only will any government have trouble establishing its credibility as an independent organizer, but the very real conflicts of interest may well lead to distortions of the forums in exactly the way that Habermas has long warned about. Thus integrating deliberation in more than piecemeal ways carries intrinsic hazards. A second issue concerns motives for participation. People who are angry about a specific issue or injustice are motivated to participate (and do), but this doesn't guarantee regular discussion on important (but boring) ongoing issues. The United States should be deliberating about health care continuously, not only when there is outrage. If forums were more fun and entertaining, people would be more likely to participate, but it's hard to see how that squares with serious discussion. With movies, television, and the Internet as endless distractions, the job of attracting participants is far more difficult than it was in the nineteenth century.

REFERENCES

Blondiaux, Loïc. 2004. "Démocratie participative et démocratie délibérative: Une lecture critique." http://www.chaire-mcd.ca/publications/conferences/Blondiaux-confi-novembre-2004.pdf.
Blondiaux, Loïc, and Yves Sintomer. 2002. "L'impératif délibératif." *Politix* 15 (57): 17–35.
Burrin, Philippe. 1986. "Poings levés et bras tendus: La contagion des symboles au temps du front populaire." *Vingtième Siècle: Revue d'Histoire* 11:5–20.
Cossart, Paula. 2010. *Le meeting politique: De la délibération à la manifestation*. Rennes: PUR.
Courtine, Jean-Jacques. 1990. "Les glissements du spectacle politique." *Esprit* 9:152–64.
Dalotel, Alain, Alain Faure, and Jean-Claude Freiermuth. 1980. *Aux origines de la Commune: Le mouvement des réunions publiques à Paris, 1868–1870*. Paris: F. Maspero.
Déloye, Yves. 1997. "Idée républicaine et citoyenneté: L'expérience française (1870–1945)." In *Culture républicaine, citoyenneté et lien social*, ed. Jean-Michel Lecomte and Jean-Pierre Sylvestre, 67–83. Dijon: CRDP de Bourgogne.
Ely, Mary L. 1937. *Why Forums?* New York: American Association for Adult Education.
Gastil, John, and William Keith. 2005. "A Nation That (Sometimes) Likes to Talk: A Brief History of Public Deliberation in the United States." In *The Deliberative Democracy Handbook: Strategies for Effective Civic Engagement in the Twenty-First Century*, ed. John Gastil and Peter Levine, 3–19. San Francisco: Jossey-Bass.
Keith, William. 2007. *Democracy as Discussion: The American Forum Movement and Civic Education*. Lanham, Md.: Rowman and Littlefield.
Mollier, Jean-Yves. 2004. *Le Camelot et la rue: Politique et démocratie au tournant des XIXe et XXe siècles*. Paris: Fayard.
Offerlé, Michel. 1993. *Un homme, une voix? Histoire du suffrage universel*. Paris: Gallimard.
Ray, Angela G. 2005. *The Lyceum and Public Culture in the Nineteenth-Century United States*. East Lansing: Michigan State University Press.
Reynié, Dominique. 1998. *Le triomphe de l'opinion publique: L'espace public français du XVIe au XXe siècle*. Paris: Odile Jacob.
Rieser, Andrew Chamberlin. 2003. *The Chautauqua Moment: Protestants, Progressives, and the Culture of Modern Liberalism*. New York: Columbia University Press.
Rosanvallon, Pierre. 2001. *Le sacre du citoyen*. Paris: Gallimard.
Roussellier, Nicolas. 2001. "La diffusion de l'éloquence en France sous la IIIe république." In *L'éloquence politique en France et en Italie de 1870 à nos jours*, ed. Fabrice d'Almeida, 41–46. Rome: École Française de Rome.
Studebaker, John. 1935. *The American Way*. New York: McGraw-Hill.
Studebaker, John, and Chester Williams. 1937. *Choosing Our Way*. Washington, D.C.: U.S. Department of the Interior.
Westbrook, Robert. 1992. *John Dewey and American Democracy*. Ithaca: Cornell University Press.

SECTION II

PUBLIC DELIBERATION AS RHETORICAL PRACTICE

Robert Hariman's observation that "democracy depends on crafting in speech and writing a distinctive form of consciousness that is simultaneously—and often awkwardly and even contradictorily—public and social" (2007, 222) might serve as a motto for this section, in which several scholarly approaches to deliberative democracy and vernacular rhetoric come together in a shared interest in exploring ways of bettering civic life by sustaining and improving communities through critical analysis. Part 1 of this section brings together studies that have as common themes the multifarious discursive challenges that meet a person wishing to participate in public debate, and the ways in which individuals and groups craft their rhetorical responses. From different disciplinary and theoretical starting points, the following four chapters discuss how participants in contemporary public debate meet the challenges of arguing effectively while also attending to other communicative tasks such as maintaining a tolerable atmosphere in spite of deep-seated disagreements or conflicts of interest. A recurring theme is finding constructive elements in communicative practices that ordinarily are considered unconstructive, such as being provocative or evasive.

Considering Norms of Communicative Behavior

In the first chapter, Italo Testa, a philosopher, challenges a commonly assumed norm of mutual respect in debate. He argues that an a priori respect for other debaters as persons is not a prerequisite for true deliberative debate, but that such respect might also have negative effects and lead to fallacious paths of thought. The demand for moral (equal) respect for persons per se as a necessary condition for public discourse could in fact hinder dialogue and prevent the search for some agreement between parties who may not respect one another as persons but nevertheless could respect as legitimate the values, beliefs, and preferences held by their counterparts. Testa argues that we must distinguish between respect as a static, a priori presupposition and respect as a dialogical achievement, and similarly between respect as equally due to persons and respect as potentially due to values, beliefs, and preferences we may not share but may still find legitimate. It is the second terms in these distinctions that should be seen as ground rules of deliberative discourse.

Niels Møller Nielsen, like Testa, sees public debate from a general and theoretical angle. Coming from the field of pragmatic-functional linguistics, he examines it as a system in which dialectical exchanges are "embedded" in rhetorical exchanges. They represent a social, rule-governed form of behavior involving communicative roles such as protagonist and antagonist, but on a different level they serve an overarching, rhetorically oriented relationship between the media as an institution and the media audience. Whereas theories of pragmatics provide useful insights in understanding conversational negotiation of argument structure and general acceptability as a form of tacit acceptance of a cooperative norm at the dialectical level, these insights are only useful once the overlying rhetorical level is integrated into the analysis.

Marie Lund Klujeff, a rhetorician and literary theorist, takes as her starting point the observation that everyday political debate often bears little resemblance to the ideals espoused by academic theorists and the norms considered to be in place. She looks to rhetorical forms often considered inappropriate in public deliberation and argues that provocation has important functions in a public debate and should not be discarded wholesale. Her case study of an Internet-based debate is grounded in Hauser's notion of vernacular rhetoric and explores the way in which this contentious debate reflected norms of civic engagement. Applying Hauser's terms activity/engagement and tolerance and discussing their possible incompatibility at a practical level, she analyzes the Gaarder-Kristol controversy over Israeli policies. Klujeff identifies traits of the provocative style and argues that it can serve the functions of structuring argument, forming opinions, constituting an engaged and reflective audience, and creating presence. Gaarder's discourse is characterized as parody functioning as "refutation by mockery" as it performs the idea it attacks.

In the final chapter in part 1 of this section, Ildikó Kaposi highlights the fact that discursive communities should not be evaluated on their adherence to traditional norms of argumentative exchange alone, but that we would be well advised to recognize that a broad range of communicative action takes place, some of which has less to do with the development of political opinions and more with affirming and maintaining the existence of the community, even when it involves exchanges that would at first glance seem offensive. In a careful study of the "pub politicking" practiced on a Hungarian online site for political discussion, she shows how this otherwise negatively marked concept is embraced by participants as they engage in construction of the boundaries of admissibility to public discussions on the forum, informed by universalistic principles and adapted to the particular circumstances on Politika Forum.

Critiques of "Elite" Discourse

In part 2 of this section, four authors turn their attention to participants in public debate who enjoy privileged positions in order to study how notions of citizenship are portrayed and realized by agents in positions of power and influence.

Kristian Wedberg looks at the literary public sphere, arguing that it holds the potential to shed new light on contemporary democratic culture. In a study of the Norwegian literary celebrity, Wedberg discusses Dag Solstad's particular polemical way of destabilizing norms regarding the manner, form, and content of a TV interview. Wedberg's starting point is a critique of Habermas's understanding of the connection between (literary) art and the public sphere, especially the lack of recognition of the rhetorical nature of an interview situation. Solstad's apparently peculiar behavior on screen is understood as a way of providing the public with an image of political rationality that challenges the paradigm of enlightened rationalism. Wedberg labels Solstad's rhetorical practice of uncooperativeness a "rhetoric of duplicity" and argues that Solstad's odd behavior can be read as a way of stratifying the audience, thereby pointing to a tension between democratic and aristocratic cultural views. Wedberg further sees a direct challenge to norms of openness and expectations of disclosure of opinion and sentiment; according to Wedberg, this is a rhetorical mode that emerges from an attempt at truthfulness.

In her chapter on "gendered war rhetoric," Berit von der Lippe analyzes speeches by three women, former U.S. first lady Laura Bush, former leader of the Norwegian Defense Committee Marit Nybakk, and Norwegian defense minister Anne-Grete Strøm-Erichsen, on the topic of the war in Afghanistan. Drawing on feminist theory and notions of hegemony and co-optation, von der Lippe launches a critique of what she regards as the silencing of Afghan people in public discourse on the war being fought in their country, and the way gender plays into the legitimation of and debate about the war, especially in the shape of a co-opted feminist discourse forwarded by leading women rhetors. Concludes von der Lippe, "no less than in the context of the cold war rhetoric of containment, war rhetoric is informed by specific masculine values," and she warns against an uncritical acceptance of the rhetoric of women's rights in connection with the war in Afghanistan for reasons of its exclusion of subaltern voices and co-optation of feminist ideas.

In her chapter on negative reactions to a well-known Danish politician's statement in connection with a terrorist attack on a Danish embassy, Lisa S. Villadsen argues that a lack of appreciation of rhetoric's role in public deliberation may be one way to explain a political debate climate intolerant of dissent at a moment of pressure. By analyzing how expressions of the need for reconsideration of Danish foreign policy made by an MP and a CEO, respectively, were immediately construed as downright treacherous by politicians from across the spectrum, Villadsen makes the point that rhetorical agency can be controversial even for elite debaters when their right to a speaking position is challenged by opponents. Reading the negative reactions as symptoms of a perceived breach of communicative norms of consensus, she suggests that a political debate climate where expressions of skepticism are construed as acts of hostility and result in attempts to exile such voices is in need of a more robust understanding of the value of public debate and the exchange of differing ideas.

The final chapter in part 2 of this section addresses issues of rhetorical citizenship from the vantage point of constitutional law and legal philosophy, as Bart van Klink and Oliver W. Lembcke examine the "rhetoric of exception." Involving suspension and violation of fundamental rights such as freedom of expression, political justification for this policy is an important area of citizenship research. The authors focus on former UK prime minister Tony Blair's rhetorical treatment of antiterror measures in the wake of 9/11 and the terror bombings in London in 2005. Blair created a sense of urgency that contributed to justifying extreme measures, and this move was supported by a clear differentiation between "friends" and "enemies" in which the latter were portrayed as radically "other." Citizens were offered three roles: as objects of care, objects of command, or objects of conviction. The analysis supports the suggestion by Schmitt and Agamben that there is little room for the rule of law in a state of exception. Moreover, the authors show how Blair's inclusive rhetoric of "us" served to undermine his persuasiveness as the British people learned more facts about the war and their disapproval of it grew.

Rhetorical Citizenship Across Communicative Settings

In part 3 of this section we suggest the possible critical scope of the concept of rhetorical citizenship through four case studies that range from the relatively "obvious" kind of setting, such as public hearings, via online debate about the status of the housing market to entertainment theater.

Public deliberation forums represent an increasingly popular way of attempting to engage citizens actively in questions of public concern, and James McDonald argues that such forums are valuable because they offer opportunities for individuals with varying degrees of expertise to learn about the issues at stake and subsequently to modify their views as they strive for collective solutions, thereby also contributing to the enactment of a rhetorical democracy based upon public deliberation. Asking by what specific rhetorical practices such learning and critical assessment of opinions take place, McDonald is particularly interested in how individual participants were able to contribute to developing alternative solutions. His analysis of a series of hearings held in Quebec, Canada, regarding the construction of a controversial gas plant finds that the principal move in participants' deliberative practices was to accept key points of the other group's argument, thus paradoxically strengthening their own ability to persuade skeptics, enabling them to find ways to negotiate disagreement and pointing to alternative solutions acceptable to both parties.

Tatiana Tatarchevskiy, aware of the prevailing sociological view that citizens in the United States today avoid public deliberative talk, has followed three grassroots groups in New York and Washington, D.C. that have sought to establish a space where strangers can meet and discuss public affairs, social issues, or philosophical questions. Interviews and observations suggest that participants are reluctant to engage in dialectical questioning of one another's premises and persuasions. Rather, they choose various tactics to mask their disagreements, such as addressing an outside opponent, adding another angle to the predominant lines of discussion, suggesting a meta-argument, or asking for clarification. This kind of rhetoric, Tatarchevskiy suggests, helps them preserve civility and at the same time allows the questioning of various sides of an issue. The question, then, is what implications such patterns in public face-to-face communication have for theories of deliberative and rhetorical democracy—which, by definition, value argumentation and contradiction.

Sine Nørholm Just and Jonas Gabrielsen, both rhetoricians, have looked at online debates concerning the real estate market on Euroinvestor, a Danish website dedicated to economic issues. The real estate market is a sector of public as well as private interest, which is why discussions of its problems and developments may be seen as transcending the boundary between the market and the public sphere. This transcendence, the authors hypothesize, may mean that debaters position themselves both as consumers and as citizens. To see if this is so, the authors look at what arguments are put forward and how they are presented. They apply *stasis* theory, drawn from ancient rhetoric, to analyze arguments and their constructive potential, and to test their theoretical and empirical claims.

Jette Barnholdt Hansen examines a song from a popular Danish revue—a traditional vaudeville-like genre of humor that mixes sketches, songs, and monologues, satirizing celebrities and topical events. In Denmark, the crisis following the Muhammad cartoons in 2006 spawned a heated controversy but also many instances of satire and humor, such as the revue song studied in this chapter. This song made a statement that arguably had the potential to defuse a hostile and polarized debate somewhat, acting as a catalyst for the understanding that "we are all in the same boat."

Covering a range from more theoretically oriented to more critically oriented attempts to understand particular forms of public debate, the case studies in this section all share a concern with teasing out what the notion of rhetorical citizenship entails in contemporary settings. As the section brings together examples of how scholars analyze and evaluate public deliberation as it takes place in different countries, different media, and different genres, it illustrates the relevance of a concept like rhetorical citizenship in settings where citizens meet to exchange ideas.

REFERENCES

Hariman, Robert. 2007. "Amateur Hour: Knowing What to Love in Ordinary Democracy." In *The Prettier Doll: Rhetoric, Discourse, and Ordinary Democracy*, ed. Karen Tracy, James P. McDaniel, and Bruce Gronbeck, 218–50. Tuscaloosa: University of Alabama Press.

PART I

CONSIDERING NORMS OF COMMUNICATIVE BEHAVIOR

4
THE RESPECT FALLACY:
LIMITS OF RESPECT IN PUBLIC DIALOGUE

Italo Testa

Deliberative politics should start from an adequate and differentiated image of our dialogical practices and their normative structures; the ideals that we eventually propose for deliberative politics should be tested against this background. In this chapter I argue that equal respect, understood as respect a priori conferred on persons, is not and should not be counted as a constitutive normative ground of public discourse. Furthermore, requiring such respect, even if it might facilitate dialogue, could have negative effects and lead to fallacious paths of thought—as seems to happen on matters of deep disagreement such as the Colorado fundamentalist/gay HIV issue I discuss below. I put forward this argument from the standpoint of argumentation theory, drawing consequences for dialogical theories of politics. Basing my argument on a pluralistic notion of public discourse—understood as a mixed discourse of persuasion, information seeking, and negotiation—I argue that respect is a dynamic, situational phenomenon and that the norm of equal respect for persons is contextually contingent in political deliberation: equal respect should be considered as a potential outcome, a discursive achievement. I understand this as a second-order consensus achieved dynamically on a provisional basis rather than as a universal condition for dialogue.

1. *Preliminary remarks: reciprocity, equality, impartiality.* Respect seems to be first of all a moral and social attitude. It is not in itself necessarily reciprocal: someone can always be respectful without being respected. Neither does reciprocity imply equality: there are various social and political practices in hierarchical societies, even in democratic ones, that express reciprocal respect under conditions of asymmetry and inequality.

One example is the Kula exchange or Kula ring—the ceremonial exchange system studied in Papua New Guinea by Malinowski and Mauss.[1] Respect is not analytically equal respect. Even those who see respect as a moral ideal of intrinsic value might not agree that its intrinsic moral value implies the intrinsic moral value of *equal* respect.

But *should* respect be equal? Should we submit it to some normative principle of equality? Some contest this, arguing that if there is a normative principle regulating respect, it is not equality. For instance, Harry Frankfurt states, "treating a person with respect means, in the sense that is pertinent here, dealing with him exclusively on the basis of those aspects of his particular character or circumstances that are actually relevant to the issue at hand." That's why "treating people with respect precludes assigning them special advantages except on the basis of considerations that differentiate relevantly among them" (1997, 8). In dealing with people we should be guided only by what is genuinely relevant. Thus respect entails impartiality and avoidance of arbitrariness rather than equality—understood by Frankfurt as "a matter of each person having the same as others."[2]

Whatever the normative principle of respect may be, it is reasonable to agree with Frankfurt that respect, even if assumed as a basic moral principle, is a defeasible value that sometimes may be overridden by other moral values: "people often prefer—sometimes for perfectly good and even admirable reasons—to be treated as though they have characteristics they do not have or as though they lack characteristics that they actually possess" (1997, 8n). We need not share Frankfurt's perspective to realize that respect is balanced against other values (I may prefer to love or be loved even at the price of not being respected or of being humiliated), and that in much social and political intercourse (such as recognition politics) respect is a "good" that is being negotiated. Hence the commitment to respect, equal or not, is not necessary insofar as it is often withdrawn in practice. In what follows we'll see particularly how all of this is manifested in dialogical practices.

2. *Against equal respect as universal a priori.* Given this, we can come closer to our argumentation theory approach. First, I aim to show in which sense "equal respect" for persons—understood as addressed universally to members of the moral community—is not a necessary normative ground for public discourse in general. This means first of all that equal

respect for persons is not a universal a priori that must be satisfied in order to enter into any form of dialogue.

Argumentation theories—for example, Perelman's *nouvelle rhétorique*, Toulmin's *fields of argument*, van Eemeren and Grootendorst's *pragma-dialectics*, Walton's *new dialectic*—do not usually introduce respect as constitutive of the normative structure of discourses. Nevertheless, Apel's discourse ethics and Habermas's moral theory of discourse have seen it as a universal necessary presupposition of entering into a dialogue to assume (even counterfactually) that certain norms are satisfied as categorical imperatives, and they have tried to derive these norms from the procedural principles of argumentation, which imply minimal ethical principles, including equal respect. (Take, for example, Habermas's principle of universalization [U]: a [moral norm] is valid just in case the foreseeable consequences and side effects of its general observance for the interests and value orientations of *each individual* could be *jointly* accepted by *all* concerned without coercion.) This means that there are dialogical commitments we necessarily and a priori endorse whenever we enter into dialogue: a contradictory idea, one could say, since commitments are given in the modality of possibility, as something we may or may not endorse, and it is not clear whether a norm we must endorse could still be qualified as a commitment.

A different view was later adopted by Habermas (1996), where he not only definitively abandoned the transcendental approach but also restricted the principle (U) to moral argumentation and formulated a more general principle for the validation of discourse named (D), consisting in a principle of impartiality: a rule of action or choice is justified, and thus valid, only if all those affected by it could accept it in a reasonable discourse. This was because Habermas acknowledged that there are different kinds of arguments—ethical-political, juridical, moral, pragmatic, prudential, negotiated, and so on—and to submit them all to the normative principle of universalization would deny their peculiarity and normative autonomy. The general principle (D) requires only impartiality for argumentative justification of norms and is detached from the requirement, typical of moral discourse, of universality and equality of rights for all possible participants. Thus (U) ceases to be the normative principle of the genus of discourse and becomes a principle regulating that specific kind of discourse (moral discourse) whose claims must be justified universally in light of an equal consideration of interests; they are thus addressed universally to all rational beings/persons as members of the moral community to whom equal respect is due. If this is to be consistent, I think it should imply that the principle of universalistic equal respect for persons—implied by (U) and not by (D)—is not a necessary presupposition of public discourse: public discourse is a mixed form of discourse where different contexts of discourse intersect and different kinds of arguments occur.

3. *Defeasible respect in dialogue.* So far I have argued that equal respect for persons is not a universal a priori in any form of dialogue. Moreover, even if some kinds of dialogue do require some form of respect from participants, this does not mean that this commitment couldn't be withdrawn or defeated. Even if we commit ourselves in the political sphere to the moral principle of universalization as a regulative ideal (not in itself political), and thus to universal equal respect for persons, this principle can always be balanced against other principles and values and eventually retracted: for instance, in political discourse there could be reasons to give priority to ethical-political considerations addressed to a specific community over those addressed to all human beings. Also, even within the moral domain we shouldn't, according to moral pluralism, understand respect for persons as an all-encompassing, indefeasible moral first principle, but rather as one consideration among others.

But even if public discourse is regulated by principles of impartiality such as Habermas's principle of discourse, Perelman's formal justice, or Stuart Hampshire's procedural principle of *audi alteram partem*, all these might be understood as normative principles of respect, since impartiality could be, following Frankfurt, the normative principle of respect. If so, what exactly is being respected here? Equal or not, would the kind of respect eventually required in dialogue be a respect for persons?

I address this question from the vantage point of Stephen Darwall's article "Respect and the Second Person Standpoint" (2005). Darwall considers the possibility that recognition respect—which according to his previous article is not necessarily personal, since we could have recognition respect also for inanimate beings such as claims, norms, institutions, and so on (1977, 38)—could come in degrees, be more or less earned, or eventually in some circumstances be retracted.

Darwall's examples concern contexts such as testimony in trials (legal discourse), cooperative search for truth (scientific discourse), advice (information-seeking dialogue), mutual inquiry and addressed criticism (persuasion, critical dialogue, or quarrel). Here we are expected, first, to acknowledge by default some authority of the person we are dealing with (as a rational being, a witness, an expert or practical advisor, and so on) and thus recognitionally respect him or her; nevertheless, it may become apparent afterward that this authority was not reliable, and we may be driven to grade our acknowledgment of authority or deny it. This is "defeasible" recognition respect: epistemic authority is "defeasibly merited," as Darwall puts it, that is, liable to be overridden under appropriate circumstances (note also that here Darwall connects defeasibility with this recognition respect of authority being conditional on epistemic merit or excellence). Darwall's point is that the specifically moral recognition respect for persons he defends is of a different kind (indefeasible and not conditional). In the aforementioned examples the authority we recognize in the second person (showing recognition respect for theoretical knowledge, practical wisdom, etc.) is ultimately an epistemic-like authority that is not essentially second-personal, expressible in the third person, whereas the specific moral authority proper to equal respect for persons is practical and essentially in the second person.

Let's assume that Darwall is right in this: it follows that equal respect is not a general principle of public discourse. Recognition respect in the second person may be proper to moral discourse but is not required in most contexts of public discourse, where we are primarily expected to acknowledge an epistemic, defeasible authority that must be expressed in the third person. Some may call this acknowledgment respect, but it need not be egalitarian in a strong sense: we could discover reasons to give different weight to the epistemic authority of different partners of dialogue, and in some contexts we should give different weight to them by default, such as information-seeking dialogues with experts.

We now must look closely at some structural features of public discourse. In order to be validity structures for discourses, distinguishing sound arguments from bad ones, argumentation theories usually assume that we must appeal to a position that has been identified as either the rational judge, the generalized other, the universal audience, the community of communication, or whatever one wishes to call it. The validity structure implies the third-person perspective of a judge: that is, the second-person standpoint must be reexpressed in the third person to be evaluated. Hence the grammar of the second person is necessary but not sufficient to articulate the grammar of public discourse. Second, the authority we acknowledge in the second person is in many cases one that we may see as an instantiation of a third-person authority: an epistemic or practical authority.[3]

In public discourse the authority of the partner is not indefeasible. Furthermore, there is no indissoluble connection between the defeasible authority we acknowledge in our partners and what they say: I need to separate your claim from your authority and look at it in the third person. *Focus on reasons, not persons.* The validity of your claim should be weighed separately from your authority; that may itself come under scrutiny and be graded at a different stage.

Of course, there are contexts of dialogue where it may be relevant that precisely *you* made that claim—as in a quarrel, where I am not committing a fallacy by reproaching you, or in negotiation, where you are protecting your own interests, but this should be not generalized to all contexts of dialogue; otherwise ad hominem attacks would always be sound. The assumption that it is always relevant *who* makes the claim—that is, a systematic *tu quoque*, or incapacity to see the second person from a third-person standpoint—might, as we'll see, engender argumentative fallacies. Of course, there are ethical-political discourses where your identity, your history, what you have suffered, may be relevant in evaluating your claim, but this is not always so in political deliberation; otherwise politics per se is reduced to identity politics.

Argumentation theories help us understand that public discourse is not a monolith but is differentiated in various contexts of dialogue with distinctive normative structures and burdens of proof (such as persuasion, inquiry, information seeking, deliberation, negotiation, eristic dialogue) (Walton 1998, 171–73)—and different kinds of arguments (moral, ethical-political, juridical, pragmatic, strategic). Even political discourse should not be modeled upon one single context of dialogue: the role of deliberation—where agents have to choose between different courses of action—should not be overestimated, since political discourse is often a mixed discourse where persuasion, practical deliberation, information seeking, negotiation, and eristic dialogue are intertwined, and where legal, strategic, pragmatic, moral, and/or ethical arguments all occur, given the circumstances. From this, deliberative politics might gain a pluralistic notion of public discourse, which implies not conflating public discourse with moral argumentation, and not posing moral equal respect for persons as the monistic principle of political deliberation.

4. *Fallacies of respect.* A further point is that making respect for persons a precondition of discourse could foster argumentative fallacies such as ad hominem attacks and refusals to enter into dialogue with people we do not (sometimes for good reasons) respect. Dialogue requires that we respect what is said, not who says it: to think that respect for the person is a necessary condition for respecting what is said may lead to fallacious paths of thinking.

   A frequent fallacy in public dialogues, particularly in political contexts, is the ad hominem argument. Fallacies are traditionally understood as arguments that *seem* valid but aren't. Argumentation theories have tried in various ways to explain what exactly is wrong in fallacies. Here I assume (following contemporary theories) that no arguments are of themselves fallacious; they become fallacious when used in ways that break the rules of the dialogical game. Following Walton's *New Dialectic* (1998), this means that there are contexts where arguments such as ad hominem are legitimate (for example, some forms of eristic dialogues) and others where they are not (for example, inquiry)—and that fallacies arise when there is a shift, not agreed on by the parties, from one context of dialogue to another (Walton and Krabbe 1995, 108): that is why the arguments might *seem* valid to someone, since the shift is covert, not perceived by anyone.

   This characterization is rather formal, and I think that much remains to be explained about what exactly happens in public dialogues where fallacies such as ad hominem are ubiquitous. If in scientific inquiry an argument is attacked on the basis of the alleged personal immorality of the scientist—he harassed a student some years ago—it is pretty clear that an illicit shift from persuasion dialogue or inquiry to eristic dialogue has occurred. But in a political context where we listen to an expert about waste disposal (i.e., an information-seeking dialogue), we may later discover that the expert wasn't impartial, as he had concealed having shares in a firm specializing in waste disposal in just the way he proposes: then a personal attack would be rather reasonable.

The theory of context shift lets us glimpse a general structure of fallacies but misses something about what is peculiar to ad hominem attacks. A definition of ad hominem is this: "a technique of argument used to attack someone's position by raising questions about the person's character or personal situation" (Walton 1998, 111). Let's reconsider our examples from the perspective of respect: in the first, bad moral character is alleged; in the second, it is alleged that the person has a hidden agenda. In the first, instead of attacking your argument on a scientific basis, I attack your argument because you are not worthy of respect as a person: you did something morally wrong, and I assume that this invalidates your argument, too. Since you are unworthy of respect, so is your argument. The respect in the first part of that sentence is personal moral respect, whereas that in the second part is epistemic respect. One could also say that the recognition respect due to the epistemic authority of the person is attacked because of the lack of moral authority of the person, which is then transmitted to the claim. I understand this "respect fallacy" as the product of an unnecessary demand for moral personal respect as a precondition of entering into dialogue; this is a moral psychological explanation but also a normative one, since it shows that it is a wrong application to dialogue of the norm of respect for a person that co-produces the fallacy. In dialogue we should be prepared to disentangle the authority of the claim from the authority of the claimer and judge it from a third-person standpoint.

The systematic conflation of the third person with the second could be the source of frequent fallacies in public discourse. Nevertheless, there can be occurrences where the moral authority of the claimer *is* relevant to judge the credibility of her or his third-person epistemic authority and in weighing the authority of what is being said—as in the waste disposal case, where the alleged hidden agenda justifies doubting the person as an objective arguer. But this cannot be the general rule. Hence the norm of personal respect in public discourse is contextually contingent, in the third person, and retractable.

I want to make a further point with regard to fallacies. The appeal to authority can amount to the fallacy *ad verecundiam*, as in a critical discussion when someone, instead of raising critical questions and giving arguments, just pays respect to some authority. But appeal to authority is by no means always fallacious, since it is pretty reasonable that in some contexts—when we seek information relevant to a decision—we appeal to experts for relevant information. So clearly epistemic authority in dialogue is gradable—not everyone counts as an expert—and if there is to be a rule of respect for personal authority in dialogue, this would be a nonegalitarian recognition respect: there can be no general rule for equal respect of personal authority, but rather a rule of impartiality and guidance by the relevant authority, treating similar cases alike and relevantly dissimilar cases differently.

5. *What about the alleged two kinds of respect?* One may argue that in analyzing the "respect fallacy" I did not draw a distinction between respect of the person per se and of particular merits and excellences. After all, wasn't the "personal moral respect" we were talking about of the second kind, that is, appraisal of the moral value of the person? So, even if one admits that moral respect in this second sense is not a precondition for entering into a dialogue, and that an unnecessary demand for it may cause fallacies, this would not prove that moral respect in the first sense is not required as a precondition of dialogue.

Here I would first like to address the distinction between two kinds of respect introduced by Darwall and followed by many authors, that is, between universal, unconditional recognition/status respect for persons per se, and particular, conditional merit/esteem/appraisal respect for persons as determinate individuals. That this is a rather recent theoretical construal resulting from processes of emancipation within the modern world does not, of course, in itself mean that such a distinction may not be somehow justified. I want to stress what has been noticed by many, that is, that in our practices these two supposedly different kinds of respect are intertwined. Adding a genealogical trait to the picture, I would say that it is from an experience of appraisal respect of concrete individuals that we may eventually come, through education and abstraction, to think of individuals—the ones we have interacted with or distant ones—as worthy of status respect as persons per se, and may form a habit of doing so.

There are reasons not to presuppose such a distinction a priori and base a discourse theory on it. First, such a distinction does not seem to be deeply rooted in ordinary language and discourse, where there is no sharp line between the alleged two senses. The distinction is rather theoretical, introduced on the basis of philosophical assumptions. Thus the burden of proof seems to be on those who introduce it. Furthermore, such a distinction depends on metaphysical notions not accepted by all (what does it mean, "a person per se"? Or "a person as such"?). Consider this application of Bernard Williams's dilemma of equality (1973): either we look at empirical features of persons, and it will be hard to find a basis that could justify equal respect for them (some empirical property found in all persons in similar measure), or we look for some transcendental capacity (i.e., some abstract moral capacity) that won't be accepted by those who doubt the very existence of such noumenical capacities (and this is exactly what those who introduce respect for persons as such tend to presuppose).[4] Finally, in the expressions "respect for a person as a person" and "respect for a person as such" there seems to be an ambiguity not easily solved: sometimes it indicates an appreciation of personality traits of the person, generally considered desirable in persons, whatever their particular roles; sometimes it indicates a widely inclusive, nonconventional status that persons have, though lacking most human excellences or even believed to be immoral (Hill 1998, 284). This indicates a need for further thinking; basing a discourse theory on such an ambiguous distinction may produce more problems than it solves.

Were the distinction between two kinds of respect better worked out and even justified from a moral point of view, we would nevertheless not need to take it preliminarily into account in developing a framework for public dialogue. As argued, either respect for persons is not relevant for dialogue in general—that you are a person per se doesn't usually affect the soundness of your argument (a computer could have a better one)—or, if relevant, respect mainly concerns issues that deal with the particular person you are (your identity or history, your alleged dishonesty, and so on).

So, even if we admit the legitimacy of the distinction between respect of persons as such and respect as an appraisal of the merits of particular persons, this should not lead us to say that the first is more than contingently connected with the kind of epistemic respect for what is said basically required in public dialogue.[5]

6. *Unwelcome consequences of personal respect.* Making moral (equal) respect for persons per se a necessary condition for public discourse could sometimes hinder dialogue and prevent the search for some kind of agreement between parties who may or may not equally respect one another as persons, but nevertheless could respect as legitimate, even if they don't agree with, the values, beliefs, and preferences held by their counterpart. Recognizing the other as an equal co-member

of a moral community could contingently facilitate dialogue and agreement between persons, but it may be unnecessary, and sometimes dangerous, if respect for what the other person says (whoever he or she may be) is the thing really to be secured.

I here develop a suggestion from Dryzek and Niemeyer (2006, 641). Arguably, respect for the moral standing of others may prevent violence against them, thus facilitating dialogue. However, respect for persons may be beside the point when it comes to generating "metaconsensus": that is, respect for persons as co-members of a moral community could be beside the point in generating dialogue between parties. For instance, respect for the moral standing of others is consistent with a refusal to engage with their claims in dialogue. Let's take Dryzek and Niemeyer's example of fundamentalist Christians who "hate the sin and love the sinner": loving sinners as persons—in this case gays and lesbians—is consistent with refusing engagement with their sinful views, that is, with their claims in public discourse on, say, HIV policies. So any connection between moral respect for persons and respect for what they say is contingent and varies from case to case. Dryzek and Niemeyer describe a dialogue on HIV/AIDS policy in Colorado, designed to produce advice for the state government. The participants were selected to represent democratic diversity and included gay activists, people with AIDS, and fundamentalist Christians active in campaigns against gay rights. We may assume that these Christians saw themselves as respecting the moral personhood of the gays per se (loving the sinner as a person per se) but disrespected certain features of their personal identity; in Darwall's terms, they may have had moral personal recognition respect but no personal appraisal respect for the others. So we have a case where moral respect for persons per se is at least insufficient to entertain dialogue: indeed, it could sometimes be an obstacle to dialogue. Note that applying the distinction between the two kinds of respect so as to create an unbridgeable gap between the person per se (to be respected) and the person with her or his individual features and circumstances (that I may disrespect) could be part of an excluding attitude, since I can always say that I respect you as a person per se while refusing to deal with your particular moral identity. Here again we have the "respect fallacy": since you are unworthy of personal (appraisal) respect, so is your argument. And the fact that I am ready to give you personal recognition respect as a person per se does not advance the situation but eventually makes it worse. I think this example illustrates that the idea of respect in the second person (either recognition or appraisal respect) as a universal precondition of dialogue is flawed. In the Colorado case no progress could be made until after the Christians set aside the entirely moral issue of the moral personhood of the others.[6] Eventually, some measures of public policy, such as moral education in school and sexually explicit material targeted at the gay community, were agreed upon, although not as components of an overlapping consensus, since these measures remained objectionable to gay activists and fundamentalist Christians, respectively. Progress could be made when each side came to recognize "the legitimacy of the values of the other side as they might have to enter public policy consideration—while not recognizing the legitimacy of the identity of the others and (on the fundamentalist side) still believing that gays and lesbians should be denied public policy protection of their rights as a matter of state policy" (Dryzek and Niemeyer 2006, 642). We could say that progress could be made when they came to distinguish respect due to persons from respect due to what is claimed.

7. *Restrictions on dialogue and its openness.* Dialogue should be possible between partners who do not respect each other equally, or even do not respect each other at all. In fact, dialogue could be the way to obtain the missing respect, and this is a reason to think that the value of public dialogue may override the value of respect. Readiness to argue with those who do not respect us (or the other way around), and to take into account their claims, could be an attitude with moral value. So I think it reasonable not to think of respect as a condition a priori, posing restrictions on access to public dialogue: otherwise the cognitive and eventually moral heuristic process of dialogue would be undermined.

Neither should we think that a priori conferred respect for persons per se in itself facilitates dialogue. Respect justified on the basis of a positive, substantive understanding—a religious, metaphysical, or even pragmatic understanding—of personhood always posits restrictions on the range of subjects to be included, restrictions that may be revealed as arbitrary.[7] This also goes for restrictions that limit the attribution of respect for persons to those belonging to the natural kind of *Homo sapiens* (fallacies of speciesism); even the usual candidates for defining features of personhood—capacity to suffer, rationality, autonomy, moral agency, and so on—are always gradable and aren't necessarily satisfied in every case (such as in seriously deficient humans). I am not saying that we shouldn't engage in discussions about personhood or that every attempt to justify a theory of personhood is flawed from the beginning. My point is that only through dialogue can we eventually discover the specific contents and bounds of personhood, and that's why respect reflecting a substantive notion of personhood shouldn't be a precondition of public dialogue itself.

On the other hand, we should be ready in dialogue even to consider arguments raised by or concerning individuals that we do not actually confer personhood on, and who may never be eligible candidates for it. Here, think not only of embryos, nonhuman animals, aliens, and robots: just recall that personal recognition respect has been historically extended and that in the past slaves, indigenous peoples, blacks, and women weren't thought of as satisfying the current criteria. In other words, views about who is entitled to respect have suffered and could still suffer from what Nancy Fraser (2005) calls *misframing*:[8] they have been framed by grammars of discourse that foreclosed the claims of some, and that may still obscure claims we cannot even imagine as possible, let alone legitimate. One should acknowledge that, just as rituals of reciprocal respect in traditional societies were ideological means to legitimize economic and social inequalities, practices of equal respect for persons nowadays could have an ideological function too. Once we accept that misframing can exist in principle, we realize that we can only treat framing disputes dialogically, as public discourse conflicts whose legitimate resolution requires unconstrained, inclusive public discussion. First-order questions of respect for persons must be handled discursively, that is, within reflexive dialogue, or metadialogue. Thus the very reflexivity of public dialogue—the fact that this dialogue can reflect on the wrong configurations that actual grammars of personhood pose for public debates—argues for the historical and contextual contingency of the value of respect for persons in public dialogue, and thus in a deliberative conception of politics and metapolitics; in other words, respect for persons is not a universal metadialogical rule.

8. *Respect and consensus of the second order.* The preceding points are not meant to suggest that no kind of respect could be part of the normative achievements of public discourse and political deliberation. The point is to distinguish clearly, on the one hand, between respect as a *static, a priori* presupposition (unnecessary and sometimes dangerous)—and

respect as a dialogical achievement, a *dynamic, a posteriori* second-order respect, and, on the other hand, between respect as equally due to persons (unnecessary as a precondition of public dialogue) and respect as justifiably due to values, beliefs, and preferences we may not share but still find legitimate (normative metarespect).

Dialogue need not a priori presuppose respect for persons but could achieve, by itself, respect justifiably due to values, beliefs, and preferences we may not share but still find legitimate—for instance, we disagree on how to prioritize certain values or preferences but still find it reasonable that others think differently about it. This normative metarespect (respecting other views as legitimate) is neither de facto nor de jure personal (as concerning the views themselves)—and should not be conceived as a *static* presupposition but as a dynamic, second-order achievement. Of course, dialogues could concern persons and the respect due to them, and it could contribute to enlarging our views and achieving better conceptions of personhood, but this still does not mean that respect for persons is a necessary presupposition of dialogue: in this case, too, what we need is to appreciate the views others hold on personhood. That's why I think that prominence in public dialogues and deliberative politics should be given to respect for the legitimacy of values, beliefs, and preferences that we may not share but that we acknowledge as legitimate.

Note that even respect for the legitimacy of values, beliefs, and preferences should not be conferred a priori, as indefeasible and unretractable. Were it so, the consequence would be that *anything goes*: there would be no way to distinguish between legitimate and illegitimate claims, and dialogue would defeat itself and its validity structure. Rather, respect for the legitimacy of beliefs, values, and preferences we may not share is something we may come to appreciate in the course of dialogue when given some reasons: for instance, we may predict that respect for the legitimacy of beliefs will be much more restricted than that for values and preferences. This implies that there will always be views that we won't hold as respectable; and this is not a bad thing in itself.

Framed this way, the issue of respect intersects with a major problem in political philosophy and argumentation theory: that of consensus. I'll give some hints as to how a concept—second-order consensus—could be useful in helping us understand consensus in deliberative politics.[9]

The consensus we need in deliberative democracy is not on first-order beliefs, values, and preferences, but rather a second-order consensus, achieved dynamically, on how to disagree on first-order views. A provisional and contestable metaconsensus on how to reasonably disagree implies a dynamic reciprocal recognition between the parties centered on the legitimacy of beliefs, values, and preferences held by the persons involved, rather than on the persons themselves.[10] This should also help us overcome those obstacles to dialogue that arise because people do not very often personally respect or esteem one another.

9. *Respect as a second-order disposition?* It may still be argued that at least some kind of respect is given to the other as a valuable counterpart in a dialogue, and that this implies a norm of reciprocity—although not of equal reciprocity, since the other could be a more or less valuable counterpart. I may not respect *you* as a person per se—maybe you are not a person under the given concept, but a computer; I may not respect you as *this* particular individual—some would say I don't esteem you; but still, as long as I am ready to enter into dialogue with you, I am treating *you* as a valuable counterpart in *this* dialogue. Does not the willingness to listen to what others say amount to some kind of nontrivial respect for persons as speakers? Even so, it does not imply that respect for persons is a condition for being able to show respect for what is said. We may simply suppose that it implies some kind of respect to be further qualified, something that a dialogical interaction promotes as its by-product. What would this respect be like? It is neither an a priori presupposition nor a condition of possibility of dialogue: dialogue could take place for strategic reasons and thus without any appreciation of you as a valuable counterpart. This respect would be best conceived as a second-order disposition that dialogue may promote and stabilize. This by no means implies that we need a priori to specify the determinate content of the other that is being recognized or respected (human individual, moral agent, rational being, talking animal, community member, and so forth). This varies contextually and should be left to the participants in the dialogue themselves. Note that it would be difficult to classify this respect either as recognition/status respect or merit/esteem respect, since it seems to have to do both with your status as a participant in a dialogue and with my appraisal of your individuality. It would be a mixed form, as I think it always is, and we should not try to overdetermine its content a priori. The bent toward a normative overdetermination of the disposition to

recognize, in order to keep public discourse open, could in fact, as I have argued, set too many restrictions on the openness of the discourse and in the end undermine the dialogical situation itself.

NOTES

1. On this, see especially Sennett 2003, chapter 8.
2. Of course, this is a rather peculiar understanding of respect and equality, and one should ask whether impartiality so understood isn't a form of equality, at least equality as expressed in the principle of formal justice formulated by Perelman: treating similar cases in similar ways and different ones in different ways (Perelman and Olbrechts-Tyteca 1958, §52).
3. This could be said not only of the supposed kind of recognition respect we have in public dialogues but also of specifically moral Kantian versions of personal recognition respect, even in Darwall's second-person standpoint (2005; for a second-person standpoint approach, compare Bagnoli 2007), where you are respected as an autonomous being and hence as an instantiation of moral law. This does not satisfy our intuition that personal respect should be an individualizing act, referring to the person as *this* individual—just you (on this, see Galeotti 2008, 29). Let's assume that equal respect bona fide should be given in a reciprocal I-thou relation of co-authority—where I demand of you, and vice versa, to be recognized as your equal. Were this reciprocal respect, it could not be required for it to be a universal principle of discourse.
4. Regarding the two versions of Darwall's specific account of universal respect, the first one, in the third person (1977), is neither specific for persons (there are kinds of recognition respect we owe to claims and norms), nor indefeasible and unconditional: this respect for epistemic authority is retractable in dialogue and conditional on epistemic merits. The second version (2005), in the second person, seems to be specific to moral respect for persons, and that's why it cannot be useful for understanding the kind of respect we eventually need in all kinds of dialogue (except for some moral dialogues).
5. An anonymous referee suggested that even if we should not show equal respect to the people we are arguing with, we should nevertheless give equal respect to the content of their arguments—in other words, show equal respect for what is said, for the reasons they advance. Even if it were possible to construe this as a case of equal respect for reasons, I doubt that this would prove that respect for persons—and in particular a priori respect for persons per se—is a necessary condition for respect for what is said. Even if some constraints in dialogue could be construed as norms of equal respect, under some particular interpretation of equality (not necessarily a universalistic one), that would not in itself imply that these are norms of equal respect for persons. The burden of proof should be on those who assume this connection and the need for a notion of personhood to account for these norms of dialogue.
6. One may object that it is not clear which sense of "moral personhood" is being invoked here. And in fact it isn't; very often, public discourses, in applying the ambiguous notion of respect for persons, make an opaque appeal to metaphysical notions of moral personhood (such as in the "loving the sinner and not the sin" case).
7. On this see also Margalit 1996, chapter 4.
8. For this notion in relation to the issue of justice, see Fraser 2005.
9. On this issue, see Cantù and Testa 2007.
10. On "legitimate disagreement," see especially Kock 2007.

REFERENCES

Bagnoli, Carla. 2007. *L'autorità della morale*. Milan: Feltrinelli.
Cantù, Paola, and Italo Testa. 2007. "Is Common Ground a Word or Just a Sound? Second Order Consensus and Argumentation Theory." In *Dissensus and the Search for Common Ground*, ed. Hans V. Hansen, Christopher W. Tindale, John Blair, Ralph H. Johnson, and David M. Godden, 1–9. CD-ROM. Windsor, Ont.: OSSA.
Darwall, Stephen. 1977. "Two Kinds of Respect." *Ethics* 88:36–49.
———. 2005. "Respect and the Second Person Standpoint." *Proceedings and Addresses of the APA* 78 (2): 43–59.
Dryzek, John S., and Simon Niemeyer. 2006. "Reconciling Pluralism and Consensus as Political Ideals." *American Journal of Political Science* 50 (3): 634–49.
Frankfurt, Harry. 1997. "Equality and Respect." *Social Research* 64 (1): 3–15.
Fraser, Nancy. 2005. "Reframing Justice in a Globalizing World." *New Left Review* 36: 69–88.
Galeotti, Anna E. 2008. "Rispetto come riconoscimento: Alcune riflessioni politiche." In *Eguale rispetto*, ed. Ian Carter, Anna E. Galeotti, and Valeria Ottonelli, 24–53. Milan: Bruno Mondadori.
Habermas, Jürgen. 1996. *Between Facts and Norms: Contributions to a Discourse Theory of Law and Democracy*. Cambridge: Polity Press.
Hill, Thomas E., Jr. 1998. "Respect for Persons." In *The Routledge Encyclopedia of Philosophy*, ed. Edward Craig, 283–87. London: Routledge.
Kock, Christian. 2007. "Norms of Legitimate Dissensus." *Informal Logic* 27 (2): 179–96.
Margalit, Avishai. 1996. *The Decent Society*. Cambridge: Harvard University Press.
Perelman, Chaïm, and Lucie Olbrechts-Tyteca. 1958. *Traité de l'argumentation: La nouvelle rhétorique*. Paris: PUF.
Sennett, Richard. 2003. *Respect in a World of Inequality*. New York: W. W. Norton.
Walton, Douglas N. 1998. *The New Dialectic: Conversational Contexts of Argument*. Toronto: University of Toronto Press.
Walton, Douglas, and Erik C. W. Krabbe. 1995. *Commitment in Dialogue: Basic Concepts of Interpersonal Reasoning*. Albany: State University of New York Press.
Williams, Bernard. 1973. "The Idea of Equality." In Williams, *Problems of the Self*, 230–49. Cambridge: Cambridge University Press.

5

DIALECTICAL CITIZENSHIP?
SOME THOUGHTS ON THE ROLE OF PRAGMATICS
IN THE ANALYSIS OF PUBLIC DEBATE

Niels Møller Nielsen

A Complex Model of Public Debate

It is widely recognized that the life of the middle sibling is often pretty tough. You don't get to be spoiled like the younger sibling, and you don't get the attention and freedom of the older one. You get the worst of both worlds. Dialectic is the middle sibling between little sister Rhetoric and big sister Logic. Seen from the logical side, dialectic lacks consistency and rigor and the obvious benefit of having a concept of truth. Seen from the side of rhetoric, dialectic is rigid and oriented toward an ideal of dispute resolution that has very little, if any, bearing on the real communication practices that rhetoric deals with.

Arguably, pragmatics is a modern theory of dialectic.[1] Its aim is to lay out the constitutive rules for rational communication, where "rational" is understood in an expanded sense—it centers not only on *logos* but covers also norms and values. In this chapter I argue that the middle sibling, in its pragmatic guise, has an important part to play in the rhetorical analysis of public debate.

Public, mediated debate is a phenomenon of great importance for democratic processes and the agency of citizenship. It needs to be studied and understood, and that task has often fallen on the disciplines of rhetoric and speech communication. They have a tendency to understand the phenomenon as a process where the persuasive force is directed at the third party, the audience. In fact, it would be a breach of the genre if one interlocutor should indeed succeed in persuading another during a normally formatted TV debate.

The triangular constellation of two (or more) interlocutors and an audience has led rhetorical analysts to adopt a so-called trialogical model that sets the debate apart from the critical discussion; a debate is defined by its trialogical persuasion, a critical discussion by its dialogical persuasion (cf. Jørgensen 1998).

I argue that whereas the trialogical model is useful for distinguishing complex, multipositional forms of communication from simple, dialogical forms, the analysis of debate is better off with a more advanced model that conceives of debate as a dialogical constellation (mapping the relationship between debate interlocutors) embedded in a monological constellation (mapping the relationship between media institution and media audience). This model is better suited to explaining various linguistic features of the debate.

While debate is clearly directed toward the persuasion of the audience, a typical feature of a debate is the presence of what I refer to as the *demonstration of dialectical virtue*, moves that are dialogical, reasonable, and aimed at achieving and preserving mutual respect and understanding between the interlocutors. I further argue that such dialectical virtues are best studied as reflections of the kind of communicative trust that is described as a constitutive rule for communication in the discipline of normative pragmatics.[2]

To make this argument, I discuss the idea of normativity as a perspective in a theory of communication. I argue that the contribution of normative pragmatics in the study of argumentative discourse is the insight that any form of language use is governed by language users' mutual expectations of the cooperative endeavor toward the goal of reaching mutual understanding. Such expectations refer to a necessary yet counterfactual ideal presupposed in the performance of communicative acts, and this ideal forms the basis of what I call dialectical virtue.

By way of conclusion, I also briefly discuss how the counterfactual ideal of language is present at a higher level of discourse—the level where democratic processes are played out. I argue that the rhetorical constellation in the model (between the media institution and the audience) is also influenced by expectations connected to a counterfactual ideal, closely associated with the ideal of language. The public space where political decisions are made can be expected to be a dialogical event to which citizens have access; however, in the absence of such access, the media are obliged to act as a substitute public sphere. I argue that such legitimacy is based partly on the demonstration of dialectical virtue in the debates.

The Hypothesis: Balancing Efficiency and Virtue

Drawing on analyses of extracts from the presidential debates of the American 2004 election, I suggest that an analysis of public debate needs to distinguish between at least two levels of inquiry, that of the relationship between the interlocutors (the dialectical level—an exchange based on normative expectations in situated context) and that between the media institution and the media audience (the rhetorical level—a strategic persuasion event in institutional context). The former is embedded in the latter, so that the dialectical level of communication in and of itself serves as a persuasive element at the rhetorical level.

The underlying hypothesis is as follows:

The public, mediated debate is felicitous when interlocutors succeed in striking a delicate balance between persuasiveness of two different kinds:

1. *Employing whatever strategic means necessary to make some viewpoint appear convincing (or to make the counterpart's viewpoint look unconvincing) to the audience.*
2. *Being communicatively virtuous, that is, by employing conversational strategies aimed at consensus—as if one would be ready to concede the other party's viewpoint, given sufficiently strong argumentation.*

These two levels influence each other reciprocally. Being communicatively virtuous (as in 2) turns out to be a strategic means for persuading the audience (as in 1), and persuasiveness of type 1 influences persuasiveness of type 2 by rendering the apparent consensus seeking hypothetical: the strategic viewpoint of audience persuasion turns the dialogue into a demonstration of dialectical virtue rather than an actual search for mutual understanding.

The Trialogical Constellation

In her 1998 paper, Charlotte Jørgensen addresses the tendency of various argumentation scholars (exemplified in Douglas N. Walton) to portray debate as inferior to the ideal of critical discussion. Jørgensen rightly observes that whereas critical discussion is often portrayed in its ideal, normative form, debate is characterized descriptively with all the shortcomings that any form of argumentation shows in practice. She suggests a normative model where both discussion and debate are seen as normative ideals, and both may be seen empirically to degrade into eristic. Theoretically, the difference between them lies only in their "constellations,"[3] discussion being dialogical and debate "trialogical" (since the third party, the audience, is the persuadee).[4]

The trialogical constellation would look something like the model depicted in figure 5.1. I tend to agree that the two forms of argumentation serve different purposes, that neither is nobler than the other, and that they should be accounted for on equal terms in a theoretical exposition of their features. However, I find that the ideal behind critical discussion is far more basic than the ideal behind debate. The ideal underlying critical discussion is consensus—that is, the normative ideal underlying normative pragmatics, and that is by no means reducible to one among many genres of argumentation. In normative pragmatics, the consensus ideal is central to the philosophical description of language use, as in the universal pragmatics of Habermas (1976).[5]

The "Trialogical" Constellation

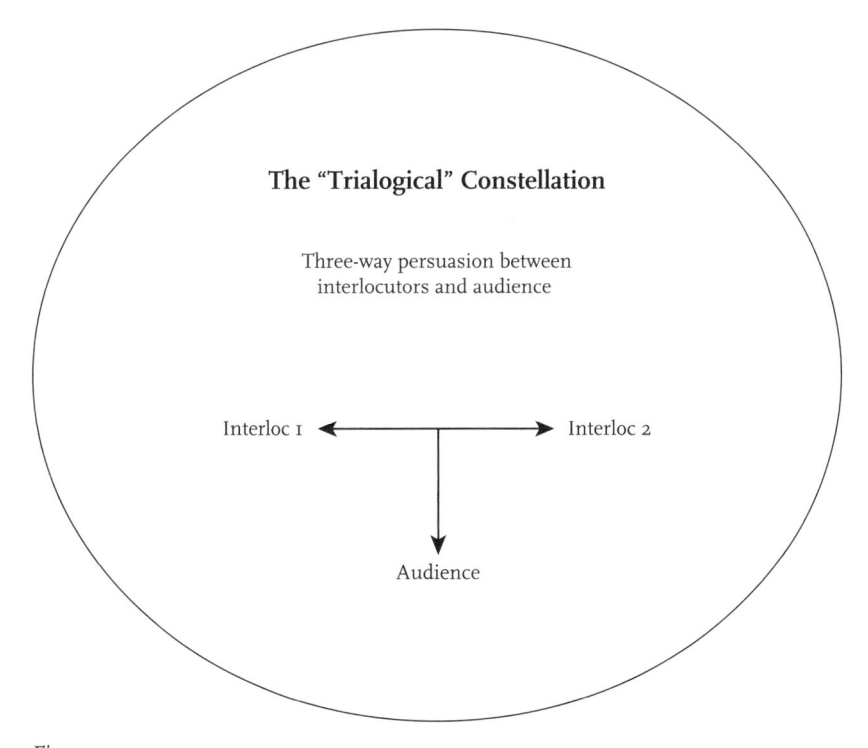

Three-way persuasion between interlocutors and audience

Interloc 1 ←————→ Interloc 2
                ↓
            Audience

Fig. 5.1

Consequently, the discussion of my hypothesis must take as its starting point the concept of normativity and the role of the normative ideal in a theory of communication. The role of the normative ideal is central to understanding how dialectical analysis complements rhetorical analysis in the analysis of public debate. The contribution of the pragmatic-dialectical analysis is to show how debates balance between strategic maneuvering and dialectical virtue in a subtle interplay between conversation and audience persuasion.

On Normativity: Factual Consequences of Counterfactual Ideals

A basic analysis of language as action indicates that in performing a constative speech act you are obliged to be truthful; in performing a regulative speech act you incur an obligation to social rightness; and in performing a representative speech act you are obligated to be sincere. These validity criteria constitutive of the general speech act types lead to the understanding that were we able to create a space where the use of speech acts was unhindered by any other forces, such as physical or social power, then communication in that space would eventually lead to consensus.

This view deliberately disregards the empirical realities of language use: all other things being equal, language is designed to make us understand one another, not to make us misunderstand one another. All other things being not so equal, it is a different matter. Habermas has made a case for this analysis in many versions, most prominently in his universal pragmatics (1976). The argument is that the orientation toward consensus exists primarily as an expectation central to the communicative competence of language users.

Habermas has often been misinterpreted on this point. He has been taken to mean that some form of a dominance-free communication sphere could exist in which language users would eventually reach consensus on some matter. These misinterpretations, however, have usually overlooked the fact that Habermas continually stresses that this ideal space, liberated of all sources of power, is *counterfactual*. It does not exist, never has existed, and never will exist. The theoretical understanding of language is abstract, universal, dealing with language out of empirical context. In any empirical context all kinds of noise and effects of social and systemic sources of power render any ideal kind of consensus impossible. This is no news to proponents of universal pragmatics; in fact, it is a central point. Lies, deception, betrayal, seduction, and other such perlocutions are only possible because they utilize the default expectation of validity criteria being respected. "You can lie only to someone who expects you to be truthful" is the vernacular version of the argument for a universal pragmatics. Hence a pragmatic approach is well equipped to deal with lies, betrayal, and linguistic seduction, since such actions can be identified as violations of presupposed norms of language.

The theoretical understanding of language as consensus-oriented behavior is important when dealing with empirical reality, because it helps us understand the expectations of the language users. Why bother to listen to one another in the first place? Because it is worthwhile—interlocutors have reasoned expectations that there is something to gain, that the counterpart has something to contribute that is useful, gives insight or understanding, is pleasurable, and so forth. Grice's theory of conversational implicature (1975, 1989) is basically an attempt at a coherent understanding of such expectations and explains how they generate inferential processes that eventually turn out as *meaning*.[6]

So pragmatics deals with communicative expectations and how they generate inferential meaning. Given that fact, pragmatics often tends to deal with the subject matter of dialectic rather than that of rhetoric. Dialectic is the field where the rules of rational conversation obtain. Various attempts have been made at giving a coherent theory of the pragmatics of argumentative discourse, notably in the work of van Eemeren and Grootendorst (1984, 1992, 2004; van Eemeren et al. 1993) and Walton (1995).

This chapter is concerned with the idea of the counterfactual ideal and its output of very real consequences. At present it is not so important that there is no final theory of the rules of conversation; what is important is that the above-mentioned theories employ a counterfactual ideal as background for understanding language. Like Habermas's analysis, Grice's cooperation hypothesis is clearly counterfactual: Gricean implicature theory explicitly understands meaning as communicative content derived not by obeying but by flouting (openly disobeying) the maxims of the cooperation principle. In argumentation theory, van Eemeren and Grootendorst relate to the counterfactual ideal of critical discussion. Common to all is that strategic language uses become meaningful only on the background of the counterfactual ideal.

Levels of Inquiry: From Conversational Organization to Institutional Discourse

Empirical, linguistic events such as public, mediated debates can be studied at different levels, giving different kinds of output. However, it is in the way these levels interact that real explanations emerge. Thus the study of debate needs to take into account the whole picture, regardless of which level is of particular interest.

I envision public, mediated debate as a phenomenon that can be understood at least at four levels[7] of contextual abstraction:

At the *linguistic* level, events are seen in *sequential context*, that is, as activities that are the product of preceding turns in the conversation and preparatory to the following turns. Empirical data consist of microlinguistic events; the discipline dealing with data at this level is *conversation analysis*.

Such sequences make up the next level, the *dialectical level*, at which events are understood in *situational context*, in order to reconstruct interlocutors' inferential processes and interactive production of dialogical meaning. Empirical data consist of speech acts and implicatural moves; the discipline dealing with them is *pragmatics*.

Such processes make up the *rhetorical level*, where communicative events must be understood in *institutional context*, in order to understand how dialogue becomes persuasive argument directed at the media audience. Empirical data consist of the broadcast event in its entirety; the discipline dealing with this analysis is *rhetoric*.

The rhetorical processes in turn make up the societal level, where institutions and other power structures are analyzed in their *cultural context*, in order to understand how the media institution reproduces itself as a late modern substitute for the public sphere. These phenomena are studied in such disciplines as *sociology* and *cultural studies*.

Most important in this context is the relationship between the middle levels, the rhetorical and the dialectical. I suggest that a model mapping both levels and their mutual relationship is more adequate than the model of the trialogical constellation.

The model in figure 5.2 depicts how debate can be analyzed as a dialectical constellation involving the discussion between the interlocutors (including the mediating journalists, present audience members, etc.), embedded in a rhetorical constellation between the media and the media audience.

I hope to highlight below how this approach may prove useful, and how analysis at the dialectical level, utilizing insights from normative pragmatics,

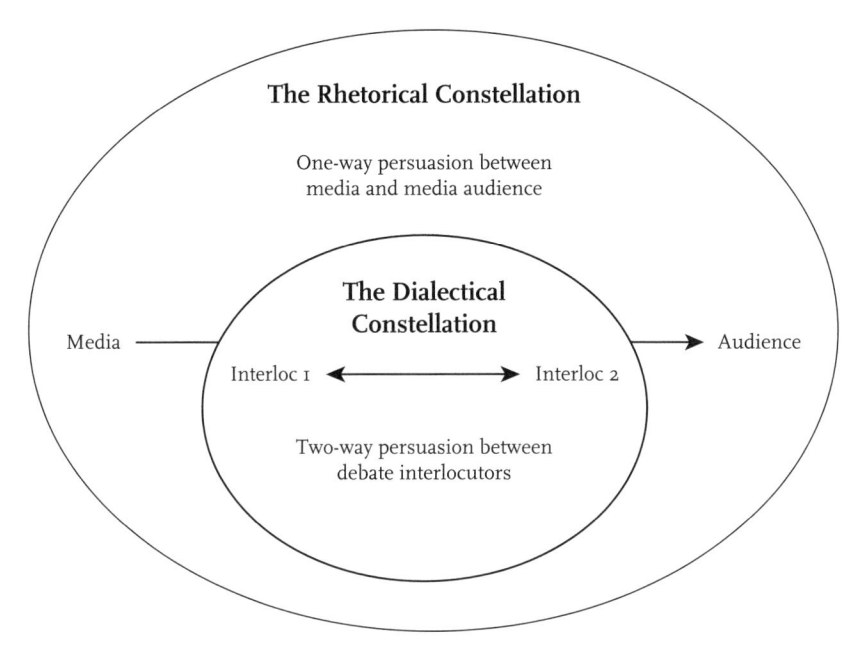

```
                    The Rhetorical Constellation

              One-way persuasion between
                 media and media audience

                       The Dialectical
                         Constellation
   Media ─────                                      ────▶ Audience
              Interloc 1 ◀─────────▶ Interloc 2

               Two-way persuasion between
                  debate interlocutors
```

Fig. 5.2

forms crucial premises for the argumentation in the overarching rhetorical situation.

Dialectical Virtues in Debates

I do not intend to give an exhaustive presentation of a piece of empirical debate. I merely present a few examples of dialectical virtues becoming apparent in debates, taken from a general election debate between John Kerry and George W. Bush in 2004.[8] The features presented are omnipresent in any debate, not specific to any one debate. Their omnipresence can indeed make them hard to spot, but I argue that the analysis of such linguistic features is important for thoroughly understanding the discourse on the higher, more broadly relevant levels of analysis.

Pragmatic Meaning: How?

Pragmatic meaning is generally thought to range on a scale from almost semantically coded meaning to fully inferential and context-sensitive implicatures. In the small excerpt chosen for analysis here, numerous examples of all kinds are present.

In (1), Bush is asked to give an account of Kerry's character as a possible future president.

> (1) And that's my biggest concern about my opponent. I admire his service. But I just know how this world works, and that in the councils of government, there must be certainty from the U.S. president.

The contrasting "but" between "I admire his service" and "I just know how this world works" is known in pragmatic theory as generating a conventional implicature—roughly a member of the class of presuppositions. The implicature is: "Kerry does not know how this world works." This is pragmatic meaning of an almost semantic nature, since it is traceable to coded meaning, in this case the functional meaning of the word "but." Bush need not state directly that he thinks Kerry is ignorant of the workings of the real world. He can rely on our communicative expectations to help us work out the implicature. As we shall see, the effort to avoid compromising the counterpart's face directly, as evident in this example, is a dialectical virtue.

An example from the other end of the scale, the so-called particularized conversational implicatures, shows how the context-sensitive kinds of implicature are only observable as dialogical phenomena: implicatures only become manifest when hearers reconstruct them.

> (2) Bush: And it is one of the things I've learned in the White House, is that there's enormous pressure on the president, and he cannot wilt under that pressure. Otherwise, the world won't be better off. . . .
> Kerry: I have no intention of wilting. I've never wilted in my life. And I've never wavered in my life.

In a Gricean framework it is to be expected that conversation relies heavily on the cooperation principle. Thus one should expect that a lot of the meaning remains unsaid—or more specifically that it is conveyed indirectly by flouting maxims, thus placing clues for the hearer to infer the full meaning. In (2), Kerry produces a counterargument, but it is directed at something Bush has implicated, not *said:* Kerry would wilt as a president.

The analysis reveals that the exchange is *rational:* while seemingly incoherent (Bush has not claimed that Kerry would wilt, so superficially Kerry's reply seems irrelevant), the counterargument is actually very precise. Being accused (indirectly, by way of implicature) of having a weak or unstable character, Kerry replies that he has never wilted, and thus, it can be inferred, that he is unlikely to do so as president.

This exchange exemplifies how argumentative conversation is often much more rational than it appears at the surface. Obviously, conducting a coherent and rational line of thought counts as a dialectical virtue.

Pragmatic Meaning: Why?

Why don't people just say what they mean? At least two answers are possible; one emanates from cognitive considerations and points out that the processing time in the articulatory part of the communicative chain is several thousand times slower than the processing time of inferential processes in the brain. So articulation constitutes a "bottleneck" in the conveyance of meaning, and hence it is economical to leave as much meaning as possible to inference (cf. Levinson 2000). Another explanation is social and deals with the necessity of maintaining social relations, which may occasionally conflict with communicative goals. Interlocutors need to "soften" potentially offending communication by leaving it indirect but still capable of being comprehended through defeasible inference.

Both kinds of motivation for pragmatic inference are at work in almost all communication, but when we want to understand how the dialectical and the rhetorical levels interact, motivations of the second kind are more important.

Returning to (1) and (2), if Bush does not explicitly articulate what he means—namely, that (1) Kerry does not know how this world works, and (2) Kerry would wilt as president—but rather leaves these meanings to be inferred by the hearer, this can be explained as motivated by the desire to maintain certain social conditions. It is important that these conditions are of different kinds and serve different functions at the dialectical and rhetorical levels.

At the dialectical level, (1) and (2) instantiate positive "facework" in the sense of Brown and Levinson (1987).[9] Bush avoids offending Kerry's positive face, that is, he preserves his need to be accepted in the social context at hand.

The debate displays various other examples of the candidates performing speech acts whose sole purpose seems to be to preserve the other's positive face:

(3) Bush: Well, first of all, I admire Senator Kerry's service to our country. I admire the fact that he is a great dad.
(4) Bush: I admire the fact that he served for 20 years in the Senate. Although I'm not so sure I admire the record.

Politeness and respect are dialectical virtues. To cooperate in reaching reciprocal understanding, you need to display acceptance and respect for the other party's competence as a language user, his knowledge and his personal and moral integrity. Such virtues, again, are almost omnipresent in (noneristic) communication, although their frequency and quality depend on genre, speech situation, and culture. However, in complex situations like mediated debates, they have quite different purposes on the overarching rhetorical level.

At that level, acts like (3) and (4) are not acts of respect or politeness but demonstrations of dialectical virtue, seeking the media audience's approval. They become rhetorical devices designed to build the speaker's ethos, not the counterpart's face. At the rhetorical level there is hardly any desire to actually support the counterpart's face, so reservations such as the one seen in (4) are to be expected: Bush admires Senator Kerry's long service in the Senate, but not "the record," which rather deflates his admiration; long service is hardly admirable in itself.

Debates are complex and require complex analytic strategies. They must be studied at the levels of dialectic and rhetoric at the same time. Most important is to discuss how requirements and norms on the two levels interact. Analysis of mediated debate is the analysis of the interplay between dialectical and rhetorical strategies.

At the dialectical level, certain features of the rhetorical level influence and constrain the conversation, which becomes artificial because the interlocutors only apparently address each other; but even so, they still employ dialectical strategies explainable within normative pragmatic theory. At the rhetorical level, communication occurs between the images of the interlocutors as media constructs and, in a one-way conveyance of meaning, the media audience. This event can be analyzed with rhetorical methods but is still constrained by features of dialectical rationality.

The Ghost of the Public Sphere: The Media Substituting the Citizen's Speaker Position

In my model, the dialectical constellation—displaying dialectical virtue—is embedded in the rhetorical constellation. In conclusion, I wish to suggest that the rhetorical level of the model depicts the media as assuming the role of a substitute public sphere seeking justification as such, thus depending on their ability to demonstrate dialectical virtues reminiscent of the ideal of the classic public sphere. I believe that this argument follows directly from the proposed relationship between the two levels depicted in the model; however, space prevents a full discussion, so it will remain a mere outline intended for further discussion.

I see the media institution, rather than the debaters themselves, as the sender of an argument intended to persuade the audience. Thus the debaters are mediated constructs playing a particular role in a process where the media seek legitimacy in the democratic process—the media need, as part of their self-image as the watchdogs of democracy, to demonstrate that they do in fact function as the revitalized public sphere often called for by intellectuals in recent decades.[10] I argue that central to such a demonstration is the emphasis on spontaneity and dialogue, however unspontaneous and undialogical debates may actually be. But it is crucial for the institutional media to have public, televised debates appear as viable substitutions for the lost art of deliberative debate, so deeply rooted in our view of ourselves as citizens in a representative democracy.

The counterfactual ideal of language, discussed above, as the cornerstone of a pragmatic philosophy of language is echoed in theories of the public sphere.[11] The bourgeois public sphere portrayed by Habermas (1971) is a historical idea rather than an empirical phenomenon. Arguably, however, it does exist as a counterfactual ideal—in a sense, universal pragmatics describes the rules for deliberative discussion in an ideal public sphere.

So, while any empirical attempt to describe late modern processes of democracy would probably uncover a range of various publics (note the plural),[12] it does make sense to discuss practices as consequences of self-understandings grounded in counterfactual ideals. In this light, we may understand the behavior of the media toward important democratic events as strongly influenced by a self-understanding not unlike the role of the bourgeois public sphere. The argument is that the media's legitimacy hinges on their function as caretakers of a public debate that can transform mass-mediated, one-way communication into something that emulates ideal discussions in an ideal public sphere.

As I have argued, debates contain demonstrations of dialectical virtues that, on a higher level, serve the rhetorical constellation. These traces of deliberative reason can be explained at this higher rhetorical level: as suggested in the analysis of the Bush-Kerry debate, dialectical rationality adopted as ethos virtues at the rhetorical level explains why debates usually do not degenerate into eristic. Debaters cannot afford to appear dialectically incompetent. They partake in the counterfactual yet highly active self-understanding of how we are supposed to decide on common issues in society: by way of rational conversation.

At the rhetorical level, that is, in the relationship between the media and the audience, the media depend on features demonstrating how one-way communication can substitute for the public sphere. Debates have the distinctive feature of being formally dialogical. While not providing an actual discussion forum, the media can instead *transmit* conversation, thus emulating public discussion. Journalists and commentators acting as mediators in debates lend their voices to the passive audience, ask the questions that people would ask, and make the challenges and critiques that people would make were they partaking in actual public discussion. Thus debates can contribute to the media's legitimacy as caretakers of the public processes of democracy.

Rhetorical citizenship is about incorporating the citizen in democratic processes, about creating positions from which citizens can become effectively engaged and influential in democracy. The central conclusion with regard to rhetorical citizenship is that there is reason to distinguish between the various levels of inquiry; when you analyze the complex interplay between the dialectical and rhetorical constellations, you are really dealing with how a substitute public sphere is *performed* in order to make the media audience conceive of itself as less isolated than it would otherwise appear to be at the passive end of one-way mass media. Thus the analysis of deliberative debate as a dialectical exchange is really an analysis of the creation of a substitute for the citizen's position as a speaker.

NOTES

1. This is a widely recognized view, especially in the Amsterdam school of argumentation studies. Cf., e.g., van Eemeren and Grootendorst 2004.
2. The word "normative" can mean a variety of things. It is broadly used to denote practices that are regulatory or in some other way aimed at social change or, in some instances, emancipation. Often this meaning has a ring of idealism to it, signaling a certain underlying morality. In the case of pragmatics, it has no moral or ethical import and does not mean "rule-setting" but "rule-governed." It refers to the notion that communicative action is based on constitutive rather than regulative rules. For this crucial distinction, cf. Searle 1969.
3. Jørgensen 1998 uses the word "constellation" to refer to the distribution of distinct participant roles in an argumentative setting.
4. As will become evident, the idea of a trialogical constellation is not viable when you look at debates as an activity taking place simultaneously on two levels, each level having its own set of sender-receiver constellations.
5. Of course, the normative background is not unique to pragmatics; indeed, the field of rhetoric defines itself as normative (cf. Kock 1997). However, it is not obvious that the idea of normativity is the same in the two instances.
6. Grice (1994) famously defines meaning as the recognition of communicative intentionality. The later developments of Grice's philosophy of language (1975) build

on this concept of meaning, involving the suggestion of particular maxims regulating the inferential understanding of the intended message based on a normative principle of cooperation.

7. The four levels are simplifications intended to clarify the point. In the context of studying empirical language data, they should be taken as closely interrelated perspectives.

8. For a transcript of the debate, see http://www.debates.org/pages/trans2004a.html.

9. Brown and Levinson's concept of face is an adaptation of the concept originally proposed by Goffman (1967).

10. See, for example, Goodnight's influential paper on the subject calling for a revival driven by critique: "If the public sphere is to be revitalized, then those practices which replace deliberative rhetoric by substituting alternative modes of invention and restricting subject matter need to be uncovered and critiqued" (1982, 227).

11. Habermas's theories of communicative action (1984) and universal pragmatics (1976) are in many respects reflections of his earlier work on the transformation of the bourgeois public sphere (1971), in that these later theoretical developments explain—on a pragmatic level—how the idea of public reason is mirrored in the validity criteria of language: basically, the ideal public sphere relies on the criteria of truthfulness, social rightness, and sincerity, as well as on the need to be shielded from the influence of power, noise, and money, in order to be the truly critical instrument of democracy.

12. Cf. Hauser's (1997) reply to Phillips (1997).

REFERENCES

Brown, Penelope, and Stephen C. Levinson. 1987. *Politeness: Some Universals in Language Usage*. Cambridge: Cambridge University Press.
Eemeren, Franz H. van, and Rob Grootendorst. 1984. *Speech Acts in Argumentative Discussions*. Dordrecht: Foris.
———. 1992. *Argumentation, Communication, and Fallacies*. Hillsdale, N.J.: Lawrence Erlbaum.
———. 2004. *A Systematic Theory of Argumentation: The Pragma-Dialectical Approach*. Cambridge: Cambridge University Press.
Eemeren, Franz H. van, Rob Grootendorst, Sally Jackson, and Scott Jacobs. 1993. *Reconstructing Argumentative Discourse*. Tuscaloosa: University of Alabama Press.
Goffman, Erving. 1967. "On Facework: An Analysis of Ritual Elements in Social Interaction." In *The Discourse Reader*, ed. Adam Jaworski and Nikolas Coupland, 306–21. London: Routledge.
Goodnight, G. Thomas. 1982. "The Personal, Technical, and Public Spheres of Argument: A Speculative Inquiry into the Art of Public Deliberation." *Journal of the American Forensic Association* 18:214–27.
Grice, H. P. 1975. "Logic and Conversation." In *Syntax and Semantics III: Speech Acts*, ed. P. Cole and J. L. Morgan, 41–58. New York: Academic Press.
———. 1989. *Studies in the Way of Words*. Cambridge: Harvard University Press.
———. 1994. "Meaning." In *Basic Topics in the Philosophy of Language*, ed. Robert N. Harnish, 21–40. New York: Harvester Wheatsheaf. (Orig. pub. 1957.)
Habermas, Jürgen. 1971. *Borgerlig offentlighet*. Oslo: Gyldendal.
———. 1976. "Was heisst Universalpragmatik." In *Sprachpragmatik und Philosophie*, ed. K. O. Apel, 174–272. Frankfurt am Main: Suhrkamp Verlag.
———. 1984. *The Theory of Communicative Action: Reason and the Rationalization of Society*. Cambridge: Polity Press.

Hauser, Gerard A. 1997. "On Publics and Public Spheres: A Response to Phillips." *Communication Monographs* 64:275–79.
Jørgensen, Charlotte. 1998. "Public Debate: An Act of Hostility?" *Argumentation* 12:431–43.
Kock, Christian. 1997. "Retorikkens Identitet." *Rhetorica Scandinavica* 1:10–19.
Levinson, Stephen C. 2000. *Presumptive Meanings: The Theory of Generalized Conversational Implicature.* Cambridge: MIT Press.
Phillips, Kendall R. 1997. "The Spaces of Public Dissension: Reconsidering the Public Sphere." *Communication Monographs* 63:231–48.
Searle, John R. 1969. *Speech Acts: An Essay in the Philosophy of Language.* Cambridge: Cambridge University Press.
Walton, Douglas N. 1989. *Informal Logic: A Handbook for Critical Argumentation.* Cambridge: Cambridge University Press.
———. 1995. *A Pragmatic Theory of Fallacy.* Tuscaloosa: University of Alabama Press.

6

PROVOCATIVE STYLE:
THE GAARDER DEBATE EXAMPLE

Marie Lund Klujeff

Everyday debates rarely live up to the ideals of reason and soundness of argumentation. Thus criticism of actual political and cultural debates is often negative. My claim is that provocative style, mordant irony, and caustic sarcasm are not simply violations of deliberative ideals but vital elements of debate, helping to shape *presence*, structure argument, form opinion, and constitute an engaged and reflective audience. My critical approach is closely coordinated with Gerard Hauser's theory of public deliberation and presents a critical scrutiny of a debate on Israel and the Jews started by the Norwegian writer Jostein Gaarder in 2006.

Adjusting the Norms: A Rhetorical Model

There is a tangible difference between idealized norms of public communication and the actual debates that constitute everyday deliberation. From a rhetorical point of view, the norms may be set too high. According to Gerard Hauser, negative evaluation is the inevitable outcome of measuring everyday debates by the high standards of ideal speech.

In *Vernacular Voices* (1999), Hauser outlines how pessimism and apathy govern our understanding of public deliberation and political processes: "We still outwardly acknowledge the importance of democratic processes but the deliberative characteristics of public discussion . . . are under assault" (24). Disillusionment with, and cynicism toward, "the public" and public deliberation are to a large degree the results of an increasingly marketing-based attitude on the part of political parties and the media, reducing political processes to negative campaigning, reliance on focus groups, and opinion polling. According to Hauser, "Commentators, critics, and theorists surveying this scene are thereby led to a single and compelling conclusion: 'the public' is moribund" (30). Hauser, however, finds that reports of the imminent demise of the public are exaggerated: "Their distortion comes from looking for 'the public' in the wrong places through conceptual lenses radically out of focus" (30). The premises are wrong, or—extending the optical metaphor—the lenses are adjusted to Habermas's rationalistic theory of public communication but are out of focus when it comes to what goes on in everyday deliberation. Hauser finds that one of the most obvious problems in Habermas's theory is the grounding of "the public" in shared interests, the idea that discursive deliberation can be defined as disinterested parties discussing some common good: "Habermas envisions a universalized public sphere populated by disinterested participants who adhere to rationalistic norms and unitary modes of expression on which they base warranted assent. This idealized vision is at odds with the rhetorical features of discourse as it is practiced in a democracy. The addressed and particularized character of discourse on public problems suggests that rhetorical assumptions are a more consonant alternative to those of ideal speech for assessing the discursive practices of actually existing democracy" (55).

Instead of defining "the public" by shared interests, Hauser introduces a rhetorical model in which "we may define a public as the interdependent members of society who hold different opinions about a mutual problem and who seek to influence its resolution through discourse" (32). Thus a public is an activity, and emphasis should be on the discursive process rather than on concrete political entities or groups. In a rhetorical model, participants need not be disinterested; in fact, personal engagement is a defining feature of persuasion.[1]

While Hauser dismisses certain aspects of Habermas's rationalistic model, he still believes that the assessment of rhetorical discourse and the critical inspection of a public sphere depend on some set of communicative norms. This is to be found in the rhetorical tradition. One obvious difference is that instead of testing the validity of discourse by universal norms, we can make judgments according to local conditions of reasoning applied by stakeholders (76). Hauser's rhetorical normative framework consists of five criteria (permeable boundaries, activity, contextualized language, believable appearance, tolerance), of which I focus on the two that are relevant to my purpose.

One criterion concerns *activity*, or more precisely, *engagement*. According to Hauser, "mass societies tend to treat audiences as passive; they are asked to purchase and to applaud. Publics, on the other hand, are presumed to have a guiding interest for which they have the potential to become active; they are asked their opinions" (77). I agree that activity and engagement among *participants* are core features in a rhetorical framework.[2]

The other rhetorical norm I adopt from Hauser is *tolerance*. Tolerance stems from the very definition of a public sphere as composed of members of society holding *different* opinions: "Because civil society is constituted by difference rather than identity, by *diversity* rather than unity, contact with alternative ideas and traditions is inevitable" (79). Tolerance, then, is a fundamental condition of communication when consensus is unlikely.

While engagement and tolerance are defining characteristics of public deliberation, as rhetorical norms they might be at odds at a practical level. This chapter explores the engaging function of provocative style and is concerned with the ways in which provocative features of style and argument initiate and constitute public deliberation as an engaged and engaging activity. Engagement and activity, however, should be weighed against other critical norms, such as tolerance of other people's opinions. The balancing of the rhetorical virtues of evoking active debate and maintaining mutual respect is not an easy critical task. I will discuss these difficulties in my critical assessment of the Gaarder-Kristol controversy.

The Function of Provocative Style

I argue that provocative style in public debate has a function, and that we err if we simply dismiss provocation as unconstructive. To fully understand the dynamics of public debates, we must study them from a relevant perspective and with relevant critical concepts. My conception of provocative style as a critical concept is an attempt to better understand properties of rhetorical discourse that are often seen, yet rarely appreciated. I draw on a few twentieth-century rhetorical theories that have established the basis for the argumentative and deliberative approach to style. Perelman and Olbrechts-Tyteca (1969) have done important work on the function of rhetorical figures in argumentation. Also relevant is their concept of *presence* as a strategic way to constitute salience. The very choice of giving presence to some elements instead of others implies their importance and pertinence to the discussion and acts directly on our sensibility, as illustrated by a Chinese parable: "A king sees an ox on its way to sacrifice. He is moved to pity for it and orders that a sheep be used in its place. He confesses he did so because he could see the ox but not the sheep" (116).

Perelman and Olbrechts-Tyteca relate *presence* to the function of certain rhetorical figures. Leaving the customary classifications of rhetorical figures, they discuss the argumentative effects of figures. One effect is to increase presence. The simplest figures for doing this are those depending on repetition, for instance, *anaphora*, or *interpretatio* (the explanation of one expression by another—not so much for clarification as to increase the feeling of *presence*) (175, 176).

Another major influence on my view of provocative style is Jeanne Fahnestock's *Rhetorical Figures in Science* (2002), a study of how (some) rhetorical figures structure argumentation and reasoning. Fahnestock sees rhetorical figures not as deviations from ordinary language but simply as linguistic choices. A figure functions as an epitome, a condensation of a longer line of argument: "In the presence of more text, it could be said, as the old manuals would put it, that the precise phrasing of this figure adds force or vividness to the whole argument. But it also is the argument itself in the most compressed form possible. If the text were to be reduced to one sentence, that one sentence, emblematic of the whole, would be the figure" (40).

Emphasizing the topical nature of figures, Fahnestock echoes an earlier study by James J. Murphy (1990), which, although short and suggestive, is particularly relevant to my position because it is not restricted to figures but suggests the relationship of topics and argumentation to style as such. Both Fahnestock and Murphy understand rhetorical figures as constitutive of meaning and argument rather than as some added quality.

This is crucial to an understanding of provocative style; style is not merely a superficial layer that can be removed with no real consequence for the argument. Style is the creator of thought, argument, and meaning. It cannot be isolated to *elocutio* but becomes part of *inventio*.

Furthermore, my idea of provocative style draws on some recent critical studies on rhetoric and style that all develop particular styles as a set of rhetorical characteristics. An example of this tendency is Robert Hariman's study of political style, in which style is taken to be a compilation of rhetorical features: "a political style is a coherent repertoire of rhetorical conventions depending on aesthetic reactions for political effect" (1995, 4). Similarly, Barry Brummett (2008) defines style as elements working together: "Style is a complex system of actions, objects, and behaviors that is used to form messages that announce who we are, who we want to be, and who we want to be considered akin to. It is therefore also a system of communication with rhetorical influence on others. And as such, style is a means by which power and advantage are negotiated, distributed, and struggled over in society" (xi).

Perhaps most evident in this respect is Karlyn Kohrs Campbell's elaborate description (1998) of the rhetorical characteristic of the feminine style.[3] The understanding of style as a coherent compendium is, however, far from novel; it is well established in the aesthetic tradition of studying style, for instance, in the application of style to period or nation.[4] But the recent studies deviate from an earlier, notably romantic identification of style as an essential quality of the artist's personality or the spirit of an epoch.[5] Instead, recent rhetorical critical studies build on an understanding of style as constitutive of argument and performative of identity, as does my own development of provocative style.

Although style, and by extension provocative style, is able to constitute both argumentation and deliberative action, some less celebrated implications need consideration as well. Provocative style is impertinence; it is a deliberate discursive trespassing against some norm of interaction. As such, the study of provocative style will reveal ad hominem arguments and sometimes even a general attitude of derogation of other people's opinions. Recapturing Hauser's rhetorical model, in provocative style the value of an engaged debate and an active public sphere is likely to be challenged by a scant tolerance. To bring matters to a head, provocations and personal attacks are often useful to debaters *because* they evoke the interest and attention of the attacked parties and other stakeholders. I return to the discussion of this evaluative dilemma in conclusion.

In the Gaarder-Kristol debate, at least, Gaarder's provocative style was a crucial catalyst to an engaged debate in an international public sphere. As such, it was no clear case of vernacular discourse in Hauser's sense: "The vernacular, by definition, is the aboriginal language used by the people of a country or district. It is the nonofficial language of the working class, peasants, certain ethnicities, and the marginalized" (2008, 443). On the contrary, the primary actors were professional writers using their language skills to fight their opponents. Still, provocative style shares some characteristics with the vernacular since it is a distinctly nonofficial discursive practice, a deliberate violation of the norms of official communication and communicative action. Similarly, vernacular language, according to Hauser, "stands apart from official ones used for public transactions within power relations, as occur in commerce, education, governance, law, and the professions" (443).

The Jostein Gaarder Debate

On 5 August 2006, Jostein Gaarder, the Norwegian best-selling author of the popular philosophical book *Sophie's World*, published an article in the Norwegian newspaper *Aftenposten*—a direct response to Israel's bombing of south Lebanon, containing a harsh critique of the state of Israel (2006b).[6]

The article opens with a denunciation: "Israel is now history. We no longer recognize the State of Israel." The main argument is that the state of Israel seems to act as if it had a divine and historical mandate for its actions. Gaarder attacks this notion from the perspective of a discursively constructed collective identity, a "we" who supposedly are more humanistic and rationalistic than the government of Israel:

> We don't believe in the notion of God's Chosen People. We laugh at this people's capriciousness and weep at its misdeeds. To act as God's Chosen People is not only stupid and arrogant, but a crime against humanity. We call it racism. There are limits to our patience, and there are limits to our tolerance. We do not believe in divine promises as a justification for occupation and apartheid. We have left the Middle Ages behind. We laugh uneasily at those who still believe that the god of flora, fauna and the galaxies has selected one people in particular as his favorite and given it silly stone tablets, burning bushes and a license to kill. We call baby killers "baby killers" and will never accept that people such as these have a divine or historic mandate excusing their outrages.

Gaarder is careful to distinguish between the Israeli government and the civilian population; his critique is aimed solely at the state: "May the world therefore have mercy upon the civilian population; for our prophecies of doom are not aimed at the civilian individuals. We wish the people of Israel well, nothing but wellness, but we reserve the right to not eat Jaffa oranges as long as they are foul tasting and poisonous." Yet he soon undermines the distinction, painting a vivid picture of hate-driven Israeli children supporting the war: "We ask ourselves if most Israelis think that one Israeli life is worth more than the forty Palestinian or Lebanese lives. For we've seen pictures of little Israeli girls writing hateful greetings on the bombs about to be dropped on the civilian populations of Lebanon and Palestine. The little Israeli girls are not cute when they burst with glee at the death and torment on the other side of the front."

Gaarder's criticism of the "rhetoric of the State of Israel" is structured as a confrontation between an ancient doctrine of vengeful Judaism and the more humanistic stance of Christianity: "We do not recognize the spiral of retribution and blood vengeance that comes with 'an eye for an eye and a tooth for a tooth.' . . . Two thousand years have passed since a Jewish rabbi criticized the ancient doctrine of 'an eye for an eye and a tooth for a tooth.' He said: 'Do unto others as you would have them do unto you.'"

The humanism of the "we" is demonstrated discursively once again in the conclusion, where Gaarder elaborates on, and thereby gives *presence* and salience to, his vision that Israel has ceased to exist. His prophecy of doom has come true, and Israelis have become fugitives: "Shoot not at the fugitives. Take not aim at them! They are vulnerable now—like snails without shells. . . . Give the Israeli refugees shelter; give them milk and honey!"

The provocative devices of Gaarder's contribution were consistent, yet simple. Instead of a sound, critical argument against Israel's policies, Gaarder produced a mockery of biblical language. His references to Jewish religious concepts as "silly stone tablets," "burning bushes," and "milk and honey" are obviously offensive to those who identify with them. Laconic, repetitive sentences imitate the prophecies of doom condemning Israel for its sins. In general, the style or tone of Gaarder's article parodies certain parts of the Bible. The effect of this stylistic choice is a line of reasoning that goes beyond a mere refutation of Israel's policies and actions. The stylistic parody functions as refutation by mockery, performing the idea it attacks: that the state of Israel has a divine mandate for its actions. As such, the style argues a point. In the subsequent debate, however, the offense in alluding to religious symbols and biblical language is bracketed from the argumentative purpose, as it is perceived as ridicule of religious belief and Jewish culture as such.

As might be imagined, a heated debate followed, on both the printed pages and the website of *Aftenposten*. Soon the debate engaged international participants, some of whom were outraged, some sympathetic. Both positions are represented in the following excerpts from two articles on the debate webpages of *Aftenposten*. The first is an open letter from Dr. Shimon Samuels (2006), the director for international relations at the Simon Wiesenthal Center in Paris. "Jostein Gaarder, the author of the literary chef d'oeuvre, *Sophie's World*, has become seriously ill, either with malice, or, perhaps, Alzheimer's or both. Translated into 53 languages and with 26 million copies sold, so many of his readers will mourn Gaarder's current loss of vision, coherence and, above all, his recruitment to the forces of darkness."

Uwe Wagner, a German citizen from Rostock, supported Gaarder. Unlike the professional spokesperson for the Wiesenthal Center, Wagner (2006) built his ethos as a person independent of organizational interests but possessing the relevant moral and intellectual qualities. He had fought for a good cause in the past (*areté*) and was therefore rhetorically in a position to insist on a more nuanced debate (*phronesis*):

> In my opinion, Mr. Gaarder is absolutely right. Millions of Jewish people were killed in the past by the German Hitler-fascists. And I myself fought against German fascists. . . . But this mass murder cannot be a justification for the reign of terror the ruling politicians of Israel organize against the Arabian people. It is an infamy to denounce Mr. Gaarder as an anti-Semitic man. The same perfidious methods we know here in Germany: you have criticism against the policy of Israel's leaders, so you are automatically an anti-Semite.

The obvious result of Gaarder's provocative style was the formation of an active public engaged in deliberation. As such, Gaarder's entry kick-started a debate that was soon taken over by other active participants. While the provocative aspects of Gaarder's style were not disputed explicitly in the examples quoted above, their effects can still be sensed. Samuels responded to the anger and dismay Gaarder's article caused by raising doubts about his sanity. Wagner, on the other hand, reproduced the indignation of Gaarder's article in his defense of the right to criticize the state of Israel without being dismissed as anti-Semitic. Both statements bear the stamp of provocative style. Thus the debaters seem to adopt, by citation or imitation, the provocative style that Gaarder's article introduced.

The provocative style was certainly picked up in a leading article in the *Weekly Standard*, an American magazine, by its right-leaning editor, William Kristol (2006), who opened by evoking the anti-Semitic sentiments of the early twentieth century:

> "How odd / of God / To choose / The Jews." Thus the British journalist (and communist) William Norman Ewer, in the early part of the last century. The reply came from Cecil Browne: "But not so odd / As those who choose / A Jewish God / But spurn the Jews." Browne's riposte may have won the poetic exchange. But Ewer's anti-Judaism prevailed in the next decades in Europe. Buried there after World War II, hatred

of the Jews flourished for the rest of the 20th century in the Middle East. Is anti-Judaism now enjoying a broader revival? It would seem so.

Kristol concluded that "Jews are under attack. And no one seems much concerned"—which is also the title of his text. Four examples backed up his claim, of which Gaarder's article was just one. On Gaarder, Kristol wrote:

> Mr. Gaarder's distaste for Israel seemed to be based on his dislike of Israel's policies, his revulsion against the God of Israel ("an insatiable sadist"), and his anger that, "for two thousand years, we have rehearsed the syllabus of humanism, but Israel does not listen." It's not clear who that "we" has been for two thousand years. But since Israel has only existed since 1948, it is presumably the Jews, not merely Israel, who have not listened. (It was, however, generous of Mr. Gaarder to call for mercy on the Jewish civilian population.)

Although these few lines fail to render an exact account of the content of Gaarder's article, Kristol pinpointed how Gaarder's argument was based on the very premise he defied (the conflation of state and religion). This inconsistency made it easy for Kristol to ignore Gaarder's recurring claim that his criticism was aimed not at civilians but at the state of Israel.

The commonsensical reasoning and the mild irony at the end of the paragraph veil the force of Kristol's particular brand of provocative style. Kristol used the piece to launch the conspiracy theory that Jews, in America as well as internationally, historically as well as today, are under attack by the powerful and the cultural elite. The humble style of his refutation of Gaarder seems to attempt to enact the vernacular by speaking in the voice of the victimized. Additionally, Kristol's provocative style is characterized by large claims with little backing, as well as a highly selective reading of Gaarder. Besides the framing of Gaarder's article as part of an international Jew-bashing trend, Kristol takes a specific expression, "an insatiable sadist," out of its exact context. Thereby Kristol disregards the fact that Gaarder, rather than denouncing the Jewish God in general, is discussing a specific tale, arguing that, "in that tale, the Lord God of Israel appears as an insatiable sadist."

To recapitulate the particulars of provocative style, the most obvious feature is its violation of decorum. In its deliberate overstepping of norms of public communication, the provocative style can be identified as a species of the vernacular. It is a nonofficial public discursive practice that is easily combined with a speaking position of the outraged, or even the victimized. Another characteristic of the provocative style is its elaborate stylistic performance of the argument. In the Gaarder example, the mimicking of Jewish concepts and biblical tone functions as a refutation of the idea of a divine mandate. As a consequence, certain biblical *topoi* are present in the argumentation, and this presence seems to be another significant feature of the provocative style. Furthermore, provocative style tends to be "cited" or copied in the responses.

Taken as a whole, the Gaarder-Kristol controversy provided ample evidence of what we may now characterize as provocative style. That the immediate effect was an active public engaged in deliberation is not to be disputed. But the debate was very far from ideal. While both debaters delivered fairly strong and strategic partisan contributions, displaying argumentative and stylistic skills, they also violated some norms of public deliberation. Gaarder's article was weakened by argumentative inconsistency that made it vulnerable to criticism. Kristol's representation of Gaarder's argument was biased and manipulative.

About one week after his initial piece appeared, Gaarder wrote another article titled "Forsøk på klargjøring" (Attempt at Clarification) (2006a). Studies of apology and atonement have demonstrated discrepancies between the speaker's explicit statements of the purpose of the speech and the strategies being used (Koesten and Rowland 2004; Villadsen 2008). In Gaarder's clarification he explained how his use of rhetorical devices caused a misunderstanding. He emphasized the emotional context of the original article, quoting the line "not as of this writing, not in the hour of grief and wrath," and explaining that it was written the same day that pictures from Qana came in. Using differentiation as a strategy, he sought to separate the stylistic and emotional aspects of the article from "the real message," and claimed that he never meant to say that Jewish religion and culture were inferior to the humanism found in Christian and Muslim history. His criticism was aimed solely at the notion of "God's chosen people," which, he said, he still understood as a divine mandate for political action.

By using differentiation strategies, Gaarder minimized the importance of his style while defending his argument. Whether as a strategy of defense or as a theory of signs, this separation of style and argument (form and meaning) is not warranted by modern theories of metaphor, rhetoric, and style. The constitutive and argumentative function of style and rhetorical figures has been established in numerous studies, including those mentioned above.[7] As for the specific case, Gaarder's attempt to separate stylistic and literary devices from the "real argument" is misplaced. Gaarder's criticism of the idea that a certain group of people should have a divine mandate to act politically is argued forcefully in the stylistic parody employed in his initial article. The style was provocative, but as such it functioned as a line of argument that Gaarder stood by in his clarification.

Although Gaarder's article provoked both offense and irritation, it also gave rhetorical salience to a conflict that Scandinavian audiences often see as "Other." It functioned as an argumentative selection of data giving *presence* to the complex problems of Israeli history, politics, and religion. Temporarily isolating the conflict from abstract world politics, Gaarder's style reclaimed its relevance for an audience responsive to allusions to "milk and honey," familiar to them from their childhood narratives. During the debate, opinions were formed ("a criticism of the State of Israel is not identical to fascism"; "Jews are under attack"). In this respect, the debate did constitute an audience and engage it in rhetorical citizenship, forming and stating opinions in order to seek influence. In assessing the specific case, I believe that its importance was far from neutralized by the offenses and attacks perpetrated by the debaters.

Critical Reflections

Having identified the features and functions of provocative style and assessed its qualities, we are still faced with the problem of conflicting norms: how do we balance those incommensurable values, an engaged public and communication ethics, on a more general level? Returning to Hauser, we find that although interests and partisan appeals are acceptable, this does not mean that anything goes. Essential to the norms of a rhetorical model is that they "offer encouragement toward the achievement of a common mind rather than advancement of vested interests" (1999, 80). Hauser, like Perelman and Olbrechts-Tyteca, draws the line at propaganda, and distinguishes between "partisan urgings, in which responsiveness to the other side and the possibility of being persuaded are assumed, and the manipulation of propaganda" (80).

A similar caution and concern for the constitutive aspects of pernicious discursive practices is found in James A. Mackin's study of Pericles' funeral oration (1991). Mackin reasons in terms of an environmental metaphor as he considers "a social system as an ecosystem that goes beyond the physical to incorporate the symbolic" (251). He traces how Pericles' oration damaged the Athenian community as an ecosystem through a process of "symmetrical schismogenesis," a progressive differentiation that resulted in polarization. In rhetorical stylistic terms, he shows how the use of antithesis to intensify partisanship at one level of the social system necessarily results in a tearing apart of community at another level.

The antithesis emphasizes the antagonism between Athens and Sparta, but at the same time it artistically creates consubstantiality and strengthens the Athenian sense of community. Yet, by reinforcing Athenian uniqueness and describing Athens as a closed ecosystem, Pericles undermined the larger communicative ecosystem of the Greek city-states. Mackin's concern is the long-term effect of this kind of rhetorical pollution of an ecosystem: "The rhetorical chasm that Pericles created by his artful use of antithesis may well have contributed to the ultimate decline of Athens" (256).

A similar distinction between context-specific practices and long-term effects may also apply to a discussion of provocative style. At least, the implications of a rhetorical style, where the reproduction of mockery and offense is central, deserve some consideration. However, a first step must be to study actual debates on their own terms. I have launched "provocative style" as a critical concept in order to enable rhetorical critics to perceive what has sometimes been overlooked in the study of public deliberation. In this way I propose that increased understanding is sustained by careful rhetorical analysis and cautious interpretation, not by assuming the worst. Also, I hope that the concept of provocative style will be able to counterbalance environmental metaphors suggesting vast and potentially irreparable damage, as well as widespread critical *topoi* such as *fear of the precedent or unlimited development* (Perelman and Olbrechts-Tyteca 1969, 281–92). As a critical tool, provocative style at least aims at enabling the critic to scrutinize debates and debate cultures on a more concrete level. The conceptualization of provocative style insists on a bracketing into stages and elements. There are engaging factors, argumentative functions, and argumentative faults, all of which should be studied and appreciated before they become part of a critical evaluation.

NOTES

1. "Discourse intent on gaining the assent of those who share the consequences of a public problem inevitably addresses them as particular individuals and groups. We adapt our arguments to our audience's readiness to attend, understand, and respond . . . through such rhetorical concerns as *kairos* (timing) and decorum. These rhetorical characteristics of addressed discourse belie the condition of disinterest" (Hauser 1999, 50). All translations in this chapter are my own unless otherwise noted.

2. Theorists of rhetoric from Aristotle through Perelman and Olbrechts-Tyteca (1969), to Edwin Black (1970), Michael McGee (1975), and Maurice Charland (1987) have discussed the concept of "audience" without reducing it to somebody being asked to purchase and applaud, and I see no reason to so reduce it now.

3. Especially as it is developed in "Hating Hillary: The Discursive Performance of Femininity," where the feminine style is summarized in a checklist: "In rhetorical terms, performing or enacting femininity has meant adopting a personal or self-disclosing tone (signifying nurturance, intimacy, and domesticity) and assuming a feminine persona, for example, mother, or an ungendered persona, for example, mediator or prophet, while speaking. It has meant preferring anecdotal evidence (reflecting women's experiential learning in contrast to men's expertise), developing ideas inductively (so the audience thinks that it, not this presumptuous woman, drew the conclusions), and appropriating strategies associated with women—such as domestic metaphors, emotional appeals to motherhood, and the like—and avoiding such 'macho' strategies as tough language, confrontation or direct refutation, and any appearance of debating one's opponents" (Campbell 1998, 5).

4. See, for instance, Wolfgang F. Müller's definition of period style: "A period style is to be understood as a set of features of expression and artistic form that are characteristic of a particular epoch (age)" (2008–9, 1271).

5. For a full account of the traditional *topoi* of style, "style as man," and "style as dress," see Müller 1981. For an abbreviated version in English, see Müller 2001.

6. The object of my analysis is the translation of Gaarder's article "Guds utvalgte folk," translated into English as "God's Chosen People" on the Simon Wiesenthal Center website. Slightly inaccurate, the translation bears the mark of (vernacular) deliberation in a globalized public sphere—as do the entries by citizens debating in a foreign language.

7. It has also been discounted in studies on metaphor by Richards 1936, Black 1972, Ricoeur 1975, Lakoff 1993, and Lakoff and Johnson 1980. See Klujeff 2011.

REFERENCES

Aristotle. 2007. *On Rhetoric.* Trans. George A. Kennedy. Oxford: Oxford University Press.
Black, Edwin. 1970. "The Second Persona." *Quarterly Journal of Speech* 56 (2): 109–19.
Black, Max. 1972. *Models and Metaphors: Studies in Language and Philosophy.* Ithaca: Cornell University Press.
Brummett, Barry. 2008. *A Rhetoric of Style.* Carbondale: Southern Illinois University Press.
Campbell, Karlyn Kohrs. 1998. "Hating Hillary: The Discursive Performance of Femininity." *Rhetoric and Public Affairs* 1:4–19.
Charland, Maurice. 1987. "Constitutive Rhetoric: The Case of the *Peuple Québécois.*" *Quarterly Journal of Speech* 73 (2): 133–50.
Fahnestock, Jeanne. 2002. *Rhetorical Figures in Science.* Oxford: Oxford University Press.
Gaarder, Jostein. 2006a. "Forsøk på klargjøring." *Aftenposten,* 12 August. http://www.aftenposten.no/meninger/kronikker/article1419237.ece.
———. 2006b. "God's Chosen People." English translation of "Guds utvalgte folk," which appeared in *Aftenposten,* 5 August. http://www.wiesenthal.com/site/apps/s/content.asp?c=fwLYKnN8LzH&b=253162&ct=2869779.
Hariman, Robert. 1995. *Political Style: The Artistry of Power.* Chicago: University of Chicago Press.
Hauser, Gerard A. 1999. *Vernacular Voices: The Rhetoric of Publics and Public Spheres.* Columbia: University of South Carolina Press.

———. 2008. "The Moral Vernacular of Human Rights Discourse." *Philosophy and Rhetoric* 41:440–66.
Klujeff, Marie. 2011. "Rhetorical Figures and Style as Argumentation." In *Studies in Rhetoric: Rhetorica Scandinavica, 1997–2005*, ed. Jens E. Kjeldsen, 302–22. Åstorp, Sweden: Retorikforlaget.
Koesten, Joy, and Robert C. Rowland. 2004. "The Rhetoric of Atonement." *Western Journal of Communication* 55:68–87.
Kristol, William. 2006. "Anti-Judaism." *Weekly Standard*, 11 September.
Lakoff, George. 1993. "The Contemporary Theory of Metaphor." In *Metaphor and Thought*, ed. Andrew Ortony, 202–51. Cambridge: University of Cambridge Press.
Lakoff, George, and Mark Johnson. 1980. *Metaphors We Live By*. Chicago: University of Chicago Press.
Mackin, James A., Jr. 1991. "Schismogenesis and Community: Pericles' Funeral Oration." *Quarterly Journal of Speech* 77 (3): 251–62.
McGee, Michael C. 1975. "In Search of 'the People': A Rhetorical Alternative." *Quarterly Journal of Speech* 61 (3): 235–49.
Müller, Wolfgang G. 1981. *Topik des Stilbegriffs: Zur Geschichte des Stilverständnisses von der Antike bis zur Gegenwart*. Darmstadt: Wissenschaftliche Buchgesellschaft.
———. 2001. "Style." In *Encyclopedia of Rhetoric*, ed. Th. O. Sloane, 745–57. Oxford: Oxford University Press.
———. 2008–9. "Epochenstil/Zeitstil." In *Rhetorik und Stilistik: Ein internationales Handbuch historischer und systematischer Forschung/Rhetoric and Stylistics: An International Handbook of Historical and Systematic Research*, ed. Ulla Fix, Andreas Gardt, and Joachim Knape, 2 vols., 2:1271–85. Berlin: Gruyter.
Murphy, James J. 1990. "Topos and Figura: Historical Cause and Effect?" In *De Ortu Grammaticae: Studies in Medieval Grammar and Linguistic Theory in Memory of Jan Pinborg*, ed. G. L. Bursill-Hall, Sten Ebbesen, and Konrad Koerner, 239–53. Amsterdam: John Benjamins.
Perelman, Chaïm, and Lucie Olbrechts-Tyteca. 1969. *The New Rhetoric: A Treatise on Argumentation*. Trans. J. Wilkinson and P. Weaver. Notre Dame: University of Notre Dame Press. (Orig. pub. 1958.)
Richards, I. A. 1936. *The Philosophy of Rhetoric*. London: University of Oxford Press.
Ricoeur, Paul. 1975. *The Rule of Metaphor: Multi-Disciplinary Studies of the Creation of Meaning in Language*. Toronto: University of Toronto Press.
Samuels, Shimon. 2006. "An Open Letter to Norway from the Simon Wiesenthal Centre (Paris)." *Aftenposten*, 6 August. http://www.aftenposten.no/english/local/article1416800.ece.
Villadsen, Lisa S. 2008. "Speaking on Behalf of Others." *Rhetoric Society Quarterly* 38: 25–45.
Wagner, Uwe. 2006. Letter to the editor. *Aftenposten*, 6 August. http://www.aftenposten.no/english/local/article1416800.ece.

7

VIRTUAL DELIBERATIONS:
TALKING POLITICS ONLINE IN HUNGARY

Ildikó Kaposi

Deliberative theories of democracy recognize the importance of "spontaneous, unsubverted circuits of communication in a public sphere that is not programmed to reach decisions and thus is not organised" (Habermas 1997, 57). This stands in marked contrast to traditional political and social thought, which generally fail to deem everyday talk significant enough to merit theorizing or systematic enquiry. From the latter perspective, talk is a "natural" part of everyday life, its pervasiveness rendering it invisible, on top of its being irrelevant to the responsible, enlightened, and capable sphere of political decision making. The resurgence of interest in everyday political talk in the wake of the "deliberative turn" in social science has challenged this view. The new approaches claim that while everyday talk is not oriented toward decision making, and is not always self-conscious, reflective, or considered, it is nevertheless a crucial part of the full deliberative system, which is made up of interrelated parts, including public forums, activists, associations, and formerly private spaces like the home and workplace. Everyday talk matters because it is how people come to understand themselves and their environment better, and it helps participants change in ways that are better for them and the larger polity (Mansbridge 1999).

However, assessing the qualities of everyday talk remains difficult because, while "deliberation" has a set of standards and criteria that define the term, the same cannot be said for the terms that characterize more informal exchanges. It even remains questionable what model of communication applies to everyday political talk: the terms "talk," "discussion," and "conversation" are used, sometimes interchangeably, to describe people exchanging information and opinions about political issues in the public and private spheres. This neglect in theorizing about talk is hardly new.

In classical rhetoric, conversation as a genre was recognized but paid little attention (Remer 1999). Cicero's writings contrasted conversation with oratory, public judicial, and deliberative speech. Unlike such forms of rhetoric, conversation was to be found in small, exclusive circles. And because conversation was speech among a select group, it was restrained, free of destructive passions that would conflict with deliberation and reason. From this perspective, conversation cannot be the main genre for politics because political speech is public, addressing large audiences, and because conversation is not directed at action in a way necessary for politics (which depends on action).

Publicness and the orientation toward specific results are also among the features by which Michael Schudson (1997) differentiates models of conversation. Schudson argues that there are two distinct ideals of conversation: the sociable model and the problem-solving model. In the sociable model, conversation need not have an end outside itself. Conversation of this kind is oriented to the pleasure of interacting with others without the necessity of persuasion. The problem-solving model of conversation, by contrast, starts from the premise that talk is justified by its practical relationship to the articulation of common ends. The focus here is on arguments declaring what the world is and should be like. Problem-solving conversation works as a model of good government, expecting reasonableness from participants in their willingness to listen to others, state their own views, and revise statements in the light of responses.

The two types of conversation, says Schudson, are necessary for democracy in radically different ways. The sociable model involves homogeneous conversation, where people talk primarily with others who share their values. The shared assumptions make the testing of opinions and ideas "safe," free from severe conflict, so that participants are likely to be reinforced in their shared views. In problem-solving conversations, heterogeneity is the norm. Talk occurs among people who do not share the same views; therefore a friendly testing of ideas is not possible. Uncertainty and doubt are penalized, conviction and certainty rewarded. This is the "truly public" mode of conversation, and it takes place in settings where talk is bound to be uncomfortable, threatening to the point where formal or informal rules of engagement are required.

The Beginnings of "the Great Conversation" Online

The rise and diffusion of the Internet added further fuel to the debates on the merits and models of political conversation. Many celebrated the new technology's potential to enhance the deliberative system by creating new arenas for political conversation. In its 1997 decision to strike down the Communications Decency Act (*ACLU v. Reno*), the U.S. Supreme Court declared that "it is no exaggeration to conclude that the internet has achieved, and continues to achieve, the most participatory marketplace of mass speech that this country—and indeed the world—has yet seen."[1] The idea that the Internet ushered in a new age of participatory politics was further echoed by early enthusiasts, who welcomed the new technology as providing the potential—at least discursively—to empower citizens or groups that hitherto lacked access to the political arena. Calls for a new media-assisted galvanization of the public (Meeks 1997), or for the end of the broadcast era and the beginning of the great conversation (Barlow 1997), endure. Some researchers argue that the information and communication technologies (ICTs), by opening up the political arena, create a new kind of politics that cuts across the boundaries between politics, cultural values, civil values, and identity processes (Bentivegna 2006). Others argue that even if ICTs are not necessarily producing "new" citizens, they "provide for new and important citizenship practices" (Hermes 2006, 306).

The political conversation spaces on the Internet help people overcome barriers such as discomfort generated by disagreement in face-to-face settings, bringing "new voices" to the public sphere (Stromer-Galley 2002). The concept of "voice" has also been used to highlight how marginalized groups are able to use the Internet as a "'safe' alternative living space" for finding their voices and gaining recognition. For such groups, the Internet offers a "speaking space" (Mitra 2001, 45) where they can not only speak out and crystalize their identities but also challenge the dominant worldview by forcing it to acknowledge and respond to them.

Challenging the dominant becomes possible for marginalized groups on the Internet because the medium enables people in subordinate positions to voice their own discourses. In this sense, the Internet exerts a profound equalizing force, as it levels access to the public arena. Online deliberation has been celebrated for its consistent reduction of the independent influence of social status (Gastil 2000), and news groups have been considered a welcome development for democracy because their communicative dynamics are seen to be activated by the substantial equality among members (Bentivegna 1998). Equality among members, the right to intervene prompted only by interest in the issue, the public character of discussion, the size of the audience, and the increased freedom of expression are elements that have made discussion groups created in cyberspace a modern version of the Habermasian public sphere, creating "an opportunity to bring the citizens back into talk politics" (Bentivegna 2006). Because of the anonymity they may guarantee and the possibility for users to reinvent their identities, some forums of online discussion are judged promising for equalizing participants and allowing the "force of the better argument" to triumph, in the Habermasian spirit (Ó Baoill 2000).

Against hopeful assessments of the Internet as approximating the ideal of a public sphere, there are those who are skeptical about the Internet's contribution to democracy. Even when citizens participate, these skeptics maintain, their online political discussions fail to live up to the standards of good deliberation (Davis 1999; Hill and Hughes 1998; Papacharissi 2002, 2004; Schneider 1997; Streck 1997; Wilhelm 2000; Witschge 2002). Instead of the free, equal, reasoned, and consensus-seeking deliberation of the ideal derived from democratic theory, online discussion forums, including well-researched Usenet groups, are noted for their manifestations of the hateful and other conflict-fueling examples of what the unrestricted communication of political views can produce. As Davis concludes in his analysis of Usenet political discussions, "people talk past one another, when they are not verbally attacking each other. The emphasis is not problem solving, but discussion dominance. Such behavior does not resemble deliberation and it does not encourage participation, particularly by the less politically interested" (1999, 177).

The question arises whether the medium of communication is responsible for the character and tone of discussion on Usenet and other political discussion forums, whether the Internet is to blame for the apparent failure of online discussion to live up to deliberative standards. The critics argue that online political discussion allows "faceless" individuals to express or "shout" anonymous views (White 1997), which results in the poor quality of discussion. The loss of social cues online is said to be conducive to harsh arguments, as it reduces the responsibility individuals have for their utterances (Kiesler, Siegel, and McGuire 1984). Nor does "faceless" computer-mediated communication necessarily liberate participants from preexisting social roles and relations (Postmes, Spears, and Lea 1998; Spears and Lea 1994). If online interaction is extended over time, the social and cultural differences between participants resurface (Jankowski and van Selm 2000). The skeptics conclude that the model of citizens pursuing consensus through rational discussion is systematically denied in the arenas of electronic politics (Poster 1995).

The democratic potential of the Internet has also been questioned on the ground that it undermines the unity and cohesion of the public.

Fears of fragmentation have inspired theorists to view the Internet as a threat to democracy on the strength of the objection that users form deliberative "enclaves" online (Buchstein 1997; Sunstein 2001). In essence, this means that the Internet allows people to personalize their information intake to the degree that they access only information and opinions they are interested in or agree with. In the fragmented speech market of the Internet, it becomes possible to avoid dealing with diverse views and to create communication enclaves whose walls are penetrated only by like-minded others. The result of deliberative enclaves can be "group polarization"; that is, people "move toward a more extreme point in the direction to which the group's members were originally inclined" (Sunstein 2001, 65). Instead of enlightened, public-oriented preferences shaped in the process of deliberation, people may end up with extreme positions on issues. Eventually, the foundations of democracy in the public sphere may be eroded, as there remain no shared, overlapping issues that people of different convictions would regard as politically relevant to their lives.

Arguably, however, much of the literature critical of online political talk fails to shed light on online discussion because of an insistence on rigidly defined criteria of ideal deliberation that do not apply in a straightforward manner to the phenomenon being researched. As Mansbridge (1999) suggests, the criteria for judging deliberative talk need to be treated and interpreted flexibly, and modified according to the circumstances in which deliberation and discussion occur.

The Hungarian Context

"Democracy" and "the Internet" are concepts that are often used universally, but the relationship between them can best be approached by examining specific democratic political contexts and online practices. My focus here is discursive engagement on the Internet in the context of a "third-wave" democracy, the Republic of Hungary.

Hungarian social scientists regularly lament the quality of public political debates in the country. Debates are seen as driven by factionalism, emotionally charged, focused not on specific issues but on symbolic matters, and "extremely egocentric and success oriented" (Dombrádi 2003, 55). Squabbling between political parties is said to pose problems for the whole public sphere because public debate has essentially become conflated with party discourses

(Hankiss 2005). Independent assessment and alternative discourse could normatively be expected from a free press, but the Hungarian media follow a path of partisanship instead of professionalized, objective norms (Ádám and Mink 2005).

Standard assessments of citizen participation in Hungary's public life suggest that it remains limited, despite the legal guarantees that ensure numerous opportunities to participate for citizens and associations on both the national and local levels. However, one area that is exempt from low participation is political discussion. The results of a 1995 cross-national survey found that Hungary had the highest percentage of people with politically relevant extensive networks. Hungarians had broad and politicized networks, "politicized" meaning that political discussion took place in the networks with remarkable frequency. Data from a national survey in 2003 also show that Hungarians are almost equally likely to discuss politics with their five important alters (Lup 2006). Nor is political discussion limited to like-minded individuals. Although the likelihood of discussing politics drops from around 80 percent with alters who have similar political views to just under 57 percent, on average, with alters whose political preferences differ, this still means frequent political discussion. The frequency of political discussion in both homogeneous and heterogeneous groups of important alters indicates an acceptance of political differences as inevitable under conditions of high polarization. It could also be a sign of "truly public" conversation, that is, uncomfortable and even threatening conversation (Schudson 1997), occurring in "safe" social settings.

Research on Hungarians' political discussions has not tackled the issue of how citizens understand and judge these practices. However, Hungarians often describe everyday political talk outside the home as *kocsmai politizálás*, or "pub politicking." This is a colloquial expression for the phenomenon of widespread political discussion in everyday situations, but it also carries negative connotations. Pubs are dubious settings of association. Although drinking can stimulate conviviality and act as an equalizing force in facilitating the mixing of socially heterogeneous company, it can also make pubs riotous hubs of sociability. The consumption of copious amounts of liquor is de rigueur in a pub, and the result is the loosening of tongues and social norms. This produces a relaxed, easy flow of conversation, where discussions need not observe the rules and norms of public debate, including soundness or consistency of positions. When the concept of pub politicking is extended beyond the confines of the pub, it carries these negative connotations.

Pub politicking becomes a metaphor for poor-quality discussion in which unsound views and opinions can be expressed irresponsibly and without much risk of retaliation. As a metaphor, it is used widely to label political talk unworthy of public attention, which—together with its amorphous manifestations—is probably why no systematic exploration of this practice has been undertaken.

Online political discussions are especially vulnerable to the surfacing of hostility, and they tend to polarize regular discussants, who vent their differences in "flaming," or an ongoing tirade of offensive comments (Lee 2005). Perceived potential threats to civility may have been among the reasons why, in the early days of Hungarian Internet communities, political discussion was not welcome in online conversation forums. In 1995, "taking political stands was still considered improper," except in forums created specifically for this purpose; therefore, "users abstained from it, and the forum participant or mailing list member who announced his political views was usually ostracized" (Bodoky and Dányi 2005, 153). This was the ruling norm on the first, and still the largest, Hungarian online group of conversation forums, where political discussion was first allowed in 1996, when it became clear that there was considerable demand for it.

Politika Forum, or Polforum, as it is often called by participants, was created in the fall of 1998 after it became clear that the original online community of the Törzsasztal[2] forum could no longer contain the traffic of political postings it attracted. Discussion on Polforum is organized around thematic threads called "topics," where participants post their contributions. Participation requires registration, but users need only provide a working e-mail address to get a password and activate their handle, commonly referred to as a "nick."[3] Discussion on the forum is moderated by unpaid volunteers recruited from the pool of active participants. Moderators do not prescreen messages; rather, they patrol and monitor topics and delete postings that break Polforum's code of conduct (the "modus moderandi," also composed by participants on a voluntary basis).

Polforum enjoys autonomy in handling its affairs, although it operates as part of a Hungarian-owned horizontal public portal called Index. Based on its traffic, Index is among the five most successful Hungarian portals.[4] However, the online communities are not part of the commercial sections of the portal. The management of Index.hu has no business strategy for the discussion forums, and while commercial pressure is thus removed from them, the forums cannot expect major investments in the technological infrastructure, either. As the portal's editor-in-chief put it, "After a while, we stopped developing the forum because we did not make a penny out of it. We don't care about it; we have nobody to look after it. To be honest, it's a mystery to me how it can still work. . . . I don't really understand what makes the thing survive" (quoted in Drótos, Kováts, and Gast 2004, 4).

Why indeed is Politika Forum such a long-running, robust institution? What is it that makes the online forum a prominent site of discussion among diverse and disagreeing elements of the Hungarian polity? What standards and practices do participants rely on to manage conflict and disagreement?

One attempt to answer these questions analyzed discussions from the perspective of how deliberative they are (Kiss and Boda 2005). Modeling their analysis on international research on Usenet discussions, Kiss and Boda analyzed select discussion threads and topics and concluded that while political forums do not seem appropriate for achieving consensus, participants are willing to make relevant and reasoned contributions to the discussion. Obscenity and ad hominem remarks are frequent, but they do not prevent the continuation of the discussion. Furthermore, the forum was found to have a great degree of autonomy, sustained by the traditions of the online community. The discussion agenda was consistently set by participants instead of merely following cues from political events, and the interpretive schemes appearing on the forum maintained their independence from political parties and their views even when a political actor initiated discussion.

Kiss and Boda raise the question of the purpose and value of discussion forums for participants who themselves note the general lack of relevance of many postings. In other words, they ask what sustains the online community in the absence of quality deliberation. Their method of coding discussion topics, measuring the volume of traffic, and counting and classifying topics, however, does not yield answers to this question. Nor does it help clarify the meanings of deliberative democracy in the political and cultural context of the Hungarian Internet. Exploring these issues would require a different research approach, one more open to the perspectives of the participants.

The question of what happens when people engage in everyday political discussion on Polforum, what meanings and interpretations participants construct for themselves on politics, democracy, and the Internet, and how these can be interpreted from a deliberative democratic perspective, led me to an ethnographic approach. Ethnography, as Hine (2000, 42) notes, is appealing for its depth of description and its lack of reliance on a priori hypotheses, and it offers the promise of getting closer to understanding the ways in which people interpret the world and organize their lives. For researching interactive online forums, Lori Kendall (1999) recommends including participant observation. If a researcher or citizen simply wanders into Politika Forum and peruses some of its topics, the first thing he is likely to notice is the harsh tone of the discussion and the great number of apparently irrelevant contributions, as if one had landed in the middle of the chaotic, ongoing conversations of virtual pub politicking.

If read superficially, these discussions are so far from ideal deliberation that it becomes easy to dismiss the whole forum as irrelevant to politics or democracy, as nothing but a repository of king-size egos and extreme opinions. In fact, one of the recurring views that forum participants express is that Polforum is like a madhouse, a case study in psychiatric abnormalities, a pub full of drunken brawling, and the like. Taking these statements at face value and scanning a few discussions may seem to support this view. And yet there is a fondness in the way the participants talk about the madness they all share in; they can talk for hours about the forum, to which they keep returning, often for years. How the forum works, what it is like to discuss politics online with these people, is revealed only if the researcher becomes part of it.

My research on Politika Forum lasted from the spring of 2002 to the end of 2003. I also went to the face-to-face meetings of the forum (held on the first Thursday of every month in Budapest restaurants) and to a summer garden party organized by one of the participants. When possible, I spent time with the participants in their homes, adopting the strategy that advises researchers to consider "off-line social contexts that participants jointly create" (Kendall 1999, 62). Long-term involvement with the forum participants, through a variety of methods, enables the proper contextualization of any aspect of their lives in other aspects (Miller and Slater 2000, 21). The Internet is not detached from any connection to "real life" and face-to-face interaction. Interpreting my findings and putting them in the context of e-participation or deliberative democracy could not be done without becoming one of the participants online as well as off, especially when the off-line component of participation is prominent, as in the case of Polforum.

Politika Forum: A Success Story?

The political context in which I started my research was the aftermath of the 2002 parliamentary elections. The 2002 political campaign by all accounts was an extraordinary time for politicized interaction in Hungarian society. Emotionally charged, embroiled in symbol, crystalizing around the personalities of political leaders, and unabashed in its reliance on black propaganda, the campaigns waged by the two main political camps were geared toward mobilizing their supporters (Fowler 2003; Kapitány and Kapitány 2002; Sükösd and Vásárhelyi 2002). Rampant political debates were said to be tearing the fabric of everyday social cooperation apart, with heated discussions about the merits of one or the other political party overtaking not only the media but also the workplace, family life, and the company of friends. It was to be expected that the discussions on Polforum, already noted for their harshness, would follow suit in the crescendo. And so they did, becoming more heated and polarized as the campaign unfolded.

Participants on Polforum express a strong sense of what produces quality discussions, and an equally strong sense of the demise of good discussion on the forum. As they said in the interviews:

> It is nothing like what it used to be. It used to be possible to hold sensible discussions, talk normally about certain issues—you can't do that now. Debates used to have reasoned arguments, counterreasoning, references; this is all gone now.

> What makes a debate good? Arguments, real reasoning that come from informed positions. I mean, if one is willing to fact-check.

> Cultured debate is free from the ad hominem and prejudice. We don't respond to each other with personal attacks in the absence of arguments.

> Index used to be very good for me and I think for many other people too. On the one hand, in proper discussions you thought through your own arguments, what you wanted to say, whether your arguments stood up logically, coherently. One did a lot of checking, read up on things.

> Classical debate does not work. [There is no] reasoning, counterargument, conclusion, crap like that.

The demise of quality in the discussions is usually attributed to a combination of the growth of the forum and the coarsening of the tone of Hungarian political life after 2000. The growth of the forum meant an increase in the number of participants as well as in the number of registered nicks, topics opened, and messages posted. In the beginning, most participants knew each other well, often from meeting in person. Growth, however, prevented the prevalence of personal ties, and the size of the active discussion population after a while undermined the working of the original civilizing force of exclusiveness. The same complaints about how the atmosphere was better, the tone more moderate, before the influx of new participants undermined civility and usefulness were also found in research on the expansion of Usenet (Pfaffenberger 1996) and by an ethnographic study of the nonpolitical Törzsasztal community on Index (Gelléri 2000). Gelléri interprets the stories of demise as a classical myth of the golden era, the retrospective appreciation of a bygone period that in fact had its share of disputes and ad hominem attacks, although the numbers of participants and topics were indeed lower on Polforum than they had been on Törzsasztal.

The same "golden era" myth may account in part for why participants describe Polforum in terms of "massification" when it was still made up of 395 identified core members at the end of 2005. But these and possibly other users had thousands of registered nicks, both active and unused, and by 2002 they had produced 724,000 postings. Polforum was becoming chaotic in the sense of having so many topics opened, so many discussions started, that it was increasingly difficult to navigate its flow. In the abundance of discussion topics, it was also becoming more and more difficult to attract attention to one's postings, and the surest way to get responses is to declare an extreme position in harsh tones. In other words, the culture of Polforum discussions does not simply favor strongly polarized views that are expressed in harsh tones; it makes such expression a rational option for generating discussion. Most participants are aware of this; they realize that what they are posting is not exactly what they think but rather a particular version of their views purged of subtlety. They may even make open references to this in the course of the discussion, as casual side remarks, as in the posting that replied to an argument about state-funded academic research by saying, "I too like to compose my messages in polarized terms, that's a specialty of Index, but I feel you were a bit unjust in your judgment."

The tone of discussion on Polforum is often described in terms of *fikázás*, a Hungarian slang word that is defined as the "forceful reviling, vituperation, degrading of an object." *Fikázás* is declarative; it is a way of expressing negative judgments without supporting them fairly with facts and sound arguments. While it is not unique to online discussions, it is more prevalent there, and it supports norms of discussion that presuppose adversity. Adversity, or the expectation that people's values and convictions differ and that these differences will ignite conflict, can be an engine of discussion. At the same time, another set of norms dictating expectations about quality debate is also present in the discussions, and these norms evoke a deliberative ideal, however distant. These norms help to counterbalance the adversary culture and maintain the political community that is created when participants engage in conversation, regardless of whether they agree with one another.

Reciprocity

The deliberative principles of reciprocity, or mutual respect, consistency of speech and action, and the need to acknowledge the strongly held beliefs of others, apply unproblematically to everyday talk (Mansbridge 1999). Participants also recognize reciprocity as an essential ingredient of quality conversation. Frank, a participant whose political preferences are for radical right-wing parties and organizations, described in an e-mail his views on good discussion:

> It can be called pleasant if there emerges a consensus. Because even though forum participants are necessarily confrontational personalities, everybody is obviously pleased if they can achieve agreement on something. I usually say that the essence of forums (and the institution of current democracy) is the initiation of dialogue. The purpose is not to have everyone agreeing with everyone else about everything—this is never going to be possible. We should just be aware of each other. Of each other's thoughts. The biggest misfortune is if there's no dialogue between different groups. If we act without being aware of each other. Of each other's feelings. With some goodwill toward the other, it can be possible to eliminate the most severe conflicts if we are in a position to make decisions.

Frank was consistent in practicing what he preached. His sincerity in professing deliberative openness started a respectful dialogue between him and "mrsnorris," an outspoken core member of left-liberal group. He was even entertaining thoughts of attending a left-liberal get-together.

Greeting is an important expression of community generated through communication. It is more frequent among friendly participants, but it does not occur as a matter of routine in each conversation, which makes it even more significant. When the right-wing participant Publius reappeared on the forum after months of absence following the 2002 elections, he was greeted with cries of "welcome back" and "welcome back on board" by people on the left. They continued to disagree and argue with him, but they voiced their pleasure in his return to the community. In this case, the greetings and Publius's thanks for them underlined the mutual respect between participants, creating an atmosphere of friendliness in which the time they spent together was clearly valued, even in political disagreement.

If not already present, mutual respect can be built through argument. The following exchange between two participants displays an appeal to external norms after they got into an argument over the validity of left-wing conceptions of what would make an acceptable right-wing party in Hungary:

ROARING REVEREND: You have already "introduced" yourself a few times, why don't you drop this hypocritical blah-blah . . .
NEWLANDER: Look, if you on your own can decide what it is that I want to say, and you know better than I do, then stop listening to my hypocritical blah-blah. Look for confrontation, I'm sure you'll find a partner for that. I would like to debate with those who have different opinions from mine but are willing to support them with reasoned arguments and are willing to listen to my arguments. Not necessarily so that we could convince each other, but that's what makes positions clearer. The ad hominem just makes the fog denser.
ROARING REVEREND: Okay, I apologize for the ad hominem remarks, but I stand by my own opinion.

In this exchange, the principle of reciprocity is appealed to successfully in the sense that it earns an apology for the participant who invokes it, even if disagreement will continue to guide the discussion. In other conversations, however, the appeal to reciprocity produces different results:

NUKIA: You're a typical case, Dear Jack. You demand concrete contributions, but you forget that You too should make contributions concrete.
JACK RABBIT: *"You're a typical case, Dear Jack. You demand concrete contributions, but you forget that You too should make contributions concrete."* Are you an organic perl implement?:)))

NUKIA: By and large your message makes absolutely no sense, Dear Jack. Try using Hungarian language, or write for the Martian Chronicles!

ZEBULUN_2000: May I help to interpret it? The Jack Rabbit nick would like to say that everybody's stupid, he's the only smart one, he's got his head even in his arse. Trust me, the control of the biological unit hiding behind the Jack Rabbit nick is not particularly complicated :)

In this conversation, the appeal to reciprocity appears as the need to find mutually acceptable arguments. The appeal also reveals nukia's relative lack of familiarity with the forum, as Jack Rabbit is known for his pugnacity and history of belligerence when engaging with others' arguments. This bit of information is supplied by Zebulun_2000, who enters the discussion to help nukia by contextualizing the nonsensical messages in Jack Rabbit's forum record. For a participant like Jack Rabbit, any criticism directed at his discussion style or person can trigger a string of postings intended to affirm his superiority. Therefore, the appeal to reciprocity, which also included a polite rebuke, was bound to be counterproductive. It also suggested nukia's lack of experience in Polforum discussions, where conversation is jointly shaped by external norms of quality and the forum's own debate culture.

Accountability

According to Mansbridge, accountability, too, needs to be interpreted broadly in the whole deliberative system, with full accountability entering the process not in its creative early stages but later, when it becomes most public. Nevertheless, participants apply the principle of accountability widely and at different levels. First, they regularly demand from one another justifications for the claims they make. Requesting the source of data that inform statements is a widespread mechanism for this. Shekhina relied on meticulous sourcing when she tried to refute stock anti-Semitic arguments. Her opponent kept making claims by referring to the Talmud, so Shekhina demanded the precise source of the references, and she was able to look up the chapter and verse and determine that it did not support her opponent's claims. At the same time, while demanding sources can be an evocation of the principle of accountability, it can also be an adversarial move. It can be presented as a challenge to the credibility of the other, as in the posting in which Wake Up Call asked his opponent, "Can you also provide a source, or did you just make up the whole thing?" Even when the source is provided, it is still possible to question its authenticity, which also implies that the person who relies on it is mistaken, deceived, or lying deliberately.

Second, the forum also makes it possible for participants to hold one another accountable for the consistency of their current and previous statements. Postings leave long records that are accessible to all. Previous postings can be looked up by clicking on the participant's name, which brings up a "data sheet" that includes a hyperlink ("Contributions") to all the topics on which the nick ever posted. Checking the earlier contributions of discussion partners can help a person decide what to make of ambiguous postings, and they can be quoted in the debate to point out inconsistencies in the arguments. Since it is a somewhat time-consuming task in the case of prolific contributors, this technique is most useful if one knows roughly which topic to look up—for this reason, it is favored mainly by seasoned old-timers.

Finally, accountability appears in the discussions about politicians, journalists, and other public figures, all of whom are standard subjects of conversation on Polforum. Participants frequently discuss the actions and statements of public figures within a framework of accountability. They demand justifications for political claims and moves, and they are quick to point out the inconsistencies between speech and action that characterize much of public life. This constant monitoring is facilitated by the online environment, for the Hungarian slice of the Internet provides a vast resource of online newspaper archives, academic, governmental, municipal, party, and politician websites, and similar sources where texts can be accessed and copied to the forum for dissection. The mechanisms of accountability in the everyday forum environment are made less clear because the public figures under scrutiny do not as a rule engage in the discussions.[5] Yet the left-right camps play out the process among participants by adopting the role of critic or defender of the public figure and answering to the claims as if acting on his or her behalf.

Reasoned Argumentation

Among the criteria for quality discussion (and good deliberation), rationality is perhaps the most difficult to realize. Mansbridge acknowledges that the standard of public reason needs to be enlarged in the context of everyday talk to include a considered mixture of emotions and reason. In the discussions on Polforum, the ongoing exchange of reasoned arguments is sometimes explicitly named as the ideal for the Internet, as in this left-wing participant's rant against the right-wingers who engaged in a smear campaign against a

Socialist politician in the 2002 elections: "[My criticisms] of course do not apply to those rightie fellows who use the net for what it was invented for, reasonable debates where people may not convince one another but both sides can find out about the opinions of the other side, and they do not cry high treason about people they got to know, after all we live in the same country." Participants realize that reasoning together to handle disagreement is a key to maintaining discussion, but it is difficult to sustain it—the frequent degeneration of the quality of the discussion, the strong left-right polarization of participants, the recognition of *fikázás* as a prevailing constituent of culture on the forum, and the abundant use of ad hominem attacks attest to this.

The political is personal in the sense that political convictions can be deeply held constituents of personal identity. Having one's politics constantly challenged may start to feel like a challenge to the person him- or herself, which puts an emotional burden on the discussion that it cannot always sustain. People can then abandon the discussion arena, or they can try to shift the discussion to a terrain that is free of emotions. Trying to reason with others is often a successful strategy of making this shift. Participants tend to respond in like tone, returning abuse for abuse but turning respectful when addressed respectfully and providing reasons for their opinions if others start reasoning with them. They may even alternate their tone within the same topic discussion, depending on whom they are responding to.

Discussions that involve highly technical issues or expert knowledge in a specialized area tend to be the most conducive to reasoned argumentation. Positions can and do still differ in these areas, but the technical language needed to engage meaningfully with issues of monetary policy, legislative provisions, or electoral systems cushions the discussion and tends to minimize outbursts of raw emotion. Legal issues, science, and the economy have produced some of the most memorable and long-running discussions on the forum. Expertise usually provides an implicit filter, although its screening function can also be spelled out, as in the case of one of the most prestigious topics, the Monetary Council's meeting. This topic has operated on an invitation-only basis since its opening in 2001. The topic opener invited seven forum participants who had built up a reputation for economic expertise to form a mirror institution to the Monetary Council of the Hungarian Central Bank (MNB). The online council holds a virtual meeting two days before the MNB meetings, members make recommendations, and the president makes a decision on monetary policy, which decision can then be compared to that of the Central Bank. Although it would have been technically possible for anyone to post to the topic, forum dwellers respected the virtual council's wish to keep the discussion closed to outsiders. A separate topic called "Virtual Monetary Council—the Gallery" was opened for wider deliberations on monetary policy, and it is here that all the other interested participants can discuss monetary policy with virtual council members. The rational discussions in the Monetary Council topics are facilitated further by the transparency characteristic of the operation of the Central Bank. Economic data and the bank's positions are widely available, easy to access, and possible to interpret according to the universal principles of finance and economics. By overriding the political, these expert codes also make it possible for left- and right-wing participants to maintain mutual respect in their common topic.

In the case of issues that are less conducive to reasoned argumentation, rationality still remains a powerful tool for indicating the acceptability of arguments, even when it is referred to under different labels. The implicit ideal of rationality informs some of the ad hominem remarks aimed at passing the judgment that some arguments and participants cannot be engaged with reasonably. Slurs that declare others to be mentally disturbed, insane, childish, adolescent, or primitive serve this purpose, as do the verbal shortcuts of calling others animal names.[6] These are last resorts, and they indicate that a person has given up on engaging in any sort of reasoned discussion with the other. Thus Zebulun_2000 calls Jack Rabbit a "really, really sick puppy" in the knowledge that sensible dialogue between them is over. In the same topic, Jacobi tells Jack Rabbit, "You have really become completely senile, demented." A flame fest is dismissed by a participant who did not take part in it with the words, "Brainwashed and counter-brainwashed. You all deserve one another." After a heated ad hominem exchange, Fang apologizes by saying, "You see, sometimes the bull in me roars out . . . and that's a big stinking animal. Then I calm down." Kite advises Toni, whose postings usually focus on the fear induced in him by right-wing politics, to "go see a doctor, because you would need treatment if you are afraid of everyone and everything, if you suffer from stronger-than-average anxieties and worries, believe me: a good physician could provide the solution to your problems."

These and many similar postings hurl epithets that make meaningful discussion or deliberation impossible. At the same time, they indicate the active construction of the boundaries of admissibility to public discussion on the forum. Particular ad hominem remarks acquire their full meaning in the process of this construction, through their contextualization in the communicative situation in which they are posted. They are not welcome for quality discussion, but they may be justified in certain cases, as when they are used to tackle opinions (such as unshakeable racism or anti-Semitism) that themselves are considered beyond reason.

The standards and practices of discussion on Polforum actually show remarkable similarity to those found on Usenet. In her content analysis of Usenet discussions on political subjects, Papacharissi (2004) found that participants preferred covert forms of impoliteness, including sarcasm and shouting. Besides sarcasm, her research found vulgarity, name calling, and aspersions among the favored expressions of aggression, but at the same time Usenet participants were highly aware of democratic ideals and frequently invoked principles like freedom of speech or diversity in discussion. Arguments were also regularly supplemented by demands that people provide evidence for their claims, and this evidence had to come from reputable sources. Given that only a fraction of Polforum participants give any indication of familiarity with Usenet, these similarities between the standards and techniques of online debate appear to suggest a universality not only of the principles of democracy but also of the ways in which people across continents use the Internet for political conversation.

Conclusion

Along with the principles of reciprocity, accountability, and rationality, the meaning of political discussion in the democratic microcosm of Polforum is also being clarified and constantly modified in the course of the conversations. This process, furthermore, is intertwined with the ongoing interpretation of democratic politics. Participants have created an online community they are trying to run on democratic principles, regularly invoking and making references to a deliberative ideal of discussion. Theirs is a discursive enterprise, and the rules that govern it include freedom and equality, accountability, reciprocity, and reasoned argumentation—the same ideals that are integral to a deliberative conception of democracy. This is remarkable because the rules, both in their formal, codified and in their informally observed versions, are as much the product of the democratic ideals that participants bring to the forum as of trial-and-error, piecemeal rule making that has been shaped through constant reinterpretation and application in the course of discussion.

Conversational rules and standards of conduct serve the purpose of maintaining communication among members of a newsgroup (McLaughlin, Osborne, and Smith 1995). In the "truly public" mode of conversation, where talk is bound to be uncomfortable and even threatening, formal or informal rules of engagement are required. If the project, as on Politika Forum, is to maintain political conversation, and to make it as meaningful for the participants as possible, then the elements of deliberation are the tried and tested principles on which to rely. The discussions will not produce consensus; indeed, they can increase the amount of disagreement. At the same time, they can eventually help participants handle moral disagreement and inform their dissensus, enabling the emergence of political community.

NOTES

1. For the text of the decision, see http://www.ciec.org/decision_PA/decision_text.html (accessed 6 October 2008).
2. "Törzsasztal" means a table maintained for regular clients in a coffeehouse or restaurant. The appearance of this concept on the Internet suggests that members of the emerging online community saw their discussions as related to the time-honored practices of coffeehouse culture. All translations are my own unless otherwise noted.
3. I have not translated the terms "topic" and "nick"; Hungarian participants used these English words.
4. Between 2000 and 2005, Index saw a 351 percent increase in the number of visitors and a 738 percent increase in the number of page impressions, or the number of times the site has been accessed or viewed by a user (Bodoky 2005).
5. It should be noted, however, that public figures do show up on the forum occasionally, often to respond to claims made about them.
6. The same categories have been used historically to deny people the political franchise, and some of them (e.g., age and insanity) continue to restrict participation in elections.

REFERENCES

Ádám, Zoltán, and András Mink. 2005. "A képviseleti vákuum nem állhat fönn az idők végezetéig: Beszélgetés Rauschenberger Péterrel" [The Representative Vacuum Cannot Last Forever: An Interview with Peter Rauschenberger]. *Beszélő*, 10 August. http://beszelo.c3.hu/cikkek/a-kepviseleti-vakuum-nem-allhat-fonn-az-idok-vegezeteig (accessed 6 October 2008).
Barlow, John Perry. 1997. "The Best of All Possible Worlds." *Communications of the ACM* 40 (2): 69–74.
Bentivegna, Sara. 1998. "Talking Politics on the Net." Paper written for the Joan Shorenstein Center, John F. Kennedy School of Government, Harvard University, August. http://www.hks.harvard.edu/presspol/research_publications/papers/research_papers/R20.pdf (accessed 6 October 2008).
———. 2006. "Rethinking Politics in the World of ICTs." *European Journal of Communication* 21 (3): 331–43.
Bodoky, Tamás. 2005. "A hírportál mint tömegmédium" [News Portals as Mass Media]. *Médiakutató* (Summer). http://www.mediakutato.hu/cikk/2005_02_nyar/05_hirportal.

Bodoky, Tamás, and Endre Dányi. 2005. "Új média" [New Media]. In *Magyar médiatörténet a késő Kádár-kortól az ezredfordulóig*, ed. Péter Bajomi-Lázár, 133–58. Budapest: Akadémiai.

Buchstein, Hubertus. 1997. "Bytes That Bite: The Internet and Deliberative Democracy." *Constellations* 4 (2): 248–63.

Davis, Richard. 1999. *The Web of Politics*. New York: Oxford University Press.

Dombrádi, Krisztián. 2003. "A posztszocialista nyilvánosság szerkezete" [The Structure of the Postcommunist Public Sphere]. *Kommunikáció, Média, Gazdaság* 1 (1): 55–65.

Drótos, György, Gergely Kováts, and Károly Gast. 2004. *Index.hu. Esettanulmány* [Index .hu: Case Study]. Budapest: Vezetésfejlesztési Alapítvány.

Fowler, Brigid. 2003. "The Parliamentary Elections in Hungary, April 2002." *Electoral Studies* 22 (4): 799–807.

Gastil, John. 2000. "Is Face-to-Face Citizen Deliberation a Luxury or a Necessity?" *Political Communication* 17:357–61.

Gelléri, Gábor. 2000. "Egy cyberközösség antropológiája" [The Anthropology of a Cybercommunity]. Undergraduate thesis, Eötvös Loránd University, Budapest. http://iszolda.hu/mese/bagoly_mondja_doga/szigorl.htm (accessed 6 October 2008).

Habermas, Jürgen. 1997. "Popular Sovereignty as Procedure." In *Deliberative Democracy*, ed. James Bohman and William Rehg, 33–45. Cambridge: MIT Press.

Hankiss, Elemér. 2005. "The Democratic Puzzle: Has Hungary Solved It?" *European Journal of Social Theory* 8 (4): 487–502.

Hermes, Joke. 2006. "Citizenship in the Age of the Internet." *European Journal of Communication* 21 (3): 295–309.

Hill, Kevin A., and John E. Hughes. 1998. *Cyberpolitics: Citizen Activism in the Age of the Internet*. Lanham, Md.: Rowman and Littlefield.

Hine, Christine. 2000. *Virtual Ethnography*. London: Sage.

Jankowski, Nicholas, and Martine van Selm. 2000. "The Promise and Practice of Public Debate in Cyberspace." In *Digital Democracy*, ed. Kenneth. L. Hacker and Jan van Dijk, 149–65. London: Sage.

Kapitány, Ágnes, and Gábor Kapitány. 2002. "Kampány és értékek: A pártok arculatának dimenziói 2002 tavaszán" [Campaign and Values: Dimensions of Party Images in Spring 2002]. *Politikatudományi Szemle* 11 (3–4): 167–98.

Kendall, Lori. 1999. "Recontextualizing 'Cyberspace': Methodological Considerations for On-line Research." In *Doing Internet Research: Critical Issues and Methods for Examining the Net*, ed. Steve Jones, 57–74. Thousand Oaks, Calif.: Sage.

Kiesler, Sara, Jane Siegel, and Timothy W. McGuire. 1984. "Social Psychological Aspects of Computer-Mediated Communication." *American Psychologist* 39:1123–34.

Kiss, Balázs, and Zsolt Boda. 2005. *Politika az interneten* [Politics on the Internet]. Budapest: Századvég.

Lee, Hangwoo. 2005. "Implosion, Virtuality, and Interaction in an Internet Discussion Group." *Information, Communication, and Society* 8 (1): 47–63.

Lup, Oana. 2006. "When Does Alters' Influence Matter? An Analysis of the Political Relevance of Personal Networks in Hungary." Paper presented at the Annual Doctoral Conference, Central European University, Budapest, 13–14 April.

Mansbridge, Jane. 1999. "Everyday Talk in the Deliberative System." In *Deliberative Politics: Essays on Democracy and Disagreement*, ed. Stephen Macedo, 211–37. New York: Oxford University Press.

McLaughlin, Margaret L., Kerry K. Osborne, and Christine B. Smith. 1995. "Standards of Conduct on Usenet." In *Cybersociety: Computer-Mediated Communication and Community*, ed. Steve Jones, 90–111. Thousand Oaks, Calif.: Sage.

Meeks, Brock N. 1997. "Better Democracy Through Technology." *Communications of the ACM* 40 (2): 75–78.

Miller, Daniel, and Don Slater. 2000. *The Internet: An Ethnographic Approach*. Oxford: Berg.
Mitra, Ananda. 2001. "Marginal Voices in Cyberspace." *New Media and Society* 3 (1) : 29–48.
Ó Baoill, Andrew. 2000. "Slashdot and the Public Sphere." *First Monday* 5 (9). http://firstmonday.org/htbin/cgiwrap/bin/ojs/index.php/fm/article/viewArticle/790.
Papacharissi, Zizi. 2002. "The Virtual Sphere: The Internet as a Public Sphere." *New Media and Society* 4 (1): 9–27.
———. 2004. "Democracy Online: Civility, Politeness, and the Democratic Potential of Online Political Discussion Groups." *New Media and Society* 6 (2): 259–83.
Pfaffenberger, Bryan. 1996. "'If I Want It, It's OK': Usenet and the (Outer) Limits of Free Speech." *Information Society* 12:365–86.
Poster, Mark. 1995. "The Net as a Public Sphere?" *Wired*, November. http://www.wired.com/wired/archive/3.11/poster.if.html (accessed 6 October 2008).
Postmes, Tom, Russell Spears, and Martin Lea. 1998. "Breaching or Building Social Boundaries? SIDE-Effects of Computer-Mediated Communication." *Communication Research* 25 (6): 689–715.
Remer, Gary. 1999. "Political Oratory and Conversation: Cicero Versus Deliberative Democracy." *Political Theory* 27 (1): 39–64.
Schneider, Steven M. 1997. "Expanding the Public Sphere Through Computer-Mediated Communication: Political Discussion About Abortion in a Usenet Newsgroup." PhD diss., Massachusetts Institute of Technology.
Schudson, Michael. 1997. "Why Conversation Is Not the Soul of Democracy." *Critical Studies in Mass Communication* 14:297–309.
Spears, Russell, and Martin Lea. 1994. "Panacea or Panopticon? The Hidden Power in Computer-Mediated Communication." *Communication Research* 21 (4): 427–59.
Streck, John M. 1997. "Pulling the Plug on Electronic Town Meetings: Participatory Democracy and the Reality of the Usenet." *New Political Science* 41–42:17–46.
Stromer-Galley, Jennifer. 2002. "New Voices in the Public Sphere: A Comparative Analysis of Interpersonal and Online Political Talk." *Javnost—The Public* 9 (2): 23–42.
Sükösd, Miklós, and Mária Vásárhelyi. 2002. *Hol a határ? Kampánystratégiák és kampányetika, 2002* [Where Is the Limit? Campaign Strategies and Campaign Ethics, 2002]. Budapest: Élet és Irodalom.
Sunstein, Cass. 2001. *Republic.com*. Princeton: Princeton University Press.
White, Charles S. 1997. "Citizen Participation and the Internet: Prospects for Civic Deliberation in the Information Age." *Social Studies* 88 (1): 23–28.
Wilhelm, Anthony G. 2000. *Democracy in the Digital Age: Challenges to Political Life in Cyberspace*. New York: Routledge.
Witschge, Tamara. 2002. "Online Deliberation: Possibilities of the Internet for Deliberative Democracy." Paper presented at the "Euricom Colloquium Electronic Networks and Democratic Engagement" conference, Nijmegen, the Netherlands, October.

PART 2
CRITIQUES OF "ELITE" DISCOURSE

8

DIS-PLAYING DEMOCRACY:
THE RHETORIC OF DUPLICITY

Kristian Wedberg

Toward the end of the nineteenth century, some European writers of literature saw themselves in a new political role. According to the influential Danish critic Georg Brandes, the vitality of a literary work from then on depended on its ability "to submit problems to debate." It was a time when the specific pathos of Zola's "J'accuse" evolved into the ethos of the public writer in general.

Brandes's motto is apparently in accord with Jürgen Habermas's thesis that the politico-historical function of the modern literary institution was to create a space where issues were genuinely *arguable*. Literature, as presented and debated in eighteenth-century theaters, literary salons, and coffeehouses, for the first time assembled a true *publicum*. Its status as such was on the one hand presupposed by the socioeconomic autonomy of the new bourgeoisie (apart from the monarchy, church, and landowners), and on the other hand by the Enlightenment idea of the autonomous power of human reason (apart from the God-given, eternal authority of the king and the church). As we can see, it was no small part that literature was supposed to play; actually, it appears to be the firstborn child of modern liberal democracy.

No doubt literary writers today are met with lesser expectations. However, some portion of this grandiose ethos still rings through: owing to what is, in Norwegian discourse, known as the poetocratic tradition, writers of literature are still "called upon" by the nation "in times of crisis," as one critic put it. The public still seems to listen when they speak. What is the content of, and the reason behind, the distinctness of these voices? Why do they resonate, and in what kind of room? And what has this to do with contemporary democracy? The premise behind these questions is that there *really is* a connection between literature, public space, and democracy. I presume that investigating literary public space will shed new light on present-day democratic culture, a presumption that resonates with Habermas's aim in *Strukturwandel der Öffentlichkeit:* to get "a systematic comprehension of our own society from the perspective of one of its central categories" (1991, 5).

As is widely known, Habermas developed a general theory of publicity based upon the historical study of European public spheres from the time of the feudal system up until late modernity. Among those spheres were what could be called "literary publics" (literary salons, *Tischgesellschaften*, coffeehouses, etc.). In this respect, my own investigation can be said to have a Habermasian discursive background, both thematically and empirically. However, I shall try to show that in order to grasp the phenomena in question one must pay close attention to aspects that tend to be neglected in the Habermasian discourse. Most important, one must consider the extent to which these public events are rhetorical performances as well as sociological symptoms. More specifically, the public texts and events must be viewed as rhetorical situations (as this concept is understood in the Bitzer-Vatz-Consigny discourse). This view entails the importance of considering and interpreting the concrete verbal and gestural conduct of the agents involved, as well as the details of the specific social setting. One might object that the focus on situational specifics and details sacrifices the social scientific goal of revealing regularities and reaching a level of universality. However, the approach of rhetorical close reading can be defended as a method of paradigmaticity. By this I mean that the readings serve as concrete examples, or paradigms, of that upon which our image of a cultural whole is sketched. It does not mean, then, that my study is antisystematic, only that it refrains from trying to construct an exhaustive discursive image of the larger public culture of which the readings are a part. In general methodological terms, my ambition is to sketch an image of overall contemporary democratic culture by means of descriptions of some of its possibilities.[1]

In sum, my analyses imply that Habermas's general theory of publicity is insufficient as a regulative ideal in the sense of a model description and normative basis for understanding public sphere phenomena. Insufficient does not mean wrong; it means that Habermas's basic sociohistorical perspective must be supplemented with a rhetorical perspective. Public situations have a fundamentally dual character: on the one hand, they are socially and culturally given; on the other hand, the meaning of a particular public speech act might be exactly to interfere with or change that given social and cultural reality. From this basic complementarity follows the thesis that all phenomena of public discourse must be seen as fundamentally dialectical, that is, processes in which some given social or cultural matter of fact is modified or crafted. It may be that this last formulation is not in direct conflict with Habermas's theses; nevertheless, the element of "crafting" entails that we keep a keener eye on possible rhetorical subtleties than is normally allowed for in the Habermasian discourse.

These general theoretical reflections can now be stated with regard to the purpose of my present empirical survey. Through close readings of some specimens of literary public discourse in contemporary Norway, I aim to show that their *exact significance* is to provide the public with an image of political rationality that challenges the paradigm of enlightened rationalism (of which the ideal of Habermasian deliberation is an example). More specifically, I argue that this image emerges as a result of a certain rhetorical practice, which I call the *rhetoric of duplicity*.

The case under consideration here is that of Dag Solstad, a successful contemporary Norwegian novelist, at least if regarded by the standards of the literary field itself (as manifested in literary prizes, critical acclaim, reviews, etc.). However, Solstad's influence is not restricted to the small-scale, highbrow literary field; it has spread to a wider public. For instance, his novels have been distributed by book clubs, he has co-written several books on football, and one of his novels has been adapted to the movie screen. But most important in our context is the fact that he regularly intervenes in public debate and shows an unusual ability to stir up public opinion. Some of these interventions even turn into public events in their own right. The media and genres of his rhetorical actions are diverse; sometimes they take the form of polemical essays, and sometimes he chooses written or televised interviews as the preferred channel of communication. A few examples: Solstad has appeared on TV talk shows (e.g., Solstad 1997b), he has appeared in a TV commercial promoting book clubs, and recently he took part in a public debate on the subject of "freedom of speech" with the Norwegian foreign minister. The result of such public appearances is that Solstad stands out not only as a celebrated writer of fiction but as an intellectual persona in the contemporary Norwegian public sphere.

Before I examine one such public occasion in some detail, it should be noted that Solstad's physical appearance is highly idiosyncratic, not to say odd. He often looks distracted and awkward. This may be explained as psychological uneasiness in situations where he is at the center of public attention. It might also simply be an expression of his personality (and I actually think this *is* part of the explanation). Still, there is something in his evasiveness and ambiguous appearance that seems deliberate to the extent that it cannot be explained simply as the mere exterior of personal, psychological, or physiological reflexes. Again, one might explain this impression of deliberate conduct as a manifestation of a habitus that has enabled him to cope with public attention. I would suggest, however, that such explanations must be supplemented by the notion that what we are witnessing is a kind of rhetorical *mode*.

I shall describe this mode by way of an example. In the 1997 TV talk show *Bokbadet* (Solstad 1997a), the interviewer drew attention to a scene from one of Solstad's novels in which the protagonist, a university professor, witnesses a murder but refrains from reporting it to the police. The interviewer asked Solstad, "Why didn't he report it?" Solstad took a long pause before replying, "Well, that is actually what the book is about." A little later on, he was asked, "But the murderer, how does [the professor] relate to the murderer?" In his characteristically introverted, nervous-looking manner, Solstad grabbed his glass of wine, lit a cigarette, and said, "Well, I don't know." Interviewer: "But surely you do know; the book says a great deal about how he relates to the murderer." Again a pause, then: "Yes, but I don't know anything besides that." A little later on: "But I ask you, do you believe in literature?" By now Solstad was making gestures and sounds that revealed his obvious dislike of the line of questioning (uttering "oof" and "uh," while suppressing a faint smile). Eventually, he asked the interviewer, "Do I have to answer?" and after she responded, "Yes, you have to answer," he abruptly replied, "No, I don't have to answer."

Solstad's replies were met with laughter from the audience, while the interviewer did not think them funny at all. On the contrary, she was clearly uncomfortable—whether embarrassed, humiliated, annoyed, or angry (or all of those combined), it is not easy to say. But all of these possible reactions seem plausible in light of what looked like Solstad's deliberate obstruction of the dialogue. Was Solstad merely ridiculing his interlocutor? Solstad's conduct in this situation was in fact interpreted, on the one hand, as childish, but on the other hand as an example of a male-domination strategy (Wold 2002).[2] There may be some truth to this, but it is not, I believe, the whole truth. Surely Solstad's irony in part stems from his obvious disapproval of the questions asked and must therefore be seen as an expression of hostility. But, as I will show, this tension is not primarily a question of mood. It is rather a question of mode, and it should be noted that it is commonly held that Solstad practices a peculiar kind of irony both in writing and in speech, a trait that is essential to the physiognomy of his public persona.[3]

In order to come to terms with this ironic mode, we must examine more closely why Solstad rejected the questions posed. The question "Do you believe in literature?" is vague, and so was understandably dismissed. However, the questions that invited Solstad to speculate on the possible motives and actions of his fictional characters were not so obviously off target. Why did he refuse to answer? What he actually said was that he did not know anything other than what is in the text. It follows that there was no point in asking him, or more precisely, no point in asking *him*. Anyone (or perhaps no one) could answer. Investigating the psyche and conduct of his fictional characters is exactly the work that had been done *in writing*. The questions posed had already been answered in the published text for everyone to read. His writing could not be supplemented or developed through public small talk.

Examples like this can be multiplied. A more recent one: in an essay on Ibsen's play *Brand*, Solstad reflects on the protagonist's hardheadedness and unbending will, his refusal to compromise and his insistence on acting in full consistency with the logic of his own principles. Toward the end of the essay, Solstad, excited by his reflections and the logic of his own writing, is led to return to the ideological convictions of his youth and proclaim, "I am a communist again!" Later, when confronted with this statement in a public debate, Solstad said that the statement was not thoroughly thought through; it was a "literary" statement (quoted in Sandvik 2008). We should also note that these examples are typical of Solstad's tendency to interfere with the reception and interpretation of his work. At one point Solstad reviewed his reviewers, stating that "everything I say is misunderstood" (Solstad 1997b, 14). In an interview he claimed that, unlike many of his colleagues, he was blessed with "good readers" (quoted in Wedberg 2003, 27). According to the literary scholar Tore Rem, this statement shows that Solstad takes an "aesthete's position" that has probably "served him well" in academic circles (quoted in Wold 2002).

The consequence of regularly making himself into a writer-gestalt in public situations is that the identity of his immediate public presence is called into question. His performance seems to imply the question "Who am I?" and the answer seems to be "On the one hand, I am Dag Solstad, the person before you here and now, but on the other hand I am the representative of Solstad the author, inscribed in my fictional work." His person has thus bifurcated into two personae: the real, present Solstad and Solstad the mythmaker. My first interpretive point is thus that what looks like a mere obstruction of dialogue is also, in terms of the hermeneutics of publicity, a doubling of personae. It is this *rhetoric of duplicity* that we must try to account for in order to reach a precise understanding of the public phenomenon in question. I shall proceed by presenting some plausible analytical and theoretical bases for such an understanding.

By relativizing the presence of himself and framing the scene as a kind of play, the role of the interviewer is accordingly redefined. As the occasion is turned into a quasi-theatrical kind of interaction that the interviewer must somehow relate to, if not go along with, she becomes conscious of her own appearance *as appearance*. Solstad is putting on an act, and implicitly his interlocutor is invited to do the same. The uneasiness shown by the interviewer could thus be a sign of the difficulty she has in deciding whether to, or how to, play this game. Before committing Solstad's behavior to a moral judgment, then, one should bear in mind that given the conception of the situation as public role playing, the journalist is *in principle* not a vulnerable, private person but rather an actor distant from her "true self." She acts the part of a public representative, and as such she is not supposed to respond emotionally; she is supposed to improvise her act according to the circumstances. My point is not that this fact would relieve Solstad of his responsibility to behave decently in the situation. I am merely claiming that if we don't acknowledge this potential motive in Solstad's performance, our analysis will miss the target. Solstad obstructs the dialogue in order to disclose a paradoxical media phenomenon: the silent agreement to pretend to have a private conversation in public. By turning the situation into a tableau of interacting personae, Solstad strips the situation of any privacy or intimacy. In this context, one might point to Joshua Meyrowitz's argument, in *No Sense of Place* (1985), that modern electronic media blur the formerly sharp distinction between strict private ("backstage") and strict public ("onstage") behavior. Public stage behavior in electronic media is thus neither public nor private, or it is both public and private at the same time. Solstad's rhetoric can thus be interpreted as a way of adapting to, or as a kind of countermove, to this generalized media situation.

Allowing for the perspective of interacting personae would also seem to be in the spirit of the recommendation made by analyst and theorist Dana R. Villa: that we had better include an understanding of the concept of *theatricality* in public life, as did scholars like Hannah Arendt and Richard Sennett (Villa 1992, 147). To Villa, theatricality is the necessary supplement to Habermas's rationalist conception of the public sphere. A principle of theatricality, mediated through masks, personae, and play, enables public actors to keep the tyrannical reign of the intimate at a distance, allowing them to remain "open to the world," in Arendt's terms (quoted in ibid., 148). This mode of self-distanced, playful public appearance might be labelled aristocratic. However, one should be careful to distinguish this mode from another kind of aristocracy—namely, a kind of self-righteous, demonstrative "splendid isolation." According to Villa, Arendt (with reference to Lessing) is precisely at odds with the typical "late modern retreat from a hostile public world" (148), a view that is expressed in Arendt's critique of the so-called inner emigration response. As a matter of fact, Solstad at one point publically declared that he was going into "inner exile," which of course he never did; nevertheless, he made it clear that this kind of retreat seemed like a reasonable, logical, and tempting line of action, given the state of contemporary public life. This is exactly the kind of response Arendt would warn us against, according to Villa, because the sense of purity and tranquility gained would be earned at the cost of "our very sense of reality" (148).

Still, we can conclude that the enactment of duplicity brings to light a tension between democratic and aristocratic cultural views. Solstad presents his rhetorical conduct so as to appeal to a hidden public, a public consisting of citizens of a presumed higher stature, that is, citizens possessing literary *Bildung*. His rhetoric implicitly stratifies the audience; the doubling of personae results in a complementary doubling of implied readers, one being the implied fool, the other, the implied gentleman. His rhetoric creates a cultural divide, and the one who recognizes this and gets on the right side of the line gets his reward immediately: he feels included among the cultivated. Rhetorical citizenship is thus awarded according to merit.

As we have already noted, Solstad protects the borders of literature against intrusion from the media. Fiction must be protected from reality; fiction is the real thing. No stupid questions can be allowed, because they would devalue his writing. He must prevent the epistemological resources allocated in the craftsmanship of writing from being vulgarized by talking. In socioeconomic terms, Solstad protects what we could call his field-specific literary capital in the market of the media economy. The currency of the communicative script of writing must not be devalued. Solstad's conduct is thus a typical case of defending his literary autonomy.

However, this socioeconomic perspective is not able to explain exactly why these literary values must be defended, apart from the trivial fact that he is a writer by profession. Is this merely a question of clearing the path for his own kind of literature, or of protecting his socioeconomic well-being as a writer? In the remainder of this chapter, I propose an interpretation that suggests that what is really at stake is a quarrel over some fundamental politico-philosophical issues. Solstad's interventions demonstrate a clash between two different normative conceptions of public discourse. He practices what the American philosopher Stanley Rosen describes as *esotericism*. The characteristics of this kind of communication might be summed up by the title of Rosen's essay: "Suspicion, Deception, and Concealment" (1999). Esotericism is a communicative mode in which the author conceals himself in his own discourse. It stands in stark contrast to the view of public discourse as an open flow of information or a mutual disclosing of opinions. Esotericism advocates secrecy and sparseness of information for the sake of a higher cultural or political good. Rosen quotes Nietzsche's *Beyond Good and Evil:* "Our highest insights must—and should—sound like follies, perhaps like crimes, when in an impermissible manner they reach ears which are not suited or predetermined for them" (1999, 2). In the same spirit, Solstad's writing must not reach the ears of an interviewer or a talk-show audience "in an impermissible manner." Solstad challenges the discursive ethos based on the principles of openness and frankness. If not denying the legitimacy of these principles altogether, he points to their possible limitations. Not everything can be said directly.[4]

This last statement is reminiscent of what rhetorician and theorist of the public sphere Gerard Hauser has described as "the rhetoric of indirection" (2009). This concept refers to a kind of rhetorical situation in which the rhetor addresses one audience directly, but with the intention of reaching another (distant, absent) audience indirectly. The performance is enacted in such a way that the message is carried beyond the limits of the immediate (private) setting in order to generate public opinion. In terms of writing between the lines (or, to paraphrase, of placing the message behind enemy lines), we recognize Solstad's strategy. However, the cases that illustrate "the rhetoric of indirection" are all examples of real, serious political struggles, the outcomes of which could sometimes be a matter of life and death (e.g., the imprisonment of Nelson Mandela, the hunger strike of Bobby Sands). Surely this does not apply to the case of Solstad.

Solstad practices a different kind of politics. I will give two examples. In 1997 Solstad published the essay "Om meddelelsens problem" (On the problem of communication) in a major Norwegian newspaper. The essay was basically an attack on what we could call the freedom of cultural self-expression. In 2008 Solstad published the essay "Om ytringsfriheten" (On freedom of speech), an essay in which he criticized the discursive role of the principle of freedom of speech. Both essays were thus candid attacks on liberal political values, attacks that can be interpreted as a protest against a widely held definition of cultural and rhetorical citizenship. Even so, something in his dogmatic stance seems dubious; it is as if he *acts* sincere. His political sincerity never loses its stain of irony.

However, esotericism is not just a matter of choosing a personal rhetorical aesthetics. Its occurrence corresponds with the shifting winds of the public climate. "The issue [of esotericism]," says Rosen, "becomes entirely explicit at the time of the Enlightenment, when it is widely held that, important as the concealment of dangerous views from the wider public may have been in the past, it is now possible for the human race to enter the age of maturity" (1999, 2). In other words, esotericism becomes explicit at exactly the time that Kant recommends the principle of publicity as the pragmatic proof test of truth, the same period that happens to serve as the historical normative model for Habermas's principle of publicity. Esotericism delimits the range of this principle: it is the rhetorical expression of its political countermovement and as such a subculture of the Enlightenment. However, it is important to notice that according to Rosen's interpretation of Nietzsche and the esoteric tradition, the kind of dissimulation we are talking about here is not merely a sociological phenomenon (although it is that); it is also a reflection of "the very nature of human experience and, still more fundamentally, . . . the way things are" (1999, 3). It corresponds to a philosophical position, namely, the view that "deception and concealment are intrinsic to existence itself. Esotericism is thus the inevitable consequence of our warranted suspicion of nature" (3). Esoteric communication is a rhetorical mode that emerges from an attempt at truthfulness.

Esotericism is found, claims Nietzsche, "wherever one believes in rank-ordering and not in equality and equal rights. . . . Everything that is deep loves the mask; the deepest things have a hatred for image and likeness" (from *Beyond Good and Evil*, quoted in Rosen 1999, 2). It is in the nature of higher and valuable things to present themselves in disguise. Higher things cannot be vulgarized in essence; they cannot be presented in floodlight. In this perspective, Solstad's conduct is the *rhetorical* counterpart to the *political* problem underlying the concept of the public sphere: the distinction between the salutary concept of *demos* and the derogatory concept of *vulgus*. As is commonly known, there is a *textus* of ambiguous etymology connecting these words: from the Greek *demos* comes the term *democratic*, but from the Latin *vulgus* comes the term *vulgar*. From Latin *populus* comes *public* but also *populist*, and from the French word *peuple* stems the Norwegian word *pøbel* (mob). From a biographical perspective, this ambiguity mirrors Solstad's deeply paradoxical (to critics, inconsistent) stance toward the political idea of democracy, as illustrated for instance in his early communist period, when he proclaimed that he wrote in the service of the people—not, however, in accord with the expressed tastes and interests of the people but with the program of his own exclusive literary circuit (named "Profil"). Many commentators are surprised that Solstad, a former communist, expresses what they consider elitist, aristocratic, culturally conservative views (Wedberg 2003, 8, 51–58). They find his political leap too great, his stance too contradictory. In my view, the concept of esotericism helps us explain this apparent contradiction. Esotericism cuts across the ideological polarities of left and right, radical and conservative, progressive and reactionary (and postmodernist and modernist, for that matter). In Solstad's intellectual project as a whole, there seems to be a permanent dialectic between cultural conservatism and political radicalism.

Also, it must be noted that Solstad has acknowledged his debt to what he calls the middle European literary tradition, seen for instance in his essay on Gombrowicz, with the resonant title "Nødvendigheten av å leve inautentisk" (The necessity of living inauthentically). I have argued elsewhere that Solstad is influenced by Milan Kundera, who also explicitly defines himself as a writer in the "central European" tradition (e.g., Kafka, Broch, Musil, Gombrowicz) (Wedberg 2003, 103–13). Kundera's youth as a communist, his later conversion to high-culture aestheticism, his contempt for the state of public life in the former Republic of Czechoslovakia (because of the ideological vulgarity and domination of Russian culture), and his reluctance to participate in public debates on political issues are all traits reminiscent of the literary persona of Dag Solstad. Even more important, an essential part of Kundera's literary theory (if such it can be called) is the notion that there is a real ideological conflict between "the common spirit of the mass media" and "the spirit of the novel" (Kundera 1992, 28). The spirit of the novel is the spirit of aesthetic judgment, a spirit that recognizes differences of value, of *distinction*. In this context, we should also note that Kundera is partly a Nietzschean. He adheres to the Epicurean principle of secrecy, as can be seen in his novel *Slowness*, a novel by which, as it happens, Solstad may have been directly influenced.[5] Kundera also speaks pejoratively of what he regards as the dominant ethos of journalism, which is not "the right to ask a question" but "the right to demand an answer" (Kundera 1995, 115).

In my analysis, it is exactly this political tension that is enacted in Solstad's public interventions and that crystallizes as a typical rhetorical-strategic possibility for a late modern intellectual. Such interventions amount to a form of resistance against what is regarded as an extreme principle of publicity, a discursive ethos of radical openness and frankness that tends to pervert itself into a general blurring of distinctions. But if Solstad is to make a difference, he has to express this resistance within the very public space that he opposes. Therefore, his point must be dramatized, staged, and demonstrated, not just stated or expressed.[6] His interventions are crafted so as to make us see the fabric of the apparently transparent liberal public sphere.

Habermas's basic conception in the *Strukturwandel*—the claim that the historically generated principle of rational publicity is essential for modern democracy—is surely correct. But this principle, in the particular shape of "communicative reason," deliberation, or any other such doctrine, is not sufficient to serve as a universal, normative politico-philosophical ideal. In our case, Solstad acknowledges the power of publicity in the very act of appearing, while simultaneously mocking its beneficiaries (the wider public, the masses), thus dismissing the principle of publicity in the very act of making use of it. His rhetorical interventions are so crafted that they undermine and disrupt the immediate public surroundings in which they appear, but their intentions are seemingly constructive: they are supposed to remind us of the limit where liberal publicness and communicative openness might turn repressive. The politico-philosophical corollary to this is that political liberalism cannot itself be grounded in liberal theory; it must be grounded in something else, something outside itself (cf. Rosen 1999, 15: "What I object to is the delusion that there is a liberal theory of liberalism which is free of the intrinsic aporia of liberalism").

These reflections lead to some conclusions with regard to the rhetoric of duplicity. Duplicity, in the technical sense of the word, means doubleness. The device of doubling personae, with its potential for expressing resistance, for maintaining artistic integrity, for playing with the interlocutor, for creating different kinds of implied readers, for anticipating and controlling the response of the audience, is generally a rhetorical device of self-empowerment. In ordinary speech, however, duplicity means dishonesty. The strategy of doubling personae has a flip side: hiding, deceiving, lying. The inherent problem in practicing the rhetoric of duplicity is thus to challenge the perverted ideal of repressive frankness without becoming morally corrupt. The playful, aristocratic relativizing of naïve public (demotic, vulgar) situations at some point turns into a self-gratifying discursive game that merely serves its own aesthetic needs. It thus remains to be seen what the alternative spaces, to which such intellectual practice points, are to be filled with. It seems that in a late modern (if not postmodern) society, these spaces are left either undescribed, or empty, or filled with politico-philosophical content that is not taken seriously. Thus the rhetorical practice in question is in danger of deteriorating into pastiches of political resistance, fragmented reminiscences of a time when intellectual interventions made a real political difference. In the last analysis, these rhetorical postures might be just that: mere postures. For all the stylistic appeal and subtle appropriations of *kairos*, it might be that the perspective behind these linguistic interventions is dangerously close to political nihilism. The merit of the interventions of a Solstad or a Kundera is that they manage to show that in an open, liberal, capitalist society something more than social and economic injustice is at stake—something more abstract, transparent, perhaps barely detectable: a dispute over the disappearance of cultural distinctions. On the other hand, by leaving the solutions to these problems unspecified and resting content with a dramatization of their nature, such intellectual practice might appear as a kind of boutique political activism.

The ethos of Habermasian deliberative democracy might be more or less effectively countered by champions of linguistic ingenuity, but their success does not move us past the politico-philosophical deadlock of late Enlightenment thought: the dialectic between the relics of positivist scientism, on the one hand, and the twin brothers of postmodernism and Marxism on the other. The rhetoric of literary subtlety and cunning is a powerful force within certain academic, intellectual, and artistic circles. As I have argued, this is understandable. It emerges from a legitimate critique of Enlightenment rationalism, whether in the form of scientism or of rather empty theories of "communicative reason." The problem, however, is that the same forces implicitly undermine not only rationalism of the reifying kind but political rationality as such. Those who enter a state of fatigue faced with the ruins of the Enlightenment or of historical utopia may turn to "poeticizing reason" (Nietzsche's "dichtende Vernunft") in order to preserve a kind of hope. But this hope is not properly grounded. *Its spokesmen give us no good reason to believe in it*. The rhetorical playfulness of intellectual writers like Solstad appeals to those who value artistic sensibility and aesthetic judgment. But these writers cannot account for the root (*ratio, raison*) of such judgment. In this respect, poeticizing reason is unreasonable.

Solstad and writers like him see the symptoms but have no diagnosis: they are doctors without a cure. In the conclusion of this chapter I can only indicate the nature of the disease. As I have tried to show, we are somehow led in the right direction by a close reading of Solstad's speech acts: they demonstrate that the problem and the solution lie somewhere in the organic relation between *playfulness* and *truthfulness*. But this mere demonstration is not enough. One must also theoretically account for the facts of human distinction, value, and judgment that, again in the words of Stanley Rosen, amount to an account of the intimate relation between *intelligibility* and *the good*. The deepest lesson to be learned from these public events is thus that residents of late modernity must carefully reconsider the relation between rhetoric and philosophy in order to resurrect political rationality of a sensible kind.

NOTES

1. When speaking of social phenomena in terms of "spheres" (Habermas), or "fields" (Bourdieu), we run the risk of inadvertently turning our local intuitive insights into global discursive systems. We should avoid reifying through geometricizing, a mechanism by which the social or cultural entity under scrutiny is imagined within the matrix of quasi-mathematical space. The problem inherent in such a spatializing procedure is that the particular case is lifted out of the situation from which it originated into a coordinate system where all cases are instances of the same; every social or historic event, every cultural phenomenon, and every literary or artistic work is aligned and formalized according to a quasi-economic continuum or monad ("the public space," "the literary field"). My ambition is rather to compose a set of cases that speak for themselves, and resonate with one another, as far as they go. And they go only as far as the point that, when transgressed, the content, value, and meaning of the specific case are lost in abstraction.

2. Among the general negative characterizations of Solstad's public persona are the views that he appears to be old and disillusioned, evasive, elitist, conservative/reactionary, cowardly, etc. On the other hand, there are generally two ways of responding positively to Solstad's interventions: he is funny and witty, or he is eloquent and stylistically refined. It must also be noted that sometimes the responses are, somewhat paradoxically, both positive and negative at once: "His opinions are intolerable, true, but how well articulated!"

3. On the issue of irony, Solstad himself (1997b) stated in an interview, "I am not ironic." The statement, however, was immediately modified by an ironic comment.

4. Solstad's style is frequently at odds with the demands of what could be called informational-economical efficiency: his sentences, paragraphs, and semiliterary anecdotes are long, slow, repetitive, and meticulous. This communicative redundancy might be considered a device of imprecision, a kind of description that captures its object indirectly (see Wedberg 2003, 34–35).

5. In a 1997 interview Solstad was asked if he had the impression that the general public dismissed him as an "old school communist." "Yes," he responded, "that's true. In a time that is all about dancing, you are old if you don't. But being a writer is different from being a rock star. We don't go around jumping for two hours" (Solstad 1997d). I have argued that the term "dancing" may be a reference to Kundera's *Slowness* (1996), in which Kundera uses the concept of "the dancer" as a description of a typical late modern public persona, a player without a political cause, a vain poseur obsessed with the ambition of being the object of public attention.

6. As Rosen observes, esotericism becomes "entirely explicit at the time of the Enlightenment" (1999, 2). In a late modern public sphere, esotericism has taken an even more refined shape: it is now not only explicit; it is the very problem with which the intel-

lectual intervention is concerned. Esotericism has become practically self-reflexive to the extent that the content of the issue has merged with the shape of its demonstration. (In a different context, John Durham Peters has described this as a general rhetorical phenomenon, namely, the case of a text that "enacts its point in the form of its saying, performing its own modus operandi" [1994, 121].) As such, I believe that these rhetorical interventions are not only symptoms of the eccentricities of a specific writer, like Dag Solstad, or simply expressions of the inner life of the Norwegian literary field. They are examples of a transhistorical rhetorical type. But, as I have tried to show, this type is not merely of academic interest to students of rhetoric; it may be important as the locus of a real contemporary ideological schism.

REFERENCES

Habermas, J. 1991. *The Structural Transformation of the Public Sphere: An Inquiry into a Category of Bourgeois Society*. Cambridge: MIT Press. (Orig. pub. in German, 1965.)
Hauser, G. 2009. "The Rhetoric of Indirection." Paper presented before the Department of Media Studies and Information Science, University of Bergen, Bergen, Norway, 18 May 2009.
Kundera, M. 1992. *Romankunsten*. Oslo: Aventura.
———. 1995. *Udødeligheten*. Oslo: Aventura.
———. 1996. *Langsomheten*. Oslo: Aventura.
Meyrowitz, J. 1985. *No Sense of Place*. Oxford: Oxford University Press.
Peters, J. D. 1994. "The Gaps of Which Communication Is Made." *Critical Studies in Mass Communication* 11 (2): 117–140.
Rosen, S. 1999. "Suspicion, Deception, and Concealment." In Rosen, *Metaphysics in Ordinary Language*, 1–14. New Haven: Yale University Press.
Sandvik, H. 2008. "Løgn eller forbanna dikt." *Bergens Tidende*, 27 May. http://www.bt.no/meninger/kommentar/sandvik/article570709.ece (accessed 15 November 2008).
Solstad, D. 1997a. "Intervju med Eva Bratholm." *Bokbadet*, 21 March. http://www.youtube.com/watch?v=remnOcZ1Ak8.
———. 1997b. "Om meddelelsens problem." *Aftenposten*, 27 June.
———. 1997c. "Om romanen." In Solstad, *Tre essays*, 7–32. Oslo: Forlaget Oktober.
———. 1997d. "Portrettet: Forsøk på meddelelse." *Aftenposten*, 5 July.
———. 1997e. "Solstad satte punktum." *Dagbladet*, 7 August.
———. 2000. "Nødvendigheten av å leve inautentisk." In Solstad, *Artikler om Litteratur, 1966–1981*, 126–39. Oslo: Forlaget .
———. 2008. "Om ytringsfriheten." *Samtiden* 2:4–19.
Villa, D. R. 1992. "Theatricality in the Public Realm of Hannah Arendt." In *Public Space and Democracy*, ed. Marcel Henaff and Tracy B. Strong, 144–71. Minneapolis: University of Minnesota Press.
Wedberg, K. 2003. "Litterær offentlighet og opplysningens dilemma." Master's thesis, University of Bergen, Norway.
Wold, B. 2002. "Harkingens estetikk." *Klassekampen*, 5 October 2002. http://www.klassekampen.no/artikler/kultur_medier/29414/article/item/null.

9

RHETORIC OF WAR, RHETORIC OF GENDER

Berit von der Lippe

The protection-of-women-and-children scenario has always been common in war rhetoric. Viewing war and security through a gendered lens may reveal "how a certain logic of gendered meanings and images helps organize the way people interpret events and circumstances, along with their positions and possibilities for action within them, and sometimes provides some rationale for action" (Young 2007, 118).

This chapter looks critically at the rhetoric of protecting and liberating Afghan women in the wake of the "war on terror." I intend to connect rhetorical inquiry with contemporary social concerns, exploring the relevance of rhetoric to current global issues of opportunity and diversity.

Increased gender awareness in general and in relation to war in particular has influenced how war stories have been told in recent decades. Feminist ideas and strategies have created a favorable environment for new concepts of gender equality. *Co-optation*, a common discursive, rhetorical, and linguistic practice, has occurred. Gendered concepts may easily be used in ways that don't reflect the original goals of those who formulated them. Because these concepts allow for multiple conflicting interpretations, a space is created for rhetoric, including empty declarations. An analysis of three women's rhetoric will shed light on this process and serve as a platform for discussing gender and war rhetoric from postcolonial perspectives, critical to Western scenarios of "protecting" Muslim women, even with military means.

I aim, on the one hand, to examine how Afghan women, and the silencing of them, are used in war rhetoric. On the other hand, I want to demonstrate how difficult it is to talk about war without co-opting the hegemonic war rhetoric and creating a *doxic* room, dominated by taken-for-granted "common sense," including its large areas of silence. Creating space(s) for racially and culturally marginalized voices, particularly those of women whose protection and liberation one claims to secure, may enlarge the field of rhetorical studies. The ensuing perspectives are wider and more diverse than the perspectives rooted in traditional neo-Aristotelian rhetoric. Rhetorical citizenship and public deliberation should be seen in a context of democratic global citizenship. My narrative about gendered war rhetoric should illuminate what is at stake at the global level when gender awareness is included, an awareness easily co-opted in the Western rhetoric of liberation.

This chapter also considers the use of panegyric, that is, formal public utterances in praise of a person or thing. In her study of foreign policy as a social construct, Roxanne Lynn Doty (1993) asks questions that I ask as subquestions: with whom is the reader, male or female, implicitly asked to identify when reading or listening to war stories? Who are the heroes or protectors, and how are they represented?

Finally, my aim is to raise questions related to gender neutrality and gender awareness in regard to security issues—issues of relevance in attempting to shape the concept of "rhetorical citizenship."

The Rhetoric of Silence

A rhetoric of silence may seem peculiar, given the Western tendency to overvalue speech and speaking out, as Cheryl Glenn (2002) writes. Within the rhetorical tradition, the focus has mainly been on who is seen and what is read or heard. Traditional rhetoric is thus mainly about successful and unsuccessful rhetoric from the perspective of the powerful. Some feminist rhetorical scholars have sought to transform the rhetorical tradition from what is seen as upper-class, agonistic, public, and male into regendered, inclusionary, dialogic, and collaborative rhetoric (Campbell 2008). Feminist rhetoric is, however, a vague concept, understood differently by different scholars. The rhetoric of silence, as understood here, will challenge this overly dichotomous perspective (male-agonistic/female-dialogic).

The question is not only whether speech or silence is more productive or appropriate. Rather, the question is about a rhetoricity of purposeful silence: when is it self-selected, when imposed? "When silence is our rhetorical choice, we can use it purposefully and productively—but when it is not our choice, but someone else's for us, it can be insidious, particularly when someone else's choice for us comes in the shape of institutional structure. To wit, a person can choose silence, but the choice isn't really hers because speaking out will be professional suicide. In short, she's been disciplined—and silenced" (Glenn 2002, 5).

Glenn is discussing rhetoric and silence within North American culture. Silence may be a means of survival or a conscious way of resistance. When silence is broken but nobody listens, one's value as a human being seems to be nil. As Jacqueline Jones Royster puts it, "What I am compelled to ask, when veils seem more like walls, is who has the privilege of speaking?" (1996, 36). Or who has the privilege to speak for Afghan women? The veiling of Afghan women is much more than the burka; more important for most Afghan women are those veils that "seem more like walls." The rhetoric of the veil—or the rhetoric of silence—occurs when the speaking subjects speak on behalf of and in place of Afghan women, erasing more or less the subjectivity of Afghan women—who then become helpless objects to be rescued by us.

Cynthia Enloe (2004, 19–42) gives examples illustrating yet another aspect of the rhetoric of silencing gender. There must be a group with sufficient power to create a center that makes some other individual or group belong to the margin: "There is yearly and daily business of maintaining the margin where it currently is and the center where it now is. It is harder for those at the alleged center to hear the hopes, fears and explanations of those in the margins, not because of physical distance—the margin may be two blocks from the White House . . . but because it takes resources and access to be heard where it matters" (20).

Viewed from "the center," be it Washington, London, Paris, Berlin, or Oslo, Afghan people seem to be at the very margin. Afghans of both genders, men as potential terrorists or potential collaborators and friends, women in need of Western protection, have been silenced, marginalized, erased, and stereotyped in different ways and with different consequences. Belonging to various tribal centers at home, Afghan men are seldom listened to from the Western center(s); neither are their lives considered worthy of our grief.

The point is that hegemonic discourses, as defined by Gramsci (1978), are offered as something you already agree with, as reflections of your own desires, needs, and wants, in which you can effortlessly recognize yourself. Hegemony seems to offer what you already want. For a short period after 11 September 2001, this kind of hegemony was not threatened in Western countries, and together with the rhetoric of silencing gender—of protecting and liberating Afghan Muslim women (and children)—it was suitable for the hegemonic discourse. The authority in this case was forcibly imposed. It was not offered to Afghan women (or men) in any subtle ways.

Co-optation takes place when the hegemonic ideology of war is not questioned and alternative war stories are silenced or marginalized. Co-optation of women's rights issues, such as gender equality, is, according to Stratigaki (2004), more likely when there is a high level of normative legitimacy for the general principle underlying the original policy goal. Gender issues are so closely linked to fundamental principles of democracy and social justice that the concept of gender equality is rarely challenged in public deliberation. The underlying intentions are most apparent in the ways that gender equality is translated into concrete policies. Feminist engagements with security and human rights issues require a constant and careful consideration of the way in which feminist claims may be transformed through the powerful and complex interplay between dominant social relations and competing discourses.

Rhetorical co-optation is often achieved through ideographs, as they offer a subtle means of transporting—and *transforming*—ideological commitments. Ideographs are the basic linguistic and structural elements of ideology and represent a collective commitment to a particular but ambiguous normative goal, justifying and legitimizing action conducted in the name of the public (Cloud 2004; McGee 1980). Ideographs are mainly abstractions, like liberty or justice. In gendering my own perspective(s), I also aim to make manifest the material aspects embedded in ideographic abstractions.

Feminism and Metamorphosis

War rhetoric, with its use of ideographs, occurs within historical situations in which gendered rhetoric can be used strategically to legitimize foreign policies. Victimization of women in non-Western cultures has been discussed in feminist studies classes for more than three decades. An imagined community of global sisterhood was advocated. Who speaks and acts in mediated war narratives seems to draw on a particular and selective use of these ideas. Patriarchal oppression and violence against women is committed "out there" by "uncivilized men." The appeal of gender and gender(ed) rhetoric will easily contribute to the appeal of "us" versus "them" (Stabile and Kumar 2005).

Global respect for women was a foreign policy priority in the rhetoric of the Bush administration. When addressing the public, both George W. Bush and Colin Powell referred to the plight of Afghan women. Several women became visible in public, as when prominent women like Mary Matalin and Karen Hughes deplored women's conditions under Taliban rule in the autumn of 2001 (Flanders 2004). Among these highly influential women was the First Lady, Laura Bush, who experienced a metamorphosis shortly after 9/11. She suddenly appeared in public as a political spokeswoman—and consoler-in-chief—on national security and international issues.

Inspired by Tasha Dubriwny (2005) as well as by S. J. Parry-Giles and D. M. Blair (2002), let us consider one of Laura Bush's six speeches to the nation, in this case one that her husband would normally have given. On 17 November 2001, a few weeks after the war in Afghanistan had begun, Bush addressed the American people: "Good morning. I'm Laura Bush, and I'm delivering this week's radio address to kick off a world-wide effort to focus on the brutality against women and children by the al-Qaeda terrorist network and the regime it supports in Afghanistan, the Taliban" (Bush 2001). This extraordinary address is represented as something nearly ordinary. The First Lady, usually standing silently by her man, has suddenly chosen/been advised to break her silence on policy issues. She does it by applying a rhetoric of everyday language on issues far from everyday events. By kicking off "a world-wide effort" for Afghan women and children, she manifests both non-traditional First Lady potency and responsibility as the global caring mother.

Sometimes she foregrounds the Afghan women only, attributing to them qualities as individuals in their own right, as in the next part of her exordium: "That regime is now in retreat across much of the country, and the people of Afghanistan—especially women—are rejoicing. Afghan women know, through hard experience, what the rest of the world is discovering: The brutal oppression of women is a central goal of the terrorists." After a few weeks of bombing, she announces an end to suppression and the retreat of the Taliban. Without blaming "the rest of the world" or the United States for passivity or neglect vis-à-vis Afghan women, Bush tells her listeners that Operation Enduring Freedom for Afghan women has nearly succeeded. Reminding the "nation" several times of Taliban atrocities, the women-and-children rhetoric gathers rhetorical strength: "Long before the current war began, the Taliban and its terrorist allies were making the lives of children and women in Afghanistan miserable."

Bush's rhetoric differs, though, from the rhetoric of the president. She avoids the dichotomy of us and them, underscoring the non-Islamic character of the Taliban's treatment of women:

> Women cannot work outside the home, or even leave their homes by themselves. The severe repression and brutality against women in Afghanistan is not a matter of legitimate religious practice. Muslims around the world have condemned the brutal degradation of women

and children by the Taliban regime. The poverty, poor health, and illiteracy that the terrorists and the Taliban have imposed on women in Afghanistan do not conform with the treatment of women in most of the Islamic world, where women make important contributions in their societies. . . . Only the terrorists and the Taliban threaten to pull out women's fingernails for wearing nail polish. The plight of women and children in Afghanistan is a matter of deliberate human cruelty, carried out by those who seek to intimidate and control.

Foregrounding the illiteracy imposed on Afghan women might be effective—the educated librarian First Lady's primary ethos is already established and serves as a pillar for her secondary ethos, the ethos both attributed to her as First Lady and resulting from this speech (see Mral 2003). The rhetoric illustrates her balancing neoconservative/maternal rhetoric (the juxtaposition of women and children) and liberal/modern feminist rhetoric (protesting women's exclusion from work outside the home).

In her conclusion Bush returns to a familiar North American form of rhetoric: "In America, next week brings Thanksgiving. After the events of the last few months, we'll be holding our families even closer. And we will be especially thankful for all the blessings of American life. I hope Americans will join our family in working to ensure that dignity and opportunity will be secured for all the women and children of Afghanistan."

This reference to Thanksgiving traditions probably reached the "hearts and minds" of most listeners. Praising traditional family values and avoiding any explicit reference to her religion, the First Lady has delivered a speech appealing to most Americans. The political position she takes is elegantly transformed into the national caring mother as well as the global caring mother, speaking on behalf of women (and children) all over the world.

In this speech, as Dubriwny (2005) demonstrates vividly, Laura Bush draws upon the tradition of the republican mother, crafting an argument for women's rights that upholds a traditional understanding of womanhood while balancing on a tightrope between the modern private/public dichotomy and liberal feminist rhetoric. Women and children function much like the abstractions "equality," "democracy," "modernity," and "liberty," despite the materiality of both women and children. According to Dubriwny, this indicates the ability of material concepts—such as the ideographs "women and children" or "the plight of women and children"—to act as ideology in certain types of discourse.

Although ideographs are culture-bound, meaning different things in different cultures, the women-and-children reference appeals to common values all over the world, at least to some extent. This indicates the ability of abstractions to obscure or veil the material/physical world. The "women-and-children" concept derives its meaning from its specific applications and works to support visions essential to rallying wartime nationalism and presenting citizens with a sense of their nation's special benevolence. Simultaneously, Laura Bush was a notable voice on important global security issues.

Liberal Norwegian Co-optation of Feminism

While the American First Lady had to balance between a neoconservative and a co-opted liberal feminist rhetoric, Norwegian female representatives of the power elite were dancing on a different tightrope. They had to reach a fairly liberal Norwegian public that valued equity feminism, focused on incorporating women into existing male-dominated liberalist ideology. At the same time, they had to avoid too close identification with both the U.S. president, "the commander-in-chief," and his wife, "the consoler-in-chief."

Instead of maternal feminism, Nordic feminism is largely characterized by equity feminism. In Norway a traditional, but liberal, social-democratic ethos with a heterosexual nuclear family at its center dominates feminist thinking. Women are seen as inherently similar to men, and gender equality has been the driving force for the feminist movement. Male dominance and power have been criticized, and one of the goals has been women's equal participation in the domestic political sphere. The state ideology is that of a welfare state with strong labor unions and labor parties, and official feminism coincides with that ideology.

The story of Norwegian foreign policy rhetoric depends in large part on Norway's remote geographical position, which, according to the hegemonic narratives, has historically permitted the state to remain aloof from international engagement. The decision to enter into military alliances was made after World War II, with Norway's admission into NATO in 1949. Solidarity, internationalism, and peace-keeping operations have been the ideographs around which Norwegian foreign policy rhetoric has been crafted and in whose name actions have been performed. According to this rhetoric, Norway never takes part in warfare; it happens, though, that the country takes part in military operations. The narrative cherishes the idea that Norway has a long-standing tradition of participation in UN-led peacekeeping activities, conflict prevention through political dialogue, mediation, and overseas development aid on a large scale (see Bergman 2004; Ingebritsen 2002).

The Norwegian Social Democrat and leader of the governmental Defense Committee from 2002 to 2005, Marit Nybakk, has for several years been Norway's most important spokesperson for co-opted feminist rhetoric and the rhetoric of silencing gender. In August 2002 Nybakk started her campaign for Afghan women within the frame of the liberal and equity feminist tradition, creating, though, no heterodox position that would allow a true polyphony on the rationale of a country's foreign policy toward Afghanistan, or unspoken silences to be spoken. Rather, a co-optation took place when she appropriated, in the very early stages of the intervention in Afghanistan, the Western hegemonic discourse on the war.

In an article titled "A War for Women's Liberation," Nybakk explained her support for the U.S.-initiated war on terror: "This is a liberation war, and a liberation war for Afghan women too. This aspect is for me the main question and the main issue. For years I have been concerned about Taliban's extreme suppression of Afghan women" (quoted in Ellingsen 2002). Nybakk thus immediately transformed or redefined the war on terror as a liberation war. Hers is the voice of a feminist using both leftist rhetoric from the 1970s and rhetoric similar to Laura Bush's. She continues with softer rhetoric: "Here in the West we have closed our eyes to the brutal treatment of Afghan women because the injustice did not strike at ourselves. Then we experienced 11 September and the US-led war to fight against the Taliban and the terror network al-Qaeda. This is indeed a necessary war." The interpellation of all people in the West, an all-embracing, nongendered "we," is characteristic of Nybakk's rhetoric; it alludes both to religious rhetoric ("the injustice did not strike at ourselves" echoes "love thy neighbor as thyself") and to an important Norwegian writer, Arnulf Øverland, and his often-quoted lines "Du skal ikke tåle så innerlig vel / den urett som ikke rammer deg selv" (You shall not tolerate so terribly well / the injustice that doesn't strike yourself). Elements of love for "the other," as prescribed in the Bible, and virile war rhetoric—"this is indeed a necessary war"—are, however, elements indicative of robust strength regardless of gender. Equality between women and men is an ideographic building block within the Norwegian rhetoric of war and peace. Laura Bush's overtly maternal rhetoric is absent from Nybakk's speech, as it is from Norwegian war rhetoric in general. Nybakk's campaign decreased in strength, and in 2004 she chose (the rhetoric of) silence. Her footprints, however, remained.

The step from benevolent altruism to patronizing rationality is short and easy to take. When Anne-Grete Strøm-Erichsen, also a Social Democrat, was appointed defense minister in the autumn of 2005, a rhetoric within a liberation/protection scenario was challenged, as most Afghan women had hardly seen real changes after five years of Operation Enduring Freedom.

Strøm-Erichsen's speech in Brussels in 2006 to the European Union members on security issues promotes self-evident truths within an apparently harmonious security discourse. Her exordium might seem rhetorically to be of limited interest; representing a non-EU state, her appreciation of being invited among friends is, though, an embrace of some importance. "First of all, let me thank the Presidency for inviting me to this Troika meeting," Strøm-Erichsen begins.[1] "The opportunity to discuss current security issues with our close European friends and allies is very much appreciated." She then, in a similarly modest and polite manner, assures the audience that "Norway will remain an active contributor to the ESDP [European security and defense policy]," emphasizing "that invitations from the EU to contribute to ESDP operations are always given serious consideration in Oslo."[2] The tightrope dance is, indeed, very different from those referred to above. Avoiding any explicit war rhetoric at home, but representing Norway's and Norwegians' trust and serious engagement in both EU and ESDP operations, she must balance soft and hard rhetoric carefully. "Norway's participation in the EU battle groups concept is a key element in our contribution to the ESDP." Before this audience Strøm-Erichsen's rhetoric may be called loyalty rhetoric, similar to that of a trustworthy pupil addressing a group of highly respected teachers.

Underscoring the need to improve NATO-EU relations, cooperation, and the value of strategic partnership, Strøm-Erichsen approaches security challenges and the complexities of peacekeeping and peace building, paying specific attention to the war in Afghanistan: "First, the international community must coordinate civilian efforts in a better way. Today the civilian aspects of our engagements, in Afghanistan and elsewhere, are often fragmented and uncoordinated. This means that the overall results are less effective."

Catastrophes for Afghan civilians are presented simply as insufficient coordination of "civilian efforts," and the problem is depicted as gender-neutral. The war in Afghanistan thus seems to be a matter of logistics rather than military occupation. "Second," she continues, "development cannot take place without the necessary level of security. There needs to be close cooperation between NATO, the EU, and the UN, as well as with other international actors, including NGOs." The harmonious unity between organizations is taken for granted, and gender is not an issue—so far.

Strøm-Erichsen, after panegyrically embracing all these Western-dominated institutions, somewhat surprisingly turns to UN Resolution 1325 (2000), which urges member states to consider women's role in new peace-support operations, and she goes on to praise the EU decision to promote "gender equality and gender mainstreaming in crisis management, in line with UN Resolution 1325." She then assumes the role of teacher, telling the audience, "This is important progress. Norway puts great emphasis on the UN resolution and has adopted a national action plan to promote gender issues." Complete harmony is finally established when she urges EU members to agree with Norway and UN Security Council Resolution 1325, emphasizing that operations should be gender-sensitive at all levels.

The rhetorical use of this resolution may be seen as a subtle form of feminist co-optation, on the following reasoning: Norway participates in Afghan peace operations. UN Resolution 1325 stresses the importance of women as participants in peace building. Norway is thus participating in establishing gender equality for Afghan women. The Norwegian minister promotes both gender equality issues and the Norwegian interpretation of participation in warfare. This rhetoric is also a subtle way of silencing the voices of Afghan women. Metamorphosis thus occurs at different levels, in different contexts, and by different means. The gender mainstreaming is so effective that the UN resolution easily fits into most war stories, no matter what is referred to.

The similarity in the rhetoric of Norwegian female politicians is to be found in their promotion of benevolent philanthropy, dressed in feminist guise. This suggests, however, that it is easier to identify with oppressed women than with strong and potent women—who might also be in need of support, however, on the basis of solidarity between equals. In the co-optation process, co-opted concepts are not necessarily rejected, but the initial meaning may be transformed and used in policy discourse for a different purpose. "Today," Stratigaki notes, "European politicians of all parties pay lip service to gender equality as a fundamental principle of democracy and social justice" (2004, 37). Co-optation often works by using the original as well as the transformed concept as an alibi. As Stratigaki observes, "It is difficult to mobilize against a claim that appears to be one's own even if it no longer is used to mean what one intended" (36).

Rhetorical flexibility may indicate both openness and ambivalence, or it may be a strategy for constructing war stories as facts. Potent Afghan women speaking for themselves about needs and aspirations based on their own experiences might have raised problems for the humanitarian rhetoric of feminist co-optation.

Rhetoric of Liberation and Protection

The abstractions so common in foreign policy rhetoric refer to a world that bears little resemblance to the real world. War rhetoric, as part of foreign policy rhetoric, is about policy as a foreign terrain as well as about activities happening on foreign territory. The success of war rhetoric is thus often greater than the success of domestic policy rhetoric, shaping the reality of foreign affairs in another manner. The didactic aspects of foreign policy rhetoric invoke and interpret the perennial ideals of its nation's greatest experiences in the past and present, and act as a guide for the future. Policy vocabulary is strongly rooted in political culture, national consciousness, and the nation's perception of itself and its enemies in the world. And the way this perception is used in political rhetoric is seldom gender-neutral (Yuval-Davis 1997; Tickner 2001).

The concepts of "liberating" and "protecting" women are still seen as essential for the legitimization of violence; they are an important myth creating sustained support for war and its legitimization for both women and men (Ahmed 1992; Cooke 2002). The liberator/liberated or protector/protected relationship is by definition unequal, and unequal relations rest ultimately on the threat or act of violence. For the liberators and protectors to wield this public superiority, there must be a certain constructed "liberated" and "protected" (Doty 1993; see also Ayotte and Husain 2005). Being seen mainly as victims might, at worst, undermine claims of women's rights.

In the real world the relation between protector and protected is often experienced as a relation between oppressors and nobody—no body. Who has the privilege of speaking "when veils seem more like walls," as Royster puts it, is an issue more important than the veiling of bodies. The interest in and the foregrounding of burka-clad, apparently voiceless Afghan women were part of a rationale for once again waging a just war and securing Afghan women (Stabile and Kumar 2005).

Gayatri C. Spivak's essay "Can the Subaltern Speak?" (1988) is as relevant now as it was twenty-four years ago. In my view, the subaltern often can speak, but the question is, "Are we really listening, and can we hear her?"

Glenn (2002) also writes about the difficulties of hearing and listening, and, like her, I wonder if hearing and listening will ever occur: "Really listening across worldviews operates as a straining toward understanding—glimpsing what lies between the 'I' and the 'other'" (Ballif, Davis, and Mountford 2000, 587). An abstract silent "local woman" in the narratives of war, as embedded in a rhetoric of silence, is often better than a corporeal speaking subaltern. When the subaltern speaks, it requires openness to her message on the part of the listener, because that message may be unsettling, something we do not want to hear. For example, Malalai Joya, Afghanistan's youngest and most outspoken parliamentarian, warned as early as December 2003 against some of the allies of the West, calling them criminals, bandits, and "the most anti-women people in the society" (Joya 2003). Four years later she wrote:

> The US government removed the ultra-reactionary and brutal regime of Taliban, but instead of relying on the Afghan people, pushed us from the frying pan into the fire and selected its friends from among the most dirty and infamous criminals of the "Northern Alliance," which is made up of the sworn enemies of democracy and human rights, and are as dark-minded, evil, and cruel as the Taliban. The Western media talks about democracy and the liberation of Afghanistan, but the US and its allies are engaged in the warlordization, criminalization and drug-lordization of our wounded land. (Joya 2007)

The Western silencing of the alliance with the warlords, whose brutality and oppression of Afghan women was similar to that of the Taliban, might have challenged the liberation-protection-scenario rhetoric. Simultaneously silencing female voices like Joya's was necessary in order for the rhetoric to succeed.

Rhetoric, Gendered (In)security, and the Creation of Spaces

In "Postcolonial Intervention in the Rhetorical Canon: An 'Other' View" (1996), Raka Shome sees the rhetorical discipline as a discipline celebrating masculine voices, built on public address, which historically has been a realm in which imperial voices are heard. Security issues are, however, one of the most gendered rhetorical fields—the stories told of history, war, defeat, victory, and glory spring mainly, and more manifestly than other discourses, from masculinized memory, ambitions, humiliation, and hope and are told mainly by males in positions of power (Enloe 1999, 2004; see also Connell and Messerschmidt 2005).

Obviously, things have changed. In the rhetoric of the protection/liberation of Afghan women, the subject, speaking on behalf of and in place of, can be a woman. Phrases like "stateswomen protecting men and children" would, however, probably still be seen as strange—all over the world. Security is perhaps the most gendered field on earth, literally speaking. Metaphorical rape—as in, say, the metaphorical rape of a country—is, for most women, seldom experienced metaphorically. Security easily merges into insecurity and becomes physical, material, gendered insecurity. J. Ann Tickner explodes the "myth of protection" in this way: "despite a widespread myth that wars are fought, mostly by men, to protect 'vulnerable' people—a category to which women and children are generally assigned—women and children constitute a significant proportion of casualties in recent wars" (2001, 49). Existing patriarchal power structures tend to be fortified, and the patriarchal oppression of women tends to increase, during warfare.

It is in the interest of political elites, in matters of foreign policy rhetoric and public deliberation, to avoid a discussion of potential political themes; this they seek to achieve by steering a part of the symbolic system toward the correct opinion, and by denying people with blasphemous views access to the tools that they might use to contest existing definitions of "reality" (Bourdieu 1979). According to Bourdieu, every society has assumptions that are never questioned because those in power want to present "something"—in many cases the most important aspects of social structures and control over them—as given and natural. The "doxic room" is where the political is seen as nonpolitical, natural, and closed to debate. In democracies, keeping the doors to this room (un)safely closed is, however, not possible. Sometimes *doxa*, or taken-for-granted assumption, is challenged, and the taken for granted becomes less taken for granted. Imperfections occur in public deliberation, but they are mainly articulated within the framework of an ideology where good intentions prevail. In war rhetoric, good intentions will prevail, as will the silencing of opposing voices.

As war rhetoric is discursively constructed around a set of intangible and malleable themes that are never static but are continually being reimagined and reinvented, a critical rhetoric can uncover the persuasive and manipulative work being done through hegemonic discourse, including feminist co-optation. Discourses are historically specific, socially situated, signifying practices, and yet they are themselves set within social institutions and action contexts. The concept of discourse links the study of language to the study of society. There is a plurality of discourses in society and therefore a plurality of communicative sites from which to speak. Feminist rhetorical scholars have sought to transform the rhetorical tradition into regendered, inclusionary, dialogic, and collaborative rhetorics. But the concept of a dialogic and collaborative rhetoric, based on shared meanings and understandings, needs to be continuously reexamined (Shome 1996). Shared meanings on security issues are shared mainly by people in positions of power, mostly men, and express the perspective(s) of the power elite(s). When alternative war stories are silenced, an injection of new voices and new ideas alongside new perspectives becomes all the more important (Ross 2009).

In an era of globalization and increasing interdependence between nation-states, no less than in the context of the cold war rhetoric of containment, war rhetoric is informed by specific masculine values. Attempts to connect structures of violence with attributes or behavioral propensities that men or women supposedly share rely on stereotypical generalizations about men and women and will, as Young observes, "often leap too quickly from an account of the traits of persons to institutional structures and collective action" (2003, 2). Good citizenship still seems to consist of cooperative obedience to authorities who claim that "we" support democracy "over there" in the ongoing war on terror.

The use of the rhetoric of women's rights in the context of the war in Afghanistan should not only make feminists uncomfortable; it should be challenged and questioned.

NOTES

1. The "Troika" represents the European Union in external relations within the scope of common foreign and security policy. All translations in this chapter are my own unless otherwise noted.
2. The ESDP is a major pillar of the EU's common foreign and security policy and the defense and military domain of EU policy.

REFERENCES

Ahmed, Leila. 1992. *Women and Gender in Islam*. New Haven: Yale University Press.
Ayotte, K. J., and M. E. Husain. 2005. "Securing Afghan Women: Neocolonialism, Epistemic Violence, and the Rhetoric of the Veil." *NWSA Journal* 17 (3): 112–33.
Ballif, Michelle, D. Diane Davis, and Roxanne Mountford. 2000. "Negotiating the Differend: A Feminist Trilogue." *Journal of Advanced Composition* 30 (3): 583–625.

Bergman, Annika. 2004. "Post–Cold War Shifts in Swedish and Finnish Security Policies: The Compatibility of Non-Alignment and Participation in EU Led Conflict Prevention." Paper presented at the ECPR conference, Uppsala, 23–28 April 2004.
Bizzell, Patricia. 2000. "Feminist Methods of Research in the History of Rhetoric: What Difference Do They Make?" *Rhetoric Society Quarterly* 30 (4): 5–17.
Bourdieu, Pierre. 1979. *Outline of a Theory of Practice*. Cambridge: Cambridge University Press.
Bush, Laura. 2001. Radio address, 17 November. http://georgewbush-whitehouse.archives.gov/news/releases/2001/11/20011117.html.
Campbell, K. K. 2008. *The Rhetorical Act: Thinking, Speaking, and Writing Critically*. Boston: Wadsworth.
Cloud, Dana L. 2004. "To Veil the Threat of Terror." *Quarterly Journal of Speech* 90 (3): 285–306.
Connell, R. W., and James Messerschmidt. 2005. "Hegemonic Masculinity: Rethinking the Concept." *Gender and Society* 19 (6): 829–59.
Cooke, Miriam. 2002. "Saving Brown Women." *Signs: Journal of Women in Culture and Society* 28 (1): 468–70.
Doty, Roxanne Lynn. 1993. "Foreign Policy as Social Construction: A Post-Positivist Analysis of U.S. Counterinsurgency Policy in the Philippines." *International Studies Quarterly* 37 (3): 297–320.
Dubriwny, Tasha N. 2005. "First Ladies and Feminism: Laura Bush as Advocate for Women's and Children's Rights." *Women's Studies in Communication* 28 (1): 84–114.
Ellingsen, Per. 2002. "Krigen er kvinnefrigjøring." *Dagbladet.no*, 11 August. http://www.dagbladet.no/nyheter/2002/08/11/345724.html.
Enloe, Cynthia. 1990. *Bananas, Beaches, and Bases: Making Feminist Sense of International Politics*. Berkeley and Los Angeles: University of California Press.
———. 1999. "Margins, Silences, and Bottom Rungs: How to Overcome the Underestimation of Power in the Study of International Relations." In *International Theory: Positivism and Beyond*, ed. Steve Smith, Ken Booth, and Marysia Zalewski, 186–202. Cambridge: Cambridge University Press.
———. 2004. *The Curious Feminist: Searching for Women in a New Age of Empire*. Berkeley and Los Angeles: University of California Press.
Flanders, Laura. 2004. *The W Effect: Bush's War on Women*. New York: Feminist Press at the City University of New York.
Glenn, Cheryl. 2002. "Silence: A Rhetorical Art for Resisting Discipline(s)." *Journal of Advanced Composition* 22 (2): 261–92.
———. 2004. *Unspoken: A Rhetoric of Silence*. Carbondale: Southern Illinois University Press.
Gramsci, Antonio. 1978. *Selections from the Prison Notebooks*. London: Lawrence.
Holst, Cathrine. 2007. "Balansefeminismens begrensninger." *Tidsskrift for Kjønnsforskning* 2:5–20.
Ingebritsen, Christine. 2002. "Norm Entrepreneurs: Scandinavia's Role in World Politics." *Cooperation and Conflict* 37 (1): 11–23.
Joya, Malalai. 2003. "Malalai Joya's Historical Speech in the Loya Jirga Meeting, Kabul, Afghanistan, 17 December 2003." http://www.malalaijoya.com/remarks.htm.
———. 2007. "The US Has Returned Fundamentalism to Afghanistan." CommonDreams.org/, 12 April. http://www.commondreams.org/archive/2007/04/12/468.
Lippe, Berit von der. 2003. "Kjønn og kropp i krig og (u)fred." *Rhetorica Scandinavica* 27:83–97.

McGee, M. C. 1980. "The Ideograph: A Link Between Rhetoric and Ideology." *Quarterly Journal of Speech* 66 (1): 1–16.

Mral, Brigitte. 2003. "Motståndets retorik: Om kvinnors argumentative strategier." *Rhetorica Scandinavica* 27:34–50.

Parry-Giles, S. J., and D. M. Blair. 2002. "The Rise of the Rhetorical First Lady: Politics, Gender Ideology, and Women's Voice, 1789–2002." *Rhetoric and Public Affairs* 5 (4): 565–99.

Ross, Susan D. 2009. "Limning Terror: Seams in the Discourse of 'Terrorism.'" *Global Media Journal* 8 (15): 1–27.

Royster, Jacqueline Jones. 1996. "When the First Voice You Hear Is Not Your Own." *College Composition and Communication* 47:29–40.

Shome, Raka. 1996. "Postcolonial Intervention in the Rhetorical Canon: An 'Other' View." *Communication Theory* 6 (1): 40–56.

Spivak, Gayatri C. 1988. "Can the Subaltern Speak?" In *Marxism and the Interpretation of Culture*, ed. C. Nelson and L. Grossberg, 271–313. Urbana: University of Illinois Press.

Stabile, C. A., and Deepa Kumar. 2005. "Unveiling Imperialism: Media, Gender, and the War on Afghanistan." *Media, Culture, and Society* 27:755–82.

Stiehm, J. H. 1982. "The Protected, the Protector, the Defender." *Women's Studies International Forum* 5 (3–4): 367–77.

Stratigaki, Maria. 2004. "The Cooptation of Gender Concepts in EU Policies: The Case of 'Reconciliation' of Work and Family." *Social Politics* 11:30–56.

Strøm-Erichsen, Anne-Grete. 2006. Speech given at the EU-Troika+5 meeting in Brussels, 14 November. http://www.eu-norge.org/Aktuelt/Nyhetsartikler/forsvarsmin/.

Tickner, J. Ann. 2001. *Gendering World Politics: Issues and Approaches in the Post–Cold War Era*. New York: Columbia University Press.

Young, Iris M. 2003. "The Logic of Masculinist Protection: Reflections on the Current Security State." *Signs: Journal of Women in Culture and Society* 29 (1): 1–25.

———. 2007. *Global Challenges: War, Self-Determination, and Responsibility for Justice*. Cambridge: Polity Press.

Yuval-Davis, Nira. 1997. *Gender and Nation*. London: Sage.

10

SPEAKING OF TERROR:
NORMS OF RHETORICAL CITIZENSHIP IN
DANISH PUBLIC DISCOURSE

Lisa S. Villadsen

This chapter explores the notion of rhetorical citizenship and suggests its relevance to studies of rhetoric in society. My analysis suggests that an underdeveloped appreciation of rhetoric's role in public deliberation can be witnessed in a case study where responses to two public statements work to exclude particular points of view and to defer discussion and thus reflect a less than tolerant debate culture. The overall trajectory of my argument is that in this and similar settings, public political debate would benefit from increased attention to various manifestations of rhetorical practice, and that the concept of rhetorical citizenship may be one avenue for cultivating such a development, particularly as a frame for explicating and negotiating the communicative norms for public deliberation.

The notion of rhetorical citizenship is new. It was created as a frame for examining the role of rhetoric on a societal plane based on an understanding of rhetoric not just as a tool for individuals to wield but as a medium for being a citizen. Theoretically, the concept springs from two strands of research: deliberative democracy and rhetorical agency. An established body of literature on deliberative democracy deals with the challenges of citizen participation in the political life of representative democracies—for example, discussing how deliberation among the citizenry may constitute a more valuable form of participation than mere voting, and how it may be realized and brought to bear on lawmaking (Rawls 1987; Gutmann and Thompson 2004; Dryzek 2002; Benhabib 1996). The concept of rhetorical agency is newer and still subject to definitional variation (Geisler 2004; Hauser 2004; Lundberg and Gunn 2005; Rand 2008). Its main concern is how rhetorical action is realized in the intersection of human intentionality and skill, on the one side, and context—understood as institutional, social, and other constraints—on the other. The term *rhetorical citizenship* embraces inquiries into social and institutional deliberative practices as well as norms and issues of access, scope, and strength of individual or group discursive initiatives in the public realm. My case material—political commentaries on statements made in response to a terrorist attack against a Danish embassy—illustrates the connection between theories of deliberative democracy and rhetorical agency. While seemingly narrow in scope and ephemeral in political significance, this type of quotidian political polemic may, by virtue of its "knee-jerk" quality, shed light on common political practice and the norms informing it.

Rhetorical Agency

In recent years, the concept of rhetorical agency has inspired scholars with a range of theoretical interests. A 2004 special issue of *Philosophy and Rhetoric* illustrated this diversity. The editor, Gerard Hauser, offers no definition of the concept but points to the dual concerns associated with it, namely, rhetoric's constitutive powers "in the ongoing construction of a human world and the consequences of symbolic choice, or questions of responsibility," and the way the concept of agency "raises questions of voice, power, and rights." The latter in particular places the concept "at the center of this era's major social, political, economic, and cultural issues" (2004, 183). Rhetorical agency concerns the fact that rhetors are both makers of rhetoric (through skill, *inventio*, etc.) and made by rhetoric (as well as by circumstance, position in society, and other institutional or social conditions). We cannot account for rhetorical action merely by reference to a rhetor's intention, nor can we completely abandon the significance of the individual in rhetorical utterances.

Cheryl Geisler identifies the core of the concept of rhetorical agency as a concern with the capacity to act. She traces three main research interests stemming from this: (1) a critique of the ideology of agency, that is, the link between rhetorical action and social change, i.e., a questioning of modernist conceptions of the subject as a self-reflexive agent capable of influencing the world in intended ways; (2) a more instrumental approach to rhetoric understood as a focus on a rhetor's skill and ability to respond to shifting circumstances; and (3) the conditions for agency—in other words, studying the means or resources with which a rhetor is able to act and, not least, the accessibility of such a position: who gets a chance to be heard? (2004, 12–14). My approach spans all three strands in its overarching concern with the ideological underpinnings of public expectations vis-à-vis rhetorical agency in a particular context. In order to describe such implicit norms, I must account for the rhetor's speaking position and use of it as reflected in contemporary reactions.

Several contributions to current theory on rhetorical agency have considered the possibilities for and strategies of marginalized and underrepresented groups to enter public political debate (Asen and Brouwer 2001; Asen 2004; Welsh 2002). This work promises to yield new perspectives on nurturing a more inclusive and constructive political culture. Here, however, we shall examine a case that seems to suggest that rhetorical agency can be contested—even when it concerns individuals usually considered "mainstream," whose opinions on current politics are normally considered relevant. The speakers in question belong to the Danish elite: one, Margrethe Vestager, is a member of Parliament and a party leader; the other, Niels Due Jensen, is the CEO of Grundfos, a large pump manufacturer. Both found their rhetorical agency impugned when making public comments on a controversial matter. I argue that this social rejection of their rhetorical agency can be read as an illustration of how closely conceptions of rhetorical agency intertwine with ideological assumptions that are highly contextual in nature. The range and nature of human action are circumscribed by social interpretations of the situation and setting. Comments that in a different context might have passed unnoticed seemed controversial and destructive in a situation characterized by uncertainty and risk. With no tolerance for dissent or even for doubt, it seems that expectations about rhetorical agency in this controversy depend on unexamined norms informed by a dichotomous and, in Kenneth Burke's terminology (1984), tragic frame of debate.

Background: The Attack in Islamabad and Initial Reactions

On 2 June 2008 the Danish Embassy in Islamabad, Pakistan, was the target of a terrorist attack. A car loaded with explosives slammed into the front wall of the embassy, killing several people and wounding between twenty and thirty others. No one took responsibility for the attack immediately afterward, and the reason for the attack remained a matter of speculation for some time. The attack was, however, generally assumed to be either a response to the so-called cartoon crisis of 2005–6 and the reprinting of the Mohammed cartoons in 2008, or a protest against Denmark's participation in the Iraq War and the country's military presence in Afghanistan.[1]

Naturally, the event demanded that Danish politicians respond to this violent act. Whether one shared the prime minister's view that it constituted "an attack on Denmark" or held a more limited understanding of it as a despicable but isolated terrorist attack on Danish property, or even as "merely" a criminal act calling for police investigation, the attack clearly represented a crisis of some significance. Absent any immediate indication of who was responsible for the attack or the reason for it, comments by Danish politicians initially focused on denouncing the act and expressing sorrow over the loss of innocent human lives and the injuries sustained.

After the immediate reactions of shock, anger, and empathy, several politicians broached the question of how Denmark should react in order to prevent and defend itself from similar attacks in the future. The dominant recommendation was to investigate the incident and uphold Denmark's diplomatic and military presence in the Middle East and thus continue the country's foreign policy and diplomatic procedures in general. In other words, Denmark should stick to its guns, as it were, in order to signal the country's determination and commitment to free speech and democracy. Alternative reactions were either ignored or denounced as "giving in" to the terrorists out of fear. As a consequence of such negative reactions to nonmainstream utterances, there thus appeared to be only two discursive options: either to show loyalty to Denmark by expressing steadfastness on the political and military fronts, or to be seen as disloyal by not supporting the official policy.[2]

Two "Unruly" Reactions

In spite of the unattractiveness of taking a nonmainstream position, there were two visible alternative reactions to the terrorist attack. One came from the leader of the Social Liberal Party, Margrethe Vestager. In line with the rest of the political establishment, her first statements on 2 June condemned the attack as inexcusable and "totally unacceptable," and she expressed her "deepest sympathy" for the victims and their relatives.[3] But later that day, on *TV2 News*, she added that she thought the incident would "lead to a discussion of Denmark's foreign policy line." Denmark, she said, ought to be more "involved in solving conflicts."[4]

For this statement, Vestager incurred aggressive criticism from a broad range of politicians for "giving in" to terror and displaying inadequate loyalty to Denmark in a moment of crisis. The prime minister, Anders Fogh Rasmussen, said that he was dismayed (*bestyrtet*) and considered Vestager's thinking "very, very dangerous," and then responded to a straw argument insinuated by himself as he rejected the possibility that terrorists would be "allowed to determine" Danish foreign policy.[5] The Social Democratic leader, Helle Thorning-Schmidt, commented that a terrorist attack was an "infinitely ill-suited background on which to discuss changes in our foreign policy and our internal discussions at home such as the one about freedom of expression," adding, "it is wrong to link a terror attack and our foreign policy." The leader of the Danish People's Party, Pia Kjærsgaard, called Vestager's comment "pathetic" (*sølle*), but also shifted the focus to domestic politics, charging Vestager with "abusing the situation to create division and—to put it nicely—[trying] to shift the blame to the parties supporting the foreign policy." Kjærsgaard thus saw Vestager's comment as primarily "an attempt at domestic policy and trying to set people up against each other."[6] Perhaps the most pointed critique came from the governing Liberal Party (Venstre); an MP, Inger Støjberg, regretted on her blog that Vestager was getting "weak at the knees" (*blød i knæene*) and "giving in to the terrorists."[7] Both she and the prime minister were quoted several times charging Vestager with "playing into the terrorists' hands" (*gå terroristernes ærinde*).[8] A few days later, on 10 June, the Liberal minister of taxation, Kristian Jensen, criticized Vestager for yielding to the terrorists and deemed her statements "a dangerous signal" to terrorists, calling her and her party "unfit" (*uegnet*) to govern. This charge was backed later that day by the prime minister, who said that one should never give terrorists the impression that one can be pressured.

Four days after the attack, on 6 June 2008, another critical voice—that of Niels Due Jensen, CEO of Grundfos—also drew heavy criticism. In an interview in the financial newspaper *Børsen* Jensen expressed concern over Denmark's current aggressive foreign policy, seeing it as an invitation to confrontation and an unfortunate escalation in the relations between Denmark and the Muslim world. He found this policy detrimental to Danish business interests and concluded that it was certainly detrimental to his company's interests.[9] Several MPs all but accused Jensen of being a traitor to his country. Conservative Party political spokesperson Henriette Kjær advised Jensen to "think in a larger perspective than next year's bottom line for Grundfos." Naser Khader, leader of the libertarian party New Alliance, called Jensen's view a "disgrace" and speculated that Jensen might feel more comfortable living under a dictatorship. Khader further denounced Jensen's "huckster attitude" (*kræmmermentalitet*) and looked forward to the day when Jensen would criticize the dictatorships his corporation traded with instead of his own country.[10] Representatives from both the Liberal Party and the Danish

People's Party (Dansk Folkeparti, DF) compared Jensen to the collaborators who, during World War II, profited from trade with the Nazis. Søren Espersen (DF) declared that Jensen had "chosen the wrong country to live in. It is a tragedy when businesspeople think like that."[11] Tom Behnke, the Conservative Party's spokesperson on national defense, stated, "It is sad that Niels Due Jensen questions the policy when we are under attack. Because it showcases that we do not stand together in Denmark, and that will make the terrorists applaud with their chubby little hands."[12] Behnke (who on 5 June, Denmark's Constitution Day, had praised the nation's constitutionally sanctioned freedom of expression) called Jensen "double dumb" (*dobbelt dum*) because he said stupid things and did so at a bad time. "It encourages the terrorists to more acts of terror," he said.[13]

Analysis

From a traditional rhetorical perspective of effectiveness, Behnke's point about the timing of Jensen's statements carries some weight. A key principle in rhetoric is *kairos:* saying the right thing at the right time. Arguably, the statements by Vestager and Jensen were ill-timed because the public felt vulnerable and at risk and was therefore perhaps less prepared for critical thinking than under normal circumstances. Evaluated by a traditional criterion of effectiveness, Vestager's and Jensen's statements fall flat because they were seen as destructive to national security and therefore unpersuasive. My purpose here, however, is to offer a different kind of reading, namely, one that examines the controversy from an angle of rhetorical citizenship. I suggest that concepts of rhetorical agency and deliberative democracy help illuminate this particular case as an illustration of how contemporary political debate can be thrown off kilter, a fact that I argue suggests that it is less normatively robust than is commonly assumed. The kind of rhetorical criticism I engage in here is thus conceptually driven and pursued with the aim of theorizing about public deliberation and the norms that inform it. In this I follow Robert Asen's call for a change in scholarly focus—from deciding *what* counts as citizenship to *how* people enact it (2004, 191). The question, in other words, is what to make of Vestager's and Jensen's enactment of their rhetorical agency.

Following Asen, who sees citizenship as "a mode of public engagement," distinguishing "the manner by which something is done from what is done" (191), and thus allowing for consideration of intention and consequently for interpretation (195), my purpose is to show how this case is a small-scale illustration of several key elements of rhetorical citizenship. Central to my reading is the theoretical assumption that the statements of the various parties were interpreted not merely as political commentary but also as performances of proper civic responsibility, *phronesis* (or lack thereof), and that the reactions to them therefore read as a debate over how a citizen may properly act rhetorically in public.

As an opposition party leader, Vestager was among the first public figures given the opportunity to comment on the attack in the media, and her right to speak initially went unquestioned. In her case, the issue of rhetorical agency is interesting in relation to the content of her statements and particularly the reception of them. Not limiting herself to an expression of her immediate emotional and political reaction, she used the opportunity to call for a reconsideration of Denmark's foreign policy, transforming the event from an epideictic to a deliberative one. As we have seen, she thus provoked massive negative reactions from politicians representing most of the spectrum.[14] Vestager's political competence and even her patriotism were severely questioned because she was seen to be suggesting that the country's foreign policy might have led to the attack and that this policy needed reexamination in light of Denmark's overall foreign policy aims. This was interpreted as a criticism, even a disavowal, of the current policy and as a wish to make it less offensive to militant Islamists so as to prevent future attacks.

The vehemence and stridency of these reactions suggest that Vestager not only hit a nerve but also challenged prevailing communicative norms in the political realm. I read the attacks on Vestager as indicating that her realization of rhetorical agency in this case was deemed both inappropriate and dangerous, and I would suggest that this reaction was informed by a political debate climate that I'll explore further presently. In the eyes of many, Vestager's rhetorical act of questioning jeopardized her performance of political citizenship and national values, and by questioning the government's foreign policy she was seen as potentially putting the country at risk. Thus she was seen as betraying her rhetorical citizenship: where many considered national agreement and emphatic verbal commitment to current policy appropriate and even proof of responsible citizenship, Vestager, in their eyes, cast serious doubt on her own patriotism and abused her rhetorical agency by making what they deemed inappropriate statements.

According to Hauser and Benoit-Barné, agency amplifies the element of risk inherent in any social interaction, and therefore the need for trust emerges (2002, 271). The reactions to Vestager may illustrate the fragility of social and political trust in times of crisis. Vestager's opponents questioned her political agency partly by expressing mistrust of her judgment on foreign policy, partly by reading her call for a discussion of current Danish foreign policy as a kind of betrayal, and partly through "guilt by association," as they cited the foreign policy endorsed by her party during the 1940s as evidence against her.

Much the same can be said about the reactions to Jensen's statements—the main difference being that, as a business leader, Jensen's own vested interests were more palpable, rendering him more immediately subject to suspicion. He was almost universally criticized for putting his own profit above the national interest. Space does not permit me to develop this argument, but there is an interesting issue of rhetorical agency here. Usually, statements made by leading industry spokespeople regarding current policy are readily used as warrants in political debate, especially by the Danish government parties, but here we see an attempt to undermine Jensen's rhetorical agency in an unusual dichotomization of economics and politics. It is possible that Jensen violated a tacit norm by explicating the economic opportunities and risks that sometimes motivate and usually accompany warfare. His bringing the topic out in the open was thus deemed crass.

Hauser and Benoit-Barné list as one of the problems besetting discussions of deliberative democracy that it is usually based on individual interests. They propose that a richer understanding would reconceive political relations as deliberation-based (2002, 263). Vestager's case foregrounds some of the challenges inherent in the predominant understanding of political debate as interest-based as opposed to being oriented toward inclusion and the civil exchange of views. Vestager's statement might exemplify a different kind of political discourse, more in line with Hauser and Benoit-Barné's ideal of deliberative democracy. From the point of view of rhetorical theory, we might regard Vestager's statements as an attempt to translate "ordinary" speaking access to a richer form of rhetorical agency: using her media access to draw attention to a topic that in her opinion is too often ignored, and inviting the Danish electorate to reconsider the country's role in international politics. This reading of Vestager's position as one that favors the deliberative formation of public opinion aligns with Aristotelian thinking on *phronesis*, the cultivation and practice of (sound) political judgment. Hauser and Benoit-Barné contrast the concept of *phronesis* with the concept of *doxa*, stating that whereas the former springs from a rhetorically based conception of political deliberation, the latter is the assumed basis of conventional interest-based understanding of political action. "Democratic participation . . . is a vehicle for moving the 'will of the people' past its status as doxa (a strongly held but weakly grounded preference), as reflected in opinion polls, and return it to the status of civil judgment envisioned by Aristotle in the *Rhetoric*" (2002, 264). Clearly, such a move toward reflection and critical examination of the means and ends of Danish foreign policy was perceived as a threat in political circles and was deemed unwise and almost treacherous to the nation's safety.[15]

Deliberative Democracy and Rhetorical Theory

Drawing on the abundant literature on deliberative democracy, several rhetorical scholars have pointed to the dearth of a rhetorical perspective in this body of theory (e.g., Keith 2002; Hauser and Benoit-Barné 2002; Asen 2004). Robert Ivie argues for understanding democratic deliberation as primarily rhetorical (2002, 277): the rhetorical tradition offers constructive ways of dealing with disagreement both procedurally and substantively because it "promotes democratic practice immediately" (rather than postponing it to an ideal future where diversity and passionate disagreement have been replaced by consensus and universal reason). Moreover, dissension is considered a natural condition to be embraced as a source of critique and thus potential improvement of the debate. Using the Burkean distinction between tragic and comic frames, Ivie sees a rhetorical conception of democratic deliberation as fundamentally comic because it displays attitudes of tolerance and contemplation and thereby engages differences with a "potentially positive expectation of political advocacy, dissent, and disagreement, conduct that otherwise is easily interpreted as a dysfunctional exercise" (278). Ivie further advocates what he calls "rowdy" rhetorical deliberation. This is characterized by "maintaining a productive tension between cooperation and competition and not privileging any single perspective to the exclusion of all others," and it thus increases the potential of preventing adversaries from being transformed into scapegoats and enemies (278). What is particularly pertinent here is Ivie's point that such robust give-and-take "helps to overturn the debilitating assumption that democracy is inherently fragile, and thus risky, in the here and now" (279).

Like Ivie, Asen is interested in the potential unruliness of citizenship (2004, 195). While neither Vestager's nor Jensen's public statements were manifestly provocative, the reactions to them treated them as improper and in violation of the norms of public commentary with regard to both timing and message. So, in a sense, they were chastised for bad or "unruly" behavior, and Vestager—by calling into question the wisdom of the nation's foreign policy—was perceived by many as questioning, or rather ignoring, notions of propriety.

Conclusion

The Danish politicians' uncritical adoption of the prime minister's language of war (labeling the violent incident in Islamabad "an attack on Denmark") effectively framed the political commentary immediately following the event as dichotomous and intolerant of questioning or hesitation regarding what a wise reaction would be; it created a debate climate aggressively bent on consensus and unity to the exclusion of alternative viewpoints, as witnessed by reactions that, to borrow a phrase, "reduced difference to total otherness" (Ivie 2002, 278). The reactions to Vestager illustrate some of the problems besetting contemporary Danish public political culture: critics of Vestager's call for reconsideration of Danish foreign policy perceived it as threatening, even destabilizing, to the credibility and security of Denmark at a time of perceived crisis. The unstated argument was that this was not the time to discuss Denmark's foreign policy because the terrorists would see it as a sign of weakness. In a crisis, the underlying assumption went, the nation must stand as one and show no sign of internal division. The crisis paradoxically closed the space for political deliberation, even for this leading politician. The reactions in effect curbed the possibility of testing competing interpretations and perspectives of the events in Islamabad as well as of foreign policy in the Middle East in general. Remarkably, this was done in a manner that reduced opposing views to unpatriotic and self-serving behavior.

I have examined the controversy from the perspective of rhetorical citizenship using primarily theory on rhetorical agency and public deliberation. My analysis of Vestager's and Jensen's statements showed that while they might have been ill-timed from a narrow, effect-oriented point of view, they might also be read as illustrations of the authentic exercise of rhetorical agency and, in virtue of their commentary on current political issues, as valuable manifestations of rhetorical citizenship suited to challenge and thereby further public discussion of Denmark's foreign policy. I have argued that the case illustrates how the reactions to these comments provides the critic with a glimpse into the unspoken and, most probably, subconscious norms that inform the particular debate culture at a given point in time. High-profile politicians interpreted the statements not just as utterances with destabilizing content but also as breaches of proper civic responsibility. Their strong condemnation of the statements suggests that they saw Vestager and Jensen as breaching norms of rhetorical citizenship.

In an a-rhetorical debate culture, where disagreement is troubling and deliberation dangerous, it seems that "proper" rhetorical citizenship isn't expected to rock the boat. A more rhetorically based conception would embrace difference as a fact to be dealt with constructively. In the words of Hauser and Benoit-Barné, "A rhetorical reading of civil society returns us to its structure as a web of rhetorical arenas in which strangers encounter difference, learn of the other's interests, develop understanding of where there are common goals, and where they may develop the levels of trust necessary for them to function in a world of mutual dependency" (2002, 271). Cases like Vestager's and Jensen's statements invite us to continue questioning the norms—spoken or unspoken—that underlie notions of rhetorical citizenship in a given national or cultural context.

NOTES

1. Because many people see Denmark as indistinguishable from countries such as Sweden and the Netherlands, some also speculated that the attack was a misdirected reaction to the Dutch anti-Islamic film *Fitna*, released on the Internet in March 2008, but in July 2008 a representative of al-Qaeda claimed responsibility for the attack and said it was an answer to the reprinting of the *Jyllands-Posten*'s Mohammed cartoons in February 2006 and to the presence of Danish troops in Afghanistan.

2. This constellation of discursive options is reminiscent of the aftermath of 9/11, when President George W. Bush, with a crystal clear binary political and ethical logic, declared, "Either you are with us, or you are with the terrorists" (address to a joint session of Congress, 20 September 2001).

3. "Vestager: 'Totalt uacceptabelt,'" *Ritzau's Bureau*, 2 June 2008. All translations are my own unless otherwise noted.

4. Vestager later explained that this comment was offered in response to a comparison between Denmark and Israel made by her political opponents in the Danish People's Party, who called Denmark "the Israel of the North"—the implication presumably being that both nations are surrounded by Islamic enemies to be combatted at any price in order to secure survival.

5. Quoted in "Sprækker i borgfreden," *Jyllands-Posten*, 3 June 2008.

6. Thorning-Schmidt and Kjærsgaard quoted in "Hård kritik af Vestager," *Politiken*, 3 June 2008.

7. "Vestager bliver blød i knæene," Inger Støjberg's blog, http://inger.dk/, 3 June 2008.

8. Støjberg later said that she had been misquoted as leaving out the word "involuntarily" in this context. "Er vi selv ude om det?" *Jyllands-Posten*, 3 June 2008.

9. "Grundfos angriber VK's terrorpolitik," *Børsen*, 6 June 2008, http://borsen.dk/nyheder/politik/artikel/1/133393/grundfos_angriber_vks_terrorpolitik.html (accessed 17 January 2011).

10. Quoted in "Khader raser over erhvervsboss," *Jyllands-Posten*, 6 June 2008.

11. Quoted in "Profeten og profitten," *Jyllands-Posten*, 7 June 2008.
12. For reasons of space I have not commented on the condescending and chauvinistic nature of this utterance.
13. Quoted in "Holdkæftbolsjet: Tom Behnke; Grundfos' Niels Due er vor tids Viggo Skjold Hansen," *Information*, 7 June 2008. In fairness, Behnke recognized Jensen's right to say anything he liked, explaining that the problem was the timing of his remarks.
14. Only the two parties furthest to the left (Enhedslisten and SF) were not represented.
15. Later, as other politicians and media commentators reflected and found Vestager's statements to be in fact both legitimate and reasonable, the criticism was moderated to calling the statements ill-timed.

REFERENCES

Asen, Robert. 2004. "A Discourse Theory of Citizenship." *Quarterly Journal of Speech* 90:189–211.
Asen, Robert, and Daniel C. Brouwer. 2001. *Counterpublics and the State*. Albany: State University of New York Press.
Benhabib, Seyla. 1996. *Democracy and Difference: Contesting the Boundaries of the Political*. Princeton: Princeton University Press.
Burke, Kenneth. 1984. *Attitudes Towards History*. 3rd ed. Berkeley and Los Angeles: University of California Press.
Dryzek, John. 2002. *Deliberative Democracy and Beyond: Liberals, Critics, Contestations*. Oxford: Oxford University Press.
Gaonkar, Dilip P. 1997. "The Idea of Rhetoric in the Rhetoric of Science." In *Rhetorical Hermeneutics: Invention and Interpretation in the Age of Science*, ed. Alan G. Gross and William M. Keith, 25–85. Albany: State University of New York Press.
Geisler, Cheryl. 2004. "How Ought We to Understand the Concept of Rhetorical Agency? Report from the ARS." *Rhetoric Society Quarterly* 34:9–17.
Gutmann, Amy, and Dennis Thompson. 2004. *Why Deliberative Democracy?* Princeton: Princeton University Press.
Hauser, Gerard A. 2004. "Editor's Introduction." *Philosophy and Rhetoric* 37:181–87.
Hauser, Gerard A., and Chantal Benoit-Barné. 2002. "Reflections on Rhetoric, Deliberative Democracy, Civil Society, and Trust." *Rhetoric and Public Affairs* 5:261–75.
Ivie, Robert L. 2002. "Rhetorical Deliberation and Democratic Politics in the Here and Now." *Rhetoric and Public Affairs* 5:277–85.
Keith, William M. 2002. "Introduction: Cultural Resources for Deliberative Democracy." *Rhetoric and Public Affairs* 5:219–21.
Lundberg, Christian, and Joshua Gunn. 2005. "'Ouija Board, Are There Any Communications?' Agency, Ontotheology, and the Death of the Humanist Subject, or Continuing the ARS Conversation." *Rhetoric Society Quarterly* 35:83–105.
Rand, Erin J. 2008. "An Inflammatory Fag and a Queer Form: Larry Kramer, Polemics, and Rhetorical Agency." *Quarterly Journal of Speech* 94:297–31.
Rawls, John. 1987. "The Idea of an Overlapping Consensus." *Oxford Journal for Legal Studies* 7 (1): 1–25.
Roberts-Miller, Patricia. 2009. "Dissent as 'Aid and Comfort to the Enemy': The Rhetorical Power of Naïve Realism and Ingroup Identity." *Rhetoric Society Quarterly* 39:170–88.
Welsh, Scott. 2002. "Deliberative Democracy and the Rhetorical Production of Political Culture." *Rhetoric and Public Affairs* 5:679–708.

II

"THIS MAY BE THE LAW, BUT SHOULD IT BE?":
TONY BLAIR'S RHETORIC OF EXCEPTION

Bart van Klink and Oliver W. Lembcke

The State of Exception

In their fight against terrorism, modern states seem to install a state of exception on a permanent basis. Special competencies are created that allow authorities to violate fundamental rights, such as habeas corpus and the freedom of speech, for an unspecified period of time. In the 1920s, state of exception became a fashionable concept in legal and political thinking in Germany and the rest of Europe (Boldt 1972, 375). Carl Schmitt's *Political Theology* (1996c) played a key role. A state of exception is defined, in Schmitt's view, by a "principally unlimited authority," amounting to the suspension of the whole existing legal order. "It is clear," writes Schmitt without further explanation, that "the state remains, whereas law recedes" (12). Moreover, "order in the juristic sense still prevails even if it is not of the ordinary kind,"[1] "because the exception is different from anarchy and chaos." The "authority" that decides on the state of exception—both on its being there and on the appropriate measures to overcome it—is the sovereign, whose decisions in extraordinary circumstances are supposed to be free from "all normative ties": "the norm is destroyed in the exception" (12). However, the decision still counts as law in some, though not in a positivist, sense of the word. The "authority" "proves that to produce law it need not be based on law" (13).[2] Although this is—"looked at normatively" (31)—a *creatio ex nihilo*, it does stem from somewhere, namely, from the state's right to self-preservation.

After decades of slumber, the concept has recently made a powerful reappearance in the work of Giorgio Agamben. In his *Homo Sacer* trilogy,

Agamben follows Schmitt in defining the state of exception as the suspension of law. The rule excludes the exception as the case to which it does not or cannot apply. However, it is the peculiar force of law to be able to maintain itself in relation to that which it has excluded. *"The rule applies to the exception in no longer applying, in withdrawing from it"* (1998, 18). This is what Agamben calls the "relation of exception," that is, "the extreme form of relation by which something is included solely through its exclusion" (18). Building on Foucault, Agamben interprets the relation of exception in biopolitical terms as a "relation of ban." This act of exclusion founds sovereign power and produces its victims at the same time. In a state of exception, certain people are, by sovereign decision, excluded from the legal order, and thereby, in the same movement, included. They are the *homini sacri* who, living in the "twilight zone" between law and fact, may be killed with impunity. Reduced to bare life or naked existence, they can be disposed of in every way by everybody, unhindered by the law.

Explicitly against Schmitt, Agamben (1998, 6, 50–51) denies that the state of exception is a "state of law"; rather, it is an "emptiness of law," a space "without" or "devoid of law," in which nothing but a fictitious relation with the previously existing legal order can be established. Whereas, in the old days, the state of exception aimed at restoring normalcy, governments seem nowadays to maintain a state of exception on a permanent basis. Especially with the institutionalization of abortion and euthanasia and the declaration of a global war on terrorism, the "juridically empty" space of the state of exception threatens to "coincide with the normal order." The state of exception is institutionalized on a permanent basis; the exception becomes the rule: "Faced with the unstoppable progression of what has been called a 'global civil war,' the state of exception tends increasingly to appear as the dominant paradigm of government in contemporary politics" (2).[3]

In this chapter we examine the role that notions connected to the rule of law play in key speeches delivered by former British prime minister Tony Blair, who had to defend exceptional measures in reaction to terrorist actions and threats.[4] In the speeches selected,[5] Blair reacts to crucial political events during his leadership, in particular the 9/11 attacks and the London bombings of 7 July 2005. Our first research question is: how are the antiterror measures justified in these speeches? Are they, legally speaking, created "from nowhere," as Schmitt and Agamben would claim, or are they still somehow connected to positive law? Second, we reconstruct the kind of rhetorical citizenship established in the speeches. Are citizens invited to discuss, criticize, and change political action? We analyze the rhetorical devices Blair uses in order to justify exceptional measures, and we evaluate whether the justifications given fit the rule-of-law framework and contribute to rhetorical citizenship.

Tony Blair: A Man with a Mission

How Is a Sense of Urgency Created?

In speeches delivered directly after 9/11,[6] Tony Blair makes clear that he considers the event a decisive and unique moment in the history of mankind: "It was the events of September 11 that marked a turning point in history, where we confront the dangers of the future and assess the choices facing humankind.... What happened on 11 September was without parallel in the bloody history of terrorism" (speech 1). In retrospect, after the invasion of Iraq, it turned out to be just the "tragic prologue" to a series of unfortunate events that would probably continue: "September 11 was not an isolated event, but a tragic prologue, Iraq another act, and many further struggles will be set upon this stage" (speech 3). Together, these events constitute a threat without precedent in human history: "If the 20th century scripted our conventional way of thinking, the 21st century is unconventional in almost every respect. This is true also of our security. The threat we face is not conventional. It is a challenge of a different nature from anything the world has faced before" (speech 4).

For Blair, 9/11 was a turning point not only in the history of humankind but also in his personal history as a leader. In a religious vein, he acknowledges that this attack, "without parallel in the bloody history of terrorism," made him see his true vocation: "September 11th was for me a revelation" (speech 4). What was revealed to him was his political mission as a world leader: "I feel a most urgent sense of mission about today's world" (speech 3). His mission is to "re-order this world around us" (speech 1) or, more precisely, to restore the world's order: "The global threat to our security was clear. So was our duty: to act to eliminate it" (speech 4). The world's security is at stake, our lives as well as our way of life:[7]

> Today the threat is chaos; because for people with work to do, family life to balance, mortgages to pay, careers to further, pensions to provide, the yearning is for order and stability and if it doesn't exist elsewhere, it is unlikely to exist here. (speech 1)

This atrocity was an attack on us all, on people of all faiths and people of none.... So we have a direct interest in acting in our self defence to protect British lives.... It was an attack on lives and livelihoods.... Our prosperity and standard of living require us to deal with the terrorist threat. (speech 2)

To fulfill his mission, Blair sees no other option than to act: "We have now no choice. So we will act; and our determination in acting is total" (speech 2). In Blair's view, the events of 9/11 constituted a "warning" that we had better not ignore: "We should act on the warning" (speech 4) and put an end to our endless deliberations: "This is not a time to err on the side of caution; not a time to weigh the risks to an infinite balance" (speech 4).[8] This means a clear break with the political culture of compromise prevalent in Europe: "The political culture of Europe is inevitably rightly based on compromise. Compromise is a fine thing except when based on an illusion. And I don't believe you can compromise with this new form of terrorism" (speech 3).

How Are "Friends" Differentiated from "Enemies"?

Blair, a true champion of inclusive speech, frequently invokes a "we." In different contexts this "we" may denote different entities. As prime minister he was, of course, authorized to speak on behalf of the British people, and he often did so. In speeches delivered after the London bombings, Blair's "we" refers in particular to the authorities involved in tracking down and prosecuting the offenders: "We will pursue those responsible, not just the perpetrators but the planners of this outrage, wherever they are. And we will not rest until they are identified, and as far is humanly possible, brought to justice" (speech 5). In his speech to the U.S. Congress, "we" functions as a sign of solidarity with the American people after 9/11: "And our job, my nation that watched you grow, that you fought alongside and now fights alongside you, that takes enormous pride in our alliance and great affection in our common bond, our job is to be there with you" (speech 3). Here, "we" obviously refers to the alliance of British and American people who stand united in their fight against terrorism (as they once stood united against fascism). Though they may be "difficult" sometimes, the American people remain our friends: "I do not always agree with the US. Sometimes they can be difficult friends to have.... The danger is they decide to pull up the drawbridge and disengage.

We need them involved. We want them engaged. The reality is that none of the problems that press in on us, can be resolved or even contemplated without them" (speech 7b).

In many cases, Blair uses "we" to denote an even wider circle of people: nothing less than "the entire international community" (speech 7c). People building this "we" are not restricted to a certain space—say, the West—but are defined by sharing a particular set of convictions: "'We' is not the West. 'We' are as much Muslim as Christian or Jew or Hindu. 'We' are those who believe in religious tolerance, openness to others, to democracy, liberty and human rights administered by secular courts" (speech 7a). "We" are not aggressive at all: "We are peaceful people" (speech 2). People like "us" can also be found in the Arab and Muslim world: "Across the Arab and Muslim world such a struggle for democracy and liberty continues. . . . [There are] many Muslims, millions of them the world over, including Europe, who want what we all want: to be ourselves free and for others to be free also; who regard tolerance as a virtue and respect for faith of others as part of our own faith" (speech 7a). According to Blair, "these are the true voices of Muslims and Arab people" (speech 7c). "They" are not our enemy but our friend.

However, as inclusion always implies exclusion (cf. Lindahl 2004), not everyone in the "the entire international community" is "our" friend. There are people who support the enemy inside this community by defending a "policy of benign inactivity" (speech 7a): "It is a posture of weakness, defeatism and most of all, deeply insulting to every Muslim who believes in freedom i.e. the majority. Instead of challenging the extremism, this attitude panders to it and therefore instead of choking it, feeds its growth" (speech 7a). Fellow citizens who are critical of the current American and European approach to terrorism, are (perhaps willy-nilly) contributing to the country's destruction:[9] "[Anti-Americanism and Euro-skepticism] are the surest route to the destruction of our true national interest" (speech 8). According to Blair, these "false friends" are siding with the enemy: "The problem we have is that a part of opinion in our own countries agrees with them" (speech 7b). "They," the "real" enemy, are the "terrorists," also referred to as "religious fanatics" (e.g., speech 1) and "extremists" (speech 3).[10] "They" are a new kind of enemy, without precedent in history: "In this century, a new and unconventional enemy has appeared: a global terrorism, based on a thoroughly warped misinterpretation of Islam, which is fanatical and deadly" (speech 8). In apparent contrast to conventional terrorist groups in Europe such as the IRA or the ETA, new Islamic terrorist groups not only aim at spreading insecurity but believe in killing people for its own sake (cf. Mendes 2008, 17). Blair describes this "new and unconventional" enemy as bloodthirsty, barbarous, and boundless:

> They have no moral inhibition on the slaughter of the innocent. If they could have murdered not 7,000 but 70,000 does anyone doubt they would have done so and rejoiced in it? (speech 1)

> These [are] fanatics who will stop at absolutely nothing to cause death and destruction on a mass scale. (speech 4)

"They" hate "us" and everything "we" stand for: "They disagree with our way of life, our values and in particular our tolerance. They hate us but probably hate those Muslims who believe in tolerance, even more, as apostates betraying the true faith" (speech 7c). In short, the enemy endorses an "evil ideology" (speech 6) and is prepared "to bring about Armageddon" (speech 4). Therefore, the possibility of compromise or communication between "us" and "them" is excluded altogether: "There is no compromise possible with such people, no meeting of minds, no point of understanding with such terror" (speech 1).

In his response to the London bombings, Blair stresses the foreign roots of the terrorist attacks: "The terrorist attacks in Britain on 7 July have their origins in an ideology born thousands of miles from our shores" (quoted in Bulley 2008, 379). The attacks were "not a product of particular local circumstances in West Yorkshire" (speech 6). As Bulley (382) paraphrases Blair, "the roots of all terrorism are foreign; they are in the Middle East, in a form of government and a form of religion which is also deeply foreign to British sensibilities."

Ultimately, in Blair's view, the differentiation between friends and enemies boils down not so much to a clash of civilizations but to a "clash about civilisation." It is a "clash between extremism and progress," "a life and death battle for freedom," "a battle about modernity," and "a battle of values and progress" (speech 7a). Blair portrays terrorism as an existential threat to the modern way of life and its liberal and hedonistic values. "All civilised people," according to Blair, "Muslim or other, feel revulsion at it" (speech 6). By implication, terrorists are banned from civilization, the "entire international community," and probably—as agents of "evil"[11]—from humanity as well.[12]

What Role Do Notions of the Rule of Law Play in Defending the Measures at Hand?

To justify the extraordinary measures to be taken against terrorism, roughly speaking, Blair resorts to two different types of discourse: a discourse of exception, in which he argues that an exceptional threat requires an exceptional response, and a discourse of normalcy, in which he states that, although the threat is exceptional, the response remains safely within the "ordinary" boundaries of custom, morality, and the rule of law (or, if not, these boundaries have to be stretched somewhat to fit). Drawing from the discourse of exception, Blair claims that "we" are facing a "new type of war"[13] that "will rest on intelligence to a greater degree than ever before. It demands a different attitude to our own interests. It forces us to act even when so many comforts seem unaffected, and the threat so far off, if not illusory" (speech 4). The exceptional threat—apparently distant but nevertheless "real and existential" (ibid.)—requires "us" "to be prepared to think sooner and act quicker" if "we" want to defend "our" values. What is needed is "progressive pre-emption" (speech 7c). "We" have no other choice than to fight: "We can no more opt out of this struggle than we can opt out of the climate changing around us" (speech 7a). "If we want to secure our way of life, there is no alternative but to fight for it" (speech 7b). Blair compares terrorism to a virus: "The virus is terrorism whose intent to inflict destruction is unconstrained by human feeling and whose capacity to inflict it is enlarged by technology" (speech 3). If "we" do not stop this virus, the result will be disorder: "Our new world rests on order. The danger is disorder. And in today's world, it can now spread like contagion" (ibid.).

Though he often invokes an "us," it is clear that, in crucial moments, Blair is primarily thinking of himself—in his capacity as the United Kingdom's prime minister and a world leader—as the one who has to act, while others may "err on the side of caution" (speech 4). In defense of his decision to go to war in Iraq, Blair argues that it is the task of leadership to expose and to fight the global threat of terrorism. He acknowledges that the invasion of Iraq stirs "bitter emotions" in his own country and may be "ill-fitting the preoccupations of the man and woman on the street" (speech 4). But this does not prevent him from taking the measures he deems necessary, building on his own judgment. By making the decision to participate in the invasion, Blair puts an end to a potentially endless deliberation in an authoritarian and authoritative manner: "Prime Ministers don't have the luxury of maintaining both sides of the argument. They can see both sides. But, ultimately, leadership is about deciding. . . . Do we want to take the risk? That is the judgment. And my judgment then and now is that the risk of this new global terrorism and its interaction with states or organisations or individuals proliferating WMD,[14] is one I simply am not prepared to run" (speech 4).

Besides appeals to his leadership and personal judgment as a last resort ("ultimately"), Blair persistently tries to get broad support for his decisions by using the discourse of normalcy. In defending his antiterror approach, he draws his main arguments from both shared ideals and shared interests. In this way, as he puts it, "a happy marriage of conviction and realpolitik" is achieved (speech 8). As a matter of fact, "we" have a shared interest in the world's orderliness, in particular for economic reasons: "All of us have an interest in stability and a fear of chaos. That's the impact of interdependence" (speech 7c). Here, British self-interest coincides with the world's general interest. Therefore, "we" have to fight terrorism collectively on a global scale and eradicate the causes of its growth, such as poverty and inequality. Moreover, as Blair argued soon after 9/11, it is "our" "moral duty" to fight for the values "we" believe in, especially freedom and justice: "So I believe this is a fight for freedom. And I want to make it a fight for justice too. Justice not only to punish the guilty. But justice to bring those same values of democracy and freedom to people round the world." The "power of community" should be combined with justice in order to become a "moral power." Justice consists of "fairness, people all of equal worth. . . . But also reason and tolerance" (speech 1). These values are not specifically Western, as some opponents have claimed, but are endorsed by the whole of humanity: "Ours are not Western values, they are universal values of the human spirit. And anywhere . . . the choice is the same: freedom not tyranny; democracy, not dictatorship; the rule of law, not the secret police" (speech 3). The best way to defend "our" security is by spreading these universal values throughout the world (speech 4). "To win, we have to win the battle of values, as much as arms. We have to show these are not Western still less American or Anglo-Saxon values but values in the common ownership of humanity, universal values that should be the right of the global citizen" (speech 7b).

This statement marks the transition from the moral to the legal sphere: universal values, such as freedom and justice, should be "the right of the global citizen." By using a normative phrase ("should be"), Blair acknowledges explicitly that citizens worldwide are not, or not yet, legally entitled to these fundamental values. However, in other passages he makes it appear as if these values are already law: "We are fighting for the inalienable right of humankind—black or white, Christian or not, left, right or a million different—to be free" (speech 3). Particularly in his defense of the Iraq invasion, Blair displays an ambivalent stance toward the law. On the one hand, he claims that the invasion is in full accordance with the right of self-defense, as granted by international law:[15] "The essence of a community is common rights and responsibilities.[16] If we are threatened, we have a right to act.... We surely have a duty and a right to prevent the threat materialising; and we surely have a responsibility to act when a nation's people are subjected to a regime such as Saddam's" (speech 4).

Iraq contravened UN Resolution 1441. Therefore, it was the United Kingdom's duty to intervene: "We had to force conformity with international obligations that for years had been breached with the world turning a blind eye" (speech 3). "Our primary purpose was to enforce UN resolutions over Iraq and WMD" (speech 2).

On the other hand, Blair pleads for amending existing international law to provide for a legal justification for interventions like this. He claims that "the rule book of international politics has been torn up": "Interdependence—the fact of a crisis somewhere becoming a crisis everywhere—makes a mockery of traditional views of national interest.... We have to act, not react; we have to do so on the basis of prediction not certainty.... And what all that means is: that this can't be done easily unless it is done on an agreed basis of principle, of values that are shared and fair" (speech 7c).

Blair's basic problem with existing international law is that it does not sanction a preemptive response: "It may well be that under international law as presently constituted, a regime can systematically brutalise and oppress its people and there is nothing anyone can do, when dialogue, diplomacy and even sanctions fail, unless it comes within the definition of a humanitarian catastrophe (though the 300,000 remains in mass graves already found in Iraq might be thought by some to be something of a catastrophe). This may be the law, but should it be?" (speech 4).

Therefore, the United Nations must be reformed: "It means reforming the UN so its Security Council represents twenty-first-century reality; and giving the UN the capability to act effectively as well as debate" (speech 4). "The Security Council should be reformed. We need a new international regime on the non-proliferation of weapons of mass destruction" (speech 3).

The cause seems to justify the means: "it is an entirely noble one—to help people in need of our help in pursuit of liberty; and a self-interested one, since in their salvation lies our own security" (speech 7a). Here we find again (as earlier in this section) an allusion to "a happy marriage of conviction and realpolitik": by liberating other people, "we" protect "our" own security.

What Role Are Citizens Expected to Play in the "War on Terror"?

In Blair's speeches, citizens take on three main roles: as objects of care, command, or conviction. People in Iraq and Afghanistan are portrayed as "people in need of our help in pursuit of liberty." They are victims, waiting for "salvation." "They need our support" (speech 7c); "we should extend a helping hand" because "solidarity" requires "us" to do so (speech 7b). Moreover, the Iraqi leadership should be empowered, so that they, not we, can "lead and win the fight against terrorism." Therefore, "they need our support, politically, in their economy and for their armed forces" (speech 8). By turning "them"—the leaders and the people of Iraq—into objects of care, they will become eventually, by means of empowerment, combative subjects in their own right, capable of fighting terrorism. In his first speech on the London bombings, Blair treats the Londoners involved also as victims who are taken care of: "we are doing our level best to look after the families," and "we will be ready to join in arrangements for a Memorial Service for the victims." On their behalf, "we will pursue those responsible. . . . We will not rest until they are identified and, as far as humanly possible, brought to justice" (speech 5).

Subsequently, when using the discourse of exception, Blair puts himself in the position of a world leader making decisions on the basis of his personal judgment; by implication, citizens are mere objects of command: they should simply follow orders. There is no time for deliberation.

Finally, some room (as well as time) for deliberation is created when Blair switches to the discourse of normalcy. Here, citizens appear in their capacity of objects of conviction who have to be persuaded that Blair's course of action is both appropriate and just: "Ranged against us are the people who hate us; but beyond them are many more who don't hate us but question our motives, our good faith, our even-handedness, who could support our values but believe we support them selectively. These are the people we have to persuade. . . . We need to construct a global alliance for these global values; and act through it" (speech 7b).

Objects of conviction are obviously not the terrorists, because any communication with them is deemed impossible, as we have seen, but the "false friends," who are anti-American or Euro-skeptical, adhere to the "doctrine of benign inactivity," which constitutes "the majority view of a large part of Western opinion, certainly in Europe." According to this "worldview," the American response to 9/11 has been "a gross overreaction" (speech 7a). These "internal" critics must be persuaded that their convictions are not simply wrong but, more fundamentally, at odds with Britain's and the world's interest in safety and order, contravening basic values such as freedom and justice, and potentially very dangerous since they feed the growth of terrorism instead of "choking" it (speech 4). Whereas, in the discourse of exception, the source of authority resides in the leader's personal judgment, Blair is asking for democratic approval now: "We should have the courage of our argument, to ask the British people for their consent in this Parliament" (speech 1). Moreover, he stresses the importance of "inter-faith dialogues" (speech 6). "In the end," the fight against terrorism is won not by arms but "by the power of argument, debate, true religious faith and true legitimate politics" (speech 6).

Rhetorical Citizenship

As this analysis shows, in his key speeches Blair does not present his antiterror measures as taken from out of the blue. His justifications draw on different normative sources: interests, values, and, occasionally, the rules and standards of international law. Only in exceptional cases, when the time for deliberation seems to have run out, does he resort to his own judgment as a world leader. His main arguments are based on a combination of practical and principled reasoning: the fight against terrorism is construed as in both the British and the world's interest, serving order and safety on a global scale, and as a defense of fundamental values such as freedom and justice. Toward international law Blair displays ambivalence, particularly in his defense of the Iraq invasion. He claims that the invasion is in full accordance with the right of self-defense, but he also acknowledges that "the rule book of international politics has been torn up" and must be amended to allow for preemptive responses.

These findings seem to confirm Schmitt's and Agamben's claim that in a state of exception there is little room for law or the rule of law. In times of crisis, when the existence of the United Kingdom is at stake, Blair—in his capacity of sovereign—presents his decisions as made on his own authority. There is no time for deliberation; "we" must act now. Or, as Schmitt (1996b, 55–56) would argue, "as far as the most essential issues are concerned, making a decision is more important than how a decision is made." Moreover, Blair decides when the threat has diminished enough to permit a return to the state of normalcy. However, it is always a partial return to normalcy: one never gets the impression that the full rights catalogue is applicable or that a true democratic dialogue has been held. Blair does not seem very comfortable with the law as it is. Only once, when justifying the invasion of Iraq, does he put forward a quasi-legal argument, based on self-defense. Legally, this argument is highly questionable, since Iraq did not constitute a real or direct threat to the United States or the United Kingdom and a UN mandate was lacking. Clare Short, the British secretary for international development, who later resigned in protest against the invasion (like Robin Cook, the leader of the House of Commons at the time), stated that "the decision by Blair's government to participate in the US invasion of Iraq bypassed government procedures and ignored opposition to the war from Britain's intelligence quarters."[17]

On other occasions, Blair tries to debunk legal counterarguments as political, referring to the allegedly political bias of his critics: "The lawyers continue to divide over it—with their legal opinions bearing a remarkable similarity to their political view of the war" (speech 4). Blair proposes to bring current international law into accordance with "21st century reality," amending the law so as to reconcile it with his conception of justice and political necessity. He may sometimes seem to act and reason as if both are already reconciled, but most often he separates law from morality and politics—"This is the law, but should it be?" In conclusion, law is not always entirely absent from the state of exception, as Blair construes it, but it is never fully present, either. Law is "tolerated" as long as it supports the fight against terrorism, and if not, it is replaced by other normative notions taken from the moral and political sphere. As a result, a "twilight zone" between law and fact in Agamben's sense is created.

The possibilities for rhetorical citizenship are also limited. In the speeches analyzed here, very rarely are Iraqi or Afghan citizens invited to discuss, criticize, or change the course of political action. As objects of care, they find themselves at the mercy of self-proclaimed acts of solidarity, such as the externally enforced regime changes in Iraq and Afghanistan. Their only hope of regaining subjectivity, in Blair's vision, lies in their one day becoming combatants in the fight against terrorism, alongside or preferably instead of Western countries. As objects of command, they have no choice but to subject themselves to sovereign decisions. Because the time for deliberation has run out, Blair's personal judgment will inevitably replace a democratic exchange of opinions. Finally, as objects of conviction, opponents are told that they must change their opinion, though it may be "the majority view of a large part of Western opinion, certainly in Europe." If not, they are accused of supporting the terrorist cause. By allegedly denying fundamental values deemed "universal" by the civilized world, they risk—just like the terrorists—being banned from civilization and, consequently, excluded from communication altogether. This situation resembles the autoimmune process, as described by Derrida (see Borradori 2003, 95–102), in which potential friends are turned into enemies ("false friends"), and enemies, subsequently, into "enemies of humanity." To put an end to this deadly process it is necessary, after many years of exceptional politics, that more opportunities be created for what Blair calls "the power of argument" and "true legitimate politics" (speech 6).

Blair's rhetorical strategies turned out not to be persuasive in the long run: the British people were increasingly dissatisfied with Blair's support for the American "war on terror" (as his steady decline in popularity demonstrates).[18] This decline of rhetorical efficacy can be attributed to the "logic" of symbolic power. If the inclusive speech Blair used in the wake of terrorist attacks is contradicted by an eroding consensus, the limits of symbolic power become apparent. As U.S. president Abraham Lincoln said famously, "it is true that you may fool all of the people some of the time; you can even fool some of the people all of the time; but you can't fool all of the people all of the time." To be sure, inclusive speech is a crucial element of political rhetoric in general.[19] Therefore, its exploitation by Blair was nothing exceptional. Instead, it was the exception—the exceptional threat of terrorism—that enabled him to use the antiterror consent of the people for his own purpose, namely, to fight terrorism on a global scale. But this process of consensus building turned out to be fragile. Critics soon reclaimed the stage and redefined the battlefield: for good reasons, they demanded a return to a state of normalcy where the rule of law is respected. It seems that whenever there is a critical audience, symbolic power based on inclusive speech is itself an exception.[20] It may be persuasive for a while, but its appeal will inevitably fade when social circumstances or current opinions change. Therefore, in the political arena symbolic power is not a static entity that can be won once and for all but must be conquered over and over again by connecting to, and sometimes manipulating, convictions (or *topoi*) that are commonly held. After an era of pseudo-inclusive speech—which in fact excluded political opponents by turning them into "enemies of humanity"—the time has come for a new rhetorical discourse that enables true rhetorical citizenship.

APPENDIX: SPEECHES BY TONY BLAIR

Speech 1   Speech delivered at the Labour Party conference, 2 October 2001, available at http://www.guardian.co.uk/politics/2001/oct/02/labourconference.labour6[21]
Speech 2   Statement on military action in Afghanistan, 7 October 2001, available at www.guardian.co.uk/world/2001/oct/07/afghanistan.terrorism11
Speech 3   Speech delivered before the U.S. Congress, 17 July 2003, available at http://edition.cnn.com/2003/US/07/17/blair.transcript
Speech 4   Speech delivered before Blair's Sedgefield constituency, 5 March 2004, available at http://www.guardian.co.uk/politics/2004/mar/05/iraq.iraq
Speech 5   Statement to UK parliament on the London bombings, 11 July 2005, available at http://www.guardian.co.uk/politics/2005/jul/11/uksecurity.terrorism
Speech 6   Speech delivered at the Labour Party's national conference, 16 July 2005, available at http://news.bbc.co.uk/1/hi/uk/4689363.stm
Speech 7a Foreign Policy Speech I, London, 21 March 2006, available at http://www.guardian.co.uk/politics/2006/mar/21/iraq.iraq1
Speech 7b Foreign Policy Speech II, before the Australian parliament, 27 March 2006, available at http://www.guardian.co.uk/politics/2006/mar/27/uksecurity.terrorism
Speech 7c Foreign Policy Speech III, London, 26 May 2006, available at http://www.isn.ethz.ch/isn/Current-Affairs/ISN-Insights/ObjectDetail/?lng=en&ord61=alphaNavi&ots627=fce62fe0-528d-4884-9cdf-283c282cf0b2&ots736=69f57a17-24d2-527c-4f3b-b63b07201ca1&id=24747
Speech 8   Speech delivered at the lord mayor's banquet, London, 13 November 2006, available at http://news.bbc.co.uk/2/hi/uk_news/politics/6145454.stm

NOTES

1. In the original German text, Schmitt (1996d, 18) wrote, "im juristischen Sinne [besteht] immer noch eine Ordnung, wenn auch keine Rechtsordung."
2. The German text contains a villain pun on "need to have law" (or "the right") and "to be right," which gets lost in translation: "die Autorität beweist, dass sie, um Recht zu schaffen, nicht Recht zu haben braucht" (1996d, 19).
3. Van Klink 2007 provides an elaborate discussion of Schmitt's and Agamben's notion of the state of exception.
4. For an analysis of speeches by Spain's prime minister, José Luis Zapatero, see Van Klink, Lembcke, and Ciocchini 2011, 316–21.
5. A list of the speeches can be found in the appendix; we have cited them parenthetically in the text by the number we've assigned them there.
6. As a Briton, Blair prefers the British date form September 11 (or 11th) (and sometimes 11 or 11th September) to the American abbreviation 9/11. For an excellent critical reflection on the events of 9/11, see Derrida's comments in Borradori 2003, 85–94.
7. Blair uses the phrase "way of life" in various speeches, among them speeches 1 and 5.

8. As Kock observes, deliberation means "to weigh something, as on a pair of scales, and what we weigh when we deliberate is decisions" (2004, 105). According to Kock, "the best we can do in public debate is to make sure that the best reasons on both sides of a case are heard, understood and given attention." This is exactly what Blair decides not to do: the time for exchanging and weighing opinions has run out; "we" have to act now.

9. This statement could be read as a symptom of the autoimmune process that Derrida describes (Borradori 2003, 95–102): terrorism threatens to destroy Western countries from within. See also van Klink and Lembcke 2007, 21–24.

10. According to Mendes, Blair treats terrorism as a strategy rather than an ontological category. In this reading, "there would not be terrorist individuals or groups by nature, but the use of the strategies considered terrorist by certain actors" (2008, 9). The question is whether this distinction can be upheld when Blair repeatedly refers to people who use terrorist strategies as "terrorists."

11. In speeches by U.S. president George Bush, the theme of "evil" is even more prominent (see Mral 2004, 20–22).

12. As Schmitt notes (1996a, 37), an intensification of the friend-enemy distinction may lead to pleas for the "endgültig letzten Krieg der Menschheit" (the absolutely last war of humanity) (1996b, 36).

13. In contrast to Bush (see Mral 2004, 17–20), Blair rarely uses the expression "war," and never speaks of a "war on terror," but prefers seemingly softer notions like a "battle" or a "fight" against terrorism.

14. That is, weapons of mass destruction. On the WMD theme, see also Mral 2004, 42–43.

15. Blair makes an explicit reference to the right of self-defense in speech 2.

16. As Bulley shows, Blair introduces the idea of an international community having rights and responsibilities in 1999 and appeals to it frequently later on (2008, 283–84).

17. Quoted in "Short: I Was Briefed on Blair's Secret Pact," *Guardian*, 17 June 2003, http://www.guardian.co.uk/politics/2003/jun/18/iraq.iraqi.

18. For some statistics, see "The Long Decline: Tony Blair's Popularity," *Guardian*, 25 April 2007, http://politics.guardian.co.uk/flash/page/0,,2065152,00.html.

19. It is, for instance, also a feature of Zapatero's speeches. See van Klink, Lembcke, and Ciocchini 2011, 316.

20. Perelman and Olbrechts-Tyteca stress the importance of the audience in rhetoric: "Since argumentation aims at securing the adherence of those to whom it is addressed, it is, in its entirety, relative to the audience to be influenced" (1969, 19).

21. All of the URLs in this list were last accessed on 1 February 2012.

REFERENCES

Agamben, Giorgio. 1998. *Homo Sacer: Sovereign Power and Bare Life*. Trans. Daniel Heller-Roazen. Stanford: Stanford University Press.
———. 2005. *State of Exception*. Trans. Kevin Attell. Chicago: University of Chicago Press.
Boldt, Hans. 1972. "Ausnahmezustand." In *Geschichtliche Grundbegriffe: Historisches Lexikon zur politisch-sozialen Sprache in Deutschland, Band A-D*, ed. Otto Bruner, Werner Conze, and Reinhart Koselleck, 343–76. Stuttgart: Klett-Cotta.
Borradori, Giovanna, ed. 2003. *Philosophy in a Time of Terror: Dialogues with Jürgen Habermas and Jacques Derrida*. Chicago: University of Chicago Press.

Bulley, Dan. 2008. "'Foreign' Terror? London Bombings, Resistance, and the Failing State." *British Journal of Politics and International Relations* 10:379–94.
Chomsky, Noam. 2006. *Failed States: The Abuse of Power and the Assault on Democracy*. London: Hamish Hamilton.
Kock, Christian. 2004. "Rhetoric in Media Studies: The Voice of Constructive Criticism." *Nordicom Review* 25 (1–2): 103–10.
Lindahl, Hans K. 2004. "Inside and Outside the EU's 'Area of Freedom, Security, and Justice': Reflexive Identity and the Unity of Legal Space." *Archiv für Rechts- und Sozialphilosophie* 4:478–97.
MacMillan, Sarah. 2007. *Blair's Community: Communitarian Thought and New Labour*. Manchester: Manchester University Press.
Mendes, Cristiano. 2008. "The Speeches of Tony Blair: The Concept of Terrorism and the Stability of Its Structures." Paper presented at the 49th annual meeting of the ISA, San Francisco, 26 March. http://www.allacademic.com/meta/p253729_index.html.
Mral, Brigitte. 2004. *"We're a Peaceful Nation": War Rhetoric After September 11*. Stockholm: Swedish Emergency Management Agency.
Perelman, Chaïm, and Lucie Olbrechts-Tyteca. 1969. *The New Rhetoric: A Treatise on Argumentation*. Trans. John Wilkinson and Purcell Weaver. Notre Dame: University of Notre Dame Press. (Orig. pub. 1958.)
Schmitt, Carl. 1996a. *Der Begriff des Politischen: Text von 1932 mit einem Vorwort und drei Collarien*. 6th ed. Berlin: Duncker & Humblot.
———. 1996b. *The Concept of the Political*. Trans. George Schwab. Chicago: University of Chicago Press.
———. 1996c. *Political Theology: Four Chapters on the Concept of Sovereignty*. Trans. George Schwab. Cambridge: MIT Press.
———. 1996d. *Politische Theologie: Vier Kapitel zur Lehre von der Souveränität*. Berlin: Duncker & Humblot.
Van Klink, Bart. 2007. "Does Necessity Know No Laws? Application of Law in a State of Exception." In *Political Philosophy: New Proposals for New Questions*, ed. José Rubio Carrecedo, 129–42. Stuttgart: Franz Steiner Verlag.
Van Klink, Bart, and Oliver W. Lembcke. 2007. "Can Terrorism Be Fought Within the Boundaries of the Rule of Law? A Review of Recent Literature in Political Philosophy." *Rechtsfilosofie en Rechtstheorie* 2:9–26.
Van Klink, Bart, Oliver W. Lembcke, and Pablo Leandro Ciocchini. 2011. "Symbolic Power: Political Rhetoric in a State of Exception." In *Bending Opinion: Essays on Persuasion in the Public Domain*, ed. T. van Haaften, H. Jansen, J. de Jong, and W. Koetsenruijter, 307–25. Leiden: Leiden University Press.
Villadsen, Lisa Storm. 2008. "Speaking on Behalf of Others: Rhetorical Agency and Epideictic Functions in Official Apologies." *Rhetoric Society Quarterly* 38 (1): 25–45.

PART 3

RHETORICAL CITIZENSHIP ACROSS
COMMUNICATIVE SETTINGS

12

I AGREE, BUT . . . :
FINDING ALTERNATIVES TO CONTROVERSIAL PROJECTS
THROUGH PUBLIC DELIBERATION

James McDonald

Whoever values free speech cannot avoid discussing the merits of public deliberation. Through public deliberation, citizens who have opposing views on issues can explain the foundations of their beliefs. In Asen's discourse theory of citizenship, public deliberation is even seen as constituting citizenship (2004, 189); individuals become citizens by discursively—and thus rhetorically—engaging one another in the public sphere.

Public deliberation occasionally receives bad press: for example, because it is often impossible to bring together all the views expressed in a process of deliberation, political authorities can dismiss the concerns of the participants in a deliberation forum and make decisions without taking their views into consideration. Furthermore, deliberation, especially about controversial issues, is often seen as an interminable process, leading to little or no consensus. Regardless of these criticisms, few rhetorical and political communication scholars contest that public deliberation must be encouraged in a variety of venues, including public consultations, the media, and legislative assemblies. Many scholars, notably Robert D. Putnam, critique the lack of public participation in contemporary Western democracies, calling for a true rhetorical democracy where "all citizens are equal, everyone has a say, everyone has a vote, and decisions are based on the most compelling arguments" (Hauser 2004, 1).

In this chapter I discuss the effects of deliberation at public consultations on a projected natural gas plant in the Canadian province of Quebec. In particular, I examine how one important rhetorical practice, namely, the acceptance of key opinions of the opposing party, contributed to the development of acceptable solutions on this divisive issue, and how the deliberation venue enabled individuals to enact their citizenship rhetorically.

Public Deliberation over Controversial Issues

Controversies are more complex than simple disagreements between two parties. According to Govier, controversies have the following characteristics: the individuals who discuss issues are in disagreement with other individuals or groups that discuss the same issues; there is a minimum of two opposing views on the issues; and the parties do not simply express their opposing points of view but argue about the issues in a process of deliberation (1999, 247). Thus public deliberation is a sine qua non of any controversy.

Bohman's definition of deliberation, which emphasizes "resolving problematic situations" through deliberation processes (1996, 27), is contested by a paradigm, supported by Brante (1993, 188–89) and Callon, Lascoumes, and Barthe (2001, 16), suggesting that controversies may be closed but not resolved. The aim of public deliberation therefore need not be to consolidate different points of view but rather to learn, understand, and test a party's beliefs about an issue by juxtaposing them with those of an opposing party (Govier 1999, 65). Thus deliberation has the potential to generate new ways of interpreting a controversy, even when the parties do not arrive at an agreement.

Those who emphasize the constitutive perspective of controversies (see Callon, Lascoumes, and Barthe 2001; Scott 1991; Govier 1999) consider these events essential for a society where individuals continually assess and reevaluate their opinions—one of the bases of a strong rhetorical democracy (Hauser 2004, 1). Critical assessment and reevaluation are considered positive because, as Goodnight states, the new ways of interpreting issues may not have emerged without public deliberation (2005, 27). Public deliberation brings new and potentially consensual ways of interpreting controversial issues to the forefront. When feminist models of communication and exchange that strive for mutual inquiry, collaboration, mutual understanding, transformation, and dialogue are put into practice, these new ways of interpreting controversies have even more potential to emerge (Putnam and Kolb 2000, 83).

In a constitutive perspective, public deliberation is a practice by which each party is exposed to the knowledge and interpretations of its adversaries. All parties involved can therefore discover, even create, new knowledge that changes their initial position. Solutions that were unthinkable at the beginning of a controversy may eventually be considered and privileged by all parties. For example, describing a controversy on the burial of nuclear waste in France, Callon, Lascoumes, and Barthe note that "in the heart of the controversy, the residents realized that a number of uncertainties remained and that the burial of the nuclear waste was only one researched solution among others" (2001, 31, my translation). They suggest that, for a rhetorical democracy to flourish, controversies should be welcomed, encouraged, stimulated, and even organized in order to implicate ordinary citizens in governmental decision making (347).

However, by which specific rhetorical practices do learning and critical reassessments of opinions take place? Acknowledging the role of these practices is important for two main reasons: to better comprehend how deliberation can have the positive influence that the literature says it has, and to be able to recognize and foster practices that enable citizens to find alternatives to controversial projects while participating in rhetorical democracy.

Controversies in contemporary democracies can arise over any number of issues. *Sociotechnical* controversies, that is, those pertaining to society, science, and technology, seem to occupy a particularly important place in the contemporary public sphere and are the subject of numerous analyses in various disciplines, including rhetoric (Benoit-Barné 2007; Govier 1999; Olson and Goodnight 1994) and the sociology of science and technology (see Callon, Lascoumes, and Barthe 2001; Latour 2004). From a deliberative and rhetorical standpoint, these controversies are particularly fascinating because multiple actors, with varying degrees of expertise, discuss heterogeneous issues that pertain to both society and science and technology (Goodnight 1991, 49–50; Callon, Lascoumes, and Barthe 2001, 32, 56, 121).

The main particularity of these controversies is their heterogeneity: the issues come from several registers, from ethics to economics, from psychology to atomic physics (Callon, Lascoumes, and Barthe 2001, 36). As Lyne affirms, "science and technology controversies are not just about science and technology. They are also about our culture, our comfort, and our metaphysics" (2005, 38). They therefore allow us to examine deliberation about both technical and social issues. The heterogeneity of the participants in deliberation forums over these controversies allows the general public to discuss technical, complex issues with experts, and it allows experts to discuss social issues with ordinary citizens. Rémy (1995, 136–44) and Callon, Lascoumes, and Barthe (2001, 31) have shown that ordinary citizens, when discussing technical issues, can think of solutions to complex scientific problems that have been overlooked by experts. The value of public deliberation on sociotechnical issues and of citizens participating actively and rhetorically is therefore clear, as the deliberation exposes both experts and citizens to solutions they may have overlooked.

To expand knowledge on the discursive dynamics of sociotechnical controversies and the rhetorical strategies used by participants in deliberation over them, Goodnight has called for empirical research (2005, 29). This chapter answers Goodnight's call, following the tradition of previous rhetorical analyses of sociotechnical controversies. Benoit-Barné discusses the influence of material entities on discussions in a public deliberation forum; Keränen (2005) examines the different ways in which the parties interpret controversial issues; Gross (1995) analyzes consensus formation among stakeholders; and Moore (2003) demonstrates how two stylistic figures, synecdoche and irony, contribute to the formation of new opinions on depleting salmon stocks in the Pacific Northwest. Moore's study largely represents the constitutive perspective of controversies, showing how controversies end up shaping public opinions and discourse. In this chapter I build on this research, demonstrating how a particular rhetorical practice contributes to the formation of new opinions in a controversy.

My research question is formulated as such: how can a particular rhetorical practice used at a public deliberation forum contribute to developing alternatives to a controversial project? While addressing this question, I also show how the participants in this deliberation rhetorically enacted their citizenship, by voicing their opinions and influencing governmental policy.

The Case of "Le Suroît"

My analysis concerns the Suroît controversy. The Suroît was a projected natural gas–fired electrical plant in Beauharnois, a suburb of Montreal. This plant was never constructed: after being announced twice by Hydro-Québec (HQ) and the Quebec government between 2001 and 2004, and being severely criticized by several groups and individuals, the project was abandoned.[1]

In October 2001 HQ initially justified the plant by Quebec's rising energy consumption: either we construct the Suroît, HQ argued, or, as of 2006, we import (more expensive and potentially unreliable) energy from neighboring provinces and states. However, despite the economic gains anticipated, the project caused public outcry because of the greenhouse gas emissions that would have come from the plant: it would have raised Quebec's emissions by 2.8 percent a year in a context where Canada was leaning toward adopting the Kyoto Protocol. The project's critics, including environmental and consumer protection groups, unions, independent experts, politicians, professors, and ordinary citizens, believed that there were better options for meeting Quebec's energy needs than a natural gas plant that would cause substantial greenhouse gas emissions for at least the next twenty-five years.

Regardless of this criticism, the government and HQ still argued that the Suroît was necessary. According to them, only a natural gas plant could fulfill Quebec's short-term energy needs, because hydroelectricity projects take at least ten years to construct. They also claimed that the Suroît would diminish greenhouse gas emissions in North America by preventing HQ from importing energy from coal- and natural gas–fired plants in New England, which pollute much more than the Suroît would have. HQ positioned itself against potential alternatives such as wind energy because it considered windmills, which generate energy only under certain conditions, unreliable.

Nevertheless, the public outcry continued, and more than a dozen groups and organizations asked the government to subject the Suroît project to public hearings at the Bureau d'audiences publiques sur l'environnement (BAPE).[2] The BAPE's mission was to determine whether the project was environmentally sound, as HQ and the government claimed. The hearings took place in September and October 2002 and led the BAPE to refuse to support the project because it would have significantly increased Quebec's greenhouse gas emissions and compromised its Kyoto Protocol objectives.

Although the BAPE's report did not bind the government to a decision, the project was subsequently abandoned. This, however, was not the end of it. After Quebeckers elected a new government in April 2003, the issue was brought back to the table by HQ, which still believed that Quebec would have an energy deficit if the plant wasn't constructed. After months of preparation, a slightly modified version of the Suroît was announced in January 2004 by the government and Hydro-Québec.

Despite the government's and Hydro-Québec's rhetorical attempts to present the new Suroît as a better project, there was fierce opposition. Environmental and consumer groups, as well as general public opinion, saw the project as the same that the BAPE had rejected a year earlier. On 1 February 2004, four thousand people protested in front of HQ's headquarters in downtown Montreal. A few days later, a public opinion survey showed that 67 percent of Quebeckers were against the construction.

The government now decided to hold another public consultation, this one at the Régie de l'énergie, a government-affiliated organization responsible for determining Quebec's energy needs and electricity costs. Whereas the BAPE had examined the environmental consequences, the Régie was to determine whether Quebec's energy needs justified the construction of the plant.

The hearings at the Régie took place in May 2004. One month later, the Régie stated in its 150-page report that the Suroît was not "indispensable" to meeting Quebec's energy needs but was still "desirable" (8, my translation). The government did not comment on the Régie's nonbinding recommendations right away, but eventually, in November 2004, it denied the authorization required by HQ to build the Suroît. After the project was officially abandoned, HQ put sustainable development high on its priority list, claiming that in the future it would always privilege green energies such as windmills and hydroelectricity.

This case has all of the characteristics of a sociotechnical controversy enumerated above, and the advantage of having been subjected to two public deliberation forums (at the BAPE and at the Régie). Let us examine how, in this controversy, a particular rhetorical practice facilitated the development of alternatives: wind energy and energy efficiency.

An Inductive, Rhetorical Approach to Analyzing a Public Deliberation Forum

While attempting to craft a method to help answer my research question, my main difficulty was the sheer amount of documentation available. For example, there were 936 pages of transcriptions from the BAPE forum and 3,215 pages from the Régie forum.[3] In these consultations, countless rhetorical strategies were used and a plethora of issues discussed.[4] Because it would be impossible to demonstrate the constitutive power of each rhetorical practice, these two questions guided my choices: which issues and which rhetorical strategies would I examine?

The answer to both questions lies in the inductive approach I applied. Upon first reading the 4,151-page corpus, it became clear that much of the deliberation revolved around potential alternatives. For example, many participants claimed that investments in wind energy and energy efficiency would make the plant unnecessary. Because the emergence of alternatives through public deliberation is a clear demonstration of the constitutive power of controversies, I decided to restrict my analysis to discussions about three ways of supplying energy: wind energy, energy efficiency, and thermal energy. I therefore set out to establish the rhetorical practices by which wind energy and energy efficiency were presented as alternatives to thermal projects such as the Suroît.

Having regrouped the discussions regarding wind energy, energy efficiency, and thermal energy into three mini-corpuses, I began my rhetorical analysis. I identified nineteen mutually exclusive rhetorical practices used by parties to support their claims. Many of these contributed to the emergence of alternatives, but for the purpose of this chapter, I focus on the most influential one: accepting the opposing party's key opinions, which I define as a rhetorical practice by which an individual, X, expresses agreement with ideas advanced by another individual, Y, even though they differ on the central issue (in this case, the construction of the Suroît). This allows X to express agreement on values, ideological principles, and opinions with Y. Jones and Rowland argue that when individuals do this, their persuasive message has a better chance of being accepted or, at least, deemed credible (2007, 79). Furthermore, the use of this practice in a public consultation is interesting because we can question whether it is simply a strategy or a manifestation of the constitutive power of public deliberation.

The vast majority of participants at the two consultations accepted the opposing party's key opinions when discussing the three issues in my analysis. The parties focused on their similarities rather than on their differences, and their positions became more similar in the course of the deliberation—eventually leading HQ to abandon the plant and focus on alternatives.

Summary of the Key Parties' Opinions

At both consultations, the anti-Suroît parties argued that the plant was unnecessary because of Quebec's significant wind energy potential. They believed that new wind energy projects, combined with hydroelectricity, would eliminate the need for the Suroît. The pro-Suroît parties argued that wind energy presented too many risks and uncertainties for HQ to rely on it to cover Quebec's energy needs. They believed that wind energy could be progressively developed, but only in parallel to the Suroît.

Many anti-Suroît parties also claimed that HQ had not sufficiently examined energy efficiency programs and that such programs could make the Suroît unnecessary. The pro-Suroît parties invoked the risks associated with energy efficiency; regardless of energy efficiency programs, they maintained, the Suroît would still need to be constructed to ensure energy security.

Finally, anti-Suroît parties claimed that thermal energy should have no place in HQ's production park because of its environmental impacts, as well as Quebec's access to cleaner energy sources. Pro-Suroît individuals claimed that only thermal energy could prevent an energy shortage, and that thermal energy projects should thus be approved.

Although opinions on these three key issues varied considerably, parties attempted to minimize their differences and accentuate their similarities. This can be seen either as an attempt to persuade adversaries and/or as a manifestation of the constitutive power of public deliberation. Specific examples of this rhetorical practice will help us understand how it contributed to the development of generally acceptable alternatives.

Accepting Key Opinions of the Opposing Party

Wind Energy

Many anti-Suroît participants presented a combination of wind energy and hydroelectricity as an alternative to the Suroît. The role of wind energy in HQ's production park was therefore a major issue. Evidently, pro-Suroît participants were unable to deny several positive aspects of wind energy, a renewable energy source that emits no greenhouse gas and could help the economy of certain regions of Quebec. Thus, even though they favored the construction of the Suroît, many pro-Suroît participants expressed their interest in developing wind energy in Quebec.

This acceptance of key opinions of the opposing party was clear in the discourse of Thierry Vandal, president of Hydro-Québec Production, at the BAPE. "We have no objection to wind energy," he stated (BAPE 2002, 1.3:42). Vandal also elaborated by giving specific references to wind energy projects that HQ had supported: "In Canada, Hydro-Québec is certainly one of the biggest buyers of wind energy, with the Nordais project, for example." Thus, instead of denying wind energy's potential contribution, Vandal presented HQ as a developer that believed in it and used it already. HQ, the main promoter of the Suroît, clearly accepted certain opinions held by its adversaries.

This rhetorical practice is important for four principal reasons. First, it can seem paradoxical that HQ, which was promoting a natural gas plant, voiced no objection to a green energy source that many consider a better alternative. Implicitly, Vandal could therefore show that he believed that a wind energy project was not equivalent to a natural gas project, because if it were, he would logically have replaced the Suroît with a wind energy project. We see this especially in his claim that he had no objections to wind energy and that

HQ was already one of Canada's leading buyers. We see Vandal arguing for the construction of the Suroît by expressing his support for the use of wind energy in some circumstances. Second, by stating that he had no objection to wind energy and that HQ was a leading buyer, he was able to silence adversaries who criticized HQ for promoting a natural gas project instead of a wind energy project. Third, he demonstrated that HQ was not dogmatically inclined to build natural gas plants; the company was promoting the Suroît because it was the best solution among a number of energy sources that had already been considered. This practice enabled Vandal to argue for the Suroît by demonstrating his support for some wind energy projects. Vandal's argument was thus well adapted to his adversaries, as he showed that he had already considered the alternative they proposed but that, in his opinion, it was not equivalent to the proposed natural gas plant. Fourth, the very fact that Vandal expressed his views on wind energy so clearly reflects the constitutive power of public deliberation in a rhetorical democracy: by touting the positive aspects of wind energy, anti-Suroît participants were able to make wind energy an option that needed at least to be considered by those promoting the Suroît. Because all participants could thus influence the agenda and the potential outcome of the deliberation, the BAPE consultation can be seen as a venue in which citizens could rhetorically enact their citizenship.

A year and a half later, at the Régie consultations, HQ's representatives continued to accept key opinions of their adversaries regarding wind energy, as shown in the following statement by Vandal: "First, Hydro-Québec Production has been active in wind energy for many years. We were among the first and we are still, to my knowledge, the biggest wind energy buyer in Canada. Again this year, we were active in supporting the wind energy project in Murdochville, in the Gaspé region" (Régie de l'énergie Québec 2004, 5:24). Here, as at the BAPE consultation, Vandal implicitly accepted certain arguments advanced by his adversaries, such as Quebec's wind energy potential. Thus, when his adversaries emphasized the positive aspects of wind energy, Vandal could simply state that he was aware of these and that wind energy was already used in HQ's production park. The effectiveness of this practice as a rhetorical strategy lies in what Vandal's adversaries are led to believe: if a wind energy project could supply the same quality of energy as the Suroît, then HQ would be promoting that type of project instead of a gas plant. Accepting key opinions put forth by the opposing party is an effective strategy that enabled HQ to argue in favor of the Suroît by demonstrating its commitment to wind energy in the past. However, as in the BAPE consultation, we can also see the constitutive power of public deliberation: first, wind energy is a key issue that Vandal must address; second, Vandal mentioned that HQ had invested in wind energy since the BAPE consultations a year and a half earlier. The opponents who advocated for wind energy therefore seem to have influenced, through their participation in the BAPE consultations, HQ's energy policy and its decision to invest more in wind energy. Accepting key elements of adversaries' arguments can thus be seen as both a rhetorical strategy and a manifestation of the constitutive power of deliberation.

Anti-Suroît participants used the same practice. At both consultations, even individuals who saw wind energy as a potential alternative to the Suroît did not deny several of the problems associated with wind energy mentioned by Suroît supporters, although they believed that wind energy, combined with hydroelectricity, could be used to stop the Suroît project. For example, Xavier Daxhelet, of Quebec's Green Party, stated at the BAPE consultation, "Wind energy, I know very well that it's not something reliable because the wind is what it is. Sometimes, there isn't any. So it's for sure that it's not something that's continuous" (BAPE 2002, 1.5:74).

This representative of the Green Party thus accepted one of his adversaries' principal premises regarding wind energy. Through this practice, Daxhelet implied that the intermittence of wind does not necessarily imply that wind energy cannot constitute an alternative to the Suroît. He was able, therefore, to present wind energy as an alternative without having to prove that wind energy is not subject to the intermittence of wind, a case that would have been difficult to make. In this sense, Daxhelet exercised his citizenship rhetorically by accepting key arguments of his adversaries, while simultaneously proposing a different interpretation of the issues and potentially influencing the outcome.

At the Régie consultations, several anti-Suroît participants continued to accept key points of their adversaries' argument with regard to wind energy. For example, Richard Legault, a representative of Helimax who considered wind energy an alternative to the Suroît, admitted, "I will not try to convince you that wind energy cannot have difficulties. In fact, we still need to improve this energy source" (Régie de l'énergie Québec 2004, 11:205). By accepting this key point, Legault encouraged pro-Suroît parties to consider wind energy as an alternative, because he showed that he was very familiar with this energy source, including its difficulties, but still maintained that wind energy projects could and should replace the Suroît. Furthermore, by acknowledging the difficulties of wind, Legault limited deliberation on them by concentrating his argument on the advantages of wind energy. By participating in the Régie deliberation and presenting his interpretation of the issues, Legault also exercised rhetorical citizenship and potentially affected the outcome of the controversy—as well as HQ's energy policy.

Energy Efficiency

When participants at the BAPE and Régie deliberations discussed energy efficiency, which many individuals consider an alternative to the Suroît, both sides accepted certain key points in the opposing party's argumentation. Danielle Piette, a representative of HQ at the BAPE consultation, recognized that, "in the past, HQ has effectively invested little in its own energy efficiency programs" (BAPE 2002, 1.2:36). By accepting, instead of refuting, her adversaries' claim that HQ had invested little in energy efficiency programs, Piette limited deliberation on this point and enabled herself to concentrate on why HQ supported energy efficiency projects but also considered the Suroît necessary. For example, Piette stated that HQ had included energy efficiency measures in its strategic plan: "By the way, the distributor, Hydro-Québec Distribution, still has energy efficiency measures that can be found in its strategic plan" (1.2:33). Thus HQ accepted that energy efficiency projects are valuable and showed that it supported these programs, despite their not being equivalent, in its opinion, to the Suroît. This rhetorical practice paradoxically enabled HQ to argue for the Suroît by accepting certain values of energy efficiency, which its adversaries considered a potential alternative to the Suroît. However, this can also be seen as a manifestation of the constitutive power of public deliberation, since the very fact that Piette mentioned that HQ valued energy efficiency shows how the anti-Suroît participants had succeeded in making energy efficiency an unavoidable option.

At the Régie deliberations, pro-Suroît participants continued to recognize the value of energy efficiency programs, despite their claim that they could not replace the Suroît. For example, Jacques Marquis, a representative of the pro-Suroît Coalition pour la sécurité énergétique du Québec, stated, "There undeniably exists a vast potential of economically viable energy efficiency measures, meaning that the cost of implementation is inferior to the cost of the better production alternatives. Reducing the demand by a more judicious use of energy also represents the solution which supports the idea of sustainable development. For these reasons, the Coalition supports all initiatives which reduce the energy demand" (Régie de l'énergie Québec 2004, 9:171).

Thus Marquis agreed with his adversaries regarding the issue of energy efficiency. By restating their arguments, he reduced their potential to refute his arguments, as they could no longer claim that pro-Suroît participants denied the potential of energy efficiency projects. Paradoxically, Marquis increased the power of his argument in favor of the Suroît, as he reduced the number of arguments his adversaries could invoke to criticize his support of the project. However, it is also important to note the common ground that the consultations allowed Marquis to find with anti-Suroît participants in terms of valuing energy efficiency. The public consultations thus enabled individuals with seemingly opposing views to find commonalities and work toward a solution acceptable to all.

The anti-Suroît participants at both consultations used the same rhetorical practice. Although many presented energy efficiency programs as a possible alternative, they also accepted some weaknesses, as invoked by their adversaries, of energy efficiency. For example, Richard Gendron, a member of the Union québécoise pour la conservation de la nature, accepted a major criticism stated by his opponents at the BAPE deliberations concerning the difficulty of making consumers invest in energy efficiency because of the low cost of energy in Quebec: "For sure, the current low costs of hydroelectricity in Québec do not necessarily encourage consumers to go out and invest in their maximum energy efficiency potential" (BAPE 2002, 2.2:79). Gendron increased his credibility by demonstrating that despite his belief in energy efficiency as an alternative, he realized that the implementation of these programs would constitute an important challenge.

The discourse of anti-Suroît participants changed little between the two consultations. Jacques St.-Amant, a member of Options Consommateurs who believed that energy efficiency projects could constitute an alternative to the Suroît, accepted his adversaries' claims that HQ could do little to force consumers to invest in such projects and that their short-term success could not be guaranteed: "It seems to us that in a short-term perspective, the energy efficiency potential is relatively limited because experience tells us that it takes a certain amount of time for people to get used to and implement those programs. That said, we believe that it is clearly an avenue to develop in a long-term perspective and an avenue which we hope the distributor will engage in more than it does right now" (Régie de l'énergie Québec 2004, 13:9).

While St.-Amant accepted a key point of his adversaries' argument against energy efficiency, he used it to promote energy efficiency projects. This rhetorical practice, in addition to increasing his credibility, enabled St.-Amant to concentrate on the advantages of energy efficiency, instead of the weaknesses invoked by his adversaries. Furthermore, we see that all participants regarded energy efficiency as having both positive and negative attributes and accepted many of the arguments advanced by their opponents. Accepting the arguments of opposing parties can thus be seen as more than a strategy: it is a positive outcome of a forum where individuals can reevaluate their own arguments and adopt new ones, even when these originate on the other side of the debate.

Thermal Energy

The debate on thermal energy was different from the debate on the two other issues. Whereas opponents of the Suroît saw wind energy and energy efficiency as alternatives, the pro-Suroît side supported thermal energy, which the anti-Suroît contingent ultimately opposed. While pro-Suroît participants tended to reject the opposing party's view of thermal energy, pro-Suroît participants openly accepted several weaknesses identified by those who were against all types of thermal energy, including the Suroît.

At the BAPE consultation, Macky Tall, a representative of HQ, made it clear that thermal energy, and thus the Suroît, would not have been HQ's first choice under different circumstances: "Our priority and our first choice is the development of hydroelectricity" (BAPE 2002, 1.1:18). Later, Tall elaborated: "We have not really changed opinions because, as we discussed in sufficient detail yesterday, the situation for HQ is that hydroelectric projects, which is our number-one energy source, cannot be constructed in the same amount of time as the Suroît. That is why we are proposing the Suroît project" (1.4:67). By accepting his adversaries' view that hydroelectricity must be the privileged energy source for HQ, Tall demonstrated that he had examined the different possibilities for responding to the energy deficit envisaged by HQ. This increased Tall's, and HQ's, credibility and enabled him to argue more effectively for the Suroît.

Jacques Marquis, a representative of the Association de l'industrie électrique du Québec (AIEQ) and a supporter of the Suroît, also accepted several of his adversaries' key opinions when referring to thermal energy, as he explained at the BAPE consultation:

> The AIEQ has always supported hydroelectricity as being the privileged source of energy production in Quebec, for both environmental and economic reasons. . . . However, in the current context, the AIEQ recognizes that Hydro-Québec Production and Distribution are obliged to use thermal energy, despite its inconveniences. For other provinces,

regions or countries, the Suroît would be the first choice from both an economic and environmental standpoint. For us, it's a second choice, but an undeniable choice and a necessary tool. (BAPE 2002, 2.4:43).

While Marquis, like his adversaries, recognized that hydroelectricity is a privileged production source, he explained that the current context did not allow it. This increased his credibility, as he showed his adversaries not only that he shared their view of hydroelectricity's advantages but also that he would have promoted a hydroelectric project if the context had been different. He was thus able, paradoxically, to argue in favor of the Suroît by acknowledging the advantages of hydroelectricity and the weaknesses of thermal energy.

The opinion of pro-Suroît participants regarding thermal energy changed little between the BAPE and Régie consultations. At the Régie, they still openly admitted that thermal energy was not their first choice but maintained that HQ had to use it because of the expected energy shortage. The acceptance of points made by anti-Suroît participants is explicit in this comment from Louis Charest, an independent citizen arguing for the Suroît: "For sure, it emits greenhouse gases. I don't hide that. Between a third and a half of a fuel residue plant, so already it's better than a fuel residue plant, or again between a third and a half of a coal-burning plant. For sure, if we compare the Suroît to a hydroelectric project, it emits more greenhouse gas emissions. That's true" (Régie de l'énergie Québec, 7:130). By acknowledging the weaknesses of the project, Charest limited deliberation on these weaknesses, solidifying his argument.

Thierry Vandal also explicitly conceded important points made by his anti-Suroît adversaries: "Listen, if I had to choose today between a hydroelectric project that could be there on the periods that we are talking about, I would have no hesitation. I would follow what you are saying. A hydroelectric project, it is the best choice that we can make for Hydro-Québec Production" (Régie de l'énergie Québec 2004, 5:282). Thus Vandal linked his opinion on thermal energy to that of his adversaries, notably the belief that a hydroelectric project is more efficient than a thermal project. "You know that thermal energy has inconveniences," he told an opponent, "and it is because of these inconveniences that between a hydroelectric project and a thermal project, we evidently choose a hydroelectric project" (6:227). He thus explicitly stated two views shared with his adversaries: thermal energy has inconveniences, and hydroelectricity has to take precedence whenever possible. Once again, this concession paradoxically enabled Vandal to argue for the Suroît.

Ultimately, the Suroît was abandoned and replaced by a project deemed acceptable by all parties, including HQ. HQ also promised to propose no new thermal energy projects in the future—a sign that HQ representatives were persuaded by the arguments of the anti-Suroît participants against all types of thermal energy.

Discussion

The rhetorical practice of accepting the key arguments of opponents had several consequences for the deliberations on the Suroît. This strategy made the alternatives to the Suroît project, notably wind energy and energy efficiency, more acceptable, as pro-Suroît participants recognized certain of their advantages. Although supporters of the Suroît believed that wind energy and energy efficiency could not replace the project, they acknowledged the advantages of these energy sources and the disadvantages of the Suroît, which later allowed them to abandon the Suroît without appearing to lose face. If the Suroît supporters had rejected all arguments for the positive aspects of wind energy and energy efficiency, it would have been much harder for them to consider these alternatives afterward.

The practice is also important because it allowed groups of people with conflicting opinions to realize that although they desired different outcomes, they did share many views, and each party had valid claims that needed to be addressed. Indeed, by emphasizing similarities, the individuals and groups involved were able to find solid common ground. Less than a year after the Régie consultation, HQ and the Quebec government announced that they would abandon the Suroît and further develop greener sources of energy—an announcement to which there was no organized opposition. Clearly, the citizens so ardently opposed to the Suroît did make a difference. The Suroît case shows that rhetorical democracy is certainly alive in some contexts.

Furthermore, anti-Suroît participants contributed to the development of alternatives to the Suroît by acknowledging some of the weaknesses of the energy sources they presented as alternatives. This concession forced them to find ways to make these alternatives more acceptable, such as proposing the construction of wind energy projects over a large and diverse geographical area, and combining several energy sources instead of relying upon one source to replace the Suroît. Thus, by accepting key opinions of their adversaries, both pro-Suroît and anti-Suroît participants contributed to the development of alternatives.

Accepting key points from adversaries was the most noticeable rhetorical practice that emerged from my analysis. It thus seems that, as Govier states, a controversy is not just about two or more parties in constant opposition with each other (1999, 251). Furthermore, the Suroît controversy suggests that sociotechnical deliberation brings points common to all parties to the forefront. Thus, through public deliberation over the heterogeneous topics that are an integral part of sociotechnical controversies, parties initially opposed realize that their opinions differ less than they first thought. The acceptance of points from opposing parties allows all participants in the controversy to find, through deliberation, key common points and perhaps even solutions acceptable to all parties—chief aims of rhetorical democracy (Hauser 2004, 1).

The Suroît controversy exemplifies how rhetorical democracy works in some instances. Through the acceptance of points made by their adversaries, participants on both sides progressively became favorable to wind energy and energy efficiency and adapted the use of these two strategies to the energy situation in Quebec at the time, notably the anticipated energy deficit. One the one hand, pro-Suroît participants came to realize that wind energy and energy efficiency did have virtues that made them viable investments for HQ. On the other hand, anti-Suroît participants realized that the alternatives they proposed had difficulties that needed to be addressed. Thus abandoning the Suroît and replacing it with wind energy projects, which were to be implemented across various regions of Quebec to ensure their reliability, and energy efficiency projects, which were to be subsidized by HQ to encourage consumers to invest in them, ended up being a generally acceptable solution to all parties involved in the deliberation process. To this day, HQ continues to support these alternatives to thermal energy and has devoted all its strategic planning to green energy sources, including hydroelectricity, wind energy, and energy efficiency.

Clearly, the rhetorical democracy enacted by citizens who participated in the Suroît controversy was not perfect, as not everyone had a say or a vote. For example, not all citizens who wished to participate were able to, because those who wanted to participate had to write a proposal that could be accepted or denied by officials of the BAPE and the Régie. There were also time limits on presentations and question periods, limiting the potential impact and outcome of the deliberation. Nevertheless, the Suroît controversy provides a case study of concerned citizens who were able to rhetorically enact citizenship by first claiming opposition to a project that concerned them, which led to the creation of public deliberation venues. Their efforts were rewarded when the project was replaced by an alternative supported not only by them but also by those who had initially advanced the controversial project.

The positive influence of public deliberation is clearly manifest in the Suroît controversy. Through public deliberation at the consultations—and enacting rhetorical citizenship by engaging in political debates that had the potential to influence governmental policies—participants were able to recognize and adopt valid arguments made by individuals who had a different opinion on the issue at stake. This suggests that public deliberation is not only about persuasive strategies but also about developing a better comprehension of important issues and consequently modifying one's initial opinion—one of the positive characteristics of controversies suggested by Callon, Lascoumes, and Barthe (2001, 347). As the number of sociotechnical controversies increases in both the short and the long term (Brante 1993, 188), research should take into account not only the persuasive strategies used in public deliberation but also how citizens, at any level of expertise, can rhetorically enact their citizenship by participating in deliberation over these issues. This will help us better understand the unfolding of the sociotechnical controversies that are, and will continue to be, omnipresent in public life.

NOTES

1. HQ is a government-owned corporation and the sole electricity provider in the province of Quebec. Since the 1940s it has had the obligation to produce and distribute energy to the population of Quebec.
2. The BAPE's mission is to inform and consult the population of Quebec on questions related to the environment and subsequently present nonbinding recommendations to the Quebec government (see http://www.bape.gouv.qc.ca/sections/bape/organisme/eng_organization_ind.htm).
3. The BAPE transcripts are available online at http://www.bape.gouv.qc.ca/sections/archives/suroit/, and the Régie transcriptions can be downloaded at http://www.regie-energie.qc.ca/audiences/3526-04/mainTranscrip3526.htm. Both sets of transcriptions are available only in their original French version, and all quotations from them in this chapter have been translated by the author.
4. Some of the rhetorical strategies I identified in my reading and analysis of the BAPE and Régie transcripts included accepting the opposing party's key opinions, metaphors, analogies, appeals to action, appeals to the majority, appeals to what is new, appeals to fear, moral appeals, appeals to tradition, appeals to authority, appeals to ignorance, appeals to the incoherence of the opposing party's arguments, *ad populum* arguments, arguments by association, arguments by dissociation, attacks against an individual, representative arguments, common sense arguments, and false dilemma arguments.

REFERENCES

Asen, Robert. 2004. "A Discourse Theory of Citizenship." *Quarterly Journal of Speech* 90 (2): 189–211.
Benoit-Barné, Chantal. 2007. "Socio-Technical Deliberation About Free and Open Source Software: Accounting for the Status of Artifacts in Public Life." *Quarterly Journal of Speech* 93 (2): 211–35.
Bohman, James. 1996. *Public Deliberation: Pluralism, Complexity, and Democracy.* Cambridge: MIT Press.
Brante, Thomas. 1993. "Reasons for Studying Scientific and Science-Based Controversies." In *Controversial Science: From Content to Contention*, ed. Thomas Brante, Steve Fuller, and William Lynch, 177–91. Albany: State University of New York Press.
Bureau d'audiences publiques sur l'environnement (BAPE). 2002. *Projet de centrale thermique à cycle combiné du Suroît à Beauharnois par Hydro-Québec.* Part I, vols. 1–7; part II, vols. 1–4. http://www.bape.gouv.qc.ca/sections/archives/suroit/docdeposes/listdocdepo.htm#Transcriptions (accessed 1 August 2006).
Callon, Michel, Pierre Lascoumes, and Yannick Barthe. 2001. *Agir dans un monde incertain: Essai sur la démocratie technique.* Paris: Éditions du Seuil.
Goodnight, G. Thomas. 1991. "Special Issue: Argumentation and Public Controversy." *Argumentation and Advocacy* 28:49–50.
———. 2005. "Science and Technology Controversy: A Rationale for Inquiry." *Argumentation and Advocacy* 42:26–29.
Govier, Trudy. 1999. *The Philosophy of Argument.* Newport News, Va.: Vale Press.
Gross, Alan G. 1995. "Renewing Aristotelian Theory: The Cold Fusion Controversy as a Test Case." *Quarterly Journal of Speech* 81 (1): 48–62.
Hauser, Gerard A. 2004. "Rhetorical Democracy and Civic Engagement." In *Rhetorical Democracy: Discursive Practices of Civic Engagement*, ed. Gerard A. Hauser and Amy Grim, 1–14. Mahwah, N.J.: Lawrence Erlbaum.
Jones, John M., and Robert C. Rowland. 2007. "Reagan at Moscow State University: Consubstantiality Underlying Conflict." *Rhetoric and Public Affairs* 10 (1): 77–106.
Keränen, Lisa. 2005. "Mapping Misconduct: Demarcating Legitimate Science from 'Fraud' in the B-06 Lumpectomy Controversy." *Argumentation and Advocacy* 42:94–113.
Latour, Bruno. 2004. *Politics of Nature: How to Bring the Sciences into Democracy.* Cambridge: Harvard University Press.
Lyne, John. 2005. "Science Controversy, Common Sense, and the Third Culture." *Argumentation and Advocacy* 42:38–42.
Moore, Mark P. 2003. "Making Sense of Salmon: Synecdoche and Irony in a Natural Resource Crisis." *Western Journal of Communication* 67 (1): 74–96.
Olson, Kathryn M., and G. Thomas Goodnight. 1994. "Entanglement of Consumption, Cruelty, Privacy, and Fashion: The Social Controversy over Fur." *Quarterly Journal of Speech* 80 (3): 249–76.
Parson, Donn W., ed. 1991. *Argument in Controversy: Proceedings of the Seventh SCA/AFA Conference on Argumentation.* Annandale, Va.: Speech Communication Association.
Putnam, Linda L., and Deborah M. Kolb. 2000. "Rethinking Negotiation: Feminist Views of Communication and Exchange." In *Rethinking Organizational and Managerial Communication from Feminist Perspectives*, ed. Patrice M. Buzzanell, 76–106. Thousand Oaks, Calif.: Sage.

Putnam, Robert D. 2000. *Bowling Alone: The Collapse of the American Community.* New York: Simon and Schuster.

Régie de l'énergie Québec. 2004. *Avis sur la sécurité énergétique des Québécois à l'égard des approvisionnements électriques et la contribution du projet du Suroît.* Vols. 1–13. http://www.regie-energie.qc.ca/audiences/3526-04/mainTranscrip3526.htm (accessed 1 August 2006).

Rémy, Élisabeth. 1995. "Apprivoiser la technique: Un débat public autour d'une ligne à haute tension." *Politix* 31:136–44.

Schwarze, Steven. 2006. "Environmental Melodrama." *Quarterly Journal of Speech* 92 (3): 239–61.

Scott, Robert L. 1991. "Can 'Controversy' Be Analyzed to Yield Useful Insights for Argument?" In *Argument in Controversy: Proceedings of the Seventh SCA/AFA Conference on Argumentation,* ed. Donn W. Parson, 20–22. Allandale, Va.: Speech Communication Association.

13
DELIBERATION AS BEHAVIOR IN PUBLIC

Tatiana Tatarchevskiy

The deliberative turn in democratic theory in the 1990s was an attempt to identify democratic processes relevant to a multicultural society (Dryzek 2000). Grappling with the increasing inability of citizens to bring their differences on moral issues into the realm of political decisions, political scientists turned to the power of talk to achieve more legitimate decision making. As Benhabib suggests, "legitimacy in complex modern democratic societies must be thought to result from the free and unconstrained public deliberation of all matters of common concern" (1994, 27). Simultaneously, with the new communication technologies, deliberation is increasingly seen as applicable in various areas of decision making in civil society, that is, in interactions and talk in public meetings, civic groups, discussions, and hearings.

While more and more theoretical voices define democracy in terms of communication (Chambers 2003; Macedo 1999; Perrin 2006), questions remain about what kinds of communication best accommodate legitimate decisions. Some believe that rational argument will provide for this legitimacy (Bohman 1999; Habermas 1995), while others argue for the importance of including all potentially concerned points of view (Benhabib 1994; Fraser 1992). Experiments with deliberative democracy tend to solve the issue by means of statistics. For example, a deliberative poll carefully selects a representative sample of participants (Fishkin 1995). To overcome knowledge disparities, participants are equipped with discussion materials. It has been suggested that these procedures, via rational argumentation, produce "considered judgments" (162) that may further be legitimately linked with political institutions.

Not only statistical representativeness is considered; openness to varying genres of expression has also been emphasized (Hauser 1999). For example, Fung recommends "testimony, story-telling, relating needs, principled advocacy, and the airing of conflicts and tensions. Facilitation will seek to assure that the weak, and not necessarily those with the best ideas or arguments, have ample time to speak and express themselves" (2003, 344).

These attempts to marry theorizing with real-life deliberative programs demand more attention from sociologists. As deliberation is a specific form of discursive behavior in public, it is important to consider it as culturally defined. As Ryfe puts it, "when deliberation is introduced in a community, people must make some sense of what it is, and what it is for. They accomplish this task by situating the practice in the context of what they know, who they are, what they do, and what they value" (2007, 2). It is important to understand these norms guiding the perceptions of deliberation to see what constitutes a legitimate deliberative practice for the participants. We must consider deliberation as behavior in public; thus the norms underlying it are those underlying such behavior. This awareness may help us to theorize better about the legitimacy of deliberative practices. Deliberative forums may be procedurally correct, but if they do not account for cultural norms, they risk staying isolated and unrepresentative, and thus not contributing to deliberative democracy (with the emphasis on "democracy").

Drawing on Goffman's view of the conventions that guide the behavior of strangers in public places, I argue for seeing deliberation through a similar lens, attuned to how the conventions of interaction between strangers may affect conversations. I illustrate my argument with a case study of a discussion group, concluding that this perspective may be of use for applied as well as normative deliberative scholarship.

Conventions of Behavior in Public Places

The public behavior of modern urban dwellers is characterized by anonymity. Strangers typically relate to one another with what Goffman calls "civil inattention"—two strangers who see each other on the street may exchange "enough visual notice to demonstrate that one appreciates that the other is present (and that one admits openly to having seen him), while at the next moment withdrawing one's attention from him so as to express that he does not constitute a target of special curiosity" (1969, 84). This principle of anonymous coexistence goes back to the early days of European urbanization. Richard Sennett, talking about eighteenth-century London and Paris, notes that the influx of population made anonymity the norm: "In the mid-19th century there grew up . . . the notion that strangers had no right to speak to each other, a right to be left alone. Public behavior was a matter of observation, of passive participation, of a certain kind of voyeurism" (1977, 27). This notion guides our daily interactions with strangers.

When strangers have to communicate, they apply preventive or corrective mechanisms that Goffman locates in people's gestures, looks, and manners. Strangers' interactions in public contain means of expressing interest and at the same time keeping distance. There is an implicit social contract in our everyday interactions with strangers according to which a person can "make himself available to others in the expectation that they will restrain their calls on his availability and not make him pay too great a price for his being accessible" (1969, 106). Even where persons are confronted with strangers at an inconveniently small distance—as in a small train compartment—all those present will remain civilly inattentive. "In such cases," Goffman writes, "a strategy is to 'thin out' the encounter by keeping it impersonal and by declining to exchange identifying names, thus guaranteeing that some kind of nonrecognition will be possible in the future" (139).

This thinning out is also observable in how people code their settings as appropriate or inappropriate for specific forms of conversation. Conversation on matters that can be divisive may be considered out of place in public. It is the sphere of the private—one's home, workplace, or circle of friends—that is understood as the proper domain for political conversation (Wyatt, Katz, and Kim 2000, 89). Outside these protective circles, people may elaborate specific group customs that allow only for a certain kind of talk. Nina Eliasoph, for example, suggests that larger societal rules, promoted by the media and state agencies, create a climate where genres of talk that presuppose in-depth critical discussion are equated with a waste of time. Analyzing discussions on political subjects in church groups, sports groups, and business organizations, Perrin finds that the affiliation of the participants affected how they discussed the same subject, even though not as part of the group's usual activity. "Protestant and Catholic groups used morality the most often, while sports and unions used it less" (2006, 138), and when groups stipulated how to solve a problem, private methods were prevalent among union members while business and church groups suggested governmental methods of intervention. But in fact such in-depth political discussion is so unusual outside experiments that it is more common to hear silence. On potentially divisive topics, sometimes not words but actions may become communicative devices, as Bender finds in her study of how ways of cutting bread and making soup for people with AIDS become means of political commentary for religious volunteers (2003).

Deliberative forums attempt to break these unspoken rules of avoiding political discussion in public. The little sociological research on deliberative forums finds that participants have no choice but to invent the rules: "Individuals will come to the practice with different senses of how to identify good and bad deliberators; they will have different ideas about what counts as deliberation and what does not" (Ryfe 2007, 9). For example, they may choose genres of interaction typical of more institutionalized environments. People may rely on conventions of talk established in more familiar settings, such as education or politics. Polletta suggests that such "conversational schemas" carry "normative expectations for what should go on" (2008, 4), and if the organizers' schemas do not correspond to the expectations of the participants, there may be disappointment on both parts. While this finding is useful, it does not address the question of why certain norms of interaction may be adopted.

The fact that strangers are put in one room to converse on matters they usually avoid may help answer this question. I suggest that in a public deliberative forum the principle of thinning out the encounter may apply, and that rhetoric may be used to achieve this goal, performing the same function as silence when strangers need to be engaged in a critical discussion in public.

Case Study

Analyzing the rhetoric in a forum that convened to discuss a political topic, I posit that participants' interactions could be termed *noninteractive rhetoric*. While one group and one discussion constitute a limited resource, I hope that this may be a good starting point for demonstrating the logic underlying people's rhetorical behavior in public in the presence of strangers.

I came across a group in New York that had devised a series of what they called salons in order to involve the public in conversation. This group was created in the winter of 2005. Members pay dues, and the group holds free forums that are open to the public as well as smaller book discussions each month. According to its mission statement, public discussion in Western society has deteriorated. Arguments on social issues in the press or on TV are too shallow and politicized, and they often target personalities rather than issues. Also, this group's organizers believe, the way people talk in public is often geared to avoiding disagreements rather than openly discussing them. The group sees this as detrimental to democracy and aims to create settings in which all views may be openly expressed and questioned.

The event I studied was a forum titled "Human Impact on Environment: Have We Gone Too Far?" that took place in the winter of 2007 on the campus of one of New York's universities. A panel of four experts was present, yet the moderator—one of the group's leaders—strongly encouraged the audience to speak throughout the event. There were about seventy people in the audience, mostly white and from the middle and upper middle class. I took notes throughout the discussion and also tape-recorded it, then transcribed the recording and double-checked the transcript against the video recording that was subsequently posted on the group's website.

This forum was a natural social experiment that allows us to see the underlying assumptions that guide participants' behavior. Most interesting to me was how people chose to react in a situation where the moderators pressed them for something unusual for many Americans: open public discussion on topics that have at their core issues of justice—in other words, "political talk."

I coded the transcript with an eye to the rhetorical components of the discussion, focusing on argumentation but not on logic or rhetoric, strictly speaking. Rather, I concentrated on the exchanges of arguments or claims and was interested in how interactive this process was—specifically, who was addressed in audience members' comments, and how.

Analyzing the transcript, I came to realize that participants on both sides of the issue worked to preserve social order and a veneer of civility in this situation of rhetorical uncertainty. Indeed, this discussion featured disagreement between the invited experts and on the part of the audience members (with the experts or with one another). However, choosing what may be called *noninteractive* kinds of rhetoric, the participants managed to preserve civil inattention.

Structure of the Discussion

The moderator and four invited speakers sat at a table on the slightly elevated stage. The moderator repeatedly emphasized that the event was not just about speakers' presentations but rather about the audience's participation in the discussion, and told the audience that "everybody can say anything." After being introduced, the experts proceeded with their presentations on the motion, speaking for about five minutes each. From the outset, they outlined several frames within which discussion was to proceed. All four agreed that human civilization is not harmful to the environment, yet they suggested different logics for talking about the topic.

The first expert, an architect from the United Kingdom, spoke within what could be called a confrontational frame, criticizing alarmist environmentalists for preventing more productive debate on the environment. He talked about the contemporary preoccupation with recycling, comparing it to an obsessive-compulsive disorder: "I think that the carbon debate [meaning that led by environmentalists] celebrates the object and by definition demeans the human. We are now celebrating time-consuming activities, which to me is the very opposite of what progress is about."

This architect blamed "carbonistas" for encroaching on free speech. To illustrate his claim he cited one university's website on global warming that said, among other things, that "telling both sides of the story can actually be a form of informational bias." But perhaps more detrimentally, in his opinion, such one-sided debate "inhibits our ability to actually produce innovative social solutions," as today's "innovation is determined by predetermined goals." He finished his speech by saying, "So I want to simply advocate that we ignore self-imposed constraints. I think we should fly more; we should see the world, we should get out of our heads, get out of our trash cans, and I think only then can we really implement meaningful, experimental, risk-open innovation."

The second expert, who combined work as an energy expert for NASA and an editorship at *Discover* magazine, disagreed with the previous speaker. He conceded that there are extreme voices on both sides—the conservative and the environmentalist—but he believed that the public view falls somewhere between the extremes. He wanted the discussion to go further than weighing the points of view on the environmentalist movement; he proceeded within what I call the philosophical frame, posing the question of how humans should better manage the planet. While the human impact on the planet's environment is undeniable, he said, the real question is, "what is our role as stewards of the planet?" To him, the answer to this question was technological innovation: "The most exciting thing is—technology got us in this mess and technology will get us out of this mess." He expressed the view that it is important to figure out how to use technology for the benefit of both humankind and the environment. Here he tried to steer the debate from the confrontation about environmentalism onto pragmatic rails, attempting to identify concrete solutions: "And the real question to me is that how's that gonna work exactly? How do we foster that, so that happens in the fastest and best way possible?" He suggested that we need to think about technology that in the long term could bring us clean energy, such as, in his opinion, the nuclear fusion reactor.

The third speaker, a professor emeritus of physics and former chair of a department of applied science at a prominent U.S. university, agreed with the second speaker. He picked up what could be called the pragmatic frame, admitting that the real challenge is how to reduce global climate change. But, for him, this meant not only the question of what source of energy to use but also what kind of institutional mechanisms might stimulate this process. He suggested that the best option was to solicit governmental support, citing a national program on solar energy initiated by Jimmy Carter, where "we made a massive social commitment to achieve a certain technological goal."

The fourth and final speaker, an award-winning science correspondent, chose to proceed with the pragmatic frame. His major point was that human civilization, as it develops its potential, will also be "restoring ecology." Unlike the previous speaker, though, he insisted that it was not so much governmental policies as free trade that would encourage innovation to protect the environment. He suggested that economic growth needs proper social institutions, such as "secure property rights, democratic governments, and open markets": "So what's my proposal? Eliminate all energy subsidies, set a price requirement, an increasing one over time, and then let hundreds of thousands of energy researchers and entrepreneurs develop and test various low-carbon technologies in the marketplace. The twenty-first century will be the century of ecological restoration if we unleash human creativity to address these problems."

Having laid out their positions, the speakers outlined avenues for audience contributions. The moderator explained that "the routine" was to collect several questions from the audience and then turn again to the speakers, who might choose what point to address. To speak, a person had to stand up and talk into the microphone handed over by a person shuttling around the room. Overall, there were four rounds of questions and four rounds of experts' responses.

Audience Reactions

The experts laid out the terms for the conversation: what kind of interaction would take place among proponents and opponents sitting in the same room? Over the four rounds of discussion, audience members made twenty-two comments. While the experts were very comfortable in directly confronting their opponents, audience members used various rhetorical protective mechanisms. The situation was unusual for them: they were seeing most of the people there for the first time, moderators pressed them for an argumentative discussion, and opponents were most likely to be in the same room; thus, in making an argument or expressing disagreement, one had to be careful. I chart some of these mechanisms below. This does not attempt to be an exhaustive list of rhetorical protective measures that can be used in a public discussion but rather a sensitizing illustration of how people confronted with a need to be involved in an argument may arrange for ways to do it, preserving a veneer of social order. I have identified the following ways of explicitly or implicitly expressing disagreement:

(1) "Asking a question." A question allows one to address the interlocutor directly and yet keep one's own position undeclared or only hinted at. Even though the organizers, insisting on the genre of debate, kept telling participants that questions should be avoided ("Do not mask your point beyond the question!"), factual or clarifying questions still made up a good number of reactions, especially when the panel was addressed (N=5). For example, the following question was open-ended, leaving the audience wondering whether the person asking it was going to argue with the first expert: "In your paper you write here that 'technological improvement may be blocked'—if I'm quoting you correctly—'if they see a potential for it to cause a detrimental impact on the environment for our future.' And I am wondering what example you can cite of a current technological improvement that environmentalists are blocking?"

This question was not answered when the experts took the floor. But questions performed another role, besides soliciting information. They allowed audience members who held the same positions to identify one another and even build tacit alliances. As the discussion progressed, information received through a question could be used by others to express their positions more explicitly. This was the case with the following question, which came to be used, albeit by another audience member, to register more expressive disagreement in the end: "I was wondering what role the government might play in this, as you mentioned about [Jimmy] Carter's solar energy initiative. Is there a need for some large-scale initiative like that? Manhattan Project or like putting the man on the moon, that might find a role in this, rather than just relying on free markets?"

(2) "Extending the argument" (N=5), that is, picking up on a previously established frame and, in elaborating it, adding new information. This was

a convenient way to express one's position implicitly, using the claims of the experts as a shield. For example, continuing within the confrontational and pragmatic frames, one of the audience members commented:

> One of the things that I noticed from debating with friends is that, at least in my experience, and it's very limited, there seems to be a direct corollary between a very adamant anticapitalism attitude and using the global warming debate as proof of the evils of capitalism. . . . I think that there's an ideological issue here that is pervasive that makes it very hard for some people, for whatever reason, to believe that capitalism and technology will actually do anything to improve the situation, whether it's global warming, hunger, or poverty, anything like that. There needs to be an ideological, philosophical kind of swaying or understanding, before some people will even accept that as an argument.

Here, following up on the words of the experts, this person conjured up an imaginary interlocutor—the abstract audience of environmentalists. Talking "through" the expert softened this person's stance but at the same time allowed him to address this audience.

Often, addressing abstract opponents by way of extending the expert's argument allowed one to ask provocative questions. For example, a person working within the experts' confrontational and philosophical frames went on to suggest how the environmentalists' terms of debate (in her view)—privileging environment above everything else—might be detrimental to health and development:

> The question is whether, really, the issue of the environment should be our number one. It seems that these days the social and political priority is when we have a lot of other problems facing humanity, particularly immediate ones of starvation and disease, a lack of economic growth in many parts of the world. I wonder to what extent the technology and innovation is the solution to some of humanity's problems? Whether we should see this through the filter of "oh, it's got to be clean!"?

(3) "Meta-arguments" (N=6) were another way to express one's position, but again avoiding direct engagement with what had actually been said and thus, again, keeping a distance. This was a way to reformulate the existing

terms of the debate by offering new terms, and a way to join the conversation without identifying any actual interlocutor other than a mythical "we." Meta-argument was especially visible when an audience member attempted to pick up on the philosophical frame of the role humans play as servants or stewards of the planet. Regarding pragmatic solutions to environmental problems, one person said, "When we speak of humanity and the global population of about 6.5 billion of people, we talk about people in waking-dreaming deep sleep. Yoga and the Veda and all the wisdom traditions seem unanimous that there are higher states. . . . It is a spiritual matter, which is to say that this is a neurophysiological matter, not simply a political matter or technological matter. Indeed, the technology comes from humanity, but we need to transform humanity." Here, attempting to switch the rails of the argument, this person relied on his own existing knowledge, referring to what had been said only in a general way. Addressing the abstract "community" allowed him to soften his disagreement with the arguments made by some of the experts within the philosophical and pragmatic frames.

(4) More direct disagreement, addressing the claims actually made on the discussion floor, was also expressed (N=6). This disagreement was often softened through such means as rhetorical questions; for example, a person arguing within the philosophical frame about the positive role of technology in the solution of environmental crises said, "I am also an engineer too, as well, so . . . the creation of technology has a problem of itself. The pollution that may be created from building up the computers. . . . And then at the end of the life cycle of the computer, you might wanna dispose of that computer. How to keep that perspective that technology is a double-edged sword? What do you do with it?"

In fact, there were only a few cases (N=3) of actual dialectical argumentation, that is, argumentation confronting on its own terms what had been actually said by an interlocutor in the same room. Here is an example of somebody arguing within the philosophical frame: "Yes, gentlemen, thank you. One thing that I wanted to raise is kind of an underlying premise. We keep talking about technology as our way out of this mess. But this mess itself seems to be the planet correcting imbalances which have been caused by parasitic organisms on it."

It is important to note that when dialectical argumentation was attempted, it was often done either by one of the experts or by somebody in the audience who identified himself as an expert. In a way, by positioning themselves as experts, these people claimed the right to interact in a more direct way.

Toward the very end of the discussion a man stood up to rebut several of the experts' claims at once:

> When I was a technology officer at Chase Manhattan Bank, when they gave out stock options to people, the criticism of the management of the bank ceased. And the only question became, "what's the stock price?" ... Our global development is not focused on whether DDT will kill malaria; it's focused on how much of that money comes back to American corporations! It's always been that way, we haven't changed that yet. . . . And finally, the human really has capacity—someone dropped it—other than technology. Technology inherently is subsetting natural and human capacities, subsetting and accelerating. There are other capacities—the gentleman who mentioned the Vedas knows some of them; some of them are not explored. We need to look in all directions, because we do have a long future ahead of us.

Thus, considering the prevalence of indirect means of making an argument and expressing disagreement, the discussion had a rather noninteractive quality. It consisted mostly of listing disjointed points that did not accomplish either the convincing or the confrontational functions that may be expected from deliberation, and hence only a few threads in this discussion were developed (such as that of the pragmatic frame).

Addressing the universal audience of environmentalists, discussing the terms of discussion rather than the claims actually made, relying on experts' frames to make a point—such maneuvers allowed participants to maintain the veneer of argumentative discussion and yet stay strangely disengaged from one another's claims. Rhetorically—that is, attempting to persuade the other side—very little was expressed; factual questions, making one's own stance indistinguishable, were used almost as often as disagreeing with others in the audience. In many ways the discussion resembled a written text, where the argument is developed in isolation from preceding arguments. While, in terms of information, such conversation was definitely dense, many chances to develop something out of face-to-face argumentation went unused. Rhetoric is a powerful tool; as some suggest, it is "a mode of altering reality . . . by the creation of discourse which changes reality through the mediation of thought and action" (Bitzer 1968, 4). Rhetoric accomplished little in this setting; at best, it served to make audible texts and discourses that might as well have been written.

The only rhetorical interaction came in establishing alliances with possible allies, seeking their presence in the room indirectly when, for example, asking factual questions. In this sense, the disjointed claims and statements made throughout the discussion worked not as an argument with one's opponent in the "here and now" but as a preparation for the argument "there and then." In this unusual situation of a forum requiring oral elaboration of argument, most participants did not express argument but *prepared* it. In a way, this way of making an argument—by addressing an imaginary audience—is typical of a society where written or mediated forms of expression have long since displaced traditions of oral speech (Ong 1982). At the same time, elaborating an argument for an imaginary audience, so typical of writing, worked also to sustain the civility of oral discussion in this case. For those present, this careful dance with a set of complex moves—making one's claim indistinctly, orienting it toward a potential argument—was a way to follow and sustain the norms of civil behavior in public that prescribe minimizing interaction with immediately present strangers. If an audience member wanted to counterargue, such a person would declare her professional identity, thus establishing her credentials for expressing disagreement openly. In this case deliberation almost required additional permission, implicitly granted via the mention of one's expertise.

Conclusion

My goal here has been to put on the agenda of deliberative democracy a sociological framework. Drawing in particular on Goffman's insight, I suggest that, because of the established histories of public interactions in Western society, in deliberative contexts participants may take precautions to keep argumentative conversation as noninteractive as possible. Further research might expand the focus of this chapter and consider variations in social norms as well as in rhetorical tools that guide deliberation as behavior in public. Perhaps there are situations in which the minimizing of rhetorical contact with strangers might be eschewed. Potential areas of research might include forums not constrained by the presence of experts, or forums on more mundane topics.

At the same time, practitioners of deliberative democracy need to account for the cultural norms that guide rhetoric and interaction in public. When deliberative experiments are staged in a society with a formalized public sociability, it is important to consider the conventions that guide behavior in such settings. If we are dealing with groups, it may be important to account for the specific group customs that govern talk; but in the case of strangers it is important to pay attention to the norms of preserving civility and anonymity, and to how these are expressed rhetorically. This particular discussion may have been extreme, asking lay participants to argumentatively confront experts in public in the company of strangers; at the same time, this extreme scenario could help us identify pitfalls that organizers and participants in deliberative forums may want to keep an eye on. For example, moderators should be prepared for participants to try and create the appearance of an argument while staying disengaged from the claims actually made. Moderators might more actively press participants to detail their arguments, in relation or response to those present. On the other hand, accounting for the conditions of late modern society, they might treat such indirect forms of expression as legitimate and orient themselves to the larger developments in the discussion: first, identifying sides in the argument, and second, seeing to it that both the pro and the con sides have an opportunity to elaborate their arguments, albeit in an indirect way, and actually express them through detailed responses to one another. Alternatively, in the case of forums attended by strangers, it may be important to hold a series of more informal meetings, where customs might develop that would allow for a more interactive conversation.

Considering deliberation as a public behavior—and understanding all the communicative difficulties it entails for a modern person—may also be an important addition to theorizing on the legitimacy of deliberation. Legitimacy of decisions may not only be sought through proper procedures that include all points of view. As we have seen, the problem is not just that one side will not let the other speak; it is also that particular norms of sociability in public prohibit participants from engaging in more involved conversation.

Deliberation is usually understood as an *exchange* of views. Orientation toward seeking common ground, toward finding mutually acceptable arguments, is seen as a major principle for deliberative democracy (Gutmann and Thompson 1996). Sometimes this mutuality among opponents is not achieved—owing to incompatible moral positions, for example. At the same time, it is important to consider the limitations that deliberation may encounter because of people's understandings of etiquette, politeness, and manners in the presence of strangers.

REFERENCES

Bender, Courtney. 2003. *Heaven's Kitchen: Living Religion at God's Love We Deliver.* Chicago: University of Chicago Press.
Benhabib, Seyla. 1994. "Deliberative Rationality and Models of Democratic Legitimacy." *Constellations* 1:26–52.

Bitzer, Lloyd F. 1968. "The Rhetorical Situation." *Philosophy and Rhetoric* 1 (1): 1–14.
Bohman, James. 1999. "Citizenship and Norms of Publicity: Wide Public Reason in Cosmopolitan Societies." *Political Theory* 27:176–202.
Chambers, Simone. 2003. "Deliberative Democratic Theory." *Annual Review of Political Science* 6:307–26.
Dryzek, John S. 2000. *Deliberative Democracy and Beyond: Liberals, Critics, Contestations.* Oxford: Oxford University Press.
Eliasoph, Nina. 1998. *Avoiding Politics: How Americans Produce Apathy in Everyday Life.* Cambridge: Cambridge University Press.
Fishkin, James S. 1995. *The Voice of the People: Public Opinion and Democracy.* New Haven: Yale University Press.
Fraser, Nancy. 2002. "Rethinking the Public Sphere: Models and Boundaries." In *Habermas and the Public Sphere,* ed. Craig Calhoun, 109–42. Cambridge: MIT Press.
Fung, Archon. 2003. "Survey Article: Recipes for Public Spheres; Eight Institutional Design Choices and Their Consequences." *Journal of Political Philosophy* 11:338–67.
Goffman, Erving. 1969. *Behavior in Public Places: Notes on the Social Organization of Gatherings.* New York: Free Press.
Gutmann, Amy, and Dennis F. Thompson. 1996. *Democracy and Disagreement.* Cambridge: Harvard University Press.
Habermas, Jürgen. 1995. "Reconciliation Through the Public Use of Reason: Remarks on John Rawls's Political Liberalism." *Journal of Philosophy* 92:109–31.
Hauser, Gerard A. 1999. *Vernacular Voices: The Rhetoric of Publics and Public Spheres.* Columbia: University of South Carolina Press.
Macedo, Stephen. 1999. *Deliberative Politics: Essays on Democracy and Disagreement.* New York: Oxford University Press.
Ong, Walter J. 1982. *Orality and Literacy: The Technologizing of the Word.* London: Methuen.
Perrin, Andrew J. 2006. *Citizen Speak: The Democratic Imagination in American Life.* Chicago: University of Chicago Press.
Polletta, Francesca. 2008. "Just Talk: Public Deliberation After 9/11." *Journal of Public Deliberation* 4 (1): 1–24.
Ryfe, David M. 2007. "Toward a Sociology of Deliberation." *Journal of Public Deliberation* 3 (1): 87–91.
Sennett, Richard. 1977. *The Fall of Public Man.* New York: Knopf.
Wyatt, Robert O., Elihu Katz, and Joohan Kim. 2000. "Bridging the Spheres: Political and Personal Conversation in Public and Private Spaces." *Journal of Communication* (Winter): 71–92.

14

HOMING IN ON THE ARGUMENTS:
THE RHETORICAL CONSTRUCTION OF SUBJECT POSITIONS IN
DEBATES ON THE DANISH REAL ESTATE MARKET

Sine Nørholm Just and Jonas Gabrielsen

The home is often perceived as the most private of places, a sanctuary, the place to withdraw to from the bustle of the world. However, there exists a historical link between real estate and citizenship. When democratization swept across Western societies, the right to vote was usually connected to owning property (as well as to being a white male); this was, for instance, the case in the U.S. Constitution of 1787 and the Danish constitution of 1849. With universal suffrage, the direct connection between home ownership and citizenship was severed. However, there is still a close bond between the individual's personal concern about his/her living situation and the public concern about housing policy. How one lives may be a private matter, but it is one that all citizens must deal with, and also a matter of great consequence at the level of society, as the financial crisis of 2008, with its roots in the infamous subprime mortgages, reminds us.

A basic distinction between private and public interests and economic and political activities underlies most theories of democracy (Terchek and Conte 2001). Specifically, Habermas (1989) has advocated a strict separation of the market and the public sphere as the basis of well-functioning deliberative democracy. Real estate, however, seems to be an issue on which private and public interests cannot be separated, and developments in the real estate market appear to be closely linked with social and political processes. This leads us to suspect that discussions of real estate transcend the Habermasian separation of the market and the public sphere. Moreover, we believe that this transcendence may mean that participants in these discussions position themselves as both private consumers and public citizens—not one or the other. At the theoretical level, these hypotheses question the underlying notion of the private-public divide as such, and in this chapter we explore rhetorical alternatives to the conception of the public sphere based on this divide. However, our main concern is analytical, focusing on how the interests of consumers and/or citizens are actually enacted in discussions of the real estate market. We propose that how people argue is a good indication of the interests that underwrite their positions, and we suggest that the classical theory of the *staseis* (plural of the Greek *stasis*) may provide an adequate tool for the analysis of the relationship between arguments and interests. Thus we seek to discern the positions of private consumers and public citizens as they appear in public discussion by studying the arguments they make, and we use this study as an indication of how private and public attitudes and concerns are interrelated rather than kept apart in actual deliberative encounters concerning real estate.

The Investing Public Goes Online—Presentation of Euroinvestor

Euroinvestor (www.euroinvestor.dk) is a Danish website dedicated to financial news and analysis. The site contains various elements and services; for instance, it runs constant updates on stock market prices and currency exchange rates, and there are sections dedicated to various types of financial news (stocks, bonds, currencies, etc.) as well as a lifestyle section. Furthermore, Euroinvestor has a rather large section on the housing economy, and as part of this section there is a forum for debate dedicated to the real estate market. The debate in this forum is the object of our analysis.

It is a central feature of this debate forum that a new string is often begun with a link to, or a copy-and-paste of, a news article or some other source of information, like the statistics on how many houses are for sale, how many are sold, and the average price. Following the initial post, the debate unfolds as a series of commentaries on the information and/or opinions presented in the link. This feature gives the debate a certain similarity to the discussions in coffeehouses and salons that were central to the rise of democracy in Europe, and in which the media also played a central role as purveyors of information and starting points for discussion. Although the debaters on Euroinvestor do not meet physically, the ways in which discussions on the website typically unfold correspond well with how we imagine coffeehouse debates: characterized by much bickering and abuse but also many reasoned exchanges of facts and arguments, and occasionally interlocutors who enter a discussion with divergent views end up agreeing with one another. Thus the debate functions as a marketplace of ideas, an arena for the clash of opinions and the possible meeting of minds.

To study the debate in its various forms and functions, and to discern how these are articulated, we selected fifty strings posted in the period August–September 2008. Thus the debates we studied were conducted before the financial crisis became a full-blown reality, but there were already many signs of an impending crisis. Specifically, real estate prices had been falling for some time, and there was a general expectation that they would continue to fall.

We chose only strings that dealt directly with the real estate market, preferring strings that discussed the state of the market. Central questions included: is the market healthy? How should we interpret the development in prices and other central statistics? What will happen in the future? How should one react? How individual debaters perceived these issues depended, of course, on their position in relation to real estate, specifically on whether they related to the market as (potential) buyers or sellers.

Our study is exploratory, and the analysis of the debate on Euroinvestor serves as an illustration rather than a comprehensive statement on the debate as such. Thus we have not studied the fifty strings systematically here; instead, we present tendencies and quote examples. In quoting postings on the site, we refer to the username of the author as well as the number of the contribution from which we quote.[1] With this information it is relatively easy to sift through the debate—the site has a search function that allows one to go directly to a specific string—and find the quoted passage in the original version.[2]

The Private Goes Public: The Habermasian Public Sphere and Its Rhetorical Counterparts

Habermas's theory of the public sphere as he originally set it forth in *The Structural Transformation of the Public Sphere*[3] is one of the most influential contributions to the study of public debate to date. Habermas draws a clear line of demarcation: the private sphere, on the one hand, includes the home, where people interact as family members, but also the market, characterized by interaction between buyers and sellers. The public sphere, on the other hand, is a space of political and cultural interaction where people meet as citizens (1989, 30).

In later work, Habermas shifted the basic divide to one separating the lifeworld from the system (1987). While this shift means that the private and public realms, as set forth in the earlier work, are now included within the same larger category of the lifeworld, it does not change the fact that Habermas is concerned with developing an ideal of public interaction that may lead to rationally based consensus and excludes the personalized reasoning and open conflict that often characterize real-life discussion. Thus "the ideal speech situation" (1970, 371) refers to norms, such as equal access to making claims and equal rights to questioning these claims, the aim of which is to enable people to convince each other through "the unforced force of the better argument" (1993, 163). This normative ideal may be argued on different grounds, but in many ways it resembles the ideal type of the bourgeois public sphere as Habermas originally construed it. That is, in providing reasons backing up the truth, rightness, and sincerity of their claims (1984, 329), people are also expected to base their arguments on the common good and bracket their social differences. Moreover, the public sphere continues to be conceived as a coherent and comprehensive locus of interaction between citizens, clearly demarcated from the state (Fraser 1992a, 117–18).[4]

In direct opposition to Habermas's thinking, Gerard Hauser argues that at the level of society public spheres must always be conceptualized in the plural, and that the partial and fragmented public spheres—that is, the many different arenas of argumentation that in combination could be said to represent the deliberative potential of society—must always be studied in the specificity of the interaction that constitutes each particular sphere (1999, 46). Specifically, Hauser suggests that we should not look at official discourses or adhere to abstract norms but should study and conceptualize public debate in the *vernacular* (85). We should look at how people actually interact and investigate the multifarious positions from which people argue and to which their argumentation points.

Hauser's view seems to be in line with the alternative to Habermas that Nancy Fraser (1992b) presents in her general theoretical critique of his position. Fraser pays specific attention to the ways in which claims are framed and argued as public and private, as well as the consequences of positioning something as belonging to either the public or the private realm. Thus, even as the public-private divide is transcended at the theoretical level, it may continue to bear on actual discussions as a means of demarcating the realm of discussion and positioning the participants.

In the following, we seek to examine how arguments function as positioning mechanisms at both the theoretical and the analytical levels, but first we turn to Euroinvestor to provide an initial description of the website as an arena for public discussion and to outline the vernacular rhetoric of this arena. In this first round of analysis we focus on how private and public reasons in the Habermasian sense are used on the website. In so doing, we do not maintain the concepts of private and public as distinct and predefined categories but rather use these concepts as starting points for studying how public and private reasoning are related in the constitution of positions, and for investigating how the private and public positions are used strategically (cf. Leff 2003, 7).

Buyers, Sellers, and Commentators: The Vernacular Voices of Euroinvestor

Prospective buyers of a home and their counterparts, the sellers of real estate, immediately emerge as central participants in the debate. They bring to bear their heavily vested interests and cast themselves in the position of buyer/seller by means of a personalized style and privately grounded reasoning. The two positions of buyer and seller are clearly constructed in opposition to each other, and in illustrating how each is established we shall also show how they construct their counterparts.

As mentioned, the analyzed debates took place when it was generally acknowledged that real estate prices were falling. Some of the debaters whom we perceive as prospective buyers relish this fact and hit sellers on the head with it: "The housing lemmings are on their way to the slaughterhouse. Ouch, ouch, OUCH!!!!!!!!!!! The largest bloodbath of the century has started" (EddieC, 6016.5). Here, EddieC's antagonistic stance toward sellers is abundantly clear from the colorful language of lemmings, slaughterhouses, and bloodbaths; rather than establishing his own position directly, it arises out of his differentiation from, and scorn for, the sellers.[5]

EddieC represents the position of a buyer who tries to bully his opponents (and, metaphorically speaking, the market as such); he is primarily interested in and directly seeks to promote the continued drop in prices. Other participants, however, stress that they are tenants and have no immediate intention of becoming homeowners: "I sold in the spring of '06, live in a nice, big, lovely, light apartment with a reasonable landlord. . . . Yes, I was lucky to sell on top and that's nice, but [I] won't become an owner again before it is absolutely necessary, and it isn't [necessary] unless the dream home is there or the market reaches a realistic level, and as I see it that won't happen for a while" (Chesspengo, 6003.7).

Although it may be argued that the underlying position of both EddieC and Chesspengo is that of the prospective buyer, they are both busy arguing that they do not wish to buy at present. Denying the desire to buy is a general strategy of prospective buyers that may be seen as a way of protecting their interests. As is clear from these two examples, the buyers want the prices to continue falling, and openly admitting to an intention to buy would not advance that interest. Thus the position of the buyer is usually implicit in criticism of sellers for continuing to operate with prices that are too high or in praise for the life of the tenant.[6]

Prospective sellers construct themselves in a similar manner, not primarily as sellers but as either owners or what we call "hypers"—those who argue that the market is healthy and that prices will continue to rise. The position of the owner is the most common and is usually constructed in opposition to being in the market, as in this example: "If the prices on the real estate market fall so much that our house is worth less than our mortgage (which is not unlikely if the downturn continues a couple of years), I won't feel any pressure. I won't give a hoot, since the house isn't for sale and I have loans with fixed interest. I might even have to pay less in property tax" (TOP10, 5854.2). Just as Chesspengo argues that current price levels will not make him buy, TOP10 argues that the prices do not affect him, either, and thus projects the persona of the happy homeowner to counter the position of the satisfied tenant.

Other homeowners construct their positions in a slightly different manner, arguing that in the long run it is always advantageous to own a home: "Saving by paying off the loan is a certain win in the long term. Yes, you can lose 5 percent one year and earn 6 percent the next. No one knows EXACTLY what happens because of normal variation. The only thing you know with 100 percent certainty is that the value of the house increases while the loan is minimized. Even if you lived in Zimbabwe that would be WIN-WIN" (poulnyrup, 6003.62).

The position of the hyper in its pure form is found in statements like this: "The prices have gone up. CHEERS" (davidoffcw, 5973.2). The direct claim that prices are rising is, however, an exception. Even hypers usually accept the fall in prices as a fact, but argue that buying nevertheless involves more expenses (owing to higher interest rates): "It is becoming ever more expensive to buy. All the tenants are sitting in their moist two-room flats and shedding tears over the lost opportunity" (fister63, 5965.5). Here, the malice of EddieC, who took such obvious pleasure in putting down sellers, is turned around; it is not the prospective sellers who are pitiful because of their losses but the prospective buyers who are fools because they will have to pay more.

Although the interested positions of (prospective) buyers and sellers dominate the Euroinvestor postings, many participants actually strive to position themselves as neutral citizens with the common good in mind. These debaters usually recognize their personal interests in the real estate market but seek to move beyond private reasoning to make general pronouncements on the present state and future developments of the market like this one: "I am not very optimistic as to the maintenance of the high level of employment, but I am, of course, colored by being in construction, where nothing seems to be happening at the moment. Also, many, many sectors correlate with the real estate market" (teder, 6018.20).

If a debater claims to be a buyer or seller, other debaters may be hostile or friendly toward that position, but only very rarely do they question whether the debater actually occupies the position that he or she claims. The position of the citizen, however, turns out to be contested; a debater's attempt to occupy that position is often challenged by other participants, and some exchanges concern who may rightly claim the coveted position. Whoever comes out as taking the more neutral and balanced stance has the upper hand and will be perceived as a credible commentator. The debaters are all interested in price developments, but they want prices to rise or fall depending on their self-interest. This makes neutrality attractive to many, and it means that attempts to claim neutrality and disinterestedness are usually contested.

The position of the citizen whose comments transcend specific interests is coveted because it is perceived as weightier than that of the buyer or seller. A debater thus allows another to take the citizen position when the latter says something to which the former can assent. This indicates that the debaters on Euroinvestor to some extent acknowledge the role and norms of the citizen in the Habermasian sense, but it also shows that the citizen position is often used strategically in order to promote one's own cause. Although the interested position of buyer/seller, on the one hand, and that of impartial citizen, on the other, are both represented on Euroinvestor, they turn out not to be in opposition to each other but inextricably intertwined. It is the interconnection of public and private stances rather than the differentiation of the two that is the central feature of the vernacular rhetoric on Euroinvestor. In the following section we seek to explain how the positions are combined at both the theoretical and the analytical level.

Arguments as a Means of Positioning—Studying Interests with the *Staseis*

In Hauser's conception of public debate, how a case is argued in a site of deliberation sheds light on the positions that constitute, and may be used strategically in, that particular context. Taking our cue from this theoretical stance, we need an analytical tool that may explain the specific ways in which debaters on Euroinvestor argue for and from their private or public positions. We contend that the classical theory of the *staseis* may serve as such a tool for studying the interrelationship of argumentation and positioning.[7] However, as Dilip Gaonkar has pointed out, it is not unproblematic to turn the practical tools of classical rhetoric into analytical concepts for present-day purposes (1997, 27). Therefore, before we can actually apply the *staseis*, we need to consider which points of the classical system might need modification in order to be applicable to public debate in general and Euroinvestor in particular.

The original theory of the *staseis* was developed to enable judicial rhetoric to determine the central point at issue in a given case (Hohmann 2001, 741). Four *staseis* were identified, and in the following these will be defined and exemplified with arguments used on Euroinvestor in order to illustrate their continued relevance and our specific use of them.[8]

The first *status* (this is Latin for *stasis* and has nothing to do with our common understanding of the term "status," though the latter probably has etymological roots in the Latin term), *status conjecturalis*, is applied when the facts are at issue: did something happen or did it not? On Euroinvestor a main controversy concerns the evolution of real estate prices; when *status conjecturalis* is used in arguments on this issue, the facts are laid out as in the following example: "Number of homes [for sale]: 76,982. New today: 510. Price drops today: 413. Price increases today: 11" (Ungee, 5930.1). Here, the implicit argument is that prices are falling.

The second *status, status definitivus,* covers disputes concerning the nature of facts: how should the events and actions be defined? The following entry on Euroinvestor follows the above-quoted post and interprets the facts presented there: "Full-blown downward accelerating price spiral" (EddieC, 5930.2). Whereas Ungee argues through the use of facts, EddieC's argument consists in defining their meaning. The example of *conjecturalis* uses neutral language and seeks to give an objective picture of the market. The example of *definitivus*, on the contrary, uses metaphors and colorful language to convey a subjective interpretation of the situation.

The third *status, status qualitatis*, refers to controversies over the evaluation of the facts: how should the events and actions be assessed? Here, an example is taken from another string in which the issue is how the current market affects the prospects for buying or selling a home: "I think it is a SUPER time to buy" (poulnyrup, 5936.25). Poulnyrup presents the evaluation and thus also the proposal as to what action should be taken in terms that are not the loudest possible, but the explicitly personal opinion ("I think") and the use of capital letters ("SUPER") clearly mark the advice as a personal estimate or evaluation.

Finally, the fourth *status, status translationis*, originally designated a plea to have one's case tried in another court because the present court lacks the proper authority. We found no use of this strategy in its pure form on Euroinvestor, but there is plenty of argumentation that shifts the terms of debate or moves the reasoning from one context to another. This shows that *status translationis* must be revised if it is to be used as a modern analytical tool, but it also suggests that such a revised concept would indeed be relevant. What we propose is to think of the move not as a physical one from one court to another but as a metaphorical shift in argumentative scene. Thus, *status translationis* is broadened to include all attempts to change the terms of arguments, to alter the premises, and thus to transcend the conditions of judgment that are otherwise generally accepted by the interlocutors. On Euroinvestor it is often taken for granted that economy functions as the bedrock of the argument, but some debaters seek to transcend this presupposition. Here is one example of how this may be done: "Buy a house because you want to live in it, not for the investment" (TOP10, 6003.3). As in the example of *status qualitatis*, clear advice concerning how one should act results from the argument; this time, however, the advice is based not on an evaluation of the current market but on a move away from reliance on the ups and downs of the market toward consideration of one's personal needs and desires. The argument is made as if it were a maxim, a general rule "about things that involve actions and are to be chosen or avoided in regard to action" (Aristotle 1991, 1394a). TOP10 articulates his personal opinion as a general premise that might replace the economic mode of arguing and acting.

It should be noted that each *status* is articulated in many different ways. For instance, the example of *status translationis* presented above relies on the argument that quality is more important than quantity (to paraphrase TOP10's position, if you need a house, then the price is secondary). However, the shift in argumentative setting can also be realized in other ways: one may replace figures with feelings through pathos (e.g., buy with your heart, an argument that is related to, yet distinct from, TOP10's statement). It is possible to broaden the scene by means of *pars pro toto* (it is actually not the real estate market that is at issue but the economy as such). And one can move beyond current developments in prices by arguing from unlimited development (in the long run, prices will always rise)—to name but a few of the options available to, and employed by, debaters on Euroinvestor.

There thus seems to be a duality to the *staseis* system: four issues, but many ways of articulating them. Hanns Hohmann captures the duality well: "the theory of stasis develops a system designed to assist rhetors in *identifying the central issues in given controversies*, and in *finding the appropriate argumentative topics* useful in addressing these issues" (2001, 741, emphasis added). The first dimension refers to the *staseis* in their general form; at the practical level the aim is to understand the nature of the dispute and decide which of the *staseis* to apply (Heath 1994). Analytically, this translates into determining which *staseis* are used by which rhetors. In practice, the second dimension has to do with actually arguing one's case, selecting the best arguments from the whole range of possibilities that pertain to the chosen *staseis* and presenting them in the most appropriate manner ([Cicero] 1981). Here, the analytical counterpart consists in explaining the various ways in which the interlocutors actually use the *staseis*.

We propose the terminology of strategies and tactics to distinguish between the *staseis* as four general categories and as an unspecified number of different articulations of these categories.[9] This conceptual pairing allows us to study specific utterances with respect to their differences (the tactical level), while also categorizing the utterances (the strategic level). Moreover, it allows us to investigate the relationship between the general categories and their specific articulations. We propose that this relationship is one of predisposition but not necessity. That is, a given tactic may be primarily associated with one of the four general strategies, but this does not mean that it cannot also appear in the service of the other strategies. For instance, the tactic of appealing to feelings (using pathos), which we have linked with *status translationis*, is also present in our example of *status definitivus*; the colorful language of the "downward accelerating price spiral" shows how EddieC relishes the situation, but it will surely send shivers down the spine of anyone who has real estate for sale. Furthermore, it could be argued that the emotional appeal forms an integral part of *status qualitatis*. This is not to say that judging the character or value of something is irrational; on the contrary, our point is that the evaluation would not be rational if it did not consider the emotions on which it relies.

Thus the tactics—for example, the use of pathos—may be associated with all four *staseis*, but in specific argumentative encounters there may be a propensity to link each tactic more closely to one strategy than to the others. These tendencies, we believe, demarcate the positions that are actually available to and constructed by the debaters—the vernacular voices of the particular arena for discussion. And it is to the study of the positions that arise from the alignment of strategies and tactics on Euroinvestor that we now turn. However, we wish only to sketch some of the possibilities in order to present an alternative to the public-private divide and to illustrate the analytical potential of the *staseis* in this regard.

Consumers, Citizens, and Everything in Between: Analyzing Euroinvestor with the *Staseis*

We perceived strong patterns of preference for particular strategies and tactics among the most active contributors to the debate. Ungee, the most frequent initiator of strings in our set of data, was usually the fastest to post new facts and figures, his favorite being the number of homes for sale. Ungee's use of *status conjecturalis* did not obscure his position as a prospective buyer; rather, the numbers were allowed to speak for themselves because they were to Ungee's liking. EddieC was the most monomaniacal of the debaters. He rarely wrote a post without including the image of the bloodbath, a tactic that falls squarely between the strategies of definition and evaluation. EddieC often cast himself as the interpreter of the numbers that Ungee supplied, but his interpretations were made with such glee that they were also strong evaluations. Another debater with a penchant for *status qualitatis* was davidoffcw, whose preferred tactic was the ad hominem argument, and Ungee and EddieC were often the victims of his attacks, as in this example: "The pride couple [i.e., the homosexuals] Ungee and EddieC are going to have to keep renting the two-room flat in Copenhagen NV [a neighborhood with a rather bad reputation]" (davidoffcw, 5934.22). Finally, *status translationis* was often used by TOP10, who rarely missed a chance to present his favorite version of the strategy: buy a house to live in, not as an investment.

From this short overview of the preferred arguments of four users, we may get an idea of the positions that these users constructed for themselves and locate them on the private-public scale. Ungee and EddieC both positioned themselves as tenants, davidoffcw and TOP10 as owners. However, using the public-private criterion, EddieC and davidoffcw may be grouped together, since they were equally subjective in their reasoning and stylistic choices. Ungee and TOP10, by contrast, made appeals that went beyond their personal interests, and they also tended to use more neutral language than the two other debaters. Whereas EddieC and davidoffcw represented the private positions of consumer/merchant in their pure forms, Ungee and TOP10 took hybrid stands.

To provide more detail as to how private and public positions may interrelate, we have conducted a close reading of one particular debate string. This string sheds light on how the various debaters both had recourse to their preferred strategies and tactics and employed a range of other argumentative moves, and thus allows us to see how the varied use of arguments affected the construction of the debaters' positions. The debate string we selected for close reading is a rather long one. Characteristically, it begins with a post by Ungee, though in this case Ungee links his post to an article in the economic newspaper *Børsen*, not to a set of figures. The article predicts that the crisis of the real estate market will continue for at least seven years, and Ungee indicates his attitude toward this prediction by writing "no need to hurry" in the subject line (6003.1).

TOP10 is among the first to comment, giving his usual advice to buy from need, not as an investment, and supporting this position with examples of friends who waited while prices were on the rise and finally bought at a high price because their living situation was becoming unbearable (6003.3). Here, TOP10 at once makes the issue specific: "if I were living in a two-room flat and expecting my fourth child, I would probably have a tendency to hurry a bit" (6003.3), and makes a general case. TOP10 clearly is not a member of the hypothetical family in the small flat but speaks on behalf of all such families. Thus TOP10 introduces a theme of interest to an important social category and to society as a whole, and a discussion of what the family should do unfolds.

In the following posts the issue is turned over by several of the debaters; some continue the discussion of whether the family should buy now or wait, some comment on what kind of property such a family might be able to afford, and some turn to the question of whether people's expectations of the home they can afford are too high. Hestehoved, in post 6003.13, introduces the idea that in the hypothetical family he is an engineer, his wife is a kindergarten teacher, and they have only one child; this definition of the family becomes paradigmatic for the following posts. Concerning what kind of house "our" family might reasonably expect to buy, a discussion unfolds on whether a "fine house" can be bought for 3.6 million Danish kroner.

Here, kosmokrator provides evidence in the form of links to houses for sale (6003.22), and the discussion moves on to whether these houses are really "fine" or whether the family should hold out for something better. Also discussed is whether an engineer and a kindergarten teacher can actually afford these houses, and much evidence—for example, statistics on the income of engineers—is provided (JohnnyB76, 6003.40). At one point poulnyrup sets up a budget for the family (6003.43), aiming to show that they can afford a very good house. The other debaters cast serious doubt on this budget, and it becomes the main issue of the remaining string, as well as the subject of an independent string (6014).

All in all, the interaction in the debate string is driven primarily by issues of common concern: what sort of home should a family that is representative of average citizens be able to buy? Can they buy this home at present? And even if they can, should they? In order to answer these questions, the debaters present a lot of evidence of the sort associated with *status conjecturalis* (actual houses for sale, income statistics), dealing with general tendencies and conditions that affect the public as such, and this evidence is usually presented in a neutral style that allows the facts to speak for themselves. Thus the strategy of *conjecturalis* is associated with the generalized interests of the citizen, and many debaters take this position.

However, *conjecturalis* is not the only strategy used in the string, and the citizen position is not the only one present. The many details the debaters provide about the hypothetical family are interpretations of the facts. Here, the tactic of the example is used in the service of *status definitivus*, and with its many specific details this tactic brings stylistic color and a distinct voice to an argument that is still based in public reasoning—a hybrid position is articulated. The other possible hybrid, private reasoning couched in the neutral tone of the citizen, is also present, but it is not very frequent in this particular string. We find it in Chesspengo's statement about not wanting to buy yet (6003.7, quoted in the first round of analysis). Here, the strategy of *qualitatis* is linked to the private interest ("the development is good for me"), but the specific tactic (argument from cause and effect: "when the prices have fallen sufficiently, then I will buy") and the tone are quite modest given one of the key messages of the comment ("I have made a fortune"). These features lend the private argument the public form of the citizen.

Finally, the private position is constructed in both form and content when the debaters turn on each other with personal attacks. For example, poulnyrup says of Hestehoved that his thinking is "messed up" (6003.52), and Hestehoved responds by calling poulnyrup a "bitch" (6003.53). Again, the general strategy is *qualitatis*, but with the tactic of ad hominem the resulting position has moved from the hybrid position to the purely private stance.

In many respects, then, the two ideal typical positions of the private consumer/merchant and the public citizen are the reference points of the debaters' constructions of their positions. However, they are by no means restricted to using either the private grounding and personal form of the ideal typical private person or the public grounding and professional form that is associated with the citizen. Instead, each debater may use many different arguments to construct his or her position; and it is the particular combination of strategies and tactics that makes each position unique.

Using the *staseis* to study how arguments position debaters' interests, then, reveals both the regularities of the debate and the construction of unique positions. Although all four strategies are present, most debaters prefer one of them. Furthermore, many tactics are used, but a smaller set dominates the discussion, since the debaters—their choice of strategy notwithstanding—tend to take up one another's tactics and use them for their own purposes. On the one hand, the debaters are clearly positioned by their choice of arguments. On the other hand, they are not limited to one (set of) argument(s). This means that the argumentative construction of the positions does not place strict constraints on the debaters; the possibility of changing strategies and employing different tactics—and thus of constructing one's position differently—remains open.

Private and Public Positions—Homing in on the Arguments

At the theoretical level, our aim has been to show the usefulness as well as the limitations of the private-public dichotomy in studies of debate or argumentation. We believe that it makes good sense to distinguish between the two dimensions, but only as a starting point for analyzing how they interrelate, not as a normative prescription for keeping them apart. We hope that the case of Euroinvestor illustrates the point that rich and lively debate actually results from the exchange of viewpoints between debaters who are positioned at the intersection of the private and the public. We do not see Euroinvestor as an example of what public debate should ideally look like. However, we do believe that the evaluation of public debate should begin with thick descriptions of how it actually functions in its particularity. No assumptions about what good debate looks like should predetermine the conclusion; the evaluation should spring from the analysis.

In the case of Euroinvestor, it is not the presence of private interests as such that hampers debate but rather the use of the specific tactic of the ad hominem argument that sometimes causes the debate to degenerate into a shouting match. When the debaters steer clear of ad hominem attacks, their private interests often lend the discussion the nerve that makes it interesting. Private reasoning, then, is not a weakness in itself, but it is not an unconditional strength, either. The real strength of the debate lies in the many ways in which the debaters combine the positions of buyers/sellers and citizens. These complex positions are not the result of two distinct modes of reasoning, the private and the public; rather, they are constructed by means of the four strategies and many tactics, which the analytical tool derived from the classical system of the *staseis* allows us to discern.

The many arguments used by the discussants and the resulting nuanced positions mean that debates on Euroinvestor are often both enlightening and persuasive—the discussants pass on knowledge of the real estate market, and they offer their advice on how prospective buyers and sellers should respond to market developments, at both the individual level and the larger social level. The information and advice may sometimes be colored by the personal stance of the discussant, but when that stance is clear (and it usually is), this is not necessarily a disadvantage. Ultimately, personal motivation is what drives the participants to enter the debate, and it is what allows them—as well as the silent reader—to identify with or distance themselves from one another.

Thus the evaluation of Euroinvestor that our analysis invites is predominantly positive. As mentioned above, we believe that the many forums for debate, which in combination make up the multifarious public spheres of society, and the specific discussions that take place in these forums should be analyzed and evaluated separately. Thus we reject Habermas's a priori conclusions about the undesirability of private reasoning in public spheres. Our position does, however, contain its own normativity, which we wish to explicate as our final point. Habermas feared that active citizens would lose political power as passive spectators, clients, and consumers. We, by contrast, have reason to hope that passive citizens will gain rhetorical agency as active spectators, clients, and consumers. That is, we believe that private interests are a good starting point for public engagement. The study of Euroinvestor has indicated that at least this specific case has the potential to create active debate around various interested positions.

NOTES

1. All strings on Euroinvestor are numbered consecutively (the oldest string in our set is 5930 and the most recent is 6039), and each contribution to a string also has a number; thus a citation of EddieC, 6016.5, refers to a posting by EddieC (username) that is the fifth contribution to string 6016.
2. The debate was conducted in Danish, but we have translated it into English; all translations are our own unless otherwise noted.
3. First published as his *Habilitationsschrift* in 1962 and belatedly translated into English in 1989.
4. In his most recent definition of the concept, Habermas characterizes the public sphere as "a network for communicating information and points of view (i.e., opinions expressing affirmative or negative attitudes)" (1996, 360). He explains how the public sphere facilitates the formation of public opinion: "the streams of communication are, in the process, filtered and synthesized in such a way as to coalesce into bundles of topically specified *public* opinions" (360, emphasis in the original). While this definition is somewhat more dynamic than the original one, the public sphere must be comprehensive if it is to fulfill the filtering and synthesizing functions that Habermas describes.
5. In that the debaters have predominantly male usernames and/or construct male personae, we have used male pronouns in most cases, but in the understanding that this use is generic and that some of the Euroinvestor users may be, and probably are, female.
6. There are, however, debaters who position themselves openly as buyers: "I am renting a place after having sold my house. . . . I am on my way. Keep the contract warm. I want to own my home again" (Mayer34, 5935.12). The rationale here may be that the prices have already dropped sufficiently, or that the development is beyond influence—prices will continue to fall no matter what one says.
7. In this chapter we seek to illustrate this point analytically rather than argue it theoretically. For a succinct theoretical discussion of the general relationship between identity formation (a close relative of what we here call positioning) and argumentation, see Maier 1996. For an example of the analytical use of the *staseis* as a means of explaining how a rhetor presents him- or herself to an audience, see Kramer and Olson 2002.
8. Our definitions of the *staseis* are based primarily on Conley 1990 and Hohmann 2001, but classical sources—Hermogenes' *On Stases* (in Nadeau's translation, 1964) and Cicero's *De Inventione* (1949)—have also been consulted.
9. We borrow the terms "strategy" and "tactic" from classical military theory, in which the former referred to overall planning, whereas the latter designated the specific actions taken to pursue the overall strategy. The idea, then, is that the four *staseis* are general strategies of reasoning that may be realized through—or articulated by means of—many different tactics, that is, specific argumentative and stylistic forms.

REFERENCES

Aristotle. 1991. *On Rhetoric*. New York: Oxford University Press.
Cicero. 1949. *De Inventione*. Cambridge: Harvard University Press.
[———]. 1981. *Rhetorica ad herennium*. Cambridge: Harvard University Press.
Conley, Thomas M. 1990. *Rhetoric in the European Tradition*. Chicago: University of Chicago Press.

Fraser, Nancy. 1992a. "Rethinking the Public Sphere: A Contribution to the Critique of Actually Existing Democracy." In *Habermas and the Public Sphere*, ed. Craig Calhoun, 109–42. Cambridge: MIT Press.

———. 1992b. "Sex, Lies, and the Public Sphere: Some Reflections on the Confirmation of Clarence Thomas." *Critical Inquiry* 18:595–612.

Gaonkar, Dilip P. 1997. "The Idea of Rhetoric in the Rhetoric of Science." In *Rhetorical Hermeneutics: Invention and Interpretation in the Age of Science*, ed. Alan G. Gross and William M. Keith, 25–85. Albany: State University of New York Press.

Habermas, Jürgen. 1970. "Towards a Theory of Communicative Competence." *Inquiry* 13:360–75.

———. 1984. *Reason and the Rationalization of Society*. Vol. 1 of *The Theory of Communicative Action*. Boston: Beacon Press.

———. 1987. *Lifeword and System: A Critique of Functionalist Reason*. Vol. 2 of *The Theory of Communicative Action*. Boston: Beacon Press.

———. 1989. *The Structural Transformation of the Public Sphere*. Cambridge: Polity Press.

———. 1993. *Moral Consciousness and Communicative Action*. Cambridge: MIT Press.

———. 1996. *Between Facts and Norms: Contributions to a Discourse Theory of Law and Democracy*. Cambridge: Polity Press.

Hauser, Gerard. 1999. *Vernacular Voices: The Rhetoric of Publics and Public Spheres*. Columbia: University of South Carolina Press.

Heath, Malcolm. 1994. "The Substructure of *Stasis*-Theory from Hermagoras to Hermogenes." *Classical Quarterly* 44:114–29.

Hermogenes. 1964. "Hermogenes' *On Stases:* A Translation with an Introduction and Notes." Trans. Ray Nadeau. *Speech Monographs* 31:361–424.

Hohmann, Hanns. 2001. "Stasis." In *Encyclopedia of Rhetoric*, ed. Thomas O. Sloane, 741–45. New York: Oxford University Press.

Kramer, Michael R., and Kathryn M. Olson. 2002. "The Strategic Potential of Sequencing Apologia Stases: President Clinton's Self-Defense in the Monica Lewinsky Scandal." *Western Journal of Communication* 66:347–68.

Leff, Michael. 2003. "Rhetorical Criticism in the Interpretive Mode: A Case Study of Martin Luther King's 'Letter from Birmingham Jail.'" Keynote address at the Second Nordic Conference for Research in Rhetoric at the University of Copenhagen. Published in Danish as "Fortolkende retorik," *Rhetorica Scandinavica* 26:6–19.

Maier, Robert. 1996. "Forms of Identity and Argumentation." *Journal for the Theory of Social Behaviour* 26 (1): 35–50.

Terchek, Ronald J., and Thomas C. Conte, eds. 2001. *Theories of Democracy*. Lanham, Md.: Rowman and Littlefield.

15
DANISH REVUE:
SATIRE AS RHETORICAL CITIZENSHIP

Jette Barnholdt Hansen

This chapter discusses Danish revue as rhetorical discourse, exploring the rhetorical character of revue and the persuasive potential and social function of this satiric voice within public debate. I focus on a song called "Did We Learn Anything?" (Lærte vi noget?) from 2006, dealing with the so-called cartoon crisis. The song is a parody of a revue classic from 1944 about the political situation in Denmark during the German occupation. I propose that collective agency may be embodied in the subtle intertextual references to the classic, thanks to an appeal to the collective memory of World War II, when Danes stood together in a difficult time. In this way the new song seems to use the old one as a historical warrant for its implicit plea for solidarity in the present situation. While I doubt that the song changed anyone's opinion of the cartoons or the newspaper that printed them, it had, I suggest, a positive influence on the public debate about the cartoons and the ensuing crisis: the appeal for solidarity apparently aimed at defusing the eristic controversy caused by the cartoons, with a divided Danish population consisting of two wings fighting each other and a silent, frightened, and frustrated majority in the middle.[1] In a rhetorical analysis of the song, I describe how this consubstantial space and sense of relief—a basis for restoring constructive debate—is established during the aesthetic performance of the song. I also aim to unveil aspects of the public role of satirical performance in general—often interpreted as a mirror reflecting political, cultural, and moral issues considered urgent by contemporary society.[2]

Historical Outline

The French word *revue* means both "inspection" and "going through." *Revue* also designates a genre in musical theater that includes satirical songs, sketches, and dance and is rooted in a particular French tradition of the seventeenth and eighteenth centuries; satirical songs (called *vaudeville*, after Vau de Vire, the valley in Normandy where such songs were first composed) that made fun of the political system were performed in the streets of the big cities. These performances were understood as a sort of oral, versified newspaper and were so popular that they were even said to threaten the power of the absolute monarchy (Marott 1991, 22; Barnes 1989, 564). Regular revues were performed around New Year's Eve in Paris from the middle of the nineteenth century, and the name "revue" might be associated with that, as the performances dealt with the passing year and satirized current events. Inspired by the French tradition, the very first Danish *revy* was performed on New Year's Eve 1849; like its French model, it commented on contemporary political and cultural issues (Kjærulff and Ramsøe 1934, 12).

Revue During the German Occupation

The song studied here revived a revue classic from World War II for satirical purposes—an interesting rhetorical choice. During the German occupation of 1940–45, when public debate was stifled, revues functioned as a mouthpiece and a "moral vernacular" for the Danish people (Hauser 2008). In spite of severe theater censorship, the revues were able to convey Danes' resentment of the Nazis and strengthen the opposition to them through subtle political satire in which veiled criticism was communicated between the lines or hidden in metaphors. A famous example is Poul Henningsen's 1940 song "Our Mouths and Hands Are Bound" (Man binder os på mund og hånd); on the surface, it dealt with sexual repression, but it was at once interpreted as referring to the restricted freedom of expression under the German occupation. The revue theaters became important gathering places where Danes practiced rhetorical citizenship by celebrating national identity and showing resistance, though not openly or explicitly, for fear of reprisals.[3] The revue songs were used for community singing as well: during the occupation many Danes met in public places, singing Danish songs to keep up their spirits. For this purpose songbooks were published that included contemporary revue songs. In this way the satirical songs (and the implicit opposition they bespoke) spread from the theaters and reached the larger Danish population; for instance, around 750,000 people gathered for *Alsang* (a community sing-along) in public places on 1 September 1940 (Høgel 1987, 9). The feeling of solidarity and relief that came from listening to these songs in the theater and then singing them shoulder to shoulder in public was arguably what the revue song on the cartoon crisis of 2005–6 was meant to achieve, by alluding to a classic from the time of the German occupation.

Revue as Epideictic Rhetoric

Throughout its history, theater critics have dismissed the revue genre, regarding revue not as "real" art but as a sort of simple, occasional theater for the masses, so strongly linked to current events that it becomes as irrelevant as yesterday's news (Kjærulff and Ramsøe 1934, 12). Some, however, have always defended the genre, as for instance the writer, architect, and critic Poul Henningsen (1894–1967), who characterized revue as "serious fun" and ascribed to it an educational social function.[4] Plenov (2000, 7) highlights the social role of the genre in his history of the revue, which he describes as "a many-sided creature. The purpose of it is to entertain and amuse; it also plays an important role as social castigator, however. When politicians and other people make fools of themselves, they shall feel the flick of the satire's whip. . . . I have tried to write a legible text without being superficial, tried to live up to the nature of the revue itself: 'The difficult light art.'"

One might add to Henningsen's "serious fun" and Plenov's "social castigator" that revues constitute important rhetorical discourse. They are comparable to other manifestations of rhetorical citizenship—a sort of direct aesthetic response to current issues. Revue material is often rewritten in order to preserve its *kairos* and relevance to the issue at hand; if something happens to a politician, a parody of him must reflect and comment on it at once. The revue aims to catch the moment and find the most topical subjects, so that the audience will always feel its pertinence. The spectators must experience their own political reality and see their own everyday life on stage, not in a literal way, of course, but twisted by the thrust of the satire. The mirror is a suitable metaphor for the genre—not, however, a magic mirror, as in "The Snow Queen" by Hans Christian Andersen, in which the reflected image always becomes a distorted caricature. Although egos are often deflated and severe social criticism is frequent, the ideal of the Danish revue has nearly always been to offer political satire in such a way that the general audience, regardless of political persuasion, and even the parodied person himself, can have fun (Kjærulff and Ramsøe 1934, 12). Sometimes the target actually feels honored, for one must have significant public presence or charisma to warrant a parody in the first place.

Revues also allow a broad cross-section of the Danish population, representing all political stripes, to enjoy fellowship on political issues, a sort of civil public camaraderie. Many corporate employees, for instance, are invited to revue performances by their companies as part of a summer party—in spite of the unwritten rule in Danish companies and public institutions that in order to preserve team spirit one should not discuss politics on the job. But because revue satire normally emerges from public debate, the performances often elicit positive comments from all sides and are therefore considered appropriate entertainment, generating corporate spirit in employees in spite of the revue's political content.[5]

It thus seems natural to approach revues as rhetorical discourse and to use rhetorical tools to describe their ontology. From a historical point of view it also makes sense to study the revues of a certain period as cultural artifacts and manifestations of rhetorical citizenship, as a sort of record of what was considered topical at the time.

To a rhetorician, the adjective "occasional," used by some critics to devalue the aesthetic qualities of the revue, points towards epideictic rhetoric, which is often defined as occasional discourse. According to Aristotle, the epideictic genre concerns the present, though it may involve both the past and the future by referring to what has happened and what can be expected to happen.[6] Epideictic audience members are mainly defined as observers (*theoroi*), but they are also judges of the rhetorical and performative capacity of the rhetor. The revue embraces the characteristic Aristotelian features of the epideictic genre as well: it addresses virtues and vices and gives out both praise and blame, though mostly blame. Some revues—the songs of the occupation years, for instance—might also be interpreted as epideictic rhetoric with deliberative and imaginative functions; as both Hauser and Sheard have explained, epideictic often anticipates political rhetoric by influencing values that lead to action later on (Hauser 1999; Sheard 1996, 784–87).

Another social function characteristic of the revue is the creation of what Kenneth Burke calls *consubstantiality*, in which a very broad audience—men and women, young and old, liberals and conservatives—is united. The members of such an audience are supposed to "act together," sharing an identity defined primarily by the concrete situation: thus, during the revue performance, the audience symbolizes the Danish people, imitating its everyday life and political reality.[7] The spectators should also be seen as important co-players: their spontaneous response and laughter give life and energy to the comic scenes, and sometimes they are even asked to participate on stage. Although sharp satire is expected in a Danish revue, the limits of decorum are usually observed—neither toothless nor too cruel parody is fun. The latter might even split the audience into opponents and supporters of the person being parodied, which would be a catastrophe for the performance. Revue satire is thus rarely as sharp as newspaper cartoons, as the cartoonist is not directly confronted with his spectators. The subject of this chapter, a song on the cartoon crisis, deals with this issue in an explicit manner.

The Cartoon Crisis

In 2005 the Danish newspaper *Jyllands-Posten* (the Jutland Post) asked the cartoonist Kurt Westergaard, among others, to draw the Islamic prophet; it took him one hour to draw Muhammad with a bomb in his turban. Together with eleven other cartoons, Westergaard's cartoon was printed on 30 September, illustrating an article on self-censorship and freedom of expression. The cartoons soon traveled around the world, giving rise to new and complex rhetorical situations and large demonstrations in Muslim countries (Kjeldsen 2008, 52–55). Three Danish embassies were attacked, ambassadors were called home, and some Arab countries boycotted Danish products, demanding an apology from the prime minister and the queen. The cartoons caused one of the worst political crises ever in Denmark.

The crisis also heightened the fear of terror already felt by many Danes after 11 September 2001 and caused a harsh controversy. Some Danes condemned the cartoons, interpreting them as expressions of intolerance that offended the religious ethics, culture, and feelings of Muslims. Many also accused the cartoonists and *Jyllands-Posten* of causing diplomatic and economic problems and of widening the gap between the West and the Muslim world. Others defended, supported, and celebrated the newspaper for practicing and upholding freedom of expression: cartoonists and other artists should not be forced to treat Muslims with special consideration, they argued; like all other religious, political, and cultural communities, Muslims had to accept satire. Most Danes, however, simply could not believe their eyes and ears. The cartoons seemed to have a domino effect that was totally out of control, affecting distant parts of the world. TV footage of the Danish flag being burned at demonstrations in several countries, for instance, was an alarming experience for many Danes. These people felt as if they had suddenly been caught up in public trench warfare. They did not participate much in the debate. On the contrary, they seemed to lose their voice, not knowing what to think or how to react.

The Purpose of Satire

As the cartoon crisis peaked, Lisbet Dahl, who for several years had been director of the Circus Revue, an annual summer revue held north of Copenhagen, was asked in a TV interview whether the revue of 2006 would refer to the cartoon crisis. She answered that of course it would, or the revue would lose its justification as a genre. But, as we learn from the website of the song's authors, Vase and Fuglsang, this was no easy topic to handle.[8] Heavy rhetorical constraints were connected with satirizing the cartoon crisis—a crisis sparked by satire that had caused severe foreign political conflicts and a controversy that split the nation. The importance Dahl emphasized had to do with the *responsive* character of revue. We might interpret political satire as a response to exigencies, to use Bitzer's famous term. If the genre understands itself as a necessary part of public debate, then the cartoon crisis had to be commented on.

John Meyer also stresses the communicative dimensions of humorous utterances in society. He outlines four basic rhetorical functions of humor—two that unite the rhetor with his audience and two that separate them: (1) *identification* creates bonds between rhetor and audience; (2) *clarification* captures the essence of a position in a humorous utterance and makes clear the attitude of the rhetor; (3) *enforcement* uses humor to reassert social norms and ridicules those who do not follow them (some identification with those who follow the norms is maintained, however); (4) *differentiation* creates contrast and divides groups or individuals (Meyer 2000; see also Gring-Pemble and Watson 2003, 137). Although all four functions can be observed in Danish revue, it is primarily characterized by the uniting functions, identification and clarification, in that the genre always tries to bring together the broad revue audience and make the intentions of the satire clear in order to get spontaneous applause and laughter. As we shall see, these uniting functions also characterize the humor of the song and help build up its appeal for solidarity.

A comic performance often confronts us with difficult or repressed topics, and laughing freely together can have a healing effect. Jokes, according to Freud, are a source of pleasure and give a sense of release or relief by replacing fear or sadness with laughter. Freud emphasizes that comic discourse has a strong illuminating force ("gedankenerhellende Kraft") that is contrary to the dominant rational thinking ("das intellektuelle Reich unserer Gedanken und Vorstellungen"); this is due to its aesthetic liberty, its playful astuteness, and its ability to look at an issue from the outside and simplify it (1905, 2–3).[9] Freud's thesis is a central warrant for this study; it explains how a satirical song with no explicit argument can possess collective agency and influence public debate (Hoff-Clausen, Isager, and Villadsen 2005). A comic narrative of a complex chain of events can help simplify things, and the laughter it provokes has a therapeutic effect, allaying fear for some people and helping others leave their trenches in order to *talk* and *listen* again. Comedy might thus help rebuild a constructive dialogue on the cartoon crisis, although the debaters would probably remain in disagreement.[10] In this way the silent majority of Danes, who had not yet formed an opinion, were offered a new opportunity to choose between opposite views of the cartoons and the resulting uproar.[11]

"Did We Learn Anything?"

Lisbet Dahl kept her promise: her 2006 summer revue addressed the cartoon crisis with a song that attracted major public attention called "Did We Learn Anything?" The Circus Revue, begun in 1935, is performed every summer in a big circus tent located at Bakken, an old amusement park north of Copenhagen, and is considered the most influential revue in Denmark. It is seen by thousands and is later broadcast on national television, often in primetime on the weekend. Leading Danish comedians have appeared there and considered it important for their careers, as in the case of Ulf Pilgaard, who performed "Did We Learn Anything?" Pilgaard has been a mainstay of the revue company for thirty years and was an obvious choice for the song, which was performed not by a dramatic character but by *the revue actor* himself. The same was true of "We Are All in the Same Boat" (Vi er alle i samme båd) in 1944—a celebrated song from the occupation years, delivered by the great wartime actor Helge Kjærulff-Schmidt—which was the model for "Did We Learn Anything?" Pilgaard received the annual Dirch Award for his performance.[12] On accepting the award, he reflected on what the song had meant to the audience. The event was reported by the newspaper *Ekstra Bladet*: "Tall Ulf looked like a shy schoolboy receiving his grade book from his class teacher, standing there with a wreath around his neck and a 10,000 DKK check in his hand. But then he said something that hit the bull's eye: 'Did We Learn Anything' had lightened the tense Muhammad cartoon atmosphere that we had lived all winter. And the number looked back to an atmosphere no less tense, 1944, the penultimate year of the occupation. Well said" (Dirckinck-Holmfeld 2006, 11).

The Performance

"Did We Learn Anything?" took center stage in the 2006 Circus Revue; it directly followed the intermission. The set featured a big allegorical cartoon by Roald Als (fig. 15.1) depicting Denmark as a boat, inspired by the

Fig. 15.1

1944 song.[13] To do a cartoon on the cartoon crisis was an interesting idea, for it parodied parody and satirized satire, apparently pointing toward the metalevel of the revue song as a satirical genre. It thus also created an effect of *Verfremdung*: on seeing the cartoon, the audience is led to consider satire as a cultural phenomenon and, when Pilgaard sings, critically to consider the Danish revue song as satire instead of being seduced by the theater illusion. Peter Stocker explains the rhetorical effect of parodic intertextuality in this way:

> Ein typisches Merkmal der parodistischen Intertextualität ist die Verwendung der Unangemessenheit als P.-Signal. Unangemessenheit entsteht, wenn die Transposition von Figuren, Motiven, Stilelementen usw. zu einer *kotextuellen oder kontextuellen Inkongruenz* führt. Wird die Transposition "störungsfrei" (d.h. unter Wahrung des *aptums*) vollzogen, müssen zusätzlich zur Transposition Verfahren *konterdeterminiearter Transformation* ("Verfremdung") hinzutreten, damit eine parodistische Wirkung erzeugt wird. (Stocker 2003, 639)

> One typical characteristic of parodic intertextuality is the use of improper language/behavior as a parodic signal resulting from a transposition of figures, motives, or elements of style, etc., that engender a *co-textual or contextual discrepancy*. If the transposition is carried out without causing "disturbance" (i.e., with consideration for *aptum*), there must be devices of *counterdetermining transformation* ["Verfremdung"] in order that a parodic effect may be achieved.

The parodic aspect is reinforced when the audience discovers the intertextual links to "We Are All in the Same Boat." That song was part of the Hornbæk Revue of 1944 and got its own chapter in the standard work on Danish revue history (Andreasen 1981, 194–96). Many older people and revue enthusiasts know it, but even if younger audience members do not, they can still follow the narrative development of the new song. The references to the source should therefore not be seen as a key that unlocks a hidden meaning; rather, they add the joy of recognition, aesthetic depth, and an appeal to the collective Danish memory of the German occupation. Evaluating the revue retrospectively, listeners probably discussed the song; in this way younger people undoubtedly learned about the intertextual references. Looking back might thus also reinforce the effect of consubstantiality by making the audience talk together and learn from one another. Pilgaard's *actio* underlined the intertextuality: he was dressed in a classic black dinner jacket and held a *rumsterstang* (barker's stick) in his hand, a percussion instrument with a human face, as did Kjærulff-Schmidt in 1944.

This parody—which also mimicked the tune, metrical structure, stage sets, and delivery of "We Are All in the Same Boat"—seems to support another underlying intention of the discourse. Mikhail Bakhtin describes varying degrees of parody: from external and crude parody to an almost complete solidarity with the parodied discourse, which he calls "romantic irony" (2002, 413). "Did We Learn Anything?" uses parody both to ridicule and to celebrate, creating a pluralistic *heteroglossia* (to use another of Bakhtin's key concepts).[14] When the prime minister, Anders Fogh Rasmussen, and the leader of Dansk Folkeparti (the Danish People's Party), Pia Kjærsgaard, are drawn in the cartoon and characterized in the song as "the captain and the mate" (stanza 2), this is allegorical parody in the narrow sense, with the purpose of revealing "something secret or concealed" (Freud 1905, 5). The situation on the boat depicts the political power structure in an exaggerated way: Dansk Folkeparti had secured a parliamentary majority, and Pia Kjærsgaard was therefore regarded as one of the most powerful political figures in Denmark. It is, however, Bakhtin's "parody of solidarity" that dominates the song as a whole, because of its tight connection to the source. Moreover, the song's being performed by the actor "as himself," as in 1944, can be interpreted as a historical persona giving voice to the genre itself—a voice heard during the occupation and again now, after the cartoon crisis (Cherry 1998). In this way the revue seems to insist on its own public purpose: to comment, satirize, and respond to urgent political exigencies. Because of this latter parodic function, the old satiric song also seems to celebrate itself.

The Text

The original 1944 song had been inspired by an even older song that had been part of the musical culture of the *navers* (traveling Scandinavian craftsmen), with a tradition going back to 1899. It has a characteristic metrical and melodic structure: incremental repetitions make each stanza longer than the previous one, and each ends with a refrain. In this way, ideas are repeated over and over.

The five stanzas of the song explain what can be seen in the allegorical cartoon onstage, while the repetitions bring out more and more details about the crisis. The satire on the Danish politicians who played a key role in the conflict is developed in this way. We are introduced to the captain (the prime minister) in the second stanza; in the third we are told that he *"thinks he steers,"* and in the fourth we learn about his unwillingness to apologize. Finally, in the fifth stanza, he is characterized as a "stubborn" captain waiting for "the rescuers from the West": the American president and British prime minister. The repetitions create a rhetorical *amplificatio* and enact the domino effect of the crisis. The culminating fifth stanza has twenty lines that not only list, once again, the main characters of the drama but also address the Danish people (represented by the audience) directly by mentioning the eristic debate among the Danish population: "friends who are enemies" because "the fat's in the fire."

Because the stanzas grow longer and longer, they become more and more difficult for Pilgaard to deliver at a fast tempo. Moreover, he has to point at the cartoon on stage while singing. In this way, the breathtaking performance of the song imitates both the dramatic course of events and the feeling that many Danes had in the thick of the political chaos, which is also recalled physically by Pilgaard's exertion and breathlessness. The audience, confronted again with the uproar over the cartoons, is taken back both intellectually and emotionally. They respond to this psychodynamic experience by laughing—undergoing what Freud saw as a therapeutic process, which may have helped them overcome some of the psychological and rhetorical consequences of the crisis.[15]

Elocutio and *Decorum*

In contrast to the original Muhammad cartoons, the satirical cartoon onstage is an expression of decorum (see fig. 15.1).[16] It is obvious that the cartoonist, Roald Als, has tried to consider all communicative constraints of the situation. While offering sharp satire and parody, as expected in a cartoon, all sides of the controversy can look at this drawing without feeling seriously offended or excluded. The original Mohammed cartoon, for instance, is only sketched; a wave seems to cover it, which can be interpreted as a visual sign of decorum. Consequently, the Circus Revue could not be accused of reproducing the original cartoon, as some newspapers in Europe did in order to support *Jyllands-Posten* and advocate freedom of expression.[17] The same decorum can be observed in the text, which satirizes all aspects of the crisis without taking sides, as when "two editors are washing their hands" (stanza 3) with "four red ears" (stanza 4) and are called "free speech fundamentalists" (stanza 5). On the other hand, "fanatics are in the streets" (stanza 4).[18]

The fifth stanza has subtle stylistic effects often found in revue lyrics. The puns are almost untranslatable: the cartoonists are "belowdecks" (*under dækket*, which also means "undercover"); the Muslim ambassadors whom the prime minister refused to meet become *ambassaudenfordør'ne* ("ambassadors" and "out of the room" are telescoped into one word); "Allah is great" becomes "Arla, which was great" (Arla is the largest Danish dairy company, which suffered economically because of the cartoon crisis). Finally, in the word *redningsVesten* (which means "life jacket" in Danish), the capital "V" creates the double meaning of "rescuers from the West."

Conclusion

The last line of "Did We Learn Anything?" refers specifically to the title of the 1944 song "We Are All in the Same Boat," but it now goes: "We are *still* in the same boat," which seems to offer an answer to the question whether we learned anything and at the same time reinforces the connection between the two songs. During the German occupation, with its strict censorship, "We Are All in the Same Boat" was courageous political satire that expressed both resentment and resistance between the lines. Like many revue songs of this period, the song established identification and consubstantiality, as is obvious from the title, which advocates solidarity among Danes—they had to support one another in a difficult time because they were "all in the same boat." Although the rhetorical situation in 2006 was completely different, the quotation from the old song was still persuasive—but in a new way and with another social function: the line "We are still in the same boat" now creates national identity and consubstantiality by appealing to the collective memory. By recalling the occupation in a song on the cartoon crisis, the size and significance of the latter is diminished; the song seems to be saying that if the Danish people could survive the Nazi occupation, they can certainly overcome the cartoon crisis (a tempest in a teacup compared to the situation in 1944), but we have to stop fighting—stop being "friends who are enemies" and realize that "we are *still* in the same boat." The song presents pointed satire based on identification and clarification, causing loud laughter, which helps the audience experience togetherness and overcome the emotional and rhetorical repercussions of the crisis. Moreover, parody, understood as complete solidarity, seems to pay tribute to revue as an art form and to underscore its legitimacy as a genre—that is, its function as an important satirical voice in public debate, even during wartime or following political chaos.

"Did We Learn Anything?" helps us explore some of the potential social functions of revue: to respond critically to current political issues, to offer an opportunity for fellowship around political issues (even with people with whom we disagree), to depict everyday life through satire, and to create identification and consubstantial space. Like other forms of epideictic discourse, revue may help Danes to redefine their identity in a globalized world and to constitute new social and cultural communities—as in the cartoon by Roald Als, for instance, depicting a multiethnic Denmark where one can no longer draw a clear line between "them" and "us" (unlike the wartime cartoon that it parodies). In our postmodern era, when traditional political, cultural, and moral values and categories are being deconstructed all the time, revue, understood as a satirical manifestation of rhetorical citizenship, is still an effective mirror that, in the words of Hamlet, may show "virtue her own feature, scorn her own image, and the very age and body of the time his form and pressure" (3.2). Revue is an important reflection of contemporary society that comments on significant topics in public debate, showing us which values one *can* appeal to, and how.[19]

NOTES

1. The song was uploaded from www.youtube.com/, and the comments from viewers seem to support my hypothesis: they express both relief and laughter. Some commentaries contain long and varied discussions on the cartoons and the crisis in 2005–6. All translations in this chapter are my own unless otherwise noted.

2. The mirror is an old theater metaphor for drama's role in society. It is, for instance, used by Shakespeare in Hamlet's speech to the actors (*Hamlet*, 3.2): "for any thing so overdone is from the purpose of playing, whose end, both at the first and now, was and is, to hold as 'twere, the mirror up to nature; to show virtue her own feature, scorn her own image, and the very age and body of the time his form and pressure."

3. A parallel function of theater and music can be observed in many countries under totalitarian rule. Czechoslovakia, for instance, developed a very rich theater tradition during Communist rule, when different types of drama expressed courageous political criticism, sometimes landing the dramatists in jail. The former president of Czechoslovakia, Václav Havel, was himself a dramatist and an insistent critic of Communism and spent long periods in jail. On 27 October 1989 he was arrested for the last time—only one month before becoming president following the Velvet Revolution. In his speech to the U.S. Congress on 21 February 1990, he reflected on his own history and spoke of "the dramatist" as an important persona.

4. This function is expressed in the finale of Henningsen's own first revue from 1929: "If you found the form a little too rude, remember that it was *serious fun*, because we really love the way forward" (Fandt De formen lidt for grov, så husk det var *alvorlig sjov*, fordi vi elsker nemlig vejen frem) (Andreasen 1981, 147–48, emphasis added).

5. Gring-Pemble and Watson 2003 stress parallel satirical features in James Finn Garner's *Politically Correct Bedtime Stories*, a work that struck a chord in the American consciousness by appealing to both opponents and supporters of political correctness.

6. See Rollins 2005 for a profound analysis of the category of presence assigned to the genre by Aristotle.

7. Burke 1969, 20–21. The concept of "consubstantiality" is also central in Sullivan 1993.

8. See http://www.vasefuglsang.dk/.

9. Freud is quoting Kuno Fischer, *Über den Witz* (Leipzig, 1889), 18.

10. Rawls 1993 characterizes this form of debate as *reasonable disagreement*.

11. Kock 2007 discusses norms of deliberative debate in similar terms.

12. The award is named after a legendary Danish actor and comedian, Dirch Passer (1926–1980), who was for several years the star of the Circus Revue. The writers, Vase and Fuglsang, were also honored as "writers of the year," partly for "Did We Learn Anything?"

13. The entire revue is available on the DVD *Cirkus revyen 2006* (http://www.star-video.dk/). "Did We Learn Anything?" can be watched on YouTube, and the Danish words are given on the writers' website, http://www.vasefuglsang.dk/.

14. *Heteroglossia* affirms the primacy of context over text. At any given time, in any given place, there will be a set of conditions that imply that a word uttered in that place and at that time will have a meaning different than it would have under any other conditions. See Bakhtin 2002, 263 and 428, and Gardiner 2004, 38.

15. On YouTube, Ulf Pilgaard's comical performance is praised to the skies, and the revue writers and cartoonist are also commended for making respectful satire using an old revue classic from the occupation. Some comments offer long and varied discussions of the cartoons and the uproar they provoked and hint at the future, which seems to support my argument.

16. The concept is often seen as synonymous with *aptum* and is described as a general rhetorical demand on the speaker: the content and form of a speech must always fit the speaker, the subject, the rhetorical situation, and the audience. In this satirical context, however, I use *decorum* in a narrower sense to characterize satire that makes fun without offending or excluding parts of the audience. This use of the term is inspired by Quintilian, who differentiates between *aptum* and *decorum*, characterizing the latter concept as "what is appropriate for the situation"—here also meaning *ethical* in relation to the speaker himself (*Institutio oratoria* 11.1.8–9). See Jørgensen 2000, 37–38.

17. The Danish weekly *Weekendavisen* and the Norwegian *Magazinet* were among the newspapers that reprinted the cartoons soon after their initial appearance. On 13 February 2008, seventeen newspapers reprinted Westergaard's original cartoon again, after some suspects had been arrested on the charge of planning to assassinate Westergaard.

18. See http://www.vasefuglsang.dk/billeder/opslagside/01.%20htmls/als.html.

19. I would like to thank my anonymous reviewer from the United States for a very careful and thorough reading of this chapter. This reviewer's comments and suggested reading opened up new perspectives on revue that I had not considered.

REFERENCES

Andersen, Øivind. 2002. *I retorikkens hage*. Oslo: Universitetsforlaget.
Andreasen, Mogens Wenzel, ed. 1981. *Politikens revyhistorie: Revyen i Danmark fra Erik Bøgh til Jesper Klein*. Copenhagen: Politikens Forlag.
Aristotle. 1996. *Retorik*. Trans. Thure Hastrup. Copenhagen: Museum Tusculanums Forlag.
Bakhtin, Mikhail M. 2002. *The Dialogic Imagination*. Austin: University of Texas Press.
Barnes, Clifford. 1989. "Vaudeville." In *The New Grove Dictionary of Music and Musicians*, 19:564–67. New York: Macmillan.
Bitzer, Lloyd F. 1968. "The Rhetorical Situation." *Philosophy and Rhetoric* 1 (1): 1–14.
Burke, Kenneth. 1969. *A Rhetoric of Motives*. Berkeley and Los Angeles: University of California Press.
Cherry, Roger D. 1998. "Ethos Versus Persona: Self-Representation in Written Discourse." *Written Communication* 15 (3): 384–410.
Dirckinck-Holmfeld, Gregers. 2006. "Endelig blev det Ulf." *Ekstra Bladet*, 21 August.
Eide, Tormod. 1990. *Retorisk leksikon*. Oslo: Universitetsforlaget.
Freud, Sigmund. 1905. *Der Witz und seine Beziehung zur Unbewussten*. Leipzig: Franz Deuticke.
———. 2002. *The Joke and Its Relation to the Unconscious*. Trans. Joyce Crick. London: Penguin Books.
Gardiner, Michael E. 2004. "Wild Publics and Grotesque Symposiums: Habermas and Bakhtin on Dialogue, Everyday Life, and the Public Sphere." *Sociological Review* 52 (1): 28–48.
Gring-Pemble, Lisa, and Martha Solomon Watson. 2003. "The Rhetorical Limits of Satire: An Analysis of James Finn Garner's *Politically Correct Bedtime Stories*." *Quarterly Journal of Speech* 89 (2): 132–53.
Hauser, Gerald A. 1999. "Aristotle on Epideictic: The Formation of Public Morality." *Rhetoric Society Quarterly* 29 (1): 5–23.
———. 2008. "The Moral Vernacular of Human Rights Discourse." *Philosophy and Rhetoric* 41 (4): 440–66.
Hoff-Clausen, Elisabeth, Christine Isager, and Lisa S. Villadsen. 2005. "Retorisk *agency*: Hvad skaber retorikken?" *Rhetorica Scandinavica* 33:56–65.
Høgel, Sten. 1987. "Fællessang på flere måder." *Modspil* 35:7–11.
Jørgensen, Charlotte. 2000. "Hvem bestemmer hvad der er god retorik? Vurderingsinstanser i normativ retorik." *Rhetorica Scandinavica* 15:34–48.
Kjærulff, Alfred, and Orla Ramsøe. 1934. *Den danske revy: Et tilbageblik over revyens historie fra 1850–1934*. Copenhagen: Arthur Jensens Forlag.
Kjeldsen, Jens. 2008. "Retoriske omstændigheder." *Rhetorica Scandinavica* 48:42–63.
Kock, Christian. 2007. "Norms of Legitimate Dissensus." *Informal Logic* 27 (2): 179–96.
Marott, Emil. 1991. *Dansk revy: 150 år dokumenteret i tekst og billeder*. Copenhagen: Borgen.
Meyer, John. 2000. "Humor as a Double-Edged Sword: Four Functions of Humor in Communication." *Communication Theory* 10:310–31.
Plenov, Leif. 2000. *Dansk revy, 1850–2000: Et uhøjtideligt tilbageblik*. Copenhagen: L & R Fakta.
Quintilian. 1920. *Institutio oratoria*. Trans. H. E. Butler. Vol. 4. Cambridge: Harvard University Press.
Rawls, John. 1996. *Political Liberalism*. New York: Columbia University Press.

Rollins, Brooke. 2005. "The Ethics of Epideictic Rhetoric: Addressing the Problem of Presence Through Derrida's Funeral Orations." *Rhetoric Society Quarterly* 35 (1): 5–23.
Sheard, Cynthia Miecznikowski. 1996. "The Public Value of Epideictic Rhetoric." *College English* 58 (7): 765–94.
Stocker, Peter. 2003. "Parodie." In *Historisches Wörterbuch der Rhetorik*, 6:637–49. Tübingen: Max Niemeyer Verlag.
Sullivan, Dale. 1993. "The Ethos of Epideictic Encounter." *Philosophy and Rhetoric* 26 (2): 113–33.

SECTION III

TOWARD BETTER DELIBERATIVE PRACTICES

The final section of the book is oriented toward the future, as it presents proposals for how to conduct or consider public deliberation in practice so that it might generate, metaphorically speaking, less heat and more light.

John Adams and Stephen West suggest that presidential primary campaign debates, as currently conducted, are not really debates but rather belong to the genre of interview-based, information-seeking journalistic discourse; they should be keyed, the authors propose, to preannounced policy issues, be moderated by nonjournalists, and follow a form of discourse more suitable to setting, vetting, and settling conflicted positions. Their chapter also recommends a revised format for presidential primary debates in which the focus is on debating rather than merely informing, and on whose plan is better or worse rather than on entertainment value or purely strategic considerations.

Like Just and Gabrielsen in chapter 14, Christian Kock looks to key notions from ancient *status* theories and proposes to generalize and integrate some of these into one coherent scheme. Perhaps most significantly, the *status legales* are seen as types of issues belonging to *status definitivus*. Rather than try to offer a new interpretation of what ancient thinkers had in mind, Kock aims to widen the applicability of ancient *status* thinking, transforming it into a tool that may help clarify, for debaters and observers alike, not only what a disagreement is essentially about but, just as important, what it is not about. Looking at current sociopolitical disagreements in this way, his chapter contends, might help debaters on opposite sides of an issue focus more on the essential points of disagreement between them—for the benefit of deliberating audiences. Broad and heated clashes between polarized factions might cool down, and observers and critics, such as argumentation scholars, rhetoricians, journalists, and educators, might acquire an additional tool for the monitoring of public argument and the teaching of rhetorical citizenship.

Georgia Warnke revisits her view, proposed in *Legitimate Differences* (1999), that even deep social disagreements may sometimes be seen as differences in *interpretation* of norms that are to a large extent shared. Rather than see ethical and political controversies as intractable, she suggests modeling such disputes on disagreements about textual interpretation; this might create fresh insights into the multiple dimensions that texts possess. Warnke illustrates this view by considering two principles, "liberty" and "respect for the sanctity of human life," as evidenced in the U.S. debate over abortion, a debate in which both sides claim allegiance to these principles, though they interpret them in quite different ways. Relying on Gadamer's account of a true second-person, dialogic "I-thou" relation, Warnke notes that when opposing interpretations meet, a dialogue might ensue that changes both subjects—since each interpretation is a contribution to an ongoing discussion rather than the last word on the matter. Warnke considers objections to the "interpretive" view of deep disagreements, such as the view that entrenched definitions are less interpretations of meaning than attempts to exercise power. But, Warnke argues, if power matters, so does interpretation: even power-driven attempts to solidify definitions work with interpretations that might still achieve an increase in mutual understanding.

16

PRESIDENTIAL PRIMARY DEBATE AS A GENRE
OF JOURNALISTIC DISCOURSE:
HOW CAN WE PUT DEBATE INTO THE DEBATES?

John Adams and Stephen West

During presidential primary election campaigns in the United States, news organizations televise what they call "debates." These so-called debates follow various formats, but most frequently journalists direct questions to panels of candidates. As the primary campaigns wear on and the number of candidates drops, the field is typically reduced to the two candidates most likely to win the primary elections. Recent election cycles have seen "losing" candidates wait longer and longer to concede and make room for emerging winners, which sometimes leads to a very extensive and prolonged series of debates. At any rate, the debates are advertised as a means of enabling the electorate to become properly informed about the candidates' perspectives on the issues raised by journalist-moderators during the debates.

Although there have been complaints about the relevance of the questions addressed to candidates at these debates, little attention has been focused on whether the events actually *are* debates. This chapter argues that they are a genre of discourse that is *called* debate but is motivated by the communicative form and culture of interview-based, information-seeking journalistic discourse, rather than the rhetorical form and culture of deliberative or argumentative discourse—that is, discourse induced by policy propositions where respondents' debatable differences are paramount, announced in advance, and persuasively settled through the genre of *academic* debate, as pursued in educational forums that stage parliamentary-style debates.[1]

Accordingly, we argue that presidential debates should be keyed to preannounced policy issues, be moderated by nonjournalists, and follow a form of discourse more suitable to setting, vetting, and settling conflicted positions.[2] As such, they would (1) dissociate debates from news broadcasts and their attendant journalistic aims, (2) clarify candidates' differences and pointedly test their deliberative capabilities, (3) afford the electorate lead time to prepare to act as judges, and (4) provide accessible public forums for deliberatively settling representative democracy's foremost question: which candidate deserves my vote?

As a practical extension of this argument, we also advocate a revised format for presidential primary debates, intended to illustrate how an improved format may more effectively position audience members as judges. The format prompts candidate responses to pertinent policy questions, thereby affording distinctions between candidates' positions and grounds for voters' decisions. It illustrates the central importance of procedural norms to public debate by deliberatively framing and rhetorically enabling well-considered citizen decision making.

Background

As a genre of discourse, debate has been practiced in Western civilization as a way of negotiating differences where certain knowledge cannot be achieved—where opinion prevails and differences of opinion are seen as legitimate. In contemporary democracies, these differences may be rhetorically negotiated by citizens who communally form decisions by weighing the pros and cons of publicly voiced arguments, achieving a level of consensus sufficient to merit a given position's acceptance by the majority.

In elections, candidates stand as bearers of conflicted positions. The differences in their positions and their conduct during debates may enable the electorate to choose the candidate who most effectively persuades the majority that his opinions represent the best judgment. His positions are therefore taken to represent the will of the majority.

In contrast to debate, an overriding interest of journalist discourse lies in seeking and communicating as much accurate information as possible. Journalists do not pit viewpoints against one another in a contest where point-counterpoint dominates the flow of genuine debate, and respondents address one another by making constructive opening arguments, rebutting each other's claims, and making constructive closing arguments. To be sure, there are so-called news programs that traffic in acrimonious exchanges between panelists, but again, play is undertaken in the guise of information seeking. Interviewees present their opinions on questions posed by the host. Procedurally and substantively, these are not debates. Rather, they often play out as quarrels dominated by interruptions and respondents talking over one another, so that none of what is said is intelligible. There is a difference between well-structured interchanges between opponents and face-to-face "flaming," which may have rhetorical appeal as entertainment—the oral counterpart of professional wrestling—but not the rhetorical efficacy of a deliberative political discourse aimed at promoting a wise decision about a contested proposition.

A number of the so-called debates between Hillary Clinton and Barack Obama in 2008 consisted of the candidates taking turns laying out their positions on issues chosen by journalist-moderators—"informing" the electorate. While this format might be a tactic in intraparty politics where positions differ only slightly, the emphasis remains on informing rather than debating. A case in point is the response to questions on immigration reform in a debate between Clinton and Obama in Austin, Texas, aired on CNN on 21 February 2008. The two candidates simply laid out their respective policy positions—neither addressed weaknesses in the other's position. In one instance, after Clinton spoke, Obama simply "added" a few things to what she had said. Both candidates listened respectfully as the other spoke, cordially nodding their heads in agreement.[3]

A few days later, in Cleveland, Ohio, the debate between Clinton and Obama was touted as sharp and pointed, but the sharpness was most evident in clashes over Obama's campaign tactics (MSNBC 2008). The distinguishing difference between the candidates was represented as strategic, as was seen in a journalist's question about a change in Clinton's tone after the Texas debate, in which her tone had been cordial, and her harsh attacks on Obama in the forty-eight hours following the debate.

After showing a clip of Clinton complimenting Obama at the Texas debate, followed by one in which she harshly took Obama to task for his campaign tactics ("Shame on you, Barack Obama!"), NBC's Brian Williams asked Clinton to explain the striking difference in tone. Williams's question seemed to assume that the change in tone was strategic—that Clinton's harsh accusations were a way of showing her toughness and "difference" from Obama along dimensions of trustworthiness; at stake was not any specific policy position but Clinton's righteous indignation over issues of fact. She was outraged, she responded, because Obama's campaign had misrepresented her position on universal health care. While the question of health care thus did arise, the difference in Clinton's tone in the two video clips concerned the issue of character as much as it did policy—Clinton's implicit point being that ad hominem arguments ("to the person") were justified if in fact Obama had misrepresented her policy in his campaign flyers.

Perhaps the alleged misrepresentation afforded Obama a platform for rebutting Clinton's position on health care (and on Nafta, too), but the thrust of the exchange was the ethics of the Obama campaign's representation of her position, not which candidate's health-care plan was better. To her credit, Clinton tried to present a key feature of her health-care policy, claiming that Obama's plan would leave out large numbers of people whereas her plan would not. It was an attempt to represent the facts accurately and lambaste Obama for misrepresenting them. Before Obama was given a chance to respond, however, Williams abruptly raised another instance of underhanded campaigning, this time the Clinton campaign's alleged circulation of photographs of Obama in traditional African garb. Apparently, this was the moderator's way of trying to balance the scales on the issue of character: had Clinton endorsed the unethical tactic of portraying Obama's African roots to play to the racism and xenophobia of sectors of the U.S. electorate? Obama refused to take the bait, claiming that he took Clinton at her word when she denied circulating the pictures; and he returned the conversation to what he considered differences between the two health-care plans. The candidates went back and forth a number of times on who was telling the truth and who was lying, before moving on to another issue.

Clearly, it was Williams's (and apparently Clinton's) intention to stir things up and thereby make news. To be sure, the candidates' "answers" may have helped determine the facts and who was to blame for what, but they did nothing to determine the relative merits of the two health-care plans. One must ask, "What was this phase of the debate about?" Clearly, it was about differences in policy, but the policies debated were more pointedly related to the campaigns' illicit tactics and the deeper issue of character. The give-and-take displayed the candidates' willingness to accuse each other of impropriety. The implicit question in the exchange was "Which candidate is more trustworthy?" As the exchange unfolded, the correct answer was probably "neither." The moderator thus prompted an exchange that brought the "debate" to a fairly unedifying place—making it more of a quarrel than a debate.

Now, perhaps these back-and-forth "attacks" were to the point. After all, most people would probably prefer an honest president. However, debates should not be dominated by accusations and counteraccusations prompted by moderators—where the questions are accusations and the responses are *apologias* followed by more accusations, rather than pointed rebuttals of policy statements. In our view, one major reason why this exchange took place was that the moderator had no sense of what kind of issue he was using his queries to settle—an issue of fact? An issue of value? An editorial commentary on candidate stridency? The same kind of baiting that is displayed nightly on evening news "talk programs," where candidates' surrogates take off the gloves and deliver low blows on behalf of their candidates?

The overall point is that there may be a place for the display of character differences, but presidential primary debates should not pit candidates against one another in contests over who's the biggest liar. These character contests, however important they may be to some, cannot be settled without recourse to some means of independently checking the facts. Moreover, we believe that voters do genuinely desire elevated political discourse. In the dispute over whether Obama's campaign misrepresented Clinton's healthcare plan, Clinton might at least have produced the offending pamphlet. The picture of Obama in African garb was shown. Why not the Obama campaign document as well? Instead of informing us on both sides of an issue, the press presents accusations and counteraccusations. This tactic, we would argue, is actually harmful to the process of debate and deliberation; instead of having enough information to weigh the issues, the voter is given only one side of the story.

The Format: Proceeding to Debate

While academic, parliamentary-style debate typically involves teams, the format we propose pits individual candidates against one another within a structure that parallels academic debate's interest in vetting a proposition through conflicting constructive position statements and focused rebuttals.[4] While it is time-consuming, this procedure will also work with debates between more than two candidates, as in the opening stages of U.S. presidential primary campaigns. We contend that journalists, instead of asking questions that seek information, or making reactive probes during the debates, should set up a series of policy debates focused on key propositions known beforehand.[5] Thus our format requires that the debates be moderated by nonjournalists, so as to dissociate the event from the ethos of broadcast news. The moderator would not have a substantive role in the debate. Rather, she or he would be responsible for ensuring that the debate simply followed the agreed-upon procedure (outlined below).

The advance publication of the debate proposition would allow the candidates and the electorate, respectively, to prepare their arguments effectively and to listen critically. It would give candidates an opportunity to construct well-considered opening and closing arguments and, moreover, to anticipate opponents' lines of argument in preparation for rebuttal. The electorate would get an opportunity to do research—to be informed not *by* the debate but *before* the debate, so that the truthfulness of candidates' statements and the wisdom and practicality of their positions could be considered more critically during and after the debate. Our only caveat would be that candidates and their surrogates remain silent on the proposition in the one-week run-up to the debate and allow a nonpartisan sorting out of possible positions and arguments for or against the proposition. Journalists could play a crucial educational role in helping voters build an information base related to the proposition and in critically engaging the upcoming debate.

Many will consider it unrealistic to expect voters and journalists to take on this level of responsibility. Nevertheless, running the debates in this way would, at a minimum, provide an opportunity for the development of a more competent electorate—one prepared to decide, not simply to seek information by observing the debates. We anticipate that the preparation phase could actually be a politically exciting time. With the proposition "out there," people could begin to develop their own arguments and rebuttals—they might actually debate with one another. Community groups and educational organizations could hold predebate debates to establish facts and test different perspectives on the proposition. In addition, a website could be created to give interested voters opportunities to learn more about debate itself, the forming of arguments and their critical uptake, and the history and culture of debate—as it intersects with an interest in citizenship and being a competent voter in a democratic society. This might also enable voters to "go central" in their expectations for good reasons, rather than relying on peripheral cues like hairstyles or the physical attractiveness of candidates as the grounds for their decisions.[6]

Accordingly, our format consists of a four-step procedure. Step 1: announcement of the proposition to be debated one week before the scheduled debate.[7] This would give voters time to research the proposition themselves, establish the facts, form their own well-considered positions, and become thoroughly informed about the candidates' positions before the debate, perhaps even debating the proposition among themselves. This is where the journalistic principle of informing the public could play its most useful role. News programs might facilitate everybody's preparation for the debate by staging predebate programming designed to offer pertinent information by objectively discussing, and speculating on, candidates' positions and the reasons for them. The debate propositions should be developed by representatives of the candidates so that they will engender an appropriate level of interest, that is, ensure that the propositions are relevant to the voters' interests and will promote debate. The remaining three steps constitute the debate. Step 2: candidates' constructive speeches; step 3: candidates' rebuttals (and possibly points of information);[8] step 4: candidates' closing speeches.

Our plan also requires that journalists' commentaries on the debates be withheld for two hours after each debate, giving voters time to reflect on and discuss the debates without journalistic interference. Of course, if this option cannot be instituted, as in "Debate Watch Overview" (CPD 2004a), viewers always have the option of turning off the TV immediately after the debate.

Further, the speaking order would be randomly determined by a computer program for each round of debates, in contrast to the current system, where, in the interest of maximizing ratings, news programs give preference to more "popular" candidates.[9] Under this system, if there were ten candidates, there would be ten opportunities for each candidate to meet the aims of each turn in the debate, for a total of thirty turns. If candidates were limited to a total of ten minutes each, the entire debate would take one hundred minutes for a ten-candidate field. As the field got smaller, the candidates would have longer turns—each candidate would have a maximum of forty-five minutes to speak. Regardless of timing, candidates would be required to allocate half their time to constructive material, with a quarter of the time reserved for rebuttal and a quarter for closing statements. There would be a single moderator for each debate to ensure that candidates stayed on point and did not exceed the time limits. For example, the moderator would ensure that the eighth candidate in line delivered a constructive speech on her or his first turn—not a rejoinder to another candidate's constructive speech delivered on her or his first turn. By setting strict rules about timing, the moderator could minimize off-topic discussion and keep candidates on track. Under the current system, candidates are free to talk about anything they wish, which only confuses the audience they are trying to persuade. In any event, the entire debate would be one hundred minutes long.[10]

Some may object that with a large candidate field, the brevity of the first few rounds of debate would not really enable a substantive engagement of the issues. It is important to note, however, that speakers always deal with time constraints, and that one of the abilities we demand of effective speakers is that they make the most of the time afforded to them, whether it is one minute or one hour. There is no ideal amount of time to give to speakers. It is our hope that staging ten debates on ten propositions during the primaries would position candidates to make their case and voters to make their decisions. Voters would have ample opportunity to judge the candidates' arguments on a set of salient issues. The debate series would enable candidates to develop their positions more fully—especially if they expect that the voters will be coming to the debates already informed, and that the debates are designed to help them to determine which candidate's position is best after critically evaluating all the arguments in each debate.

Conclusion

At present, the Commission on Presidential Debates (CPD) sponsors the U.S. presidential election debates. These debates focus on domestic and foreign policy, with one town-hall-style debate between them (where uncommitted voters ask the questions). It is gratifying to see that the CPD's new format gets close to approximating a debate, even to the point of including a question phase not unlike the points of information allowed in academic, parliamentary-style debate, in which candidates may question each other and the moderator sets "eight ten-minute issue segments" related to each debate's general theme (see CPD 2007). Nevertheless, the language on the CPD's website emphasizes the "educational value" of the debates: "Each of those debates will be divided into 8 ten-minute issue segments; the moderator will introduce each segment with an issue on which each candidate will comment, after which the moderator will facilitate further discussion of the issue, including direct exchange between the candidates, for the balance of that segment. Time will be reserved for closing statements by each of the candidates in each debate" (CPD 2007).

Kirk and Fahrenkopf, co-chairs of the CPD, note that this format is aimed at increasing the educational value of the general election debates. "Our mission is to promote voter education. The public deserves to hear and see the candidates offer and defend their positions on the critical issues facing our country in the most thoughtful and in-depth manner that television time constraints will allow. Loosening the constraints within the ninety minutes debate will allow for more serious examination of complicated questions. This change will also open the possibility of the moderator inviting candidates to question each other. We want voters to benefit from as full an explanation of a topic as possible, and we feel certain that the candidates will welcome this change for the same reason" (CPD 2007).

While the format is certainly commensurate with the CPD's mission and intends to provide an appropriate level of engagement of complex questions, it sets up the event as a discussion, not a debate. The differences between a discussion and a debate may be subtle, but they are significant. A discussion implies that the candidates have not yet formed their own positions—that they may change their minds during the conversation. In addition, it uses "explanation" as the term to characterize the candidates' intention as they talk about their positions. We would rather use the word "justify" to characterize what the candidates are supposed to do in their comments. However, the overarching interest in providing voters with the opportunity "to hear and see the candidates offer and defend their positions on the critical issues facing our country in the most thoughtful and in-depth manner that television time constraints will allow" is laudable and clearly anchors at least a part of their intention in putting the candidates in the position of arguing their different points of view. That said, we do not believe that "loosening the constraints" of the format or having the candidates sit at a table together will make the event more effective. Again, we want to see a formal debate in which candidates stand and face one another, with a specified number of turns and with clear expectations of what each turn will accomplish. Giving the moderator the opportunity to probe candidate responses, as in the CPD format, puts the debate into a journalistic context similar to that of an interview, where the discourses may be viewed as informative and the moderator's role is to ensure that listeners *understand* what is being said, or the moderator may give a candidate a chance to restate or refashion a statement in response to probing. We want to see candidates stand and deliver—to speak without the aid and comfort of a moderator—and thus to allow voters to evaluate the arguments for and against a given proposal, rather than merely gather information about where candidates stand on a given issue. Again, we want to emphasize the importance of putting a debatable proposition before the electorate in advance. There is no doubt that the CPD, by giving voters a general idea of what's going to be discussed, gives them an opportunity to consider the broad themes of domestic and foreign policy before the event, but it does not give them direction to focus specifically on a particular issue, to examine existing, well-publicized candidate positions, or to evaluate them in detail before the event, all of which is necessary if voters are to be optimally prepared to listen critically.

Presidential debates are a good thing—a *very* good thing. For better or worse, no matter how they are staged, they *do* play an important role in the rhetorical pursuit of deeply democratic aims by publicly displaying candidate differences and their discursive engagement. Nevertheless, no matter how well intentioned the debates may be, there is always room for improvement. We believe that having more debates, and better-structured debates, with propositions announced in advance, will make the debates more interesting and motivate voters to participate more enthusiastically and pointedly in the event as well-informed citizens—as deciders rather than as consumers of information.

Finally, we must admit that the operative constraints on televised (or mediated) debates are daunting. As the CPD points out, the event is structured to deal with "television time constraints" (CPD 2007). Rhetorically speaking, time is always a consideration. We wish to see our candidates deal effectively with the time constraints—to make strategic choices about what needs to be said and how best to say it within the time they've been allotted. We see the time constraint as a rhetorical challenge that invites candidates to make the most of what they have—to project their practical wisdom by using a limited resource in a way that is to their advantage. We fear that the real disadvantage of the time constraint is that ninety minutes of presidential debating may be beyond the scope of an average person's attention span. We'll see.

In the end, it will be interesting to see how many people watch the presidential election debates, and watch them through to the end. From the CPD's records we know, for the years when data were available, approximately how many people viewed or listened to debates (CPD 2004b). However, we do not know at what point in the debates the samples were taken. Were they taken at the start of the event, the middle, near the end? Regardless of when viewership samples are drawn, with the advent of streaming media on the Internet and its capacity for asynchronous viewing, it may be difficult to determine how many people will actually view the debates as they are happening.

More than a hundred thousand people turned out to listen to Barack Obama speak in public during his July 2008 visit to Germany. How many Americans will tune in to the debates when the Democratic and Republican candidates are on the scene? Why will they tune in? When will they tune out? We believe that giving people a proposition to mull over, research, and talk about before a debate will create a level of suspense that will motivate more people to tune in and *stay* tuned in because of the effort they've already put into preparation. If our proposed format were to be adopted, we believe that we would be able to answer these crucial questions in the affirmative: will voters be able to use the debates as sites of critically informed decision making? Will they be real debates?

NOTES

1. By "academic debate" we mean a structured debate held as part of a competition at the college level. Many debate formats are followed in academic debate; see, for example, the Wikipedia article "British Parliamentary Debate." We emphasize the procedural aspects of academic debate, as (more or less) pursued in parliamentary-style debate—with some modifications relevant to the aims of campaign debates.

2. A history of debate formats for presidential debates is posted at the Commission on Presidential Debates website (http://www.debates.org/) under "Debate History."

3. See CNN 2008. We limit our focus to Clinton and Obama owing to the protracted and deeply divided two-person contest. They provide a good example of a one-on-one intraparty candidate debate.

4. We may consider allowing points of information during rebuttals, where the target of a rebuttal may be to raise an objection or point out a flaw in the speaker's remarks. To some extent, including this option would parallel a feature of the new format for presidential debates hosted by the Commission on Presidential Debates, in which candidates are allowed to ask follow-up questions of one another if permitted by the moderator. See CPD 2007 for the debate format.

5. Making propositions known beforehand marks another difference between our proposal and parliamentary-style debates, where the propositions are unknown until the debate, at which time they are announced and debaters are given a specified amount of time to prepare their opening speeches. This also differs from academic debate, where a single proposition is debated for an entire academic year, and it is often the quantity of arguments, not their quality, that seems to be a determining factor in judging them.

6. The terms "central" and "peripheral" are drawn from the "elaboration likelihood model" of persuasion (Petty and Cacioppo 1986), which suggests that if people have a strong interest in a decision and see themselves as competent to decide, they will demand information and rational, argument-driven discourse to facilitate their decision making. In the opposite case, they depend more on peripheral cues—speaker appearance, sound bites, physical setting of the discourse, etc. While it is certainly true that some decisions are best made on the basis of peripheral cues, one would like to think that voting for one's president would demand a more complex discursive route to decision. Sadly, this is not the case, as campaign advertisements clearly attest. However, our proposal might help people take the central route, as they are given a proposition beforehand and the opportunity to conduct research, frame their own arguments, make explicit what their reasons are, and debate the proposition among themselves.

7. For example: "Resolved, that the United States should institute a universal healthcare plan." Even if all candidates agreed on this point, they would be compelled to offer the *best* plan.

8. If acknowledged, an opponent might ask the current speaker a rebuttal question, using no more than fifteen seconds. The moderator could determine whether to permit the question. Points of information could allow viewers to see how candidates spontaneously handle unanticipated queries and criticisms, providing an additional basis on which to judge their qualifications and the substantive import and relevance of responses to points of information.

9. This would eliminate the possibility of candidates complaining about always getting the first question, or always having to speak first.

10. This might need to be reconsidered. We would like to stage two or three mock debates to pilot-test our format. One possible problem is that a large field of candidates

would dictate very short opening speeches if the debate was limited to one hundred minutes. This might actually lead observers to use peripheral cues, as more in-depth arguments would be out of the question.

REFERENCES

"British Parliamentary Debate." 2008. Wikipedia, 11 September. http://en.wikipedia.org/wiki/British_Parliamentary_Style (accessed 10 October 2008).
CNN. 2008. "Obama, Clinton Agree to Disagree." CNNPolitics.com, 22 February. http://edition.cnn.com/2008/POLITICS/02/21/debate.main/index.html#cnnSTCVideo (accessed 5 August 2008).
Commission on Presidential Debates (CPD). 2004a. "Debate Watch Overview." http://www.debates.org/index.php?page=debatewatch-overview (accessed 25 January 2012).
———. 2004b. "1858 Debates–2008 Debates." http://www.debates.org/index.php?page=debate-history (accessed 25 January 2012).
———. 2007. "Commission on Presidential Debates Announces Sites, Dates, Formats, and Candidate Selection Criteria for 2008 General Election." 19 November. http://www.debates.org/index.php?mact=News,cntnt01,detail,0&cntnt01articleid=9&cntnt01origid=27&cntnt01detailtemplate=newspage&cntnt01returnid=80 (accessed 25 January 2012).
MSNBC. 2008. "Obama, Clinton Debate in Ohio." MSNBC TV, 26 February. http://www.msnbc.msn.com/id/21134540/vp/23361919#23361919 (accessed 5 August 2008).
Petty, R. E., and J. T. Cacioppo. 1986. *Communication and Persuasion: Central and Peripheral Routes to Attitude Change.* New York: Springer.

17
A TOOL FOR RHETORICAL CITIZENSHIP:
GENERALIZING THE *STATUS* SYSTEM

Christian Kock

In this chapter I suggest how to generalize and integrate ancient *status* theories into one coherent scheme. I submit that an approach to public argument that integrates principles from *status* thinking could be an important element in what we may call "rhetorical citizenship." I do not pretend to offer a new and more accurate interpretation of what certain ancient thinkers wrote or had in mind but aim to present a tool that can help present-day debaters, as well as observers in deliberative debates, narrow down the range of a dispute and identify the reasons that may be decisive for winning adherence. By deliberative debates I mean all kinds of social disagreement over action.

When debaters disagree, each debater has a strategic interest in knowing the precise reasons why opponents differ, because arguing against those reasons is probably the best way to change one's opponents' minds. The deliberating observer, looking for enlightenment on an issue, also has an interest in knowing the exact reasons why the debaters differ, because these are probably just the ones that will best help him decide for himself.

In public debates, however, such a precise understanding of where standpoints differ, and why, is often lacking—in debaters as well as observers. Debaters routinely misrepresent and radicalize their opponents' standpoints. They often neglect or distort the reasons underlying these standpoints, or attribute altogether imaginary reasons to their opponents. Debaters impute base motives to their opponents that the opponents have not expressed and never would express. Frequently, debaters assume that anyone who disagrees with them on a specific point has a coherent cluster of views, all equally repugnant, on everything. Thus debaters may see any opponent as representing one hostile, monolithic block. From there the step is short to personality slurs. Partisanship and polarization rule. Debaters see their own standpoint as righteous; divergent positions are seen not only as divergent but as opposite, usually in a dichotomous sense: there are only these two positions, nothing in between, no neutral ground—a situation well analyzed by Govier (2007). There is a characteristic *widening* of the front zone where the two sides clash, and a concomitant entrenchment of positions.

Litigation lawyers understand the need to focus their argument and present a pointed, "coordinative" argumentation—to use the terminology of Snoeck Henkemans (2000)—rather than a set of unconnected reasons. A study by Jørgensen, Rørbech, and Kock (1994, 1998) of televised political debates, where representative audiences voted on issues before and after each debate, showed the coordinative strategy as superior: "single-ground" debaters won eleven times and lost three (binomial test: $p = .0574$); "multiple-ground" debaters lost twelve times and won only twice ($p = .0130$).

Theories of *stasis* (or *status*) were developed in antiquity to help forensic debaters focus on the point(s) at the heart of a dispute. Central to these theories were the *status rationales*, the conjectural, the definitional, and the qualitative, which correspond to the questions: What are the facts? How are the facts to be categorized? What particular circumstances characterize them?

The *status rationales* problematize the facts at issue, but another component of *status* thinking was the *status legales*, questions problematizing the "laws" or rules by which the facts were to be judged. In most versions of the theory there are four *status legales*. In all, the debater argues that there is no clear one-to-one match between a norm or law and the fact at issue. A debater may resort to *ratiocinatio/collectio* when no existing norm applies to the fact; instead, he draws an inference by analogy from an existing norm about something else. A second legal *status* is *ambiguum:* a norm may be vague or ambiguous, so it might apply to the fact or it might not; we might say that the formulation of the norm is too abstract for us to be certain whether the fact is covered by it or not. A third legal *status* is *scriptum et voluntas*. We may see this as the converse case: here there is also a norm, but its overt meaning is too specific. Taken literally, it might not cover the fact, but the argument is then that it should be understood in a broader sense, according not to the letter but to the spirit. The fourth legal *status* is *leges contrariae;* this means that there are two or more norms that may both apply but that argue for different conclusions.

A leading modern legal theorist, Robert Alexy, in explaining why a judicial verdict will not always follow deductively from a correlation of facts and rules, mentions essentially the same four conditions: the vagueness of legal language, norm conflicts, lack of a relevant norm, and a contradiction between letter and intent (1983, 17); this adds credence to the claim that the four *status legales* usefully articulate problems inherent in attempts to correlate rules and facts.

The order in which I present the *status legales* above is not arbitrary. First, the argument is that there are *no* applicable norms at hand. In the second and the third cases, *one* norm might apply, but it is either too abstract or too specific. In the fourth case, *more norms than one* apply, supporting opposite conclusions, and the issue is one of priority.

Other theorists in modern times have attempted to broaden the relevance of ancient *status* thinking to cover practical, political, or deliberative debate (most recently Hoppmann); others have developed theories of argument or communication that have much in common with *status* thinking (e.g., Brockriede and Ehninger 1960; Benoit 1995; Marsh 2006). I too argue that the usefulness of *status* theory is not limited to legal argument, but I further contend that it should be applied to practical argument in the broadest sense, and (unlike Hoppmann 2008 and others) not just from the defender's point of view but from the viewpoints of any of the debaters involved, as well as audiences, observers, and critics. Like many of these theorists, I would stress the analogy between practical and legal argument. The difference is mainly that in legal argument most of the norms are formal rules written down explicitly in statutes, etc., recognized by all involved as valid; in practical argument, such as political debate, they are mostly vague, informal, unwritten, and not necessarily recognized as valid by all, or as valid to the same degree. Moreover, in practical argument the norms are most often not explicitly cited, and they are much more heterogeneous than legal rules. We might call them "multidimensional" (Kock 2003, 2006): some are prudential, perhaps exclusively concerned with economy; others are ethical, concerned with moral or honorable conduct or notions of fairness or justice; still others are formal and legal, for example, considerations as to whether a given policy is constitutional or in accordance with international law. The *status* system offers a typology of potential problems in correlating facts and norms, and as such it is just as useful in political and ethical debates as it is in legal argument.

Besides merging these two domains, I propose another merger that has not, to my knowledge, been suggested by previous theorists: the *status legales*, I suggest, may be seen as subdivisions of the *status* of definition. In the *status* of definition, we discuss how a fact can be subsumed under a rule or norm. The *status legales* are about the same kind of discussion, but they approach it from the other end, applying norms to facts. They are useful because they specify the problems that this application may engender. Many *status* theories in the rhetorical tradition are curiously underspecified on this: while the qualitative *status* is hierarchically subdivided at several levels, the *status* of definition often gets short shrift (e.g., in Hermogenes). My point is that disputes about correlating facts and norms are innumerable and varied, in particular when we include deliberative disputes; but the four usual *status legales* provide a model for how to distinguish and specify such disputes.

Ancient *status* theorists, notably Hermogenes, also included lists of so-called practical *status*, basically naming the main warrants that could be invoked in political reasoning, such as legality, justice, advantage, feasibility, honor, consequence; the earliest such list is to be found in the anonymous *Rhetorica ad Alexandrum*. But the items on the list are the same "multidimensional" norms that clash in political debates today. For example, one debater recommends a policy as advantageous, while another opposes it as dishonorable. Such clashes, common in politics, ethics, and everyday life, parallel the *leges contrariae* in legal argument.

So the three central moves in my proposed reformulation of *status* thinking are these: (1) generalizing the legal concept of laws/rules into a broader concept of regulatory norms, applicable also to political, ethical, or personal issues; (2) seeing the four *status legales* as specifications of the *status* of definition; and (3) seeing the "practical" issues as specifications of the heterogeneous norms that clash in political and other practical debates.

The complete, reformulated *status* system for practical debates is given in the following table. I have identified the cells in the table with letters and numbers, supplied terms from ancient *status* theories, and given examples of the different types of disagreement. The columns represent *status* types and their subtypes according to my reinterpretation. The rows include (1) the traditional classical terms for the three *status rationales*, which I retain as a ground structure; (2) the exact nature of the issues debated under each of the three main *status;* (3) references to a set of concepts used in works of "informal logic" (such as, e.g., Govier 2009) that identify three aspects of an argument that, in my view, correspond closely to the three *status rationales;* (4) subtypes (discussed below) of the three main *status* types; (5) rhetorical characterizations of these subtypes; (6) some explanatory comments; and (7) specific examples of issues or debates belonging under the subtypes, most of which are discussed below.

Table 17.1 *Status* system for practical debates

1	Classical terms	1. *Status conjecturae*—Conjecture	2. *Status finitionis*—Definition (the *status legales* are inserted here: C4–F4)	
2	What are we debating?	What are the <u>facts</u>?	What <u>norms</u> apply to the facts? (Legal norms [statutes], ethical norms, ideological norms, value concepts, *doxai*, "common sense," formal and informal *topoi*)	
3	Counterpart in argumentation theory	Truth/acceptability	Relevance	
4	Classical subtypes		Assimilation	Ambiguity
			Ratiocinatio	*Ambiguum*
5	Rhetorical problems and strategies	Give proof, increase probability	*No* norms clearly apply	*One* disputable (vague) norm applies
			Argument from either *consequences* or *analogy*	*Interpretation* of norm to either include or exclude facts
6	Comments	What is the case about, independent of value concepts and policy preferences?	Mostly about novel phenomena	Many debates in politics and ethics belong here (cf. Warnke)
7	Examples	WMDs in Iraq? Man-made global warming?	Cloning, file sharing, stem cell research	Abortion
	A	B	C	D

(continues)

Table 17.1 *Status* system for practical debates *(continued)*

1	Classical terms	2. *Status finitionis*—Definition (the *status legales* are inserted here: C4–F4)		3. *Status qualitatis*—Quality	
2	What are we debating?			What <u>specific features and circumstances of the facts</u> should be considered?	
3	Counterpart in argumentation theory			Weight, strength, "sufficiency," "good grounds" (= *gradual and quantitative* considerations)	
4	Classical subtypes	"Letter and intent"	Conflict of law	Counterplea	Counterstatement
		Scriptum et voluntas	*Contrariae leges*	*Antilepsis*	*Antistasis*
5	Rhetorical problems and strategies	*One* disputable (strict) norm applies	*Two or more* contradictory norms apply	Norm recognized, but breach justified by extraordinary circumstances	Norm recognized but regretfully disregarded
		Distinction between *literal* and *intended* meaning	Arguments to show that norms on own side have *more relevance and/or weight* than those on other side	"It is just"	"It is necessary"
6	Comments	Often a last resort in argument	Many debates in politics and practical ethics belong here "Conductive reasoning" (cf. Wellman, Govier) "Value pluralism" (cf. Berlin et al.) "Incommensurability" (cf. Raz et al.) "Normative metaconsensus" (cf. Dryzek) may apply Types of norms invoked include: – legality – justice – advantage – feasibility – honor – consequence	All these resemble, or are even identical with, those issues where contradictory norms apply (F5); the difference, if any, is that in the qualitative status (as we are here), one argues for an exception to the strict application of a certain general norm, the relevance of which is not contested	
7	Examples	Anti-abolitionist: "Black slaves not intended by 'all men created equal'"; Nobel Peace Prize given to non-peace causes	Invasion of Iraq: spreading democracy, deposing a tyrant, self-defense vs. legality, human and material costs, resulting chaos Muhammad cartoons: defense of free speech internationally vs. gratuitous offense to minority locally	Brutus killing Caesar; liquidation of informers under German occupation; "whistle blowing"	Torture, "extraordinary rendition," "illegal combatants"
	A	E	F	G	H

1	Classical terms	3. *Status qualitatis*—Quality			
2	What are we debating?				
3	Counterpart in argumentation theory				
4	Classical subtypes	Counteraccusation	Transference	Mitigation	Mortification
		Antenklema	*Metastasis*	*Syngnome*	
5	Rhetorical problems and strategies	Norm recognized, breach blamed on object of breach	Norm recognized, breach blamed on external party	Norm recognized, breach attenuated	Norm recognized, breach deplored, forgiveness asked
		"They asked for it"	"They made us do it"	"Mitigating circumstances"	"I apologize"
6	Comments				
7	Examples	"They broke all the rules, so we respond in kind"	"We were under orders"	Victim gets back at tormentor	"I misled people, including even my wife. I deeply regret that."
	A	I	J	K	L

All of this is intended as a typology of contemporary social and political disagreements. If public debaters saw disagreements in terms like these, they might be more likely to avoid the characteristic widening of fronts and less likely to impute imaginary standpoints, policies, reasons, intentions, and personality traits to one another. Arguers as well as observers might become more clearly aware of the norms that the case for each side is based on, and they would have more reason to explicate those norms and scrutinize them. Educators might help bring a better understanding of argumentation into school curricula, including the understanding that this chapter aims for of how disputes may be narrowed down to their essentials, rather than being seen as all-out ideological clashes. Journalists might be less prone to portray such disputes as dramatic clashes and more willing to lay out the essential points of disagreement in current social debates. And academics might do more to explicate the nature and norms of deliberative debate and to analyze and criticize ongoing debates for what they are.

I should stress that in proposing the "system" I lay out in this chapter, I am particularly addressing academics and educators in rhetoric, argumentation, critical thinking, and related fields. I would readily agree that the breakdown of types of issues that I am proposing here is probably too complicated or cumbersome for use by the general public—not so much because "ordinary people" are unable to understand it but because they would hardly be sufficiently patient with such close or detailed analysis. Ancient *status* theory, admittedly, was designed for academics. Another circumstance that might raise doubts regarding the practical applicability of the system proposed here is that the purpose of *status* theory was to facilitate invention, that is, to help these academic professionals develop effective arguments against opponents' views, rather than to find points of convergence and common ground. So it is true that neither ordinary citizens nor political candidates or other partisan debaters can be expected immediately to take this system to heart. However, the potential practical relevance that I do see in it resides, at least initially, in its usefulness for educators, academics, and other critics and commentators of public debate in determining when such debates are broader, more polarized, and less focused than they might be on what the disagreement is essentially about. Such observers might then explain this core of the controversy to the public audience, and, while pointing out what it is really about, they might make clear what it is *not* really about. An awareness of this would foster, I submit, a wish in some members of the public to hear more about the core of the issue and less about the rest of the controversy, including false versions of opponents' views, personality slurs, etc. Some audience members (voters) might even be more persuaded by debaters who focus on core issues, mainly because they would be of more help to undecided voters trying to make up their minds. Conversely, some voters might be inclined to turn away from candidates and debaters who fail to so focus. Thus, eventually, public candidates and debaters themselves might find that an increased awareness of what the core issues are, and what they are not, might in fact be to their own benefit, even strategically. This is the main reasoning on which I suggest that the "system" proposed here, and the awareness it aims to foster, might be useful and socially beneficial.

Sometimes, for instance, such an increased awareness might make clear that a dispute is about an issue where no preexisting norm indisputably applies (cell C5). That understanding might stimulate both parties to formulate a relevant norm, perhaps by considering consequences of the act or policy at issue. Such discussions might be particularly productive in new domains like digital technology. For example, web-based file sharing is a novel and disputed practice in which debaters tend to invoke old norms to little avail: on one side, norms relating to theft and piracy, on the opposite side, freedom of information, etc. A more constructive debate might start from the insight that no existing norm applies indisputably because the practice is indeed novel. A similar type of consideration might apply to both novel and anticipated phenomena in fields like biotechnology, for example, stem cell research, human cloning, and others.

In other cases, reflection on a given dispute might lead arguers and/or observers to the insight that both sides actually agree on the norms or values invoked and that their disagreement is about interpretation; in other words, they disagree on whether the issue in question can meaningfully be subsumed under a norm they both support per se (cell D5). This is the sort of "interpretive" dispute that Georgia Warnke (1999) has analyzed, using the abortion debate in the United States as her prime example. Both sides in that debate are undoubtedly "pro-life," seeing the preservation of human life as an important norm, but they may disagree as to whether the removal of a new human fetus, or fertilized egg, constitutes the taking of a human life. Similarly, both sides are probably "pro-choice," insofar as they see letting people choose instead of having their choices dictated as a good thing per se, particularly when a person's own body is concerned; but they have an interpretive disagreement about whether a woman's decision to have a new fetus removed from her body can be subsumed under this norm.

Practical disagreements corresponding to the *status* known as *scriptum et voluntas* (cell E5) are less common; as mentioned, the *scriptum* is often lacking in practical argument, most of the norms invoked being unwritten (and implicit). However, an important historical example might be the abolition debate in the United States, in light of the famous statement in the Declaration of Independence about all men being created equal and possessing, among their unalienable rights, that of liberty; Stephen Douglas, in the 1858 debate with Lincoln at Jonesboro, made a clear *scriptum et voluntas* argument by declaring, "Thomas Jefferson meant only English people when he said, 'All men are created equal and all men should be free.'" A recent example occurred in Norway, whose parliament awards the Nobel Peace Prize; a critic accused the Nobel committee of having awarded the prize to other causes than peace, but the counterargument was that the wider interpretation under which, for example, Al Gore and the Intergovernmental Panel on Climate Change won it were "in the spirit" of Nobel's will.

More common—in fact, perhaps the standard case in practical argument—are disagreements where both debaters can actually be shown to recognize the norms invoked by both sides, and even each other's interpretations of these norms. For example, two debaters disagreeing on abortion might agree that the removal of even a new fetus does indeed constitute the taking of a human life, but at the same time they might also agree that denying a woman the right to have such a fetus removed does indeed constitute a denial of her free choice concerning her own body and is thus a bad thing. In that case, we have a dispute of the kind we find in cell F5: there is agreement that *two* norms clearly apply, and there is no disagreement on the interpretation of them, but these norms point to contradictory conclusions. The dispute is now whether one of them can be said to be *more* relevant to the facts than the other, and especially whether the argument relying on one of these norms can be made to appear *weightier or stronger* than the other. So we are talking about perceived *degrees* of weight or strength. This is the practical counterpart of the *status* of *leges contrariae*. We may think of all those cases, not just in politics but also in our personal lives, where two or more normative concepts are used as warrants on opposite sides of an issue. To cite a political example, some people supported the invasion of Iraq in 2003 with reference to (a) defense against terrorism, (b) dissemination of democracy, and (c) the need to overturn a tyrannical regime; but others opposed it with reference to (d) its illegality under international law, (e) the loss in human and material terms that would follow, and (f) the political chaos that would most probably result. All of these considerations were in some sense at least potentially relevant to the issue. This plurality of relevant contradictory considerations made the issue a case of what Trudy Govier and others, following Carl Wellman (1971), have called "conductive reasoning," that is, a situation where it is necessary somehow to weigh the pros and cons. Such situations also exemplify the condition that, since Isaiah Berlin, has been called "value pluralism": there may be several norms that a given culture, and even a given individual, finds relevant to a certain issue but that nevertheless speak for opposite decisions. Other philosophers (see, e.g., Raz 1998) have emphasized that such norms may be "incommensurable"; that is, it cannot be determined in an objective way whether one or the other norm should have priority in a given case. This, I would suggest, has to do with the fact that the set of relevant norms is multidimensional. In legal argument the *status* of *leges contrariae* makes us aware of such situations, but if we widen the scope of *status* thinking to social and political disagreements we are reminded that similar contradictions are also common there, in fact much more so. Arguably, there can be no real deliberation about an issue without an understanding that relevant considerations on both sides must somehow be weighed against one another.

Another concept that may be relevant in such situations is that of *normative metaconsensus*, as defined by the political theorists John Dryzek and Simon Niemeyer, that is, "agreement on recognition of the legitimacy of a value, though not extending to agreement on which of two or more values ought to receive priority in a given decision" (2006, 639); the term "normative metaconsensus" may be said to correspond to Rescher's "axiological consensus" (1993, 130).

As is readily seen, the "practical issues" (e.g., legality, justice, advantage, feasibility, honor, consequence, as cited in cell F6) illustrate the multidimensionality of the open set of norms that may be invoked on both sides in debates on contentious political issues, as well as some of the different categories of norms constituting this multidimensionality. There is no need to insist that the list just cited, or any other, is exhaustive; the main point is that the set of applicable, relevant norms is multidimensional. From this follows incommensurability, so that there is no objective or philosophically compelling way to decide the issue: although a given, relevant norm speaks for one line of action, another relevant norm usually speaks for the opposite line of action. Thus debaters invoking a certain norm should not lightly assume that "their" norm alone decides the matter; instead, they have an obligation to engage in conductive reasoning and compare the reasons on the two sides, making a case for why their own side outweighs the other. Also, a debater should not lightly accuse her opponents of rejecting or betraying the values or norms that she herself relies on; as we have seen, often there is normative metaconsensus between opponents, even though they do not seem to recognize this themselves. Thus both supporters and opponents of the Iraq invasion would probably agree on values such as spreading democracy and respecting the law; their dispute concerns the *priority* in the specific case of one norm over the other.

Often, normative metaconsensus probably also exists between two opponents in the abortion controversy: "life" and "choice" are probably values that both recognize, but their dispute may center on priorities or on interpretation—the dispute stems from the fact that both of these key concepts are ambiguous or vague.

The examples so far all illustrate disagreements corresponding to the four traditional *status legales* (columns C–F in the table). But the other *status* types are equally relevant for identifying types of social disagreement and demarcating their true scope. The conjectural *status* may remind practical debaters that many disagreements are, and should be limited to, questions of *what is the case*, and they should be debated as such, independently of values and policy preferences. Unfortunately, in political debates this separation is often suspended. For example, in the controversy over the Iraq War there was a tendency for advocates of activist, strike-first foreign policy to believe, *for that reason*, that Saddam Hussein had WMDs; liberal war skeptics, by contrast, were inclined to believe, *for that reason*, that Saddam did not. Similarly, in the debate on global warming, adherents of conservative economic policies and unrestrained growth may be inclined to believe, *for that reason*, that there is no anthropogenic global warming calling for strong measures, while environmentalists and people skeptical of economic growth might, *for that reason*, tend to accept the reality of man-made global warming. But no one's beliefs about factual issues like the presence of WMDs in Iraq or the reality and magnitude of man-made global warming should be induced by the values or policy preferences they endorse; moreover, debaters should not lightly suggest that their opponents' beliefs on such issues are thus induced.

As for the third main *status* category, that of "quality," notice first that only a gradual transition, rather than a sharp boundary, separates it from the *status* of definition. In particular, our fourth subtype of the definitional status (F5, corresponding to the *contrariae leges*), is very similar to what Hermogenes calls *antilepsis* (translated by Heath 1995 as "counterplea"), for which our counterpart is G5. The difference is that whereas in F5 cases the argument concerns the balancing of two contradictory norms, in G5 the argument is that extraordinary, perhaps unforeseeable, circumstances call for a suspension of, or an exception to, a norm whose relevance is fully recognized.

Examples of "counterplea" might be Brutus's defense for murdering Caesar; or there is the issue of people in occupied countries during World War II who liquidated fellow civilians for acting as informers to the Nazis. In Denmark, for example, about four hundred civilians were killed by members of the resistance, against whom no legal steps were subsequently taken. Other examples might include the case of "whistle-blowers," where, for example, intelligence officials divulge information they consider vital to public safety; they thus break a law they have pledged to observe, yet their conscience tells them that owing to extraordinary circumstances this breach is just and necessary. Arguably, such cases might also be described as clashes of two contradictory norms—one formal and another vague, informal one.

From cell G5 the passage through cells H5–K5 is gradual. In all of these cells, the issue is the breach of a norm whose relevance is not contested. As we move toward K5, there is less that speaks for an outright exception to that norm; whereas in G5 the argument is whether the breach represents justice of a different order, in H5 it is merely necessary, although regrettable. Issues belonging here might be the use of torture, "extraordinary rendition," or the indeterminate detention of "illegal combatants" so as to prevent acts of terrorism. Few argue that these practices represent justice in the traditional sense, but many argue that owing to exceptional circumstances they are necessary. The last practice also has a tinge of I5 in it: for example, we sometimes hear its advocates arguing that Guantanamo detainees, being "the worst of the worst," have "broken all the rules" and thus "deserve" whatever treatment they get. In J5 no form of justification is claimed—the breach is merely presented as inevitable because forced by a superior power. In K5 neither justification nor inevitability is claimed, only mitigating circumstances that lessen the gravity of the breach. In L5 no mitigating circumstances remain except one: the remorseful apology of the accused. In the nature of these cases, however, these latter two types of argument are more or less endemic to defense rhetoric and are uncommon in practical argument as such.

All of this exemplifies an important general benefit that may follow from seeing social disagreements in terms of this generalized *status* typology: it may help opponents in public debate, *as well as* their audience, the deliberating public, to realize not just what exactly separates the two sides but also what does not. Their dispute is narrowed down but not necessarily resolved. On the contrary: the dispute might become more intense because the argumentative resources of the opposite sides might be more sharply focused on the exact disagreement that does separate them, for example, the interpretation of the concept of "life." The full argumentative resources of the debaters are then concentrated on that issue rather than being diffusely distributed across a much wider target area that assumes speculative motives and character traits of opponents, etc. Such a focused debate would be likely to generate more insight, more enlightenment, and thus probably more informed attitude formation (and change) in debaters as well as observers.

It should be emphasized again that in proposing this application of *status* thinking to social, ethical, and political disputes, I do not expect to see consensus emerge on vexed and complex issues like the ones I have mentioned. The belief that rational argumentative discourse will necessarily lead to consensus, or toward it, has been championed by Habermas in philosophy and by "pragma-dialectics" in argumentation theory (van Eemeren and Grootendorst 2004). However, as Rawls (1989, 1993) and others have maintained, there are good reasons why people may never agree on controversial topics where values are involved, thus Rawls's term "reasonable disagreement." Among these reasons is precisely the fact that people may, even within the bounds of absolute reasonableness, interpret or prioritize values differently.

Nevertheless, although consensus cannot be expected to emerge, in some cases it actually might. But if it does not, the acknowledgment of normative metaconsensus is also an achievement. For one thing, it might reveal that a dispute is probably not an all-out clash between two monolithic blocs that utterly reject each other's values. The polarization and trench warfare we often see in public debates would lose some of its fuel. Also, debaters on both sides might find better and more persuasive arguments for their views. The *status* system in antiquity had this kind of purpose. The reason why it might work in this way is that it makes it easier for debaters, as well as observers, to focus on the decisive point of disagreement. If a debater could change her opponent's mind about that reason, then and only then she might change the opponent's mind about the whole issue. The situation is similar for undecided observers: a debater is most likely to make them take her side if she focuses on the decisive point of disagreement and makes them accept her case on that precise point as the stronger one.

As a final illustration, let us consider the debate about the Muhammad cartoons published by the Danish newspaper *Jyllands-Posten* in 2005. In Denmark, most people supporting the right-leaning government, but also some left-leaning academics and intellectuals not known as government supporters, saw the publication of the cartoons as a praiseworthy act in support of freedom of speech, and in defiance of threats and violent acts calling for its suppression. Other debaters, however, mostly on the left but also some from the business and diplomatic communities, argued that the publication of the cartoons was a harmful, gratuitous gesture. The controversy reached its peak in February 2006, when Prime Minister Fogh Rasmussen used the words of Christ from Matthew 25:32, turning them against writers and others who had failed to defend the cartoons: "as far as I am concerned, the sheep have been separated from the goats" (Larsen 2006). In October 2008 the debate was revived in another leading newspaper, *Politiken*, in an exchange between its editor, Tøger Seidenfaden, a leading critic of the cartoons, and Frederik Stjernfelt, a well-known academic who supported them (Mogensen 2008). Seidenfaden repeated that the cartoons were an act of gratuitous harassment of a minority not deserving such treatment, namely, all those peaceful Muslims in Denmark who seek integration but who might be hurt and alienated by such an act. Stjernfelt, a self-declared Enlightenment thinker, objected that the cartoons were part of a global fight for freedom of speech, argued against special rights for cultural groups, and rebuked Seidenfaden for wearing "blinkers" and seeing only "the tiny Danish corner" of the issue while ignoring the global aspects.

As an observer, one might wonder why two highly intelligent and articulate debaters did not see more clearly the simultaneous relevance of two different norms, both of which they undoubtedly both supported. In other words, there probably was normative metaconsensus between them, but they did not realize it. Stjernfelt persisted in assuming that opposing the cartoons meant betraying the principle of freedom of speech, and he appeared insensitive to the relevance of the "harassment" argument; Seidenfaden, on the other hand, appeared similarly insensitive to the global context, in which some Muslim forces did in fact want to curtail freedom of speech by legislation or violence, and he was unwilling to concede that the cartoons might relevantly be seen in that context.

In an interview with another Danish daily, the celebrated German writer Hans-Magnus Enzensberger took a clear stand but at the same time showed an awareness of the contradiction: by one set of norms that he endorsed he would criticize the cartoons, while by another norm that he endorsed even more strongly, he would still support them: "I defend those malevolent, idiotic, dreadful, distasteful Muhammad cartoons. Should those responsible for them put up with murderous threats? No, no, no" (Kassebeer 2009).

Debaters as well as observers might have been reminded by a *status*-based approach to social disagreements that the debate was not between believers in one supreme principle and believers in another supreme principle; it was about which of two principles, both recognized by both sides, should be prioritized in the specific case.

More generally, I suggest that democracies like ours need a greater awareness among debaters, audiences, the news media, and educators that social disputes should not be seen as all-out clashes, as they may often be narrowed down to focused disagreements on more specific points—in which either side might have a better chance of persuading people unsympathetic to their positions. I suggest that the insights contained in ancient *status* theory as reinterpreted here can help bring about such awareness. We probably all want to avoid the plight of the two lovers in Matthew Arnold's famous poem "Dover Beach," who feel that

> we are here as on a darkling plain
> Swept with confused alarms of struggle and flight,
> Where ignorant armies clash by night.

REFERENCES

Alexy, Robert. 1983. *Theorie der juristischen Argumentation: Die Theorie des rationalen Diskurses als Theorie der juristischen Begründung*. Frankfurt am Main: Suhrkamp.
Aristotle. 1937. *Rhetorica ad Alexandrum*. Trans. Harris Rackham. Books 22–38 of *Problems*, vol. 16 of *The Works of Aristotle Translated into English Under the Editorship of W. D. Ross*, trans. Walter Stanley Hett. Loeb Classical Library 317. Cambridge: Harvard University Press.
Benoit, William L. 1995. *Accounts, Excuses, and Apologies: A Theory of Image Restoration Strategies*. Albany: State University of New York Press, 1995.
Berlin, Isaiah. 1998. "The Pursuit of the Ideal." In Berlin, *The Proper Study of Mankind: An Anthology of Essays*, ed. Henry Hardy and Roger Hausheer, 1–16. New York: Farrar, Straus and Giroux. (Orig. pub. 1988.)
Braet, Antoine C. 1987. "The Classical Doctrine of Status and the Rhetorical Theory of Argumentation." *Philosophy and Rhetoric* 20:79–93.
Brockriede, Wayne, and Douglas Ehninger. 1960. "Toulmin on Argument: An Interpretation and Application." *Quarterly Journal of Speech* 46:44–53.
Dryzek, John S., and Simon J. Niemeyer. 2006. "Reconciling Pluralism and Consensus as Political Ideals." *American Journal of Political Science* 50:634–49.
Eemeren, Frans H. van, and Rob Grootendorst. 2004. *A Systematic Theory of Argumentation: The Pragma-Dialectical Approach*. Cambridge: Cambridge University Press.
Elster, Jon. 1986. "The Market and the Forum." In *Foundations of Social Choice Theory*, ed. Jon Elster and Aanund Hylland, 103–22. Cambridge: Cambridge University Press.
Govier, Trudy. 2007. "Two Is a Small Number: False Dichotomies Revisited." In *Dissensus and the Search for Common Ground*, ed. Hans V. Hansen, Christopher W. Tindale, J. Anthony Blair, and Ralph H. Johnson. CD-ROM. Windsor, Ont.: OSSA.
———. 2009. *A Practical Study of Argument*. 7th ed. Belmont, Calif.: Wadsworth.
Habermas, Jürgen. 1996. *Between Facts and Norms: Contributions to a Discourse Theory of Law and Democracy*. Trans. William Rehg. Cambridge: Polity Press. Originally published in German as *Faktizität und Geltung: Beiträge zur Diskurstheorie des Rechts und des demokratischen Rechtsstaats* (Frankfurt am Main: Suhrkamp, 1992).

Heath, Malcolm. 1995. *Hermogenes on Issues: Strategies of Argument in Later Greek Rhetoric.* Oxford: Clarendon Press.

Hohmann, Hans. 1989. "The Dynamics of Stasis: Classical Rhetorical Theory and Modern Legal Argumentation." *American Journal of Jurisprudence* 34:171–97.

———. 2001. "Stasis." In *Encyclopedia of Rhetoric*, ed. Thomas O. Sloane, 741–45. New York: Oxford University Press.

Hoppmann, Michael. 2008. *Argumentative Verteidigung: Grundlegung zu einer modernen Statuslehre.* Neue Rhetorik, vol. 5. Berlin: Weidler Buchverlag.

Jørgensen, Charlotte, Lone Rørbech, and Christian Kock. 1994. *Retorik der flytter stemmer: Hvordan man overbeviser i offentlig debat.* Copenhagen: Gyldendal.

———. 1998. "Rhetoric That Shifts Votes: A Large-Scale Exploratory Study of Persuasion in Issue-Oriented Public Debates." *Political Communication* 15:283–99.

Kassebeer, Søren. 2009. "Ytringsfriheden må for enhver pris forsvares." *Berlingske Tidende* (Copenhagen), 18 February.

Kock, Christian. 2003. "Multidimensionality and Non-Deductiveness in Deliberative Argumentation." In *Anyone Who Has a View: Theoretical Contributions to the Study of Argumentation*, ed. Frans H. van Eemeren, J. Anthony Blair, Charles A. Willard, and A. Francisca Snoeck Henkemans, 157–71. Dordrecht: Kluwer Academic Publishers.

———. 2006. "Multiple Warrants in Practical Reasoning." In *Arguing on the Toulmin Model: New Essays on Argument Analysis and Evaluation*, ed. David Hitchcock and Bart Verheij, 247–59. Dordrecht: Springer.

Larsen, Jesper. 2006. "Verden ifølge Fogh: Interview, Anders Fogh Rasmussen." *Berlingske Tidende* (Copenhagen), 26 February.

Marsh, Charles. 2006. "The Syllogism of Apologia: Rhetorical Stasis Theory and Crisis Communication." *Public Relations Review* 32:41–46.

Mogensen, Lars Trier. 2008. "Interview: Frihed for Frederik såvel som for Tøger." *Politiken* (Copenhagen), 4 October.

Rawls, John. 1989. "The Domain of the Political and Overlapping Consensus." *New York University Law Review* 64:233–55.

———. 1993. *Political Liberalism.* New York: Columbia University Press.

Raz, Joseph. 1998. "Incommensurability and Agency." In *Incommensurability, Incomparability, and Practical Reason*, ed. Ruth Chang, 110–28. Cambridge: Harvard University Press.

Rescher, Nicholas. 1993. *Pluralism: Against the Demand for Consensus.* Oxford: Clarendon Press.

Ryan, H. R. 1982. "Kategoria and Apologia: On Their Rhetorical Criticism as a Speech Set." *Quarterly Journal of Speech* 68:254–61.

Snoeck Henkemans, Francisca. 2000. "State-of-the-Art: The Structure of Argumentation." *Argumentation* 14:447–73.

Warnke, Georgia. 1999. *Legitimate Differences.* Berkeley and Los Angeles: University of California Press.

Wellman, Carl. 1971. *Challenge and Response: Justification in Ethics.* Carbondale: Southern Illinois University Press.

18

INTERPRETIVE DEBATES REVISITED

Georgia Warnke

In modern multicultural democracies, individuals and groups can share a set of norms, principles, and practices without necessarily agreeing on their meaning. These norms and principles are inscribed in our written or unwritten constitutions, our ways of life, our ethical practices, and our political assumptions. Principles of liberty and equality are not simply beliefs in the heads of individuals but norms underwriting practices of voting, transferring power, selection of job candidates, and the like. To be sure, the principles may be honored more in the breach; nonetheless, they make up the substance and texture of our public life. At the same time, in most modern democracies we grow up within different cultural traditions, possess different heritages, priorities, and values, and take different histories, experiences, and commitments seriously. For these reasons we often understand the meaning of both our common norms and principles and our shared practices differently from one another. Indeed, it is often when we try to apply our norms and principles to our practices that our differences come to light. For example, if the U.S. Constitution enshrines the principle of equality, Americans can still differ on whether equality means equal political rights or substantively equal access to economic opportunity.

We often think that differences over the meaning of our norms, principles, and practices necessarily lead to intractable ethical controversies over our concrete policies. Certainly, current disputes over immigration, affirmative action, and marriage between same-sex partners seem to confirm this idea. Nevertheless, in this chapter I want to contest it. I take up two principles, liberty and respect for the sanctity of individual human life, and I look at one controversy, the controversy in the United States over abortion. My aim is to investigate an alternative to intractable controversy, one that models our ethical and political differences on our differences over texts, and models our ethical and political disputes on our literary discussions. Both texts and the text analogues of norms, principles, and practices involve the interpretation of meaning. In the literary domain, interpreters assume that they will understand the meaning of a given text differently from one another, and they use their differences to gain insight into the multiple dimensions the text possesses. In the case of texts, we embrace our differences and develop them in order to further the literary traditions of which we are a part. In this chapter, I argue that we should also embrace our different understandings of our norms, principles, and practices and develop them in order to further the ethical and political traditions of which we are a part. I also want to defend these debates against the criticism that they are naïve about power.

Abortion Debates and Literary Discussions

At least part of the American debate over abortion can be seen as centering on the question of how we are to interpret the principle of liberty and the principle of respect for the sanctity of individual human life as they are embedded in the ethical and political culture of the modern West. In general, these principles reflect a commitment to individual freedom and bodily integrity. But what does this commitment entail? For many of those who take the so-called pro-choice position in the abortion debate, the principle of liberty means that individuals have inviolable rights to make their own decisions about their private lives. Government agencies cannot tell them where to live, what career to pursue, or with whom to fall in love. Likewise, no public entity can force them to bear a child. Instead, as long as a fetus is part of a woman's body and dependent upon it for survival, the decision to carry a pregnancy to term is a private and personal one. In contrast, for many of those who take the so-called pro-life position in the abortion debate, the principle of liberty means that individuals are responsible for their own lives and for the decisions they make and have made. Liberty does not mean that one can make a decision and then refuse to accept responsibility for it. Thus, while for some in the pro-life movement, the principle of liberty suggests the permissibility of abortion in the case of rape or incest, it does not suggest its permissibility simply because an individual has unprotected sex or changes her mind.[1]

With regard to the principle of respect for the sanctity of human life, many who take the pro-life position assume that it means respect for biological human life (Dworkin 1993, 82). Human life is inviolable as a natural bodily fact, no matter where it exists or what its circumstances are. Indeed, it is pure hubris for anyone to decide that fetal malformations, for example, or individual handicaps mean that a particular human life is not worth living or saving. Moreover, insofar as a fetus is a human life, the circumstance that it is located inside a womb has no significance for the question of whether it has an intrinsic worth for which respect is due. If the life of a one-day-old infant is sacred and inviolable, then so too is the life of a three-week-old fetus. For many who take the pro-choice position, however, the principle of respect for the sanctity of human life signifies respect for human capacities for self-creation and meaning making (Dworkin 1993, 84). Human life is precious and inviolable not as a mere biological fact but because human beings build lives for themselves and have significant relationships to other human beings. They love and are loved. Hence the moral weight of aborting a pregnancy must be weighed against the moral weight of gestating a fetus when it endangers inviolable human life conceived of in these terms—in other words, when it endangers the future prospects or physical or psychological health of the mother, or when the life that might be created is one that can only be unbearably painful for the child and its family.

How should we think about these differences in the way different groups can understand the same principles? On the one hand, those who take opposed positions on the permissibility of abortion claim allegiance to the same principles of liberty and respect for the sanctity of life. On the other hand, in relation to the question of abortion, they interpret the meaning of these principles in quite different ways. Is it possible, then, to resolve the abortion debate? How does it help that the two sides in the controversy adhere to shared norms? The answer I want to consider here takes its start from literary discussions in which we share a common text but can nevertheless understand it in different ways. The different ways we can understand a shared text may stem from the different historical and cultural traditions to which we belong, or from the different theoretical frameworks we bring to the text, or from the different concerns and different reasons we have for reading it. Thus, if we read Nabokov's *Lolita* from a perspective influenced by life in the Islamic Republic of Iran, we may read it very differently than if we read from a perspective of life in the United States (Nafisi 2003, 37). However, we relish such differences in textual understanding. We read literary criticism and popular reviews of books because we are interested in the way other readers understand the books we have read or may read. Indeed, we read the books themselves because we want to discover how their authors understand a subject in which we take an interest, and because we think the way they understand it might help us to develop our own understanding of it. As interpreters we can come to the same texts and to the subjects they address from very different vantage points and with very different interests, experiences, and concerns. Although we may therefore differ from one another in our understanding, we take these differences to be an advantage. They can help us to see aspects of a text we failed to see previously, or to understand an issue or topic in a way that we previously could not.

Hans-Georg Gadamer provides a way of clarifying this structure of textual understanding in his examination of three possible forms of relation between what he calls an "I" and a "thou." The first I-thou relation takes an objectivistic form, or what we might call a third-person approach: in exchanges with another, the "I" takes an observational attitude and withdraws him- or herself from any interactive engagement in the exchange. Rather, the "I" surveys the "thou" and views his or her statements as reactions to stimuli rather than as claims that do or do not have merit or that require a substantive response. As a mode of textual interpretation, a third-person approach avoids dealing with the content of a text and tries instead to figure out what motivates it. Objectivistic interpreters might focus on the psychological causes behind textual claims or themes, or the text's place in the writer's biography, or its historical and cultural influences. What objectivist interpreters do not do, however, is engage the text in its substantive context. The concern is not what its point or points actually are or how they may illuminate the subject matter the text considers. Rather, the text is interesting only to the extent that it helps us to explain the individual writer and/or his or her circumstances, points us to cultural or historical influences, and the like. As Gadamer puts this point, "We understand the other person in the same way that we understand any other typical event in our experiential field—i.e., he is predictable" (358).

The second I-thou relation on which Gadamer comments takes an empathetic form, or what we might call a first-person approach, in which one insists that one knows what someone else is experiencing as well as or better than he or she knows it him- or herself. If an objectivistic approach relies on detached and indeed silent observation, an empathetic approach tries to speak for the other. Here, the "I" claims to know how the "thou" feels or to experience just what the "thou" is experiencing. As a mode of textual interpretation, first-person interpretation tries to reexperience the flow of artistic, literary, or critical production as it happened. To understand a text is to understand it as its author understands or understood it. The result, according to Gadamer, is that the other "loses the immediacy with which it makes its claim" and is simply "pre-empted" (359). Instead of listening to or engaging the substance of a text, a first-person stance claims already to know it from the inside. The result mirrors the result of objectivistic interpretation: a failure to take up textual claims or themes as claims or themes that do or do not have merit. For objectivistic interpretation, these claims or themes are simply causal effects; for empathetic interpretation, they reflect knowledge or experience with which the interpreter is already familiar. In each case, the relation between I and thou is a relation between a subject and an object.

In contrast, the central feature of the structure of the third I-thou relation is that it is a relation between two subjects. In this sort of relation, we take a second-person and dialogic stance toward another subject, experiencing the other "as a Thou" and letting him or her "really say something to us" (Gadamer 1992, 361). We engage the "thou" as a partner in dialogue, one who raises claims, evinces emotions, or expresses ideas that we neither simply observe nor identify as already our own. Instead, we take them up in their substance, as content that we consider, want to develop further, of which we approve or disapprove or with which we agree or disagree. The result is a widening or transformation of our own perspective. Indeed, crucial to Gadamer's account of a second-person, dialogic I-thou relation is the extent to which dialogue changes both subjects. In engaging with and taking up each other's claims, ideas, and expressions, we follow the logic of the subject matter they concern and come to understand it differently, whether we agree with each other or not. Gadamer refers to Socratic dialogue to make this point: "The maieutic productivity of the Socratic dialogue . . . is certainly directed toward the people who are the partners in dialogue, but it is concerned merely with the opinions they express, the immanent logic of the subject matter that is unfolded in the dialogue. What emerges in its truth is the logic, which is neither mine nor yours" (368). Indeed, even if we maintain our original outlook, we do so now with a different view of both its vulnerabilities and its strengths.

Gadamer takes textual interpretation to be similarly dialogic. We read a given text because we are interested in its subject matter and think it might be edifying. In reading and trying to understand, we engage with its content and adjudicate its validity and significance. Gadamer himself focuses on the relation of present interpreters to texts of the past, but his model conceives of text and interpreter as interlocutors. Whether the relation is between interpreter and historical text, interpreter and present text, or two interpreters about a text, the structure is that of a dialogue in which the object of attention is the substantive content of what the other or the text says. Of course, the text cannot speak for itself, so the interpreter must articulate both his or her own claims and those of the text. Nevertheless, Gadamer points out that in reading a text we necessarily assume that the points it makes or the sentiments it expresses are not our own but those of the text. Otherwise, we have no reason to read the text in the first place.

Moreover, he insists, if we read books because we are interested in what they say about their subject matter, we pursue our interest by posing queries or problems to them. Implicitly or explicitly, we want to know something we do not yet know and are open to the answers the text provides. Gadamer claims that all genuine questions are open questions, questions to which one does not know the answer in advance. On the one hand, open questions are focused; they spring from a lack of certainty or a concern about a particular area. In asking a question, the good questioner discloses his or her presuppositions and the context in which what is still unknown to him or her exists. On the other hand, open questions are unbounded insofar as they allow for unexpected answers. Questioners who ask open questions leave themselves vulnerable to any answer their interlocutor returns. Lawyers never ask a question in court to which they do not know the answer. Yet the same does not hold for genuine questions. We ask them because we do not know, but want to know, the answer. In making this point Gadamer returns to Socratic dialogue:

> To someone who engages in dialogue only to prove himself right and not to gain insight, asking questions will seem easier than answering them. In fact, however, people who think they know better cannot even ask the right questions. In order to be able to ask, one must want to know, and that means knowing that one does not know. In the comic confusion between question and answer, knowledge and ignorance that Plato describes, there is a profound recognition of the priority of the question in all knowledge and discourse that really reveals something of an object. Discourse that is intended to reveal something requires that that thing be broken open by the question. (363)

To take an I-thou relation to texts and their interpretation, then, is to ask questions of them. These questions are our questions. They stem from our concerns and our literary and historical horizons or contexts. These theoretical and historical contexts can differ from those of the text in which we are interested and from the theoretical frameworks and historical horizons from which others have approached, or will approach, the text. For this reason, our dialogue with the text is a particular one, and so too is its conclusion. Because it is part of history, because it takes up certain concerns and relates the text to particular touchstones, and because history continues, any particular interpretation of a text is a contribution to an ongoing discussion rather than the last word on the matter. Indeed, interpretations and discussions of the meaning of particular texts end only when those texts are no longer of interest, not when an interpreter issues a final statement on what they mean. Questions and answers about our texts and their meaning thus compose an ongoing literary tradition. Such traditions persist because interlocutors continue to take an interest in the texts and interpretations at their base and because their dialogues continue to produce new dimensions of meaning.

Before returning to the debate over abortion, it is worth pointing to one last feature of Gadamer's account of interpretation. Although he depicts the three possible I-thou relations as equally available options, the third, as it turns out, serves as the foundation for the other two. The first I-thou relation is a relation between a subject and an object. In its literary guise, the relation entails that the interpreter is interested primarily in causal questions. The issue is what caused the author to say what she or he said or what influences the text itself exerted on other texts. The second I-thou relation is a relation between a subject and him- or herself. In its literary guise, the relation means that the interpreter is interested primarily in re-creating the process of creation. The attempt is to transpose oneself into the mind of the author and reexperience his or her experiences as he or she experienced them. Nevertheless, in both objectivistic and empathetic cases, the interpreter must understand what the text says. If the interpreter is concerned with explaining its causes and effects, he or she must understand its content in some way or other in order to trace the causes and effects of this particular content. Likewise, if the interpreter is concerned with re-creating the process of creation, he or she must understand what is created in order to pick out the relevant processes from all the impulses, thoughts, and intentions the author might have had. Understanding the meaning of what is said or written, then, is the prerequisite to getting at the causes, effects, and process of creation relevant to it.

Interpretation in the Abortion Debate

Suppose that we apply Gadamer's account of these three I-thou relations to the debate over abortion. The first, the objectivist or third-person relation, surely leads to some of the stridency of the debate in its current form. It leads some pro-choice advocates to concentrate on tracing the claims of those who are pro-life back to traditional lifestyles and sexist views about women, while leading some pro-life advocates to concentrate on tracing the claims of those who are pro-choice back to libertine lifestyles and prejudices against religion. Both of these foci can generate insults that the two sides hurl at one another. Thus National Right to Life (www.nrlc.org/) refers to those who take a pro-choice position as "the abortion industry," while NARAL Pro-Choice America (www.naral.org/) consistently links pro-life positions with an extreme right-wing agenda. Both equate the other with Hitler and both claim that the other is interested not in ethics but in power. In sum, they focus not on the substance of the other position but only on the motivation for holding it.

The second I-thou relation, the empathetic or first-person relation, is perhaps more productive, since at least it leads each side to express sympathy rather than contempt for the other. Some pro-life literature thus claims to know how circumstances and/or significant others can pressure a woman to seek an abortion. Such literature also claims to know and to offer help with the regret and sorrow experienced by women who have had abortions (see, e.g., the website of the Elliot Institute, www.afterabortion.org/). Likewise, some pro-choice literature claims to know how guilty a woman can feel for the position in which she finds herself. This literature also claims to know the ongoing pain of giving children up for adoption (see, e.g., the website of Adoption.com, http://poetry.adoption.com/poems). Yet neither side in fact listens to the other. Pro-choice advocates counter claims about postabortion syndrome with statistics indicating that women rarely regret the decision to have an abortion, while pro-life advocates counter claims about the burdens and pain of unwanted children or adoption with testimonials on the joy of unexpected pregnancies. With such sympathy or empathy, as Gadamer points out, the possibility of dialogue is foreclosed. As it turns out, each position on abortion feels only its own emotions and talks only to itself.

In contrast, the third I-thou relation, a second-person or genuinely dialogic relation, tries neither to objectify the other position nor to identify with it. Instead, in the debate over abortion each position takes the other seriously as a possibly legitimate interpretation of shared principles. The starting point here is the structure of interpretation and an acknowledgment that any position on abortion, including one's own, issues from a particular set of concerns, historical influences, and cultural allegiances that reflects, at best, only one perspective on the meanings of the principles of liberty and respect for the sanctity of life. Even if plausible or legitimate, no interpretation can exhaust either principle's scope, if only because the principles have a past and future history. The way they have been applied in the past influences how we understand them now, just as the way we understand them and the issues to which we apply them will influence future interpretations. Principles, like texts, become part of an ongoing tradition with ever-changing concerns and issues, and thus ever-different lights to shed on its content. Just as changes in our circumstances, historical vistas, concerns, and preoccupations mean that we can always find new meanings in a text, changes in our circumstances, historical vistas, concerns, and preoccupations mean that we will never exhaust the possible meanings of our principles.

Yet, to the extent that the various positions on abortion recognize that each is only an interpretation, while perhaps a plausible one, each position asks questions of the others. If, for example, one position claims that respect for the sanctity of life means respect for biological life, we might ask what the limits of such respect are. Should we respect the biological life of mass murderers and thus condemn the death penalty as well? In order to preserve biological life, should we demand better communal support for health care, more solutions to world poverty, and better defenses against genocide? Equally, if the pro-choice position claims that respect for the sanctity of life includes respect for the lives human beings create for themselves, what are the limits of this respect? If that respect is meant to tell against giving birth to a life that is destined to be unbearably painful, who decides what is unbearable? Can we decide for others when a life is not worth living? Which sorts of psychological burdens on a mother constitute good enough reasons to abort? Likewise with regard to interpretations of the principle of liberty: on the one hand, we can ask whether liberty does not require bodily integrity and, on the other, when liberty becomes license.

As in the case of literary discussions, when we ask questions of interlocutors in an interpretive debate over abortion, we do so not because we suppose that we have better answers but because we are interested in the subject and in developing our own view of it. We ask questions because we want to discover answers. We do not suppose that we can find the one right answer to the question of what our principles mean. Instead, the dialogue in which we are engaged leads to more questions and more answers. With respect to the principle of the sanctity of life, how are biology and sociability related to each other? Do we want a world of designer babies in which all so-called defects are eliminated from the start? Do we want a world in which we force families to raise children they have neither the skill nor the desire nor the economic wherewithal to raise? With respect to the principle of liberty, are there limits on the freedom of individuals to lead the lives they want, and how are freedom and responsibility related? As in the case of our discussions of literary texts, questions and answers open up new dimensions of our principles and splinter off into different conversations that reveal yet more new dimensions.

To be sure, this account of interpretive debate raises the question of whether we are ever to expect solutions to the issues it encompasses. Are we to suppose that the dispute over the permissibility of abortion resembles a tree endlessly growing new branches and ending only if and when people simply lose interest in it, as they sometimes lose interest in particular texts? Perhaps, conversely, we might argue that ethical and political issues differ from literary texts precisely because we must resolve them; we need to resolve our differences over the permissibility of the ethical and political practices we already possess and decide what to do about emerging issues. In other words, because literary interpretations do not have a relation to practice, can we not argue that the analogy between literary discussions and political and ethical debates simply fails to hold?

In answering this question, we should note how little action and decision have accomplished in resolving the debate over abortion. The debate only intensified after the first U.S. Supreme Court decision in *Roe v. Wade*, and it has not subsided either with subsequent decisions or with a series of violent and nonviolent demonstrations. To the contrary, victories on the part of one position on abortion merely galvanize the other side.

Theoretical solutions have been no more successful. As an example, take the solution that Ronald Dworkin offers (1993, 157). Dworkin thinks that inasmuch as both pro-life and pro-choice positions enshrine respect for the sanctity of human life, we must conceive of both as religious positions. In the United States, we recognize the constitutional principle that each person has an equal right to the free exercise of his or her religion. Thus, according to Dworkin, those for whom respect for the sanctity of human life requires terminating a particular pregnancy have the right to practice their religion and terminate the pregnancy; equally, those for whom respect for the sanctity of human life requires not terminating a particular pregnancy have the right to practice their religion and not terminate it. Despite the symmetry of this solution, it fails to indicate why we cannot understand the principle of the free exercise of religion differently, particularly since we understand respect for the sanctity of human life differently. To this extent, Dworkin's solution merely replaces the debate over abortion with a debate over what does and does not constitute a religion, and this debate presumably has its own set of opposing positions.

Neither judicial decisions nor philosophical solutions thus succeed in putting an end to the abortion controversy. Since it insists on continuing, we might consider whether our best option is not to decide along which set of I-thou relations we want it to proceed. The third, dialogic I-thou relation has at least two virtues in this regard. First, it potentially eliminates the nastiness and ferocity that currently mark the debate in the United States. As long as we acknowledge that both our own and the other position are, at best, plausible interpretations of shared principles, the meanings of which have more than one dimension, we can acknowledge our differences without attributing them to stupidity or spite. Instead, we can focus on the substance of the differences and consider what we might be able to learn from them. Moreover, the upshot of this mutual learning can be a decrease in the extent of the disagreement between the two sides. The second virtue of dialogic interpretive debate is that, even without a decrease in the range of disagreement, violence is precluded. Our history has taught us that we do not need to bomb or kill those who understand books differently than we do. We can likewise learn not to bomb or kill those who understand shared principles differently. Instead, we can ask what we might accomplish by engaging with those differences and using them to strengthen our understandings of the complexity of our principles.

However, at least two additional objections arise with regard to the idea of dialogic I-thou interpretive debate. The first concerns the way in which interpretations become entrenched as definitions, and the second concerns the entanglement of such definitions with issues of power.

Critique of Interpretation

Interpretive traditions are part of what it means to live as a historical being. In both the literary and the ethical-political domain, they hand down to us ideas about what is and is not important and how to think about our lives, our worlds, and our futures. Indeed, the orientation that traditions provide first makes understanding possible. They supply a context or framework within which to place that which we are trying to understand, without which we would have no means of relating to it at all. Only because we are familiar with novels, for example, can we approach a particular text as a novel. Only because we are familiar with religion can we consider whether positions on respect for the sanctity of life qualify as religious. Insofar as we belong to a tradition that includes particular forms of religion and to a Western literary tradition that includes novels, the world is opened up to us in a particular way and allows us to grasp its meanings for us.

Nevertheless, because the ways we understand are rooted in the interpretive traditions to which we belong, our world already contains interpreted meanings for us before we can adjudicate those meanings or consider whether they make sense. We already understand the world and its meanings in certain ways before we begin to question or reflect on these ways. Terence Hawkes makes this point with regard to Shakespeare's *Hamlet*, a play we already know before we read it for the first time because the world we live in is already influenced by it. We read other theatrical and real-life dramas in terms of it; we use its terminology and we quote its lines without even knowing we do so.

> The play helps to shape large categories of thought, particularly those which inform political and moral stances, modes and types of relationship, our ideas of how men and women, fathers and mothers, husbands and wives, uncles and nephews, sons and daughters ought respectively to behave and interact. It becomes a means of first formulating and then validating important power relationships, say between politicians and intellectuals, soldiers and students, the world of action and that of contemplation. Perhaps its probing of the relation between art and social life, role-playing on stage and role-playing in society, appears so powerfully to offer an adequate account of important aspects of our own experience that it ends by constructing them. In other words, *Hamlet* crucially helps to determine how we perceive and respond to the world in which we live. (1992, 4)

Although we can always spin out new evolutions of a tradition, employing new questions and answers to climb to new branches of the trees it forms, we cannot, Hawkes suggests, climb down from the particular tree in which we find ourselves or compel it to grow in entirely new ways. We cannot go back to the start of a tradition and make it unfold differently. Indeed, many if not most of our interpretations come to seem so inevitable that they define or construct their objects and function as simple definitions. Because of the culture in which we grow up, we understand certain objects to be tables, for example. Indeed, to us they simply are tables, and the historical developments and conceptual associations necessary to understanding them *as* tables are lost from view. That one eats or writes on them, sits at them instead of under them, places things on them—all of these assumptions form the context for understanding them as tables and are historically embedded. At the same time, it is difficult for us to conceive of the capacity not to conceive of particular objects as tables. Interpretive orientations are necessary to understanding an object *as* the object we take it to be. Moreover, those orientations can misfire, as when what we initially take to be a table turns out to be a platform for making a speech or an altar in a church. Nevertheless, in most cases, the interpretive work necessary to understanding an object as the object we take it to be is so "rudimentary," to quote Michael Walzer, "that we are unlikely to recognize much more in it than the assignment of a general name to the object. And then we expect people of normal understanding to remember the name" (2008, 41). The same is true of the definition of abortion. Despite their differences, both the pro-life and the pro-choice positions understand abortion as ending a life. In fact, it is because it ends a life that one position sees it as a form of disrespect while the other sees it as a possible form of respect. The pro-life position claims that abortion is always or almost always murder and the unjustifiable ending of a human life. Fetuses differ from human beings only in their unborn status. Thus, if we allow for ending the lives of fetuses, we must be prepared to allow for infanticide and homicide. The pro-choice position conceives of abortion as at least sometimes justifiable and as the ending merely of a potential life. Because there is a difference between lives and potential lives, justifying abortion does not require us to extend that justification to infanticide or homicide. Fetuses may be potential humans, but the moral prohibition against killing is a prohibition against the killing of actual humans.

Yet, in addressing themselves to the question of whether respect for the dignity of human life justifies ending a fetus's life, neither side in the abortion debate is able to question the characterization of abortion as ending a life. Rather, the idea that abortion ends a life seems a question less of interpretation than of definition. Consider what follows. The pro-choice argument depends for its plausibility on a clear distinction between fetuses and infants, so that the reasons that may justify ending a fetus's life do not extend to ending a child's life. But if only birth signals the difference between fetuses and infants, then why is that not simply a difference in location, as the pro-life argument in fact maintains? And if we try to uphold the difference by distinguishing between human lives and persons, for example, we come up against yet more unanswerable questions. For the characteristics of persons to which we are likely to point, such as rationality, consciousness, the ability to communicate, and self-awareness, result either in excluding beings we would like to include, such as sleeping infants or those with

Alzheimer's disease, or in including beings we would like to exclude, such as parrots. In sum, as long as we understand abortion as ending a life, the pro-life argument seems to stand on firmer ground than does the pro-choice.

To test the firmness of this ground, we need only look at the debate over an abortion method originally known as "intact dilation and evacuation." Although the procedure was initially developed as a safer alternative to older suction methods of abortion, the pro-life position succeeded in renaming it a "partial-birth" abortion and in doing so made its proscription almost inevitable. The law's description of the banned procedure is particularly telling: a partial-birth abortion is "one in which (a) the person performing the abortion deliberately and intentionally vaginally delivers a living fetus until, in the case of a head-first presentation, the entire fetal head is outside the body of the mother, or, in the case of breech presentation, any part of the fetal trunk past the navel is outside the body of the mother, for the purpose of performing an overt act that the person knows will kill the partially delivered living fetus; and (b) performs the overt act, other than completion of delivery, that kills the partially delivered living fetus" (Ludlow 2008, 32–33). Note that the fetus is not simply a fetus but a living fetus, that the action "kills" this living fetus, and that the mother is a body. This definition already decides the issue of the procedure's permissibility and does so in a way that preempts any attempt to speak about the mother as a person or her relative safety during this procedure as compared to alternative methods. In sum, we might say that because abortion is defined as ending a life, the pro-choice position has already lost the abortion debate. We might also say that because it cannot dislodge embedded definitions, interpretive debate is of little consequence. It may encourage us to listen and try to learn from one another, but what we already collectively assume far outweighs what we can learn.

The second objection to interpretive debate makes matters even worse, for it suggests that interpretive debate naïvely overlooks the power struggles that take place at the origins of the interpretations that become entrenched as definitions. Interpretations of abortion or partial-birth abortion are not, the objection contends, sincere attempts to understand the procedure or whether it plausibly conforms to commitments and values we take seriously. Instead, they are forms of speech employed rhetorically with the sole purpose of winning victories. What are handed down in traditions and discussed, modified, and transmitted in them are less interpretations of meaning than attempts to gain power. It follows that, rather than take interpretations of meaning at face value and try to learn from them, as interpretive debate does, we need to investigate historical struggles in order to see how certain interpretations win the power to entrench themselves as definitions.

With regard to the current debate over abortion, Kristin Luker's history of the controversy (1985) provides an excellent starting point for this kind of investigation. Until the founding of the American Medical Association in 1847, the traditional and widespread understanding of abortions, at least those before the third or fourth month, identified them with contraception. The presence of a fetus was never certain until "quickening," or until a mother could actually feel it moving inside her. Thus abortions before 1847 were medical procedures undertaken for the health of the mother. The AMA, however, wanted to improve the status of what it saw as "regular" physicians as against other sorts of healers, such as midwives. Abortion became its vehicle for doing so. Regular physicians were generally better off than other healers and possessed the resources for some education and advanced training, however dubious that training might have been in the nineteenth century. Nevertheless, the livelihoods of regular physicians were under constant threat from the proliferation of other healers. In order to distinguish themselves from these healers and to lay claim to a larger population of potential patients, regular physicians began to argue that they possessed superior knowledge and, in particular, superior knowledge of human pregnancy. Moreover, they maintained that, according to their superior knowledge, fetuses developed in a continuous biological process from conception to birth. Thus abortion in fact ended human lives. But they also maintained that abortion was sometimes justified in order to save the life of the mother. Like later pro-choice advocates, they included under the life of the mother both the mother's physical life and her social, emotional, and intellectual life. Luker suggests that their point was self-serving. Pregnancy involved two human lives and became a medical condition, while abortion became a medical procedure. Both required the care and expertise of physicians, not midwives or other healers. The definition of abortion as the end of a life, and as legitimate only when necessary to save another life, thus issued from the victory of the regular physicians over their competition.

Luker suggests that other interests were at play here and that other definitions of abortion remained available. Indeed, we continue to call miscarriages spontaneous abortions, and one can imagine that we might have quite plausibly gone on associating at least early abortion not with ending lives, or even ending potential lives, but instead with contraception and other medical interventions such as caesarian births and vitamin supplements. Nonetheless, physicians gained control of pregnancy and abortion, with the consequence that by 1900 most states had laws on their books according to which only medical doctors could decide when an abortion was necessary and only they could perform it.

This history of the definition of abortion as ending a life makes three points. First, it reiterates the difficulty with the pro-choice position. Simply to insist that abortion is a personal choice overlooks the extent to which its identification *as* abortion encompasses an identification with ending a life that was first established in the nineteenth century. Second, it illustrates the extent to which apparently "natural" definitions and identifications are the results of specific events and struggles. In the case of abortion, it indicates the way our current definition traces its roots, at least in part, to the attempt by regular physicians to preserve their livelihoods and upgrade their status. Third, it shows the potential problem with an interpretive approach in general, for insofar as participants simply ask questions of one another that focus on the content and substance of their respective positions, they fail to deal with the elements of power behind that content and substance. These dialogic interactions may help to elaborate the implications of alternative interpretations of common meanings. Yet they arguably neglect the power struggle at the root of the meanings they discuss, and they take interpretations seriously when they ought instead to look at the motivations that constructed them.

At the same time, if interpretive approaches neglect the role of power in the victory of certain interpretations over others, reconstructive approaches arguably minimize the importance of interpretation. In describing Gadamer's three options for I-thou relations, we found that the first two, causal explanation and self-relation, necessarily work through the third, through an understanding of the content of what is said or written. The same holds for struggles for power. Efforts to entrench definitions of abortion employ understandings of meaning. These understandings may reflect attempts to solidify status and position rather than sincere efforts to understand principles and practices. Nevertheless, even attempts to solidify status and position must operate with interpretations of meaning, and these interpretations are thus available for dialogic reconsideration as well as questions about their substance. This reconsideration will always be indebted to prior interpretations and definitions. It is, for instance, far from clear that most Americans could now simply equate abortion with contraception or other interventions into pregnancy. At the same time, if power matters, so too does interpretation. The equation of abortion with ending life may have issued from a strategy to legitimate the regular physicians and gain power for the

AMA. Nevertheless, the equation might still be plausible. Likewise, we can still explore and ask questions about it.

Conclusion

What might be the effect of an interpretive dialogue on the ethics of abortion? If each side were genuinely to engage with the other, what might be the result? Suppose the pro-life position were to examine the substantive content of a pro-choice understanding of the principle of respect for individual human life. Could it not begin to see that in certain cases certain people might legitimately find the alternative to abortion abhorrent, cases, for instance, in which one or more fetuses must be aborted in order to secure the health and well-being of the infants to develop from fetuses in the same womb? Likewise, suppose the pro-choice position were to examine the substantive content of a pro-life understanding of the same principle. Could it not begin to see that in certain cases certain people might legitimately find abortion abhorrent, cases, for instance, in which women repeatedly use abortion as a means of birth control? If the pro-life position were to find abortion acceptable in some cases other than rape and incest, and if the pro-choice position were to find repeated abortions unsavory, a large part of the divide could be overcome.

Interpretive dialogue over the meaning of the principle of liberty might also lead to an increase in mutual understanding. While pro-choice advocates might learn to stress a link between liberty and responsibility, pro-life advocates might learn to consider whether there are any other circumstances in which we would punish a lack of responsibility by blocking any relief from its consequences—whether those consequences were raising a child in dangerous circumstances or giving the child up for adoption and worrying about her or his welfare for the rest of one's life. Likewise, while the pro-life position might learn to recognize the psychic and physical harms of bringing some pregnancies to term, the pro-choice position might learn to consider whether one should always try to control all facets of life. As a result, the pro-life position could begin to reconsider certain punitive and even castigatory aspects in its reaction to abortion, while the pro-choice position could begin to reconsider the slippery slope of technological interventions into childbirth, which might end in cloning and the like.

The result of such reconsideration could be compromise. Indeed, the result might look very much like the Supreme Court decision in *Roe v. Wade*, a scheme to make abortion progressively more difficult in relation to its length. Yet even at its best interpretive dialogue need not lead to consensus. Were it to do so in literary fields, university English departments would lose their raison d'être, of course. In multicultural democracies what is at least as important as consensus is the articulation and investigation of interpretations, the struggle to keep them open as interpretations, and the prevention of their calcification as fixed definitions. One might object that we surely possess some interpretations the calcification of which is warranted, the definition of death, for instance. If we must accept the possibility and even plausibility of different understandings of human life, surely death is simply death. To the contrary, we might insist that our understanding of the meaning of death is the least likely of our interpretations to calcify into a definition. Different cultures and religions have always differed in their ideas of what death is, as have members of the same culture and religion. Moreover, while we can understand texts in different ways depending on our assumptions, questions, and the like, the case of death presents an even more open set of possibilities, because the "text" is one that we can never read to the end.

NOTE

1. This analysis of the pro-life position on liberty comes from numerous classes and conversations with students.

REFERENCES

Dworkin, Ronald. 1993. *Life's Dominion: An Argument About Abortion, Euthanasia, and Individual Freedom.* New York: Knopf.
Gadamer, Hans-Georg. *Truth and Method.* 1992. 2nd rev. ed. Trans. Joel Weinsheimer and Donald G. Marshall. New York: Continuum.
Hawkes, Terence. 1992. *Meaning by Shakespeare.* New York: Routledge.
Ludlow, Jeannie. 2008. "Sometimes It's a Child and a Choice: Toward an Embodied Abortion Praxis." *NWSA Journal* (Spring): 26–50.
Luker, Kristin. 1985. *Abortion and the Politics of Motherhood.* Berkeley and Los Angeles: University of California Press.
Nafisi, Azar. 2003. *Reading Lolita in Tehran.* New York: Random House.
Walzer, Michael. 2008. "Objectivity and Social Meaning." In *Thinking Politically: Essays in Political Theory,* ed. David Miller, 38–52. New Haven: Yale University Press.

ABOUT THE CONTRIBUTORS

John Adams
holds a PhD in speech communication from the University of Washington. He serves as coordinator of the Colgate Speaking Union, Colgate University. His current research focuses on rhetoric's place in constituting communities. His most recent publication is "Hope, Truth, and Rhetoric: Prophesy and Pragmatism in Service of Feminism's Cause," in *Feminist Responses to Richard Rorty* (2010).

Paula Cossart
holds a PhD in political science and is assistant professor of sociology at Charles de Gaulle University–Lille III, assistant director of the Research Centre Individus, Épreuves, Sociétés (CeRIES), and a member of the Institut universitaire de France. Her current research concerns the historical sociology of participatory democracy. She is particularly interested in the genealogy of deliberative facilities. Among her recent publications is *Le meeting politique: De la délibération à la manifestation (1868–1939)* (2010).

Jonas Gabrielsen
is associate professor of rhetoric and communication at Roskilde University, Denmark. His main interest is rhetorical theory, especially the concept and theory of topics. He has also studied political rhetoric, business rhetoric, and public speaking. Recent publications include (with Tanja Christiansen) *Talens magt* (The Power of Speech) (2010) and several papers on argumentation, framing, and *stasis*.

Jette Barnholdt Hansen
is associate professor of rhetoric in the Department of Media, Cognition, and Communication at the University of Copenhagen. Her research interests include the relationship between rhetoric and aesthetics, epideictic rhetoric, and all aspects of orality and performativity. In 2010 she published *Den klingende tale: Studier i de første hofoperaer på baggrund af senrenæssancens retorik*, a book on Italian court opera seen from a rhetorical perspective.

Kasper Møller Hansen
is professor of political science at the University of Copenhagen. His research focuses on deliberative democracy, elections, referendums, voting behavior, public opinion, and alternative methods of public consultation. His recent publications on deliberative democracy include "The Sophisticated Public: The Effect of Competing

Frames on Public Opinion" (2007), "How Deliberation Makes Better Citizens: The Deliberative Poll on the Euro" (2007), and "The Equality Paradox of Deliberative Democracy: Evidence from a National Deliberative Poll" (2010).

Sine Nørholm Just
is associate professor in the Department of Business and Politics at Copenhagen Business School. Her research centers on issues of meaning formation in public debate; she has, for instance, studied the rhetorical constitution of the European Union. In her most recent work she has turned to the study of rhetorical market formation, focusing on the case of the real estate market.

Ildikó Kaposi
is assistant professor of communication and media at the American University of Kuwait. Her research interests include new media and democracy, the political economy of the press, political communication, and media in the Arabian Gulf. Recent publications include (with Mónika Mátay) "Radicals Online: The Hungarian Street Protests of 2006 and the Internet," and (with Stephen Coleman) "A Study of E-Participation Projects in Third-Wave Democracies."

William Keith
is professor of communication at the University of Wisconsin–Milwaukee. His research interests include the history of public participation in the United States, communication pedagogy and disciplinarity, and the rhetoric of science. Recent publications include *Democracy as Discussion* (2007), "Argumentation in Science and Technology Studies," in *Handbook of Science and Technology Studies* (2007), and "On the Origins of Speech as a Discipline: James A. Winans and Public Speaking as Practical Democracy."

Bart van Klink
is professor of legal methodology at Vrije Universiteit, Amsterdam. His research interests include the methodology of law, interdisciplinary research, terrorism, legal reasoning, and rhetoric. Recent publications include *Law and Method: Interdisciplinary Research into Law* (2011), co-edited with Sanne Taekema, and several papers focusing on the "state of exception."

Marie Lund Klujeff
is associate professor at Aarhus University, Denmark. Since 2010 she has been the Danish national editor of the Scandinavian journal *Rhetorica Scandinavica*. She is a committee member of the Rhetoric Society of Europe. Her current fields of interest are rhetorical style, constitutive rhetoric, and deliberation.

Christian Kock
is professor of rhetoric in the Department of Media, Cognition, and Communication at the University of Copenhagen. He has published in English and Danish on

argumentation, political debate, credibility, political journalism, the history of rhetoric, literary aesthetics, reception theory, versification, musical aesthetics, and writing pedagogy. He is a frequent commentator on political debate and journalism in the Danish national media. His latest book, *De svarer ikke* (They Are Not Answering) (2011), dissects the sad state of political debate in Denmark.

Manfred Kraus
is akademischer Oberrat (senior tenured lecturer) in the Department of Classics at the University of Tübingen, Germany. His scholarly interests include the history and theory of rhetoric, the theory of argumentation, early Greek philosophy, Greek poetry and literary criticism, the history of education, and Byzantine and Renaissance studies. He is the author of *Name und Sache: Ein Problem im frühgriechischen Denken* (1987) and of numerous articles and book chapters.

Oliver W. Lembcke
is senior lecturer in political science at Friedrich Schiller University in Jena, Germany. His research interests include political theory and legal philosophy, the history of political ideas, and political system analysis. Recent publications include *Hüter der Verfassung: Eine institutionentheoretische Studie zur Autorität des Bundesverfassungsgerichts* (2007) and a paper titled "Balancing Law and Politics: The Contribution of Political Theory."

Berit von der Lippe
is associate professor of language and mass media in the Department of Communication, Culture, and Languages at the Norwegian School of Management, Oslo. She is the author and co-author of books on semiotics, mass media rhetoric, and *Metaforens potens* (1999), a collection of essays on philosophy, language, and metaphors, as well as articles in various journals on rhetoric and economics, rhetoric and gender, and war rhetoric. Postcolonial theories have become an integral part of her work, as have the concepts of the rhetoric of silence, co-optation, and epistemic violence.

James McDonald
is a PhD student in the Department of Communication at the University of Colorado at Boulder. His current research examines both the role of material entities in shaping public deliberation and the strategic deployment of material entities in marketing campaigns designed to promote gender and racial diversity in the information technology field. His work has appeared in the journals *Communication*, the *Canadian Journal of Communication*, and *Organization Studies*.

Niels Møller Nielsen
is associate professor of Danish in the Department of Culture and Identity at Roskilde University, Denmark. His research deals mainly with language use and pragmatics, especially with regard to the study of argumentation as a theoretical

concept and as a practice in the public sphere. He has recently published a monograph in Danish, *Argumenter i kontekst* (2010), and he is also the author of *Counter Argument: In Defence of Common Sense* (2005).

Tatiana Tatarchevskiy
holds a PhD in sociology from the University of Virginia. Her primary research interests include contemporary cultures of publicness, offline and online. She currently teaches sociology at Sacred Heart University in Fairfield, Connecticut.

Italo Testa
is assistant professor in the Department of Philosophy at Parma University, where he teaches political philosophy. His research interests include argumentation theory, critical theory, social ontology, and the history of social philosophy from German idealism to contemporary pragmatism. He has published monographs and articles on recognition and intersubjectivity, and he is the co-author, with Paola Cantù, of a philosophical introduction to contemporary argumentation theories, *Teorie dell'argomentazione: Un'introduzione alle logiche del dialogo* (2006).

Lisa S. Villadsen
is associate professor of rhetoric and head of the division of rhetoric in the Department of Media, Cognition, and Communication, University of Copenhagen, Denmark. She is the editor-in-chief of the scholarly journal *Rhetorica Scandinavica*. From 2007 to 2009 she held a grant from the Danish Council for Independent Research, Humanities for the researchers' network Rhetorical Citizenship: Perspectives on Deliberative Democracy, which hosted the conference "Rhetorical Citizenship and Public Deliberation" at the University of Copenhagen in October 2008. Her research interests are rhetorical criticism and contemporary rhetorical theory. Recent publications include *Retorik: Teori og Praksis* (2009), co-edited with Charlotte Jørgensen, and chapters and articles focusing on issues of rhetorical agency, rhetorical citizenship, and the meaningfulness of official apologies.

Georgia Warnke
is distinguished professor of political science at the University of California, Riverside, and director of the Center for Ideas and Society. Her research interests include critical theory, hermeneutics, and feminism. She is the author most recently of *After Identity: Rethinking Race, Sex, and Gender* (2010) and *Debating Sex and Gender* (2010).

Kristian Wedberg
is a PhD candidate and member of a research group in rhetoric at the Department of Media Studies and Information Science at the University of Bergen, Norway. He is writing a dissertation on the interventions of Norwegian intellectual writers in

the public sphere. He is also working as a research assistant for Professor Anders Johansen at the same institution, and is currently preparing a seminar called The Language of Knowledge, a contribution to the academic study of nonfiction prose.

Stephen West
is a 2009 graduate of Colgate University, where his research interests focused primarily on rhetoric and the promotion of democracy. He currently works as a consultant for the Advisory Board Company in Washington, D.C., advising university procurement departments on best-practice organizational and strategic processes.

INDEX

Page references in *italics* refer to figures; those followed by *t* refer to tables, by n, to notes with note number.

abortion, and state of exception, 182
abortion debate
    Gadamer's dialogic I-thou relation and, 302–4; and moral principles as culturally determined, 303–4
    hardened opinions, causes of, 303
    modeling of on literary interpretation, 298–99; and appreciation of moral principles as culturally determined, 303–4; benefits of, 306, 312–13; causes of differing interpretations, 298, 303–4; dialogic relation as goal of, 305–6, 313; and interpretation as foundation of all meaning, 311; and opening of dialogic questioning, 304–5; power struggles underlying debate and, 309–12; and relishing of differences in interpretation, 298–99; solidification of interpretations and, 306–9
    partial birth abortions, 309
    principle of liberty and: dialogic reevaluation of, 312; differing interpretations of, 297; as shared underlying value, 298
    Roe v. Wade (1973), 305, 312–13
    and sanctity of human life: dialogic reevaluation of, 312; differing interpretations of, 297–98; power struggles underlying conception of, 309–12; as shared underlying value, 298; solidification of U.S. cultural views on, 308–9
    status system and, 283*t*, 287, 288, 290
accountability
    in deliberative democracy, 14
    as standard for political discourse; broadening of interpretation of, 128; Politika Forum and, 128–29
ACLU v. Reno (1997), 117

action, appeal of *vs.* discourse, 59
ad hominem attacks, fallacy of respect and, 75–76
ad vercundiam fallacy, 76–77
advertising, and Sophist philosophy, modern relevance of, 40
Afghanistan War rhetoric
    and Afghan women's right to speak, usurping of, 155, 162–65, 166
    co-optation of feminist rhetoric in: concerns generated by, 165–66; in Norwegian rhetoric, 159–63; in U.S. rhetoric, 156–59
    creation of doxic room in, 153
    ordinary Afghans as objects of care in, 190, 192
Afghan people, marginalization of, 155–56
Afghan women
    limited gains from War, 161
    privilege to speak for, usurping of, 155, 162–65, 166
    transformation of into objects to be rescued, 155
    views on War, 164
Aftenposten (newspaper), 106, 107
Agamben, Giorgio, on state of exception, 181–82, 191
Alexy, Robert, 280–81
Als, Roald, 256, 256–57, 259, 261
"Amateur Hour" (Hariman), 1
American Association for Adult Education, 52
American Medical Association, 310
American Mercury Presents: Meet the Press (radio program), 56
American Speaks, 59
American Town Meeting of the Air (radio program), 56
anaphora, and presence, 104
Anonymus Jamblichi (anon.), 32
antilepsis, 284*t*, 290–91
antilogía (antilogic), in Sophist philosophy, 36, 39

Antilogiai (Protagoras of Abdera), 35
Antiphon of Rhamnus
  as Athenian citizen, 33, 40
  or function of rhetoric, 41
  as sophist, 32
  Tetralogies, 37
  On Truth, 35–36, 38
Apel, K. O., 71
appeals to authority, validity of, 76–77
appraisal respect, *vs.* recognition respect, 77–78, 79–80
appropriateness (*prépon*), in sophistic rhetoric, 30, 31
Arendt, Hannah, 144–45
argument, extension of, as rhetorical protection measure in public discussion, 225–26
argumentation scholars, on debate *vs.* critical discussion, 88–89
argumentation theories, on respect, 71–75
Aristophanes, 32
Aristotle
  on civil deliberation, 1
  on deliberation and democracy, 2
  on epideictic rhetoric, 252
  on *phronesis*, 176
  Rhetoric, 39
  on rhetoric, 29
  On Sophistical Refutations, 28
  on Sophists, 28
Asen, Robert, 6, 174, 177–78, 199
Association de l'industrie électrique du Québec (AIEQ), 211–12
Athens
  democracy in, 33
  political instability in, 33
  rules of debate in, 35
  as Sophists' home ground, 32–33
  transition to literacy culture, 34
axiological consensus, 289

Bagnoli, Carla, 84
Bakhtin, Mikhail, on degrees of parody, 258
BAPE (Bureau d'audiences publiques sur l'environnement) hearings on Le Suroît electrical plant, 203, 206–12
Barthe, Yannick, 200–201, 215
behavioral norms for public places, and deliberation
  case study: audience use of rhetorical protection measures, 224–29; expert behavior in, 227–28, 229; format of discussion, 221–24; indirect establishment of alliances in, 228–29

  importance of addressing norms, 219, 229–30
  norms as inhibiting factor, 219–21
  overcoming of norms, strategies for, 230
Behnke, Tom, 174
Bender, Courtney, 220
Benhabib, Seyla, 218
Benoit-Barné, Chantal, 175, 176–77, 179, 202
Berlin, Isaiah, 284*t*, 289
Bessette, J. M., 21
Beyond Good and Evil (Nietzsche), 146
Blair, D. M., 157
Blair, Tony
  on international law, needed reforms in, 189, 191, 192
  on Iraq War, justifications for, 189, 192
  on London bombings, 184, 186, 190
  on Muslims, values of, 185
  rhetorical efficiency, dwindling of, 193
  speeches by, 194
  and state of exception, 191–92; citizens role under, 190; critics' demand for lifting of, 193; defense of, 182–83, 187–90, 191; rule of law and, 192
  on terrorism as existential threat, 186
  on United Nations, needed reforms in, 189
  and war on terrorism: citizens' role in, 190–91; dwindling of support for, 193; friends and enemies in, 184–86; necessity of, 183–84, 187, 191; necessity of immediate action, 187–88, 192–93; normal political culture, inapplicability of, 184, 186; ordinary Afghans and Iraqis as objects of care in, 190, 192; rhetorical citizenship and, 192–93, 195n8; rule of law and, 187–90, 192; supporters of benign inactivity, damage done by, 185, 190–91, 193; values being defended in, 185–86, 188
Blondiaux, Loïc, 58
Boda, Zsolt, 122
Bohman, James, 19, 20, 200
Bokbadet (TV talk show), Solstad on, 142–43
Boulangists, and French *Réunion politique*, 57
Bourdieu, Pierre, 165
bourgeoisie, rise of, and public function of literature, 139
Brand (Ibsen), Solstad essay on, 143
Brandes, Georg, 139
Brante, Thomas, 200
Brouwer, Dan, 6

Brown, Penelope, 95
Brummett, Barry, 104–5
Brutus, murder of Caesar by, *status* system and, 284*t*, 291
Bulley, Dan, 186
Bureau d'audiences publiques surl' environnement (BAPE) hearings on Le Suroît electrical plant, 203, 206–12
Burke, Kenneth, 171, 252
Bush, George W.
  and binary response to terrorism, 179n2
  co-optation of gender equality, in Afghanistan War rhetoric, 156
  presidential election debates of 2004, 87, 93–96
Bush, Laura, co-optation of gender equality, in Afghanistan War rhetoric, 157–59
Bush administration, co-optation of gender equality, in Afghanistan War rhetoric, 156–59

Callicles, 32
Callon, Michel, 200–201, 215
Campbell, Karlyn Kohrs, 105, 113n3
"Can the Subaltern Speak?" (Spivak), 163–64
Carnegie Corporation, 51
cartoon crisis (Denmark, 2005), 253–54. *See also* "Did We Learn Anything?" (Danish revue song)
  fear and conflict generated by, 253–54
  journalistic solidarity in, 259, 262n17
  status system and, 284*t*, 292–93
Chambers, S., 19
Charest, Louis, 212
Chautauqua movement, in United States, 47
Chautauqua Society Literary Circles, 47
Christian-gay dialogue, and precondition of respect, 79–80
Cicero, 116
Circus Revue, 254, 255, 256–57, 259
citizens. *See also* engagement of citizens
  as constituencies, in liberal tradition, 2–3
  ordinary, inclusion of in rhetorical citizenship, 6–7
  role in deliberative democracy, 4–5
  role in liberal representative government, 2–3
  role in war on terrorism, Blair on, 190–91
citizenship. *See also* rhetorical citizenship
  as discursive phenomenon, 1
  forums as training in skills of: French forums, 49; U.S. forums, 48
  liberal tradition on: representative government in, 2–3; rights as central focus of, 1
  origins of concept, 40
  public deliberation as constitutive of, 199, 205, 206, 207–8, 209
  and real estate, historic link between, 232
  in republican tradition, 1–2
City Club of Cleveland, Ohio, 56
city-states of Middle Ages and Renaissance, deliberative democracy in, 13
civic traditions, education in, U.S. forum movement and, 48
civil inattention, as norm of behavior in public places, 219–20, 222
civil rights movement, U.S., and appeal of action *vs.* discourse, 59
clarification, as rhetorical functions of humor, 254
Clemenceau, Georges, 53–55
Clinton, Hillary, and presidential primary debates (2008)
  limited useful information conveyed in, 269–70
  moderator's lack of intelligent focus in, 270–71
cloning, as issue, and *status* system, 283*t*
Clouds (Aristophanes), 32
Coalition pour la sécurité énergétique de Québec, 209
Cohen, J., 21–22
Cole, Thomas, 34
Commission on Presidential Debates (CPD), 274
common good. *See* polity, common good of
communicability of truth, Sophists on, 37
communication, public
  in deliberative democracy, best practices for, as issue, 218–19
  norms of: Hauser on, 102–3; idealized, 101–2, 112; localized *vs.* universal validity of, 102
Communications Decency Act, 117
communication technology, and deliberation, availability of, 218
communitarianism, Tocqueville and, 16
community
  creation of, through mutual respect, 126–27, 133
  fragmentation of, by Internet, 118–19
conductive reasoning, 284*t*, 289
consensus
  and deliberative democracy, 7

consensus *(continued)*
    as normative ideal underlying critical discussion, 88–91; counterfactuality of, 90–91, 97; and generation of meaning, 91; and strategic language, 91
    Rousseau on, 15
    on values issues, as impractical, 292
constitutive power of public deliberation, Le Suroît electrical plant debate and, 199, 205, 206, 207–8, 209
consubstantiality
    Danish revue and, 251–53, 254
    and "Did We Learn Anything?" performance, 249, 251, 257–58
context
    Danish reactions to terrorism and, 171
    in debate analysis, 91
    and fallaciousness, 75–76
    and rhetorical agency, 169–70, 171
controversy. *See also* abortion debate; provocative style
    closing of without resolution, 200
    constitutive perspective of, 200
    defining characteristics of, 200
    feminist models of communication and, 200
    importance of to rhetorical democracy, 201
    sociotechnical (*See also* Le Suroît electrical plant debate): benefits of, 201; foregrounding of common beliefs in, 213; increasing importance of, 201, 215; research on, 202
    sources of in contemporary democracies, 201
conventional implicature, in presidential election debates of 2004, 94
conversation. *See also* discussion; everyday political talk; public places, behavioral norms for
    on Internet, views on, 116–19
    problem-solving model of, 116
    public mode of, necessity for rules of engagement in, 116
    sociable model of, 116
conversational analysis, in debate analysis, 91
conversational implicature, Grice on, 91
Cook, Robin, 192
co-optation of feminist rhetoric, 153, 156, 162
    in Afghanistan War rhetoric: concerns generated by, 165–66; in Norwegian rhetoric, 159–63; in U.S. rhetoric, 156–59

    ideographs and, 156, 158–59, 160
coordinative argument, modern *status* system and, 280
Cosby, Ned, 19
Courtine, Jean Jacques, 55
CPD. *See* Commission on Presidential Debates
crisis, rhetorical agency in times of, 175–76
Critias of Athens, 32, 33, 40
critical discussion
    consensus as normative ideal underlying, 88–91; counterfactuality of, 90–91, 97; and generation of meaning, 91; and strategic language, 91
    vs. debate, 88–89
critical observation of public rhetoric, need for, 5
cross-disciplinary approach, benefits of, 8
Crowley, Sharon, 29
Czechoslovakia, Communist, role of theater and music in, 261n3

Dahl, Lisbet, 254, 255
Danish cartoon crisis. *See* cartoon crisis (Denmark, 2005)
Danish Embassy (Islamabad), attack on, 171
    Jensen's response to, 173; denunciations of, 173–74, 177–78; and fragility of trust in times of crisis, 176; and rhetorical citizenship, 176–77, 178–79; timing (*kairos*) of, 174
    mainstream response to, closing of debate by, 172, 178, 179
    motive for, 171, 179n1
    Vestager's response to, 172; denunciations of, 172–73, 177–78; and fragility of trust in times of crisis, 175–76; and rhetorical citizenship, 174–75, 176–77, 178–79; timing (*kairos*) of, 174
Darwall, Stephen, 72–73, 77, 79, 84n4
Davis, Richard, 118
Daxhelet, Xavier, 208
debate
    academic, formats for, 277n1
    in classical Athens, rules regulating, 35
debate(s), political. *See also* presidential election debates of 2004; presidential primary debates
    demonstrations of dialectical virtue in, 87, 93–96
    interplay of dialectical and rhetorical strategies, 96

levels of contextual abstraction in, 91
polarized: Internet and, 119; modern *status* system as remedy for, 279–80
and rhetorical practice, benefits of attention to, 169, 177–78
traditional function of, 268
trialogic model of, 86–87, 89, 89
vs. critical discussion, 88–89
debate(s), political, complex two-level model of, 87, 88, 91, 92–93, 93
interlocutors' dialectical constellation, 88, 92, 93; balance of persuasiveness and dialectical virtue in, 88; as content for media presentation, 87, 96–98
media-audience level (rhetorical constellation), 88, 92, 93; interlocutors as constructed content for, 87, 96–98; as substitute public sphere, 87, 96–98
deception, consensus ideal as precondition for, 91
decision-making process, in deliberative democracy, 14
Defence of Palamedes (Gorgias of Leontini), 36
deliberation, public and private components of, 4–5. *See also* public deliberation
deliberative democracy
accountability in, 14
basis in individual interests, problems inherent in, 176
body of literature on, 169
communication in, best practices for, as issue, 218–19
constitution of political equality in, 14
decision-making process in, 14
and deliberation-based public debate, 176–77
deliberation in, standards for, 13–14
history of concept, 13, 14–19; insufficient scholarly recognition of, 19, 22–23
as inclusive, 6
legitimacy in, 14
and liberal and republican traditions, unification of, 22
and listening, necessity of, 3–5
need for, in multicultural society, 3, 4
possibility of in modern states, 2–3
practical, quotidian view of, 5–7
representatives' role in, 3–4
and rhetorical practice, benefits of attention to, 169, 177–78
rhetoric as essential to, 2

as "rowdy" deliberation, 7, 177
as scholarly interest: ; reasons for rise of, 21–22; rise of, 19–23, 20, 21, 23, 24
and statistical analysis, 218
deliberative democracy turn, 19–23, 20, 21, 23
multicultural society and, 218
reasons for, 21–22
deliberative theories of democracy, on everyday political talk, 115
democracy. *See also* deliberative democracy
in ancient Athens, 33
deliberation as essence of, 2
as frame of mind *vs.* institutions, 6, 18
Koch on, 18
origins of concept, in Sophist philosophy, 39–40
principles of: and Politika Forum Internet discussion group, 132; universal awareness of, 132
Democracy in America (Tocqueville), 16
democratic consciousness, as simultaneously public and social, 61
democratic global citizenship, rhetorical citizenship and, 154
democratic theory, public-private distinction in, 232
Derrida, Jacques, 193
Dewey, John, on deliberation, 17–18
dialectic
pragmatics as modern theory of, 86
vs. rhetoric and logic, 86
dialectical level of contextual abstraction, in debate analysis, 91
dialectic virtue
definition of, 87
demonstrations of in debates, 87, 93–96
dialogic I-thou relationship
and abortion debate, 302–4; dialogic relation as goal of, 305–6, 313; modeling of on literary interpretation, 298–99; and moral principles as culturally determined, 303–4; principle of liberty, reevaluation of, 312; sanctity of human life, reevaluation of, 312
and textual interpretation, 300–302
"Did We Learn Anything?" (Danish revue song), 249
decorum observed in, 259–60, 262n16
and diffusion of cartoon crisis tensions, 249, 255, 256, 258–59, 261n1
Dirch Award for, 255–56
heteroglossia in, 258, 262n14
as parody of parody, 257

"Did We Learn Anything?" *(continued)*
  as parody of "We Are All in the Same
    Boat" (1944 revue song), 250; and
    consubstantiality, generation of, 249,
    251, 257–58, 260; pluralistic parodic
    forms in, 258; and *Verfremdung*
    effect, 257
  performance of, 255–56, 256–57, 262n15
  puns and stylistic effects, 260
  set for, 256, 256–57, 259
  and social functions of revue, 261
  structure, effect created by, 258–59
  Verfremdung effect of, 257
  writing of, 254
Diels, Hermann, 32
differences, ethical and political. *See also*
    abortion debate
  differing interpretation of shared moral
    norms as source of, 296
  modeling of on literary interpretation,
    296–97; and celebration of
    differences, 297
differentiation, as rhetorical functions of
    humor, 254
dilemma of equality, 78
Dionysodorus, 32
Dirch Award, 255–56
disagreement
  diffusing of, rhetorical tradition and, 177
  in public discussion: expert credentials
    and, 227–28, 229; softening of,
    behavioral norms and, 224–29
discourse. *See also* political discourse; public
    discourse; vernacular discourse
  as concept, linking of language and
    society through, 165–66
  as constitutive of civic engagement, 1
  vs. action, U.S. civil rights movement
    and, 59
discussion. *See also* critical discussion
  current presidential primary debates
    as, 275
  vs. debate, 88–89
disinterested citizens, as unrealistic
    model, 102
Dissoi logoi (*Twofold Arguments*; anon.), 32, 39
diverse society
  and deliberative democracy, need for, 3, 4
  and deliberative turn, 218
  effective communication in, and
    rhetoric, need for, 4
  issues of political fragmentation and, 3
  and neosophistic turn, 30
Doty, Roxanne Lynn, 154

Douglas, Stephen, 288
doxa
  in Sophist philosophy, 36, 37–38, 39
  vs. phronesis, in public debate,
    176–77, 179
doxic room, 165
  creation of, in Afghanistan War
    rhetoric, 153
  democracy and, 165
Dreyfus affair, and French *Réunion
    politique*, 57
Dryzek, John
  on deliberative democracy, 4, 21–22
  and deliberative democracy turn, 19, 20
  on normative metaconsensus, 284t, 289
  on respect in dialogue, 79–80
  on rhetoric, correct use of, 5
Dubriwny, Tasha, 157, 158
Dworkin, Ronald, 305
education, as means to democracy,
    Koch on, 18

Eemeren, Franz H. van, 71, 91
eikós (plausibility), in Sophist philosophy,
    38, 39
Ekstra Bladet (newspaper), 255–56
Eleatic theory of ontological truth, 36
Eliasoph, Nina, 220
Elliot Institute, 303
Elster, J., 16
Ely, Mary, 51–52
Encomium of Helen (Gorgias of Leontini),
    36, 37
enforcement, as rhetorical functions of
    humor, 254
engagement of citizens
  in democracy: impediments to, Hariman
    on, 199; necessity of, 199
  discourse as constitutive of, 1
  in forums: and equal participation, limits
    on, 54; motives for participation, as
    problematic issue, 59–60
  need for, to avoid technocracy, 18
  as realistic norm of public
    communication, 102–3, 112n1
  as result of Gaarder-Kristol debate, 108,
    110, 111
  tension between tolerance and, 103, 105,
    111–12
Enlightenment
  and esotericism, 147, 150, 151n6
  late, politico-philosophical deadlock of, 150
  and public function of literature, 139
Enloe, Cynthia, 155

INDEX 327

Enzensberger, Hans-Magnus, 293
epideictic rhetoric, Danish revue as, 252
equality, political. *See also* gender equality
  in ancient Athenian democracy, 33
  constitution of, in deliberative democracy, 14
  respect in public discourse and, 69–70
  Rousseau on, 15
equality dilemma (Williams), 78
equal right to speak, in ancient Athenian democracy, 33
esotericism
  defined, 146
  Enlightenment and, 147, 150, 151n6
  self-reflexivity of, 151–52n6
  in Solstad, 146–48; and late Enlightenment dilemma, 150; and philosophical grounding of liberalism, 149; and rationalism, undermining of, 150–51; and recognition of differences of value, 147–48; as resistance against extreme, leveling publicity, 148–49; and undermining of rationality, 150
Espersen, Søren, 174
Euroinvestor real estate forum, debates in, 233–34
  buyers and sellers: construction of distinctive styles, 236–38, 242–45, 246; private reasoning of, 236–37, 244–45
  and private sphere as springboard for public engagement, 246
  and public vs. private spheres: in construction of positions/identities, 236–38, 242–45, 246; intertwining of, 238, 243, 246
  research on, methodology of, 234
  staseis as analytic tool for: four *statuses*, uses of, 239–42, 246; situation-specific use of tactics and strategies, 242–45
  as type of virtual coffeehouse, 233
European political culture, and post-September 11th state of exception, 184
European writers, political role, adoption of, 139
euthanasia, and state of exception, 182
Euthydemus, 32
Euthydemus (Plato), 28
everyday political talk
  assessing quality of, 115
  deliberative theories' interest in, 115
  models relevant to, 115
  research on, 115–16
expert credentials, and disagreement in public discussion, 227–28, 229
extraordinary rendition, as issue, *status* system and, 284t, 291

facework, in debates, as demonstrations of dialectical virtue, 95–96
Fahnestock, Jeanne, 104
fallaciousness of arguments, as context-dependent, 75–76
Federal Forum Project, 51–53
feminism, Nordic, 159
feminist rhetoric
  and controversy, closing of, 200
  co-optation of, 153, 156, 162; ideographs and, 156, 158–59, 160
  co-optation of in Afghanistan War rhetoric: concerns generated by, 165–66; in Norwegian rhetoric, 159–63; in U.S. rhetoric, 156–59
  as inclusive and collaborative, 154, 166
feminist style, 105, 113n3
figures, rhetorical
  as constitutive of meaning, 104–5, 110–11
  and presence, 104
file sharing, as issue, *status* system and, 283t, 287
Fishkin, James S., 19, 21–22
Fitna (2008 film), 179n1
Fogh Rasmussen, Anders, 172–73, 258, 259, 293
Ford Hall Forum (Boston), 47
foreign policy rhetoric, detachment from reality, 163
forum cranks/hounds, 52
forums
  crisis of republicanism as motivation for, 46
  debate format for, problems inherent in, 52
  failure, causes of, 58–59
  French *Réunion contradictoire*, 53–55; degeneration of, 56–58; format and organization of, 54–55; popularity of, 50, 53; raucous debate in, 55
  French *Réunion politique*, 48–50; demonstrations of force in, 57–58; and equal participation, limits on, 54; government goals for, 48–49; as open, democratic forums, 50; political impotence of, as issue,

forums *(continued)*
    50, 58; private, government's concerns about, 50; and truth, faith in inevitable triumph of, 49–50; venues for, 53
    government involvement, issues in, 59
    motives for participation, as problematic issue, 59–60
    online. *See* Internet discussion groups
    in United States, 47–48; as adult education, 47, 51, 58; characteristic structure of, 51–52; decline, reasons for, 56; effectiveness of, 52–53; Federal Forum Project, 51–53, 56; history of, 47; modern remnants of, 56, 59; political impotence of, as issue, 48, 58–59; purposes of, 48; subjects addressed in, 48; venues for, 51
Foucault, Michel, 182
fragmentation of political community, Internet and, 118–19
Fragments of the Presocratics (Diels and Kranz), 32
France
    Réunion contradictoire, 53–55; degeneration of, 56–58; format and organization of, 54–55; popularity of, 50, 53; raucous debate in, 55
    Réunion politique, 48–50; demonstrations of force in, 57–58; and equal participation, limits on, 54; government goals for, 48–49; as open, democratic forums, 50; political impotence of, as issue, 50, 58; private, government's concerns about, 50; and truth, faith in inevitable triumph of, 49–50; venues for, 53
Frankfurt, Harry, 70
Fraser, Nancy, 81, 235
freedom of assembly, in France, adoption of, 49
freedom of speech
    in ancient Athenian democracy, 33
    Mill on, 17
    reasons for, 17
Freeman, S., 16
Freud, Sigmund, on humor, 254–55, 259
Fung, Archon, 218–19

Gaarder, Joseph, 106, 110. *See also* Gaarder-Kristol debate
Gaarder-Kristol debate
    engagement of citizens as consequence of, 108, 110, 111
    provocative style in, 105, 106–11
    and rhetorical figures as constitutive of meaning, 110–11
Gadamer, Hans-Georg. *See* I-thou relation, Gadamer's three forms of
Gaonkar, Dilip, 239
gay-Christian dialogue, and precondition of respect, 79–80
Geisler, Cheryl, 7, 170
Golléri, Gábor, 125
gender awareness, war rhetoric and, 153
gender equality, co-optation of, in Afghanistan War rhetoric, 155
    concerns generated by, 165–66
    in Norwegian rhetoric, 159–63
    in U.S. rhetoric, 156–59
Gendron, Richard, 210
Glenn, Cheryl, 154–55, 163–64
globalization, and deliberative democracy turn, 22
global warming, as issue, *status* system and, 283*t*, 290
gnoseological relativism, 36
Goffman, Erving, 219–20, 229
Gomperz, Theodor, 28
Goodnight, G. Thomas, 99n10, 200, 202
Gorgias (Plato), 34
Gorgias of Leontini
    Defence of Palamedes, 36
    Encomium of Helen, 36, 37
    and epistemic function of rhetoric, 41
    political sympathies of, 39–40
    as Sophist, 32, 33
    On What Is Not, or On Nature, 36–37
Govier, Trudy, 200, 213, 280, 288–89
Gramsci, Antonio, 155
Greece, ancient, deliberative democracy in, 13
Grice, H. P., 91, 98–99n6
Grootendorst, Rob, 71, 91
Gross, Alan G., 202
Grundtvig, N. F. S., 18
Guantanamo prison, as issue, *status* system and, 291
Guthrie, W. K. C., 29
Gutmann, A., 19

Habermas, Jürgen
    bourgeois public sphere of, 96, 99n11
    on communicative action, 99n11
    on consensus as natural result of rational argument, 292
    and deliberative democracy turn, 19, 20, 22

general theory of publicity: esotericism and, 147; supplementing with rhetorical perspective, 140–41, 144
on ideal speech situation, 235
on lifeworld-system divide, 234–35
on literary publics, 140
on norms of discourse, 71–72
on politico-historical function of modern literary institution, 139
on principle of impartiality, 71–72
on principle of universalization, 71
on public and private spheres, separation of, 232, 234–35, 246
on public sphere, formation of public opinion in, 247n4
Strukturwandel der Öffentlichkeit (*The Structural Transformation of the Public Sphere*), 22, 140, 149, 234
universal pragmatics of, 89, 90, 99n11
unrealistic vision of public discourse in, 102
Hampshire, Stuart, 72
Hariman, Robert
on democracy and rhetorical practice, 1
on democratic consciousness, 61
on democratic participation, 5
on political style, 104–5
Hauser, Gerard A.
on deliberative democracy, 176
on epideictic rhetoric, 252
and *Philosophy and Rhetoric* special issue, 170
on *phronesis* vs. *doxa*, 176–77, 179
on public debate, arguments used in, 239
on public debate as constitutive of public sphere, 5–6
on public rhetoric, 101–3, 105, 111
on public spheres, as plural, 235
on rhetorical agency and risk, 175
on rhetoric of indirection, 146
on vernacular rhetoric, 6, 105
Havel, Václav, 261n3
Havelock, Eric, 34
Hawkes, Terence, 307
hegemonic discourse, and marginalization of Afghan people, 155–56
Henkemans, Snoeck, 280
Henningsen, Poul, 250, 251, 262n4
Hermogenes, 282, 290
heteroglossia, in "Did We Learn Anything?" (Danish revue song), 258, 262n14
Hippias of Elis, 32, 33
Hobbes, Thomas, 15

Hohmann, Hanns, 241
homini sacri, 182
homo mensura statement, 36
Homo Sacer (Agamben), 181–82
Hoppmann, Michael, 281
Hornbæk Revue, 257
HQ (Hydro-Québec). *See* Le Suroît electrical plant debate
Hughes, Karen, 156
humor
four rhetorical functions of, 254
healing function of, 254–55
illuminating function of, 255
Hungary. *See also* Politika Forum (Polforum)
media partisanship in, 120
parliamentary campaign of 2002, 123–24
political debate in: citizens' views on, 120–21; raucous nature of, 119–20, 123–24
political participation in, 120
principles of democracy, awareness of, 132
Hydro-Québec (HQ). *See* Le Suroît electrical plant debate

ideal speech situation, Habermas on, 235
identification, as rhetorical functions of humor, 254
identity, rhetorical style and, 104–5
identity formation, argumentation and, 239, 247n7
ideographs
in co-optation of feminist rhetoric, 156, 158–59, 160
defined, 156
in Norwegian foreign policy, 159–60
women-and-children concept as, 158–59
ideology
French faith in inevitable victory of truth over, 49–50
and rhetorical agency, 170–71
illegal combatant detentions, as issue, *status* system and, 284t, 291
implicatures
conversational, Grice on, 91
in debates: and creation of pragmatic meaning, 93–95; as exhibition of dialectical virtue, 95–96; motives for use of, 95
inclusivity, deliberative democracy and, 6
incommensurable norms, 284t, 289
Index (Hungarian Web portal), 121–22, 133n4

indirection, rhetoric of
　as protection measure in public debate, 224–29
　in Solstad's public appearances, 146
individualization of society, and deliberative democracy turn, 22
informers, liquidation of in wartime, as issue, *status* system and, 284t, 291
institutional context, in debate analysis, 91
intact dilation and evacuation, 309
international law, Blair on needed reforms in, 189, 191, 192
Internet
　empowering potential of, lack of conclusive data on, 4
　and fragmentation of political community, 118–19
　political conversations on, views on, 116–19
　and voice for marginalized groups, 117
Internet discussion groups. *See also* Euroinvestor real estate forum; Politika Forum
　abusive and offensive comments on, 121
　as form of public sphere, 117–18
　and standards of deliberation, 118, 119
interpretatio, and presence, 104
interpretation(s). *See also* literary interpretation of texts
　of shared moral norms, 296
　solidification into unexamined knowledge, 306–9
Iraq, issue of WMDs in, *status* system and, 283t, 290
Iraq War
　Blair on justifications for, 189, 192
　as issue, *status* system and, 284t, 288–89, 290
　ordinary Iraqis as objects of care in, 190, 192
Israeli policy, Gaarder-Kristol debate on, 105, 106–11
I-thou relation, Gadamer's three forms of, 299–300, 302. *See also* abortion debate
　application of to abortion debate, 302–4
　dialogic form of relation: application of to abortion debate, 303–4; as basis of other two forms, 302; differences in interpretation, sources of, 301–2; textual interpretation and, 300–302; and widening of individual perspectives, 300
Ivie, Robert, 7, 177

Jarratt, Susan, 29, 31
Jensen, Kristian, 173
Jensen, Niels Due
　response to attack on Danish embassy, 173; denunciations of, 173–74, 177–78; and fragility of trust in times of crisis, 176; and rhetorical citizenship, 176–77, 178–79; timing (*kairos*) of, 174
　rhetorical agency, impugning of, 171
Jones, John M., 205
Jørgensen, Charlotte, 88–89, 280
journalists' role in presidential primary debates
　in current format, 267, 269
　in recommended true debate format, 271, 272
Joya, Malalai, 164
jury deliberation
　in ancient Athens, 35
　Tocqueville on, 16–17
Jyllands-Posten (*Jutland Post*; newspaper), 253, 259, 292

kairós (opportune moment)
　and critiques of Danish foreign policy, 174
　Danish revue and, 251
　in sophistic rhetoric, 30, 31
Kataballontes (*Overthrowing Arguments*; Protagoras of Abdera), 35, 36
Kendall, Lori, 123
Keränen, Lisa, 202
Kerferd, G. B., 29
Kerry, John. *See* presidential election debates of 2004
Kettering Foundation, 59
Khader, Naser, 173
Kiss, Balázs, 122
Kjær, Henriette, 173
Kjærsgaard, Pia, 173, 258, 259
Kjærulff-Schmidt, Helge, 255, 258
Koch, Christian, 195n8
Koch, Hal, 18–19
Kock, Christian, 280
Kranz, Walther, 32
Kristol, William, 108–9. *See also* Gaarder-Kristol debate
Kuhn, Thomas, 41
Kula exchange (Kula ring) system, 70
Kundera, Milan, 148, 150

Kyoto Protocol, and Le Suroît electrical plant debate, 202, 203

"Lærte vi noget?". *See* "Did We Learn Anything?" (Danish revue song)
Lascoumes, Pierre, 200–201, 215
Leff, Michael, 29, 31, 41
legal arguments
  and relative nature of truth in Sophist philosophy, 37–38, 40
  and *status* system, 280–81
Legault, Richard, 208
legitimacy
  of deliberation, norms of public behavior and, 230
  democratic: in deliberative democracy, 14; public deliberation as source of, 218
  of media, self-understanding of, 96
Levinson, Stephen C., 95
liberal political values, Solstad's attacks on, 146–47
liberal tradition
  on citizenship: representative government in, 2–3; rights as central focus of, 1
  as dominant tradition, 1
  growing irrelevance of in postmodern society, 4
Lincoln, Abraham, 193
linguistic level of contextual abstraction, in debate analysis, 91
liquidation of informers in wartime, as issue, *status* system and, 284t, 291
listening, necessity of in deliberative democracy, 3–5
literary interpretation of texts
  dialogic, Gadamer on, 300–301
  differences in interpretation: as part of ongoing literary tradition, 302; sources of, 301–2
  modeling of abortion debate on, 298–99; and appreciation of moral principles as culturally determined, 303–4; benefits of, 306, 312–13; causes of differing interpretations, 298; dialogic relation as goal of, 305–6, 313; and interpretation as inescapable foundation of meaning, 311; and opening of dialogic questioning, 304–5; power struggles underlying debate and, 309–12; and relishing of differences in interpretation, 298–99;
  solidification of interpretations and, 306–9
  modeling of ethical and political differences on, 296–97; and celebration of differences, 297
literary publics, Habermas on, 140
literary texts and events, as rhetorical performances, 140–41
literature, 18th century, as *publicum*, 139
Locke, John, 15
logos
  definition of, 34
  in Sophist philosophy, 34–35, 36–37
Luker, Kristin, 310
Luskin, Robert, 19
lyceum movement in United States, 47
Lyne, John, 201

Mackin, James A., 111–12
Madison, James, 19
Malinowski, Bronislaw, 70
Manin, B., 21–22
Mansbridge, Jane, 128, 129
Marquis, Jacques, 209–10, 211–12
Matalin, Mary, 156
Mauss, Marcel, 70
McComiskey, Bruce, 29, 30, 31
meaning
  consensus ideal and, 91
  Grice on, 98–99n6
  implicatures in debates and, 93–95
  rhetorical figures as constitutive of, 104–5, 110–11
media
  blurring of public and private spaces by, 144
  legitimacy, self-understanding of, 96
  and necessity listening in deliberative democracy, 4
  news program discussions, as arguments rather than debates, 268–69
  public figures' theatricality as insulation from, 144–45
  and Sophist philosophy, modern relevance of, 40
  theatricality of, Solstad's exposure of, 144
meta-arguments, as rhetorical protection measure in public discussion, 226–27
Meyer, John, 254
Meyrowitz, Joshua, 144
The Mild Voice of Reason (Bessette), 21

Mill, John Stuart, 17
Milwaukee Turners, 56
misframing, and personhood as basis of respect, 81
modality, as concept, 6
modern states, possibility of deliberative democracy in, 2–3
Monetary Council of the Hungarian Central Bank (MNB), Politika Forum mirror institution, 130–31
Moore, Mark P., 202
moral norms, shared
  as basis of social institutions, 296
  differing interpretations of, 296
mortification, in *status* system, 285t, 291
Moss, Roger, 29
multiculturalism. *See* diverse society
Murphy, James J., 104
Muslims, values of, Blair on, 185

NARAL Pro-Choice America, 303
National Right to Life, 303
Neel, Jasper, 29
Neosophistic turn, 29–31
  modern relevance of Sophist philosophy, 40–41
  and Sophists of ancient Greece, as separate issues, 31
New Dialectic (Walton), 75
news programs, discussions on as arguments rather than debates, 268–69
Niemeyer, Simon, 79–80, 284t, 289
Nietzsche, Friedrich
  Beyond Good and Evil, 146
  on esotericism, 147
Nobel Peace Prize, as issue, *status* system and, 284t, 288
"Nødvendigheten av å leve inautentisk" (Solstad), 148
noninteractive rhetoric, 221, 222
normative, as term, 98n2
normative metaconsensus, 284t, 289–90, 292, 293
normative metarespect, 81–83
normative pragmatics
  consensus ideal in, 88–91; as counterfactual, 88–91, 97; and generation of meaning, 91; and strategic language, 91
  and dialectic virtue in argumentative discourse, 87, 93–96
norms, shared moral
  as basis of social institutions, 296
  differing interpretations of, 296

norms of public communication. *See also* behavioral norms for public places, and deliberation; respect in public discourse, as normative ground
  Hausner on, 102–3
  idealized: negative evaluations of everyday discourse as product of, 101–2; provocative style and, 112
  incommensurable, 284t, 289
  localized *vs.* universal validity of, 102
  multidimensionality of, 281, 289–90
Northern Alliance, Afghan views on, 164
Norway
  foreign policy rhetoric: and co-optation of gender equality rhetoric, 159–63; ideographs in, 159–60
  poetocratic tradition in, 139
No Sense of Place (Meyrowitz), 144
Nybakk, Marit, 160

Obama, Barack, presidential primary debates (2008)
  limited useful information conveyed in, 269–70
  moderator's lack of intelligent focus in, 270–71
obstructionists, in French *Réunion politique*, 56–57
Olbrechts-Tyteca, Lucie, 103–4, 111
"Om meddelelsens problem" (Solstad), 146
"Om ytingsfriheten" (Solstad), 146
On Sophistical Refutations (Aristotle), 28
On Truth (Antiphon of Rhamnus), 35–36, 38
On Truth (Protagoras of Abdera). *See* Kataballontes
On What Is Not, or On Nature (Gorgias of Leontini), 36–37
The Open Society and Its Enemies (Popper), 29
opportune moment. *See* kairós (opportune moment)
Options Consommateurs, 210
other, stance toward, Gadamer on, 299–300
"Our Mouths and Hands Are Bound" (Henningsen), 250
Øverland, Arnulf, 160
Overthrowing Arguments (*Kataballontes*; Protagoras of Abdera), 35, 36

Papacharissi, Zizi, 132
Papua New Guinea, Kula exchange (Kula ring) system, 70
Parmenides of Elea, 36

INDEX   333

Parry-Giles, S. J., 157
partial birth abortions, 309
participation. *See* engagement of citizens
particularized conversational implicatures, in presidential election debates of 2004, 94
partisan urgings *vs.* propaganda, and limits of provocative style, 111–12
Pateman, Carole, 21
Perelman, Chaïm, 71, 72, 103–4, 111
Pericles, 33, 111–12
Perrin, Andrew J., 220
personhood, as basis for respect, 80–81
Peters, John Durham, 152n6
Phaedrus (Plato), 38
Philosophy and Rhetoric (2004 special issue on rhetorical agency), 170
phronesis
    Aristotle on, 176
    vs. doxa, in public debate, 176–77, 279
Piette, Danielle, 209
Pilgaard, Ulf, 255–56, 258, 262n15
Plato
    and Eleatic theory of truth, 36
    Gorgias, 34
    and neosophistic turn, 30
    Phaedrus, 38
    Protagoras, 34
    on rhetoric, 29
    Sophist, 32, 34
    on Sophists, 28
Plenov, Leif, 251
poetocratic tradition, in Norway, 139
polarized debate. *See also* provocative style
    Internet and, 119
    modern *status* system as remedy for, 279–80
Polforum. *See* Politika Forum
political debate. *See* debate(s), political
political discourse
    standards for, and Politika Forum conversation: democratic principles, embrace of, 132; members' recognition and support of, 127–28; reasoned argumentation, 129–32; standards of accountability, 128–29; standards of reason, 122; standards of reciprocity, 126–28
political processes, cynicism about, as product of idealist norms, 101–2
political rhetoric
    inclusive speech in, 193
    symbolic power in, 193
Political Theology (Schmitt), 181

politicians, lack of trust in, and deliberative democracy turn, 22
politics
    goals of, good life of all citizens as, 2
    and Sophist philosophy, modern relevance of, 40
Politika Forum (Polforum), 122
    autonomy of, 122
    establishment of, 121
    members; acceptance of standards of reasoned argumentation, 129–32; face-to-face meetings of, 123; views on conversation quality, 123
    ownership and financing of, 121–22
Politika Forum, conversation in
    and creation of community, 126–27, 133
    ethnographic approach, benefits of, 122–23
    existing research on, 122
    familiarity necessary for understanding, 123
    Forum growth and, 124–25
    members' views on, 124
    provocative style of conversation [*fikázás*], 124–26; as convention, 125–26; and norms of political conversation, 126, 127, 130–32; as rational means of generating discussion, 125, 126; technical and expert knowledge and, 130–31
    standards for, as hybrid form, 128, 132
    and standards of political discourse: democratic principles, embrace of, 132; members' recognition and support of, 127–28; reasoned argumentation, 122, 129–32; standards of accountability, 128–29; standards of reason, 122; standards of reciprocity, 126–28
    structure and regulation of, 121
    as truly public mode of conversation, 132–33
Politiken (Danish newspaper), 293
polity, common good of
    as basis for rational decision, in Habermas, 235
    necessity of focus on, 4
    as outside liberal tradition's focus, 3
    and public deliberation: determination of common good, 3; Mill on, 17; refocusing of individual attention onto common good, 19; Rousseau on, 15–16; Tocqueville on, 16–17
    training citizens to consider, through public forums, 49

Polletta, Francesca, 221
Polus, 32
Popper, Karl, 29
the possible/potential (*to dunatón*), in sophistic rhetoric, 30, 31
"Postcolonial Intervention in the Rhetorical Canon" (Shome), 164
postmodern era, and social function of revue, 261
Poulakos, John, 30, 41
  critiques of, 30–31
  "Toward a Sophistic Definition of Rhetoric," 29
Poulakos, Takis, 29–30
Powell, Colin, 156
pragmatics. *See also* normative pragmatics
  in debate analysis, 91
  as modern theory of dialectic, 86
prépon (the appropriate), in sophistic rhetoric, 30, 31
presence
  and constitution of salience, 103–4
  provocative style and, 111
presidential election debates of 2004, demonstrations of dialectical virtue in, 87, 93–96
presidential primary debates
  audience, difficulty of measuring, 276
  current format(s) for, 267; advantages and disadvantages of, 274–75; as discussion, not debate, 275; as interview-based questioning, rather than true debate, 267, 268–69, 275; lack of intelligent focus in, 269–71; moderator's role in, 270–71, 274, 275
  journalists' role: in current format, 267, 269; in recommended true debate format, 271, 272
  moderator's role: in current format(s) for, 270–71, 274, 275; in new debate format, 267, 271, 273
  Obama-Clinton debates of 2008: limited useful information conveyed in, 269–70; moderator's lack of intelligent focus in, 270–71
  theoretical function of, 268
  true debate format for, 271–74; benefits of, 267–68, 274, 275–76; characteristics of true debate, 267; pre-announcement of debate topic, 271–72, 275, 277n5; procedure for, 272–73; selection of debate topic, 272–73; structure of debates, 273–74,
277n4, 277n8; time constraints and, 276, 277–78n10; voters' role in, 272, 273–74, 276, 277n6
  voters' desire for elevated political discourse, 271
principle of impartiality, Habermas on, 71–72
principle of universalization, Habermas on, 71
private sphere, as springboard for public engagement, in Euroinvestor real estate forum, 246
private *vs.* public sphere
  arguing of claims within context of, 235
  in Euroinvestor real estate forum: in construction of positions/identities, 236–38, 242–45, 246; intertwining of, 238, 243, 246
  real estate discussions as poised between, 232–33
  separation of: in democratic theory, 232; Habermas on, 232, 234–35
problem-solving model of conversation, 116
Prodicus of Ceos, 32
propaganda *vs.* partisan urgings, and limits of provocative style, 111–12
Protagoras (Plato), 34
Protagoras of Abdera
  Antilogiai, 35
  Kataballontes (*Overthrowing Arguments*), 35, 36
  political activism of, 39
  as Sophist, 32, 33
  on truth in argument, 37
protector-protected relationship, and war rhetoric on protection of women, 163–64
provocative style, 103–5
  and balancing of engagement and tolerance, 105, 111–12
  as deliberate trespassing against norms, 105, 109
  engagement of citizens as result of, 108, 110, 111
  in Gaarder-Kristol debate, 105, 106–11
  limits of, 111–12
  in Politika Forum online forum, 124–26; as convention, 125–26; and norms of political conversation, 126, 127, 130–32; as rational means of generating discussion, 125, 126; technical and expert knowledge and, 130–31
  and presence, 111

and rhetorical figures as constitutive of meaning, 104–5, 110–11
rhetorical theories on, 103–4
usefulness of concept, 112
vernacular discourse and, 105, 109
public
Hauser's definition of, 102
misdefinition of concept, 101–2
public communication
in deliberative democracy, best practices for, as issue, 218–19
norms of: Hausner on, 102–3; idealized, 101–2, 112; localized *vs.* universal validity of, 102
public deliberation
and behavioral norms for public places: expert behavior, 227–28, 229; format of discussion, 221–24; importance of addressing, 219, 229–30; indirect establishment of alliances in, 228–29; as inhibiting factor, 219–21; overcoming, strategies for, 230; use of rhetorical protection measures, 224–29
citizens' responsibility to monitor, 5
and common good of polity: determination of, 3; Mill on, 17; refocusing of individual attention onto, 19; Rousseau on, 15–16; Tocqueville on, 16–17
as constitutive of citizenship, 199, 205, 206, 207–8, 209
criticisms of, 199
culture of written/mediated communication and, 229
cynicism about, as product of misdefinition of the public, 101–2
definition of, 13–14
as essence of democracy, 2
excessive, Rousseau on, 16
generation of new ideas approaches by, 200–201
history of concept, 14–19
importance of, 199
legitimacy of, norms of public behavior and, 230
media-presented debates as simulacrum of, 87, 96–98
officials' willingness to ignore, 199
rhetorical practices, effective, importance of identifying, 201, 215
rowdiness of, as healthy, 7, 177
as sine qua non of controversy, 200

sociological perspective on, benefits of, 219, 229
as source of legitimacy in democracy, 218
standards of: in deliberative democracy, 13–14; and Internet conversations, 118, 119
theory of, 200–202
unprincipled self-interest as only alternative to, 18–19
public discourse. *See also* respect in public discourse
as dialectical, 141
normative structures in: importance of understanding, 69; variations in, 74–75
validity structures in, 73–74, 84n3
public figures, theatricality of
as insulation from intimate exposure to public, 144–45
vs. inner exile, 145
public meetings, as site for production of citizens, 46, 47–48, 57, 58. *See also* forums
public participation. *See* engagement of citizens
public places, behavioral norms for, 219–21
and deliberation: expert behavior, 227–28, 229; format of discussion, 221–24; importance of addressing norms, 219, 229–30; indirect establishment of alliances in, 228–29; norms as inhibiting factor, 219–21; overcoming of norms, strategies for, 230; use of rhetorical protection measures, 224–29
public-politician gap, and deliberative democracy turn, 22
publics, as practical concept, 5–6. *See also* polity, common good of
public sphere
as composite of many spheres, 235
Habermas on, 96, 99n11
Internet discussion groups as, 117–18
literature, 18th century, as, 139
media-presented debates as simulacrum of, 87, 96–98
public *vs.* private sphere
arguing of claims within context of, 235
in Euroinvestor real estate forum: in construction of positions/identities, 236–38, 242–45, 246; intertwining of, 238, 243, 246

public *vs.* private sphere *(continued)*
  real estate discussions as poised between, 232–33
  separation of: in democratic theory, 232; Habermas on, 232, 234–35
"pub politicking" in Hungary, 120–21
Putnam, Robert D., 199

questions, as rhetorical protection measure in public discussion, 225
Quintilian, 262n16

Rawls, J., 19, 20, 292
real estate, and citizenship, historic link between, 232
real estate discussions, and public *vs.* private sphere, 232–33. *See also* Euroinvestor real estate forum
reason
  French faith in, 49–50
  as standard of political discourse, Politika Forum online discussion and, 122, 129–32
reasonable disagreement, 292
reciprocity, as standard for political discourse
  and community, creation of, 126–27, 133
  Politika Forum conversation and, 126–28
recognition respect, 72
  defeasible (epistemic) *vs.* indefeasible (moral) forms of, 72–73, 76
  and respect fallacy, 76
  vs. appraisal respect, 77–78, 79–80
Régie de l'énergie, hearing on Le Suroît electrical plant, 203–4, 207, 208, 209, 212
reification through geometricization, 151n1
relation of exception, 182
relativism of modern culture, and Sophist philosophy, increasing relevance of, 40–41
Rem, Tore, 143
Rémy, Élisabeth, 201
representative government
  liberal model of, 2–3, 4
  Rousseau on, 15
representatives
  role in deliberative democracy, 3–4
  role in liberal conception of democracy, 2–3
republicanism, crisis in, as motivation for forums, 46
republican tradition on citizenship, 1–2

Rescher, Nicholas, 289
"Respect and the Second Person Standpoint" (Darwall), 72–73
respect in public discourse. *See also* reciprocity; recognition respect
  argumentation theories on, 71–75
  as conditional and defeasible, 70, 72–75
  dynamic *a posteriori vs.* static *a priori* forms of, 81–83
  and equality, 69–70
  as goal, rather than precondition, 80, 82
  as impediment to dialogue, 78–80
  as moral and social attitude, 69
  as normative ground, 70–71; and ad hominem attacks, 74, 75–77; and refusal to engage in dialogue, 74, 78–80; second-order disposition toward respect as, 83–84
  normative metarespect, 81–83
  personal recognition *vs.* personal appraisal respect, 77–78, 79–80
  personal *vs.* epistemic respect, 72–73, 76
  personhood as basis for, 80–81
  reciprocity of, 69–70
  respect for ideas *vs.* persons, 75, 84n5
  as restriction on subject of dialogue, 80–81
  universal, unconditional *vs.* individual, conditional forms of, 77–78
  as universal a priori, 70–72
Réunion politique (France), 48–50
  demonstrations of force in, 57–58
  and equal participation, limits on, 54
  government goals for, 48–49
  as open, democratic forums, 50
  political impotence of, as issue, 50, 58
  private, government's concerns about, 50
Réunion contradictoire (France), 53–55; degeneration of, 56–58; format and organization of, 54–55; popularity of, 50, 53; raucous debate in, 55
  and truth, faith in inevitable triumph of, 49–50
  venues for, 53
revue, Danish. *See also* "Did We Learn Anything?" (Danish revue song); "We Are All in the Same Boat" (Danish revue song)
  consubstantiality generated through, 249, 251–53, 254, 257–58
  critical views on, 251
  decorum observed in, 253, 259

as epideictic rhetoric, 252
under German occupation, 250–51
history of, 250
and *kairos*, 251
lighthearted fun as goal of, 251–52, 253
and rhetorical citizenship, 251, 252
and rhetorical functions of humor, 254
social functions of, 261
rhetoric. *See also* Afghanistan War rhetoric; feminist rhetoric; *logos*; war rhetoric
benefits of attention to, for political debate, 169, 177–78
defined, 2
as essential to deliberative democracy, 2, 7
influence of Sophist philosophy on, 39
as practical conception, 5–7, 8
reputation of, 29
rhetorical pollution of an ecosystem, provocative style and, 112
rhetorical protection measures, in public discussion with strangers, 225–29
and rules of persuasion, establishment of, 41
traditional, as upper-class and male, 154, 164
Rhetoric (Aristotle), 39
Rhetorica ad Alexandrum (anon.), 282
rhetorical agency, 170–71
as bridge between traditional and poststructuralist views of rhetoric, 7
contesting of, in Danish reactions to terrorism, 171
context and, 169–70, 171
focus of research in, 169–70
and fragility of trust in times of crisis, 175–76
issues in, 7
rhetorical analysis. *See status* system, modern
rhetorical citizenship
and alternative responses to crisis, willingness to entertain, 174–75, 176–77, 178–79
Danish revue and, 251, 252
definition of, 46
democratic global citizenship and, 154
disciplines relevant to, 8
focus of research in, 170
and ordinary citizens, inclusion of, 6–7
origin of concept, 169
as republican view of citizenship, 2

Le Suroît electrical plant debate and, 208, 209, 213, 214–15, 217
and war on terrorism, 192–93, 195n8
rhetorical democracy, importance of controversy to, 201
rhetorical figures
as constitutive of meaning, 104–5, 110–11
and presence, 104
Rhetorical Figures in Science (Fahnestock), 104
rhetorical level of contextual abstraction, in debate analysis, 91
rhetorical performances
close reading of, as paradigmatic method, 140
literary texts and events as, 140–41
Solstad's ironic rhetorical duplicity as, 141–44
rhetorical style
as compilation of rhetorical features, 104–5
as performative of identity, 104–5
rhetoric of duplicity, in Solstad's public appearances, 143–44
content of, as undetermined, 149–51
as insulation from public intimacy, 144–45
and stratification of audience, 145
rhetoric of indirection
as protection measure in public debate, 224–29
in Solstad, 146
rhetoric of silence, 154–56
Afghan women and, 155, 163–65, 166
Rhetoric to Alexander (anon.), 39
Roe v. Wade (1973), 305, 312–13
Rørbech, Lone, 280
Rosen, Stanley, 146, 147, 151, 151n6
Rousseau, Jean-Jacques, 15–16
Rowland, Robert C., 205
Royer, Daniel, 29
Royster, Jacqueline Jones, 155, 163
rule of law, in war on terrorism, Blair on, 187–90, 192
Ryfe, David M., 219

St. Amant, Jacques, 210
salience, presence and, 103–4
Samuels, Shimon, 107–8
Schiappa, Edward, 30–31, 34, 41
schismogenesis, symmetrical, 112
Schmitt, Carl, 181, 191–92

scholarship on deliberative democracy,
    increasing volume and breadth of,
    19–23, 20, 21, 23
Schudson, Michael, 116
Scott, Robert, 29, 41
Seidenfaden, Tøger, 293
Sennett, Richard, 144, 219–20
senses, unreliability of, in Sophist
    philosophy, 36
September 11th terrorist attacks
    binary response to, 179n2
    Blair on, 183–84
    state of exception created following, 183
Sheard, Cynthia M., 252
Shome, Raka, 164
Short, Clare, 192
silence, self-selected vs. imposed, 154–55
silence, rhetoric of, Afghan women and,
    155, 163–65, 166
Simon, Jules, 49–50
Simon Wiesenthal Center (Paris), 107
Sintomer, Yves, 58
situational context, in debate analysis, 91
slavery, as issue, *status* system and,
    284t, 288
Slowness (Kundera), 147
sociable model of conversation, 116
social contract, Rousseau on, 15
social status, Internet and, 117, 118
societal level of contextual abstraction, in
    debate analysis, 91
sociological perspective on deliberation,
    benefits of, 219, 229
sociotechnical controversy. *See also* Le Suroît
    electrical plant debate
    benefits of, 201
    foregrounding of common beliefs in, 213
    increasing importance of, 201, 215
    research on, 202
Socrates
    Aristophanes on, 32
    Gadamer on, 300, 301
Solstad, Dag
    attacks on liberal political values, 146–47
    on Ibsen's *Brand*, 143
    Kundera and, 148
    literary career of, 141
    and middle European tradition, 148
    "Nødvendigheten av å leve
        inautentisk," 148
    "Om meddelelsens problem," 146
    "Om ytingsfriheten," 146
    physical appearance of, 141–42
    politics of, 146–47, 147–48
    public's view of, 151n2, 151n5
    rambling verbal style of, 151n4
Solstad's public appearances
    as attack on norms of public discourse,
        145–46
    on *Bokbadet* (TV talk show), 142–43
    esotericism in, 146–48; and late
        Enlightenment dilemma, 150;
        and philosophical grounding of
        liberalism, 149; and rationalism,
        undermining of, 150–51; and
        recognition of differences of value,
        147–48; as resistance against
        extreme, leveling publicity, 148–49;
        and undermining of rationality, 150
    and exposure of media theatricality,
        144–45, 149
    as ironic rhetorical mode, 142–43
    as protection of fiction from reality, 145
    range of mediums and genres in, 141
    rhetoric of duplicity in, 143–44; content
        of, as undetermined, 149–51; as
        insulation from public intimacy,
        144–45; and stratification of
        audience, 145
    rhetoric of indirection in, 146
Sophist (Plato), 32, 34
sophistic rhetoric, characteristics of,
    Poulakos on, 30
sophistry, as term, 28, 32. *See also*
    Neosophistic turn
Sophists of ancient Greece
    and concept of democracy, influence on,
        39–40
    as diverse group, 31, 33
    figures included in, 32–33
    legal arguments and truth in, 37–38
    on *logos*: as instrument of regulated
        competition, 34–35; and truth, 36–37
    and neosophistic turn, 29–31
    political sympathies of, 33–34, 39–40
    reputation of, 28
    on truth, 35–39; as functional concept,
        38–39; nature-based vs. custom-based
        forms of, 38–39; relevance to modern
        issues, 40–41
    vs. contemporary neosophistic
        appropriation, 31
sovereignty, new global interdependence
    and, 189
Spivak, Gayatri C., 163–64
Sprague, Rosamond Kent, 32

state of exception
    Agamben on, 181–82
    in Blair regime, 191–92; citizens role under, 190; critics' demand for lifting of, 193; defense of, 182–83, 187–90, 191; rule of law and, 192
    definition of, 181, 182
    history of concept, 181
    and *homini sacri*, 182
    as permanent, in war on terrorism, 181, 182
statistical analysis, deliberative democracy and, 218
status, practical, 282
status ambiguum, 280, 283t, 287
status antenklema, 285t
status antilepsis, 284t, 290–91
status antistasis, 284t
status conjecturalis (status conjectural), 239, 242, 244, 280, 283t, 290
status definitivus (status definitional; *status finitionis*), 239, 241, 242, 244, 280, 283t–284t, 290
    status legales as subdivisions of, 281–82
status legales, 280–81
    as subdivision of *status definitivus*, 281–82
status leges contrariae, 280, 284t, 288–90
status metastasis, 285t
status qualitatis (status qualitative), 240, 241, 242, 244–45, 280, 284t–285t, 290
status ratiocinatio/collectio, 280, 287
status rationales, 280
status scriptum et voluntas, 280, 284t, 287–88
status syngnome, 285t, 291
status system, modern
    applicability to arguments in general, 281
    applications, examples of, 287–94
    in Euroinvestor real estate forum debate: four *statuses*, uses of, 239–42, 246; situation-specific use of tactics and strategies, 242–45
    and general arguments: applicability to, 281; multidimensionality of norms in, 281, 289–90
    and normative metaconsensus, 284t, 289–90, 292, 293
    and positioning/identity formation, 239
    practical statuses in, 282
    practical uses and benefits of, 279–80, 286, 291–92, 294
    statuses in, structure of, 239–41, 280–82, 283t–285t

    strategic and tactical levels of, 241
    updating of ancient system, 239, 279
    variety of tactical techniques in, 240–41
    versions of, 281
status translationis, 240–41, 242
stem cell research, as issue, and *status* system, 283t
Stjernfelt, Frederik, 293
Stocker, Peter, 257
Støjberg, Inger, 173
Stratigaki, Maria, 155, 162
Strøm-Erichsen, Anne-Grete, 161–62
Strukturwandel der Öffentlichkeit (*The Structural Transformation of the Public Sphere*; Habermas), 22, 140, 149, 234
Studebaker, John, 51
Supreme Court, U.S.
    ACLU v. Reno (1997), 117
    Roe v. Wade (1973), 305, 312–13
Le Suroît electrical plant debate
    abandonment of project, 202, 204, 213
    agreement with opposition, as rhetorical strategies: analysis of, 213–15; examples of, 206–13
    anti-Suroît parties: arguments of, 205–6; influences on pro-Suroît parties, 208
    BAPE (Bureau d'audiences publiques sur l'environnement) hearings, 203, 206–12
    and constitutive power of public deliberation, 199, 205, 206, 207–8, 209
    energy efficiency as alternative energy source, 205, 209–11
    greenhouse gas emissions as issue in, 202
    hydroelectricity as alternative energy source, 203, 205, 211–12
    overview of, 202–4
    pro-Suroît parties, arguments of, 205–6
    public opinion in, 203
    Régie de l'energie hearing, 203–4, 207, 208, 209, 212
    rhetorical analysis of, methodology for, 204–5
    and rhetorical citizenship, 208, 209, 213, 214–15, 217
    rhetorical strategies in, 205, 215n4
    thermal energy, views on, 205–6, 211–13
    wind energy as alternative energy source, 203, 205, 206–9
"Suspicion, Deception, and Concealment" (Rosen), 146

symbolic power, in political rhetoric, 193
symmetrical schismogenesis, 112

terrorism. *See also* cartoon crisis (Denmark, 2005); war on terrorism
   Bush's binary response to, 179n2
   as existential threat, Blair on, 186
Tetralogies (Antiphon of Rhamnus), 37
Thompson, D., 19
Thorning-Schmidt, Helle, 173
Thrasymachus of Chalcedon, 32
Tickner, J. Ann, 165
Tisias, 38
Tocqueville, Alexis de, on deliberation, 16–17
to dunatón (the possible/potential), in sophistic rhetoric, 30, 31
tolerance
   as realistic norm of public communication, 103
   tension between engagement and, 103, 105, 111–12
torture, as issue, *status* system and, 284t, 291
Törzsasztal (online forum), 121, 125, 133n2
totalitarian rule, role of theater and music in, 26n3
Toulmin, Stephen, 71
town hall meetings, modern, as political theater, 59
truth
   French faith in inevitable triumph of, 49–50
   in Sophist philosophy, 35–39; as functional concept, 38–39; nature-based *vs.* custom-based forms of, 38–39; relevance to modern issues, 40–41
Twofold Arguments (*Dissoi logoi*; anon.), 32, 39

unanimity, Rousseau on, 15
Union québécoise pour la conservation de la nature, 210
United Nations, needed reforms in, Blair on, 189
United States, forums in. *See* forums, in United States
UN Resolution 1325, 161
UN Resolution 1441, 189
Usenet
   discussion on, 132
   growth of, and decline in quality of conversation, 125

value pluralism, 284t, 289
values issues, consensus on, as impractical, 292
Vandal, Thierry, 206–7, 208, 212
vaudeville, origin of, 250
Verfremdung, in "Did We Learn Anything?" performance, 257
vernacular discourse
   provocative style and, 105, 109
   stylistic performance as characteristic of, 110
vernacular rhetoric, 6, 105
Vernacular Voices (Hauser), 101–2
Vestager, Margrethe, response to attack on Danish embassy, 172
   deliberation-based public debate and, 176–77, 177–78
   denunciations of, 172–73
   and fragility of trust in times of crisis, 175–76
   rhetorical agency, impugning of, 171, 175
   and rhetorical citizenship, 174–75, 176–77, 178–79
   timing (*kairos*) of, 174
Vickers, Brian, 30
Villa, Dana R., 144–45
Vitranza, Victor, 30
voice for marginalized groups, Internet and, 117
voters, and true debate format for presidential debates
   education gained through, 272, 277n6
   role of, 272, 273–74, 276
voting
   deliberation as necessary precursor to, 18
   Koch on, 18

Wagner, Uwe, 108
Walton, Douglas, 71, 75, 88, 91
Walzer, Michael, 308
"A War for Women's Liberation" (Nybakk), 160
Warnke, Georgia, 287
war on terrorism. *See also* state of exception
   in Blair regime: citizens' role in, 190–91; dwindling of support for, 193; friends and enemies in, 184–86; necessity of, 183–84, 187, 191; necessity of immediate action, 187–88, 192–93; normal political culture, inapplicability of, 184, 186; ordinary Afghans and Iraqis as objects of care in, 190, 192; rhetorical citizenship

and, 192–93, 195n8; rule of law and, 187–90, 192; supporters of benign inactivity, damage done by, 185, 190–91, 193; values being defended in, 185–86, 188
state of exception as permanent in, 181, 182
war rhetoric. *See also* Afghanistan War rhetoric
gender awareness and, 153
ideographs and, 156, 158–59, 160
as male-dominated, 164–65, 166
protection-of-women-and-children scenario in, 153, 157–1589, 163–64, 165
and reinforcement of patriarchal oppression, 165
and silencing of opposing voices, 165–66
"We Are All in the Same Boat" (Danish revue song), 258
"Did We Learn Anything?" parody of, 250, 257–58; and consubstantiality, generation of, 249, 251, 257–58, 260; pluralistic parodic forms in, 258; and *Verfremdung* effect, 257
origin of, 258
performance of, 255
structure of, 258–59
Weekly Standard (periodical), 108–9
Wellman, Carl, 288–89
Westergaard, Kurt, 253
What is Democracy (Koch), 18–19
whistle-blowers, as issue, *status* system and, 291
Williams, Bernard, 78
Williams, Brian, 269, 270–71
women, and French *Réunion politique*, exclusion from, 54

Xenophanes of Colophon, 36

Young, Iris Marion, 7, 166